T0189973

Communications
in Computer and Information Science 1921

Editorial Board Members

Joaquim Filipe ⓘ, *Polytechnic Institute of Setúbal, Setúbal, Portugal*
Ashish Ghosh ⓘ, *Indian Statistical Institute, Kolkata, India*
Raquel Oliveira Prates ⓘ, *Federal University of Minas Gerais (UFMG),*
Belo Horizonte, Brazil
Lizhu Zhou, *Tsinghua University, Beijing, China*

Rationale

The CCIS series is devoted to the publication of proceedings of computer science conferences. Its aim is to efficiently disseminate original research results in informatics in printed and electronic form. While the focus is on publication of peer-reviewed full papers presenting mature work, inclusion of reviewed short papers reporting on work in progress is welcome, too. Besides globally relevant meetings with internationally representative program committees guaranteeing a strict peer-reviewing and paper selection process, conferences run by societies or of high regional or national relevance are also considered for publication.

Topics

The topical scope of CCIS spans the entire spectrum of informatics ranging from foundational topics in the theory of computing to information and communications science and technology and a broad variety of interdisciplinary application fields.

Information for Volume Editors and Authors

Publication in CCIS is free of charge. No royalties are paid, however, we offer registered conference participants temporary free access to the online version of the conference proceedings on SpringerLink (http://link.springer.com) by means of an http referrer from the conference website and/or a number of complimentary printed copies, as specified in the official acceptance email of the event.

CCIS proceedings can be published in time for distribution at conferences or as post-proceedings, and delivered in the form of printed books and/or electronically as USBs and/or e-content licenses for accessing proceedings at SpringerLink. Furthermore, CCIS proceedings are included in the CCIS electronic book series hosted in the SpringerLink digital library at http://link.springer.com/bookseries/7899. Conferences publishing in CCIS are allowed to use Online Conference Service (OCS) for managing the whole proceedings lifecycle (from submission and reviewing to preparing for publication) free of charge.

Publication process

The language of publication is exclusively English. Authors publishing in CCIS have to sign the Springer CCIS copyright transfer form, however, they are free to use their material published in CCIS for substantially changed, more elaborate subsequent publications elsewhere. For the preparation of the camera-ready papers/files, authors have to strictly adhere to the Springer CCIS Authors' Instructions and are strongly encouraged to use the CCIS LaTeX style files or templates.

Abstracting/Indexing

CCIS is abstracted/indexed in DBLP, Google Scholar, EI-Compendex, Mathematical Reviews, SCImago, Scopus. CCIS volumes are also submitted for the inclusion in ISI Proceedings.

How to start

To start the evaluation of your proposal for inclusion in the CCIS series, please send an e-mail to ccis@springer.com.

Rabindra Nath Shaw · Marcin Paprzycki ·
Ankush Ghosh
Editors

Advanced Communication and Intelligent Systems

Second International Conference, ICACIS 2023
Warsaw, Poland, June 16–17, 2023
Revised Selected Papers, Part II

Springer

Editors
Rabindra Nath Shaw 🆔
Chandigarh University
Mohali, India

Marcin Paprzycki 🆔
Systems Research Institute
Warsaw, Poland

Ankush Ghosh 🆔
Chandigarh University
Mohali, India

ISSN 1865-0929   ISSN 1865-0937 (electronic)
Communications in Computer and Information Science
ISBN 978-3-031-45123-2   ISBN 978-3-031-45124-9 (eBook)
https://doi.org/10.1007/978-3-031-45124-9

This Springer imprint is published by the registered company Springer Nature Switzerland AG
The registered company address is: Gewerbestrasse 11, 6330 Cham, Switzerland

Paper in this product is recyclable.

Preface

The book features selected high-quality papers presented at the International Conference on Advanced Communication and Intelligent Systems (ICACIS 2023), organized by Warsaw Management University, Poland during June 16–17, 2023, through online mode. The conference got an overwhelming response and received more than 200 papers from all around the world. All submitted papers have gone through a single-blind review process with an average of three reviews per paper. The acceptance rate was less than 25%. The presented papers are published in this proceedings volume. The book focuses on current development in the fields of communication and intelligent systems. Advances in artificial intelligence and machine learning have spawned fresh research activities all around the world in the last few years, examining novel approaches to constructing intelligent systems and smart communication technologies. The book covers topic such as Wireless Communication, Artificial Intelligence and Machine Learning, Robotics & Automation, Data Science, IoT and Smart Applications. The book covers both single- and multi-disciplinary research on these topics in order to provide the most up-to-date information in one place. The book will be beneficial for readers from both academia and industry.

We are thankful to all the authors that have submitted papers for keeping the quality of ICACIS 2023 at high levels. The editors of this book would like to acknowledge all the authors for their contributions, and the reviewers. We have received invaluable help from the members of the International Program Committee and the chairs responsible for different aspects of the workshop. We also appreciate the role of the Special Sessions Organizers. Thanks to all of them, we had been able to collect many papers on interesting topics, and during the conference we had very interesting presentations and stimulating discussions.

We hope that the volume will provide useful information to professors, researchers, and graduate students in the areas of Computer Science Engineering, Electronics and Communication Engineering and associated technologies along with AI and IoT applications, and all will find this collection of papers inspiring, informative and useful. We also hope to see you at a future ICACIS event.

Rabindra Nath Shaw
Marcin Paprzycki
Ankush Ghosh

Organization

General Chair

Marcin Paprzycki   Systems Research Institute, Polish Academy of
                                        Sciences, Poland

General Co-chair

Ankush Ghosh   ADSRS Education and Research, India

Conference Chair and Chairman, Oversight Committee

Rabindra Nath Shaw   Chandigarh University, India

Technical Chair

Monica Bianchini   University of Siena, Italy

Publication Chair

Sanjoy Das   Indira Gandhi National Tribal University,
                                        Regional Campus Manipur, India

Publicity Chair

Prashant R. Nair   Amrita Vishwa Vidyapeetham, India

Advisory Committee

Bimal K. Bose   University of Tennessee, USA
Muhammad H. Rashid   University of West Florida, USA
Muhammet Koksal   Halic University, Turkey

Contents – Part II

Contents – Part I

About the Editors

Dr. Rabindra Nath Shaw is a global leader in organizing International conferences. His brand of world leading conference series includes IEEE International Conference on Computing, Power and Communication Technologies (GUCON), IEEE International Conference on Computing, Communication and Automation (ICCCA), IEEE IAS Global Conference on Emerging Technologies (GlobConET), International Conference on Electronics & Electrical Engineering (ICEEE), International Conference on Advances in Computing and Information Technology (ICACIT) etc. He holds the position of Conference Chair, Publication Chair, and Editor for these conferences. These Conferences are held in collaboration with various international universities like Aurel Vlaicu University of Arad, University of Malaya, University of Siena. Many world leaders are working with Dr. Shaw in these conferences. Most of these conferences are fully sponsored by IEEE Industry Applications Society, USA. He is also an expert in organizing International Seminars/Webinars/Faculty Development Programme in collaboration with leading institutes across the world.

Dr. Marcin Paprzycki received the MS degree from Adam Mickiewicz University, Poznań, Poland, the PhD degree from Southern Methodist University, Dallas, Texas, and the doctor of science degree from the Bulgarian Academy of Sciences, Sofia, Bulgaria. He is an associate professor with the Systems Research Institute, Polish Academy of Sciences. He is a senior member of the ACM, a senior fulbright lecturer, and an IEEE Computer Society distinguished visitor. He has contributed to more than 500 publications and was invited to the program committees of more than 800 international conferences.

Prof. Ankush Ghosh is Senior member of IEEE, Fellow of IETE has received his Ph.D. (Engg.) degree from Jadavpur University, India in 2010. He was a research fellow of the Advanced Technology Cell- DRDO, Govt. of India. He was awarded National Scholarship by HRD, Govt. of India. He has outstanding research experiences and published 6 edited books; 4 from Springer & 2 from Elsevier; 3 National & 8 International patents and more than 120 research papers indexed in Scopus/Web of Science. He is serving as an editorial board member of several international journals including Chief Editor. He has more than 15 years of experience in teaching, research as well as industry. His UG and PG teaching assignments include Microprocessor and microcontroller, AI, IOT, Embedded and real time systems etc. He has delivered Keynote/Invited lecture in a number of international seminar/conferences, refreshers courses, and FDPs. He has guided a large number of M.Tech and Ph.D. students. Dr. Ghosh is an active member of IEEE and organized a number Seminars and workshops in association with IEEE. He is an editor & organizing committee member of the Conference series GUCON, ICCCA, ICEEE, ICACIT. He is a He is a Start-up India Mentor and Global Startup Advisor of Wadhwani NEN. He has reviewed and mentored more than 50 start-ups. He has received award for contributing in Innovate India programme from AICTE- DST, Govt. of India in 2019 and

2020. He has received an appreciation award from AICTE, DST, TI, IIMB, NSRCEL, and myGOV for fostering students to strengthen the ecosystem bridging Government, Academia, and Industry in the year 2021.

Comparative Analysis of Deep Learning Architectures for Garbage Classification

Dipmala Salunke[✉], Shrikrushnakumar Sondge, Sumit Deshmukh,
Bhushan Dhamankar, Sairaj Chidrawar, and Rohit Kangule

Department of Information Technology, JSPM's Rajarshi Shahu College of Engineering
Tathawade, Pune, India
dtsalunke_it@jspmrscoe.edu.in

Abstract. Recently, the importance of waste management has increased not only in India but also worldwide, the impact of which is creating serious mess in today's world. Some of the stats are showing that around 10 to 15 million tons garbage is making its way from the most of the metro cities in India. The Recycling phase is the most basic step due to which it enables cost effective recycling and which is harmless for environment. With the increasing development in the country, Smart Garbage Classification System is a necessity. Solid waste separation is done by laborer's which is not effective, can lead to errors and it is not feasible due to ever increasing garbage. The purpose here is to build a fully functional model that can recognize the waste type and categorize it into different categories. The model here implemented include VGG16 (Visual Geometric Group), also studied VGG19, Inception3 and AlexNet for the same purpose. During this study, it shows that VGG16 outperformed all other models. This chapter will ensure a better way for waste management thereby leading to increase in segregation speed and with best outcomes. With the integration of algorithms based on deep learning, the garbage classification problem can be effectively solved for the target database.

Keywords: Deep Learning · Convolutional Neural Network · VGG16 · Image Processing · Garbage Classification

1 Introduction

One of the things that the world is producing in large quantities on Earth is waste. The World Bank estimates that two billion and eleven million tonnes of waste go into landfills globally each year. Nearly 33% of this is not coped with in a way that is safe for the environment. Because of this garbage or waste management need to be treated cautiously. This waste if not managed properly it'll be very dangerous for humans as well as other living things. One of the best meanings of dealing with waste is everything related to the safe disposal or re-use of waste. For the successful management of waste, we need to classify waste into different categories. So, how to adequately handle garbage has emerged as a pressing issue that must be addressed immediately. Garbage classification is a prerequisite for waste management, it is the foundation for reduction, recycling and

R. N. Shaw et al. (Eds.): ICACIS 2023, CCIS 1921, pp. 1–11, 2023.
https://doi.org/10.1007/978-3-031-45124-9_1

harmless treatment of garbage. The foremost perks of trash categorization are outlined below: (a) Some home rubbish includes dangerous elements, and garbage that is difficult to decompose causes considerable damage to the soil. If recoverable garbage can be extracted by categorization, landfill volume can be reduced by 70% as classification requires lot of land area. (b) Reduce waste pollution as well as protect our environment by every means. If we perform disposal in current manner, it causes very unpleasant smell as well as gives invitation to various diseases such as Dengue, Malaria. If we use proper methods as well as supplies 25%–40% of our garbage can be recycled. We can say that time to time garbage classification, reuse and recycling can effectively solve the problem of waste.

Currently, the waste management in different countries is performed manually. Manual garbage classification is an extensively utilised strategy. Grievously, it takes an enormous amount of time as well as require very much man power which is not recommendable in today's IT oriented world. Also, there are some automated approaches for garbage classifications using some colonial Machine Learning algorithms were used, however the precision of identification was not up to the mark. The development of deep learning has made the use of convolutional neural network or CNN more widely employed in the detection of images during the last few years [22]. Strategies based on deep learning are beneficial for the reason that sophisticated computing power, enormous volumes of data, and the creation of new algorithms are readily available. In the last few years, algorithms using deep learning have produced intriguing results for trash categorization. By the previous studies, various research is conducted to divide up garbage, however the amount of the dataset varies. There is no open or normative resource for crap pictures. So, to gain some good outcomes, we are creating our own dataset by grabbing some photographs from the internet and capturing some more garbage images, gathering all of them, and utilising them as our dataset. This chapter analyses the performance of several deep learning algorithms in garbage classification, focusing on VGG16, VGG19, Inception3, and AlexNet.

2 Literature Review

The proper separation process of waste needs to be managed so as to lessen the amount of risk on our health and ecosystem. The solid waste separation is done by laborers which is time consuming and can cause errors during the separation. It is also not feasible due to large amounts of garbage. Using Deep Learning a real time Garbage Classifier can be developed. Deep Learning is emerging due to its availability of graphic processing units, multiple hidden layers, CNNs, ANNs. CNNs have been used successfully for Image recognition in various fields. Ishika Mittal established a self-learning trash sorting system employing CNN and multiple datasets – Garythung Yang, Waste classifier master, Trash net, Real images. On the Trash net dataset, the model reached a highest test accuracy of 89% where the waste was classified into organic and recyclable waste [1]. Md. Samiul Haque Sunny et al. employed ATD (Automatic Teller Dustbin) using R-CNN and Modified AlexNet. The model classified waste into 2 sets organic and inorganic with a validation accuracy of 96% [2]. Sidharth R et al. focused on separating waste into 4 categories namely – cardboard, metal, plastic and paper. The model attained a thoroughgoing testing precision of 76.19% using CNN where Softmax was used as activation function [3]. Shanshan Meng et al. compared several methods, they used SVM, ResNet 50, HOG + SVM and Simple CNN to classify the waste. They were able to attain a classification accuracy of 91.40% using ResNet 50 which was increased to 95.35% when the data was augmented [4]. Shamin N, has employed smart garbage segregation and management using CNN algorithm and IoT architecture [5]. Joao Sousa et al. suggested two-step technique preserves the benefits of contemporary object detectors (such as Faster R-CNN) while allowing the classification job to be handled in higher resolution bounding boxes. The greatest correctness attained with the data enrichment was 67%, while the mAP was 81.4% resulting from coupling with the Faster R-CNN [6]. Wang Hao considered the model named VGG16 which is employed to tackle the challenge of identifying and classifying household waste. Following data betterment, a VGG16 convolutional neural network is created on the TensorFlow framework utilising the RELU activation function and a BN layer to expedite the model's convergence speed while guaranteeing recognition precision. After real experiments, the accurate classification rate of the trash classification system claimed in this study based on the VGG16 network is 75.6%, which corresponds to the demands of daily usage [7]. Patipol Tiyajamorn AlphaTrash, a mechanism that can be connected to a standard curb-side trashcan and used to sift out deposit garbage automatically, presents a potential solution. The system can classify rubbish with a 94% exactitude [8]. Jie Yang and Zeyi Zhang from china decided to design a mobile app along with the hardware structure with the help of the ResNet-34-based grouping method. Optimizing the grid assembly into 3 aspects: multi-feature synthesis of provided pictures, reuse of characteristics of the surplus unit, and creation of an entirely novel activation mechanism are all part of the process. They were able to enhance the systems accuracy by 1.01% and the evaluation's labelling accuracy is approximately 99% [9]. Farzana Shaikh et al. proposed a system where they are able to separate bio-degradable and non-bio-degradable waste, There claimed study was able to pull the correctness of 88% for bio-degradable waste with less execution time than the existing system of 1.3 s. And an accuracy for non-bio-degradable waste of 84% with again less execution time than the existing system of 1.56 s. They were able to enhance the model by getting the accuracy as the existing model but consuming less time than them [10]. Ming Zeng et al. proposed a classification algorithm that can do several tasks. Whereas one assignment identified four key kinds of household waste and other task achieve recognition of 10 subclass garbage. A total of 10 subclasses and 10624 images were used for training. Selection of the foundation for optimised performance, data augmentation, learning rate improvement, and label smoothing is performed after which the optimized model reaches an accuracy of 96.35% [11]. S. Sudha projected framework which can learn by itself and hence can constantly reinvent itself in case of novel content. Its advantages for us would include simple breakdown, less danger to our health, and a speedier procedure as the model keeps updating itself. Their suggested idea and method are incredibly efficient, and the algorithm that uses deep learning operates more effectively providing a very high accuracy rate [12]. Wei Chen of Tianjin Key Laboratory of Information Sensing and Intelligent Control in China creates a ResNet18 convolutional neural network structure based on the attention-grabbing system for reprocessed garbage categorization. The concentration feature is included after convolution to let the model concentrate on the most noteworthy data in the feature map. The model may instinctively gather trash features for categorization, such as: glass, metal, plastic and paper. The algorithm has an accuracy rate of 92% in the categorization of recyclable rubbish, indicating that it can efficiently categorise recyclable garbage [13]. Bowen Fu et al. had created deep learning-based trash categorization system with embedded Linux system. Their system is divided into three fields, First, with the aid of a Raspberry Pi 4B, create the master board for the hardware system. Second, a novel GNet model for trash categorization based on transfer learning is proposed, as is an upgraded MobileNetV3 model. Third, a graphical user interface (GUI) based on Python and QT is implemented to provide a human-computer interaction system to simplify system modification and surveillance. The prediction accuracy of the suggested system of classification was 92.62% [14]. ANH H. VO has created a smart garbage sorter system using sophisticated sensors. Their research provides a viable approach for autonomously classifying trash based on deep neural networks. Their research creates DNN-TC, a deep neural network model for garbage categorization that is a development on the ResNext model to increase predicted performance. The results of the research show that DNN-TC achieves 94% and 98% accuracy for the Trashnet and VN-trash datasets, respectively [15]. Karthikeyan S et al., their research presents a DDR-net (Double fused Deep CNN using ResNext) advanced classification model, which is an augmentation of the ResNext model augmented by double fusion and regularisation. The suggested model may be applied in real-time to any classification configuration process that feeds the garbage picture as input via a camera, and actuators can be actuated based on the model's output. With an accuracy of 97.81%, the DDR-net classifies solid wastes into their appropriate categories [16]. Janusz Bobulski and Mariusz Kubanek focused on the trash accumulated in landfills might be utilised as secondary raw materials, with a value estimated at a couple hundred million dollars. They presented a system based on deep learning and convolutional neural networks for this purpose. The results of their testing with the suggested technology obtained an average efficiency of 74% [17]. Aghilan M suggested solid waste handling in huge metropolitan areas using automated garbage classification system. For the optimization purpose they had used Adam method. Adam combines the best properties of the Ada Grad and RMSProp algorithm. Their proposed system had come to final accuracy of 79% by performing various trial and run methods which got the accuracy around 63%, 70% and 72% [18]. Olugboja Adedeji et al. proposed system which is able to classify garbage. They recommended a predictive waste material detection based on a 50-layer leftover net pre-train (ResNet - 50) CNN model, as well as SVM to categorise trash. Bys using this system, they had achieved accuracy around 87% [19]. Yujie He Qinyue Gu Maguo Shi TrashNet was utilised as their dataset, and garbage was sorted into six basic sections. For their model, they first worked on Convolutional Neural Networks (CNN), but then changed AlexNet by removing two layers and using two classifiers, softmax and Support Vector Machine (SVM). Using this proposed system, they have had achieved 79.94% accuracy [20].

3 Methodology

3.1 Dataset Preparation and Pre-processing

Around 2001 photos have been gathered by the authors in a dataset that needs to be categorised across several trash categories. Dataset contains various garbage images like carboard, pieces of plastic, glass, metal cans, etc. Each image had been scaled down in size to 224 × 224 and stored in its appropriate folder. ImageDataGenerator was used for combining data and to increase the gainable insights by slightly modifying the images.

3.2 Proposed Architecture

VGG16 is a type of CNN model architecture who won ILSVR competition in year 2014 which is computer vision competition. It was excellent computer vision model architecture at that time. The image of dimension (224, 244, 3) is input provided to vgg16 model. Starting two layers have identical padding and 64 channels of 3 × 3 sized filters in total. Following, there is (2, 2) stride max-pooling. Following two convolution layers with 128 filters and a (3, 3) filter size, there is a maximum pooling layer having the same properties as the preceding layer. After that there is 2 convolution layers with total 256 filters and having filter size (3, 3). There are then two sets of three convolution layers, each containing 512 filters and a size of (3, 3), and all of them possess the same pooling. In conclusion, we can observe that in VGG16 model follows arrangement of convolution and max pooling layers throughout the architecture consistently. At last, it has 2 fully connected layers followed by softmax which is used to provide output. This is a huge network with about 138 million parameters.

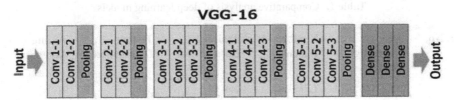

Fig. 1. The typical VGG 16 architecture

Figure 1 shows the sequence of layers in VGG16.

The block diagram for a garbage classification system in Fig. 2 shows how the dataset is obtained, pre-processed, and labelled. In order to expand the dataset and improve the model's accuracy, data augmentation is applied [21]. To classify image into different categories, various models, including VGG16, VGG19, IncpetionV3, and AlexNet, were implemented to train and test the dataset.

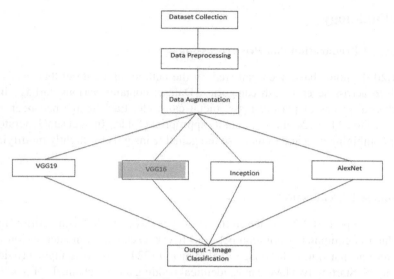

Fig. 2. Block Diagram

4 Results

2,001 images in total were scanned belonging to different categories of garbage. Out of those images 1,603 were utilized for training and 398 images were utilized for model testing. The model went through training on this dataset using different deep learning models like VGG16, VGG19, Inception V3, AlexNet.

Table 1. Comparative analysis of deep learning models

Sr. No.	Deep Learning Model	Number of Epochs	Training Dataset Size	Testing Dataset Size	Testing Accuracy
1	VGG16	120	1603	398	91.89
2	VGG19	32	1603	398	82.78
3	InceptionV3	40	1603	398	79.39
4	AlexNet	50	1603	398	16.75

Figure 3 shows the model architecture for VGG16. Our highest accuracy for the VGG16 model was 91.89%, which is ideal as shown in Fig. 4.

```
Layer (type)                    Output Shape                Param #
=========================================================================
input_1 (InputLayer)            [(None, 224, 224, 3)]       0

block1_conv1 (Conv2D)           (None, 224, 224, 64)        1792

block1_conv2 (Conv2D)           (None, 224, 224, 64)        36928

block1_pool (MaxPooling2D)      (None, 112, 112, 64)        0

block2_conv1 (Conv2D)           (None, 112, 112, 128)       73856

block2_conv2 (Conv2D)           (None, 112, 112, 128)       147584

block2_pool (MaxPooling2D)      (None, 56, 56, 128)         0

block3_conv1 (Conv2D)           (None, 56, 56, 256)         295168

block3_conv2 (Conv2D)           (None, 56, 56, 256)         590080

block3_conv3 (Conv2D)           (None, 56, 56, 256)         590080

block3_pool (MaxPooling2D)      (None, 28, 28, 256)         0

block4_conv1 (Conv2D)           (None, 28, 28, 512)         1180160

block4_conv2 (Conv2D)           (None, 28, 28, 512)         2359808

block4_conv3 (Conv2D)           (None, 28, 28, 512)         2359808

block4_pool (MaxPooling2D)      (None, 14, 14, 512)         0

block5_conv1 (Conv2D)           (None, 14, 14, 512)         2359808

block5_conv2 (Conv2D)           (None, 14, 14, 512)         2359808

block5_conv3 (Conv2D)           (None, 14, 14, 512)         2359808

block5_pool (MaxPooling2D)      (None, 7, 7, 512)           0

flatten (Flatten)               (None, 25088)               0

dense (Dense)                   (None, 6)                   150534
=========================================================================
Total params: 14,865,222
Trainable params: 150,534
Non-trainable params: 14,714,688
```

Fig. 3. VGG 16 model architecture

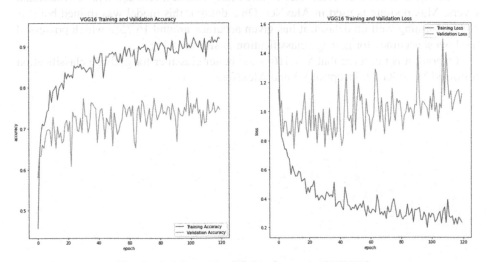

Fig. 4. Training and validation accuracy of VGG16

5   Discussion

As demonstrated in the Table 1 VGG16 model outperforms the other algorithms with an accuracy of 91.89%. Since, instead of having large numbered hyper-parameter, VGG16 focuses on having convolutional layers of 3 × 3 filter with stride 1 and always use same padding and maxpooling layer of 2 × 2 of stride 2, the model performed well on the dataset.

The VGG19 model was tested with an accuracy of 82.74% as depicted in Fig. 5.

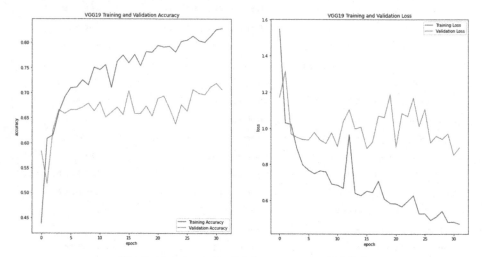

Fig. 5. Training and validation accuracy of VGG19

The Inception V3 model also performed well with 79.39% accuracy and 72.11% validation accuracy according to Fig. 6.

The AlexNet network comprises of three fully linked layers and five convolutional layers. Max pooling is used in AlexNet. On a dataset, this model was trained but it is not performing well on dataset, it has given accuracy around 16.75% which possessed the lowest accuracy for garbage classification as shown in Fig. 7.

Overall, it is observed that VGG16 is the better classifier for garbage classification followed by VGG 19, InceptionV3 and AlexNet.

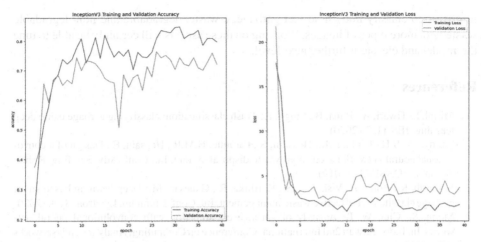

Fig. 6. Training and validation accuracy of InceptionV3

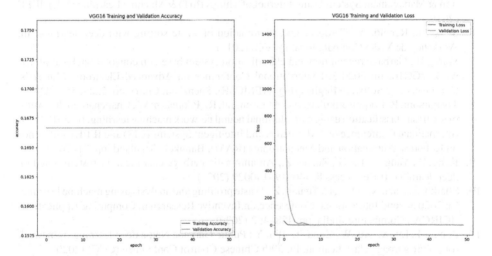

Fig. 7. Training and validation accuracy of AlexNet

6   Conclusion

Garbage disposal is becoming a global problem and to resolve this problem garbage segregation becomes very essential. In this chapter, different deep learning models like VGG16, VGG19, Inception3 and AlexNet have been trained on 2001 images and it shows that VGG16 outperformed all the others models with an accuracy of 91.89%. But, the performance of AlexNet is below average on this particular dataset. The proposed model is capable of classifying images of garbage in 6 different categories namely: plastic, rubber, metal, cardboard, paper and glass.

By integrating deep learning algorithms, the challenge of garbage classification in the target dataset can be effectively addressed and resolved. The system can be further improved to classify household wet garbage, e-waste, degradable and non-degradable waste with more types of images. Working on these aspects will certainly be able to tune the model and elevate it further next level.

References

1. Mittal, I., Tiwari, A., Rana, B., Singh, P.: Trash classification: classifying garbage using deep learning. JES **11**, 7 (2020)
2. Sunny, Md.S.H., Dipta, D.R., Hossain, S., Faruque, H.M.R., Hossain, E.: Design of a convolutional neural network based smart waste disposal system. Int. Conf. Adv. Sci. Eng. Robot. Technol. (ICASERT) (2019)
3. Sidharth, R., Rohit, P., Vishagan, S., Karthika, R., Ganesan, M.: Deep learning based smart garbage classifier for effective waste management. Int. Conf. Commun. Electron. Syst. (2020)
4. Meng, S., Chu, W.-T.: A study of garbage classification with convolutional neural networks. In: Indo–Taiwan 2nd International Conference on Computing, Analytics and Networks (ICAN2020)
5. Shamin, N., Mohamed Fathimal, P., Raghavendran, R, Prakash, K.: Smart Garbage Segregation & Management System Using Internet of Things (IoT) & Machine Learning (ML). IEEE (2019)
6. Sousa, J., Rebelo, A., Cardoso, J.S.: Automation of waste sorting with deep learning. In: Workshop de Visão Computacional (WVC) (2019)
7. Wang, H.: Garbage recognition and classification system based on convolutional neural network VGG16. In: 2020 3rd International Conference on Advanced Electronic Materials, Computers and Software Engineering (AEMCSE), Shenzhen, China, pp. 252–255 (2020)
8. Tiyajamorn, P., Lorprasertkul, P., Assabumrungrat, R., Poomarin, W., Chancharoen, R.: Automatic trash classification using convolutional neural network machine learning. In: 2019 IEEE International Conference on Cybernetics and Intelligent Systems (CIS) and IEEE Conference on Robotics, Automation and Mechatronics (RAM), Bangkok, Thailand, pp. 71–76 (2019)
9. Kang, Z., Yang, J., Li, G., Zhang, Z.: An automatic garbage classification system based on deep learning. IEEE Access **8**, 140019–140029 (2020)
10. Shaikh, F., Kazi, N., Khan, F., Thakur, Z.: Waste profiling and analysis using machine learning. In: 2020 Second International Conference on Inventive Research in Computing Applications (ICIRCA), Coimbatore, India, pp. 488–492 (2020)
11. Zeng, M., Lu, X., Xu, W., Zhou, T., Liu, Y.: Public Gargabe Net: a deep learning framework for public garbage classification. In: 39th Chinese Control Conference (CCC) (2020)
12. Sudha, S., Vidhyalakshmi, M., Pavithra, K., Sangeetha, K., Swaathi, V.:An automatic classification method for environment: Friendly waste segregation using deep learning. In: 2016 IEEE Technological Innovations in ICT for Agriculture and Rural Development (TIAR), Chennai, India, pp. 65–70 (2016)
13. Rawat, R., Rajawat, A.S., Mahor, V., Shaw, R.N., Ghosh, A.: Surveillance robot in cyber intelligence for vulnerability detection. In: Bianchini, M., Simic, M., Ghosh, A., Shaw, R.N. (eds.) Machine Learning for Robotics Applications. SCI, vol. 960, pp. 107–123. Springer, Singapore (2021). https://doi.org/10.1007/978-981-16-0598-7_9
14. Fu, B., Li, S., Wei, J., Li, Q., Wang, Q., Tu, J.: A novel intelligent garbage classification system based on deep learning and an embedded linux system. IEEE Access **9**, 131134–131146 (2021)
15. Vo, A.H., Hoang Son, L., Vo, M.T., Le, T.: A novel framework for trash classification using deep transfer learning. IEEE Access **7**, 178631–178639 (2019)
16. Karthikeyan, S., Sivakumar, M., Jeysiva, A.P., Maheshkumar, C.: Application of deep learning for solid waste trash classification using deep CNN. In: Proceedings of ACM/CSI/IEEECS Research & Industry Symposium on IoT Cloud for Societal Applications (2021)

17. Rajawat, A.S., Rawat, R., Shaw, R.N., Ghosh, A.: Cyber physical system fraud analysis by mobile robot. In: Bianchini, M., Simic, M., Ghosh, A., Shaw, R.N. (eds.) Machine Learning for Robotics Applications. SCI, vol. 960, pp. 47–61. Springer, Singapore (2021). https://doi.org/10.1007/978-981-16-0598-7_4

18. Aghilan, M., Arun Kumar, M., Mohammed Aafrid, T.S., Nirmal Kumar, A., Muthulakshmi, S.: Garbage waste classification using supervised deep learning techniques. Int. J. Emerg. Technol. Innov. Eng. **6**(3) (2020)

19. Adedeji, O., Wang, Z.: Intelligent waste classification system using deep learning convolutional neural network. In: 2nd International Conference on Sustainable Materials Processing and Manufacturing (SMPM) (2019)

20. Kumar, A., Das, S., Tyagi, V., Shaw, R.N., Ghosh, A.: Analysis of classifier algorithms to detect anti-money laundering. In: Bansal, J.C., Paprzycki, M., Bianchini, M., Das, S. (eds.) Computationally Intelligent Systems and their Applications. SCI, vol. 950, pp. 143–152. Springer, Singapore (2021). https://doi.org/10.1007/978-981-16-0407-2_11

21. Salunke, D., Peddi, P., Joshi, R.: The significance of image augmentation in deep learning: a review. Int. J. Adv. Res. Comput. Commun. Eng. **11**(3) (2022)

22. Mane, D.T., Moorthy, R., Kumbharkar, P., Upadhye, G., Salunke, D., Ashtagi, R.: Pattern classification using supervised hypersphere neural network. Int. J. Emerg. Technol. Adv. Eng. **12**(8) (2022)

Developing an Automated System for Pothole Detection and Management Using Deep Learning

P. D. S. S. Lakshmi Kumari[1]([✉]) [iD], Gidugu Srinija Sivasatya Ramacharanteja[1],
S. Suresh Kumar[2] [iD], Gorrela Bhuvana Sri[1], Gottumukkala Sai Naga Jyotsna[1],
and Aki Hari Keerthi Naga Safalya[1]

[1] Department of Information Technology, S.R.K.R. Engineering College (A), Bhimavaram, AP,
India
divyapannasa@gmail.com
[2] CSE Department S.R.K.R. Engineering College (A), Bhimavaram, AP, India

Abstract. The economy greatly benefits from the use of roads as a platform for
mobility. Roadway potholes are one of the primary problems with transportation infrastructure. Accidents frequently occur because of these potholes. Many
research have advocated using computer vision methods to automate pothole identification, including various image processing and object detection algorithms.
The system must be easy to use, economical to set up, and capable of automating pothole identification quickly and accurately. In this study, we constructed
effective deep learning convolution neural networks (CNNs) to identify potholes
accurately and quickly and to enhance training results and lower computational
costs. In addition to that, the performance of YOLOv7 and Faster R-CNN with
ResNet50 (FPN) backbone is also contrasted in this paper. According to the trial
findings, the YOLO's speed makes it more useful for real-time pothole detection.

Keywords: YOLOV7 · Faster-RCNN · ResNet50 · PyTorch Pothole Detection

1 Introduction

Roads are a nation's primary source of mobility when it comes to offering nation-
wide commuting options. Road infrastructure makes it possible to link people and carry
commodities, enhancing commercial prospects, job access, economic growth, and the
nation's healthcare system. Although high-quality roads boost the nation's GDP, poor
road infrastructure can be deadly for the wellbeing of drivers and passengers as well as
the condition of vehicles. This poor road infrastructure is caused due to many reasons
like heavy traffic, poor maintenance, bad weather conditions and wear and tear etc. One
of the main anomalies of poor road infrastructure is potholes. Potholes are basically
concave depressions in the road surface that need to be repaired since they cause terrible
events like accidents, unpleasant driving experiences, and malfunctioning automobiles.
Sometimes these potholes may lead to fatal accidents.

R. N. Shaw et al. (Eds.): ICACIS 2023, CCIS 1921, pp. 12–22, 2023.
https://doi.org/10.1007/978-3-031-45124-9_2

A few initiatives are being made utilizing various strategies to automate the pothole identification system on roads. Few are based on sensors. Some are based on 3-D reconstruction Processing of images, and some are model-based. Pothole detection methods based on sensors use vibration sensors. The vibration sensor may mistake joints, cracks in the road as potholes or fail to detect potholes in the middle of a lane, which can lead to false readings that may be false positives or false negatives which can compromise the accuracy of detecting potholes. In three-dimensional reconstruction techniques, the 3-dimensional road data captured by using lasers and cameras are used to detect potholes. The clarity of data can be compromised by the camera misalignment that could reduce detection accuracy and require expensive design and computing work to recreate the pavement surface.

Even though standard image processing techniques for pothole detection offer a high degree of accuracy, they still require difficult tasks like manually bringing out features and modifying the image processing variables and stages for various road conditions. The development of model-based pothole identification and recognition algorithms has been driven by the advancement of image processing techniques and the accessibility of inexpensive camera equipment. Using conventional ML techniques, a trained model for spotting potholes in 2-dimensional digital images was created. They use a lot of computation power and still manage to attain great accuracy. Specialists are required to manually bringing out the features in order to increase the pothole detection accuracy of ML algorithms. Convolutional neural network (CNN) methods, which are capable of concurrently automating the functioning of feature extraction and classification, were employed in deep learning (DL) approaches.

We proposed a pothole detection system using YOLO (YOU ONLY LOOK ONCE) and Faster-RCNN. We are using the current version of YOLO (YOLOv7) for this study, and we also want to contrast the performance of single stage detector YOLO and two stage detector Faster-RCNN.

2 Literature Survey

Seung-Ki Ryu, Taehyeong Kim, Young-Ro Kim, 2015 [1]. The authors proposed the Image-Based Pothole Detection System for the ITS Service and Road Management System in 2015. The three steps of this system are as follows: Segmentation, candidate region extraction, and decision-making. To begin, dark areas for pothole identification are extracted using a histogram and the morphological filter's closure operation. Next, prospective regions of a pothole are retrieved using a variety of criteria, including size and compactness. Lastly, by comparing pothole and background features, it is determined if the candidate regions are potholes or not.

Hsiu-Wen Wang, Chi-Hua Chen, Ding-Yuan Cheng, Chun-Hao Lin, and Chi-Chun Lo, 2015 [2]. An approach for real-time pothole detection for intelligent transportation systems was put forth by the authors in 2015. Based on mobile sensing, the authors provide a strategy for locating potholes. The pothole information is obtained by applying the Euler angle mechanisms to the data of accelerometer to normalise it. In addition, the interpolation techniques like spatial interpolation approach is employed to minimise locality mistakes in GPS data. The results of the trials demonstrate that the suggested approach can accurately identify classes with no false positives, and the recommended approach performs with a greater degree of accuracy.

K. Vigneshwar, B. Hema Kumar, 2016 [3]. Utilizing image processing techniques, the authors suggested Detection and Counting of Potholes in 2016. To achieve better results, the authors suggested a system where image processing is based on different Gaussian-Filtering and clustering based image segmentation approaches. According to the findings, segmentation based on edge- detection is favoured for its specificity and segmentation based on K-Means clustering was preferred for its quickest computation time.

Jeong-Joo Kim, Choi Soo-il, 2017 [4]. In 2017, Implementation of Pothole Detection System Using 2d Lidar was the idea put out by the authors. By using information from cameras and 2D lidar, the scientists have suggested a method for detecting potholes. These lidar cameras' major application is their capacity to capture a large region with fine detail. After the data is captured, a number of techniques are applied, including filtering, classification, line extraction, and gradient of data function. The performance of pothole recognition from video data and the combination with 2D lidar was improved.

Asif Ahmed, Samiul Islam, Amitabha Chakrabarty, 2019 [5]. In 2019, The identification and comparison of potholes using image processing algorithms is suggested by the authors. To detect every form of pothole, the topic chosen employs 4 different image segmentation approaches. The approaches Image Thresholding, Canny Edge Detection, K-Means clustering, and Fuzzy C-Means clustering were all worked on. After that, several scenarios were examined to see how well the various image segmentation approaches worked. In terms of accuracy and precision results were produced. Also, the outcomes were contrasted with one another in order to assess their viability.

Aparna, Yukti Bhatia, Rachna Rai, Varun Gupta, Naveen Aggarwal, Aparna Akula, 2019 [6]. The authors have presented Convolutional Neural Networks based Potholes Detection Using Thermal Imaging in 2019. This technique is able to identify potholes from thermal imagery. Real-time pothole detection is an option. A deep learning-based strategy has been used to this. Thermal photographs of roads with and without potholes are used as input in a model built on a convolutional neural network (CNN). The model recognizes and identifies if the feeded in image contains a pothole or not after being trained on this data.

Z. Hasan, S. N. Shampa, T. R. Shahidi and S. Siddique 2020 [7]. In 2020, The authors suggested using smartphone cameras and CNN's to detect potholes and speed bumps. In this study, we have created a model that uses computer vision and machine learning methods to identify undesirable potholes, deep ridges, and speed bumps. In order to train their machine learning algorithms, they have created a unique dataset, which they've named Bumpy. In their study, they offer a method for identifying speed bumps, deep ridges, and potholes using a pre-trained Tensorflow model.

Surekha Arjapure, D.R. Kalbande, 2020 [8]. In 2020, Road Pothole Detection Using Deep Learning Classifiers is the solution put out by the authors. A deep learning method was suggested by the authors. It is suggested to use a Mask Region-Based Convolutional Neural Network to precisely detect and segment such potholes in order to anticipate and determine their extent. The 291 photos in the database were painstakingly gathered on Mumbai's city streets and close-by motorways. The manual VGG Image Annotator tool is used to manually annotate the dataset. Potholes are identified as a zone of interest using Mask Region-Based Convolutional Neural Network (Mask RCNN).

Bucko, Boris, Eva Lieskovská, Katarína Zábovská, and Michal Zábovský, 2022 [9]. In this paper You Look Only Once version 3, often known as Yolo v3, a computer vision model library, is used to automatically detect potholes. Driving in low light or bad weather inherently limits our ability to see road damage. Visual object detection performance is likewise negatively impacted by such unfavourable circumstances.

B, M.P., K.C, S., 2022 [10]. The main objective of this paper is to train and evaluate the YOLOX model for pothole identification. YOLOX is an object detection technique. The YOLOX model is trained using a dataset of potholes, and the results are examined by assessing the model's accuracy, recall, and size, which are then contrasted with those of other YOLO algorithms.

3 Methodology

From the related work, we have observed some drawbacks like low accuracy, high computation power needed, high cost setup and etc. To fill this research gap, we proposed Pothole detection system using YOLO and Faster-RCNN

A. YOLOv7

YOLO is shortly named for 'You Only Look Once'. This is an algorithm that identifies and recognizes various objects in a image. In YOLO, an object is detected as a regression problem and lay outs the class probabilities for all detected images. YOLO is a single stage object detector which passes all components of the object detection into a single neural network. The CNN is used to predict various class probabilities and bounding boxes simultaneously. The YOLO algorithm consists of various variants. In this study we are using the version 7 of YOLO (Base YOLOv7) (Fig. 1).

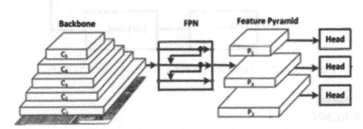

Fig. 1. Architecture of YOLOv7

The image data is fed to backbone. Backbone is stack of several pre-trained weights. The extracted features from backbone is feed to sequential network FPN. FPN is the neck of the yolo architecture. Here in FPN, convolution and pooling is done and produces feature pyramid. The feature pyramid is feeded to head where all the computation is done. Finally the head will predict the class label of corresponding feature

These are the steps needed to follow:

a) Data Collection.

We have created a custom datasets with the help of images downloaded from different sources like Kaggle, Roboflow and etc.

b) Data Annotation.

Annotating or labelling the images in the dataset using any data annotation tool. We have used labelImg for image annotation.

iii) Data hierarchy.

Split the images and labels into train and val folders.

iv) Training.

- We trained our custom pothole dataset with the help of official YOLOv7 GitHub repository.
- We have made few changes to some of the files in the repository like changing the number of classes and class names.
- After all changes made, we trained, validated our custom dataset on google colab with pre-trained weights respectively

v) Testing.

We have tested a video of potholes with our custom model weights and got predictions (Fig. 2).

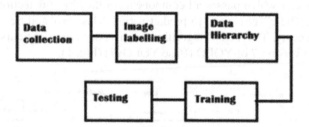

Fig. 2. Simple overview of pothole detection using YOLOv7

B. FASTER-RCNN

Faster – RCNN is short term for Faster Region based convolutional neural network, it is updated version of Fast-RCNN which is updated version of R-CNN.

Faster-RCNN contains two modules:

- **RPN**: For generating featured maps of anchor boxes
- **ROI pooling**: It is used for making all feature maps of anchor boxes to same size (Fig. 3)

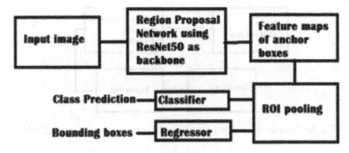

Fig. 3. Architecture of Faster-RCNN

The image is passed to region proposal network. In region proposal network, the CNN produces the feature maps of anchor boxes of foreground regions. Anchor boxes are nothing but bounding boxes used for region proposals which are of different dimensions. Foreground regions are the regions which contains the object. The output of the RPN is feature maps of anchor boxes. This output will be feeded to ROI pooling layer which makes all feature maps equal in size. Then the classifier identifies the object for the respective feature map and regressor will give a bounding box around the object.

These are the steps needed to follow:

a) Data Collection.

- we have created a custom data from internet sources like Kaggle.
- This dataset was annotated.

b) Directory setup.

- We have six python scripts, input folder, checkpoints folder, Test predictions folder
- The project directory consists of following details.
- The input folder contains the images and annotations required for training and also contains images for testing
- The savedmodel folder contains the model saved after the training
- Test_predictions folder contains the results produced after testing

c) Training.

•Run the train.py script

d) Testing.

- Run the test.py script (Fig. 4)

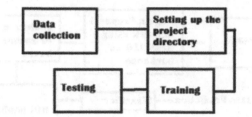

Fig. 4. Simple overview of pothole detection using Faster-RCNN

4 Experiments and Results

After training the YOLOv7 model with our custom dataset, we got batches of trained images. We can see them below (Fig. 5).

Fig. 5. Batches of Trained Images of YOLOv7

In training, for some set of epochs, a trained model will be saved in weights folder. At last, the best model out of all epochs will be saved. This will look like below (Fig. 6).

Fig. 6. Best Model saved after training the YOLOv7

Using this best model we can test our custom videos/images. Below is the frame of pothole prediction from a video (Fig. 7).

Fig. 7. YOLOv7 Prediction frames from an input video

For Faster-RCNN training, we set up the number of epochs to 8 (from epoch 0 to epoch 7) (Table 1).

Table 1. Loss values of each epochs

Epoch No	Loss Value	Time taken for each epoch
0	0.2209340971360504	~84 min
1	0.15503743677671766	~83 min
2	0.13977767626044735	~166 min
3	0.13120384020374815	~82 min
4	0.12274352340981623	~83 min
5	0.11972583682694185	~ 82 min
6	0.11648200763393216	~83 min
7	0.11067249564457707	~82 min

The predictions of Faster-RCNN is as follows (Fig. 8):

Fig. 8. Predictions of Faster-RCNN

5   Evaluation Metrics

True positives: Model predicted "yes" and the prediction is correct
True negatives: Model predicted "no" and the prediction is correct
False positives: Model predicted "yes" and the prediction is wrong (actually it was "no")
False negatives: Model predicted "no" and the prediction is wrong (actually it was "yes")
Precision: It is the proportion of correctly predicted forecasts to all predicted predictions
that were predicted as "true."
Recall: It is the proportion of correctly predicted forecasts to all true positives
From the obtained graphs, we can see our YOLO model has precision and recall about
90% and mAP@0.5 is somewhat near to 0.9. Since it is a object detection, accuracy is
termed as the ratio of number of correctly predicted potholes to all the pothole images
(Table 2).

Table 2. Comparison with related work

Evaluation metrics	Proposed Method	[9]	[10]
mAP@0.5	0.9	0.747	0.85.6
Methodology	FASTER RCNN	SPARSE RCNN	Darknet-53

From the above confusion matrix, it is clearly means that our model predicts 97%
correctly. i.e., out of 100 actual potholes it can clearly predict 97 potholes correctly
(Figs. 9 and 10).

This means we have 97% accuracy for the custom yolo model.

For Faster-RCNN, we have tested 100 images of potholes and we got 85% accuracy
that means it predicts 85 images correctly (Table 3).

Although YOLO has higher accuracy, it didn't predict the smaller potholes as
potholes and Faster-RCNN predicts tiny potholes as potholes but it has lower accuracy.

From all these metrics, we can say our YOLOv7 model is best enough for real time
application in aspect of speed and accuracy.

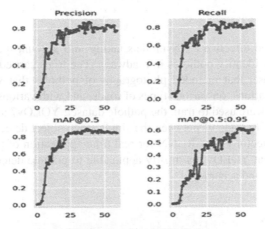

Fig. 9. Results of YOLOv7

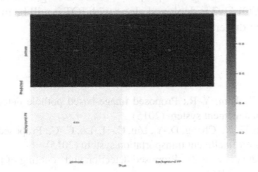

Fig. 10. Confusion Matrix

Table 3. YOLOv7 vs Faster-RCNN

PARAMETERS	YOLOv7	Faster-RCNN
Image size	640	800
Batch size	16	2
No. of Epochs	60	8
Training time per epoch	28.56 s	4920 s
Training time	0.476 h	11.4 h
Average Frames per second	25	0.312
Accuracy	97%	85%
Able to detect tiny potholes	No	Yes
Able to detect from Larger distances	Yes	No

6 Conclusion

This research created effective CNN models taking into account the requirements to reliably and quickly identify potholes in roadways. The trials carried out in this study made use of a dataset that included photographs of potholes that were taken under various lighting situations, on various types of roads, and with various forms and sizes. Two distinct CNNs were used to train the pothole dataset: YOLOv7 and Faster-RCNN.

Our main aim is to tradeoff between the single stage object detector YOLOv7 and two stage object detector Faster-RCNN for real time application of pothole detection. We can conclude that YOLOv7 is mostly applicable to pothole detection in real time because of its speed and accuracy.

7 Future Work

There is a scope for combining this project with IOT to get more realistic pothole detection system. If YOLOv7 is deployed along with IOT it will be more useful as there is a chance to alert the driver with a beep sound.

References

1. Ryu, S.-K., Kim, T., Kim, Y.-R.: Proposed image-based pothole detection system for its service and road management system (2015)
2. Wang, H.-W., Chen, C.-H., Cheng, D.-Y., Lin, C.-H., Lo, C.-C.: Proposed a real-time pothole detection approach for intelligent transportation system (2015)
3. Vigneshwar, K., Hema Kumar, B.: Proposed detection and counting of pothole using image processing techniques (2016)
4. Kim, J.-J., Soo-il, C.: Proposed implementation of pothole detection system using 2d lidar (2017)
5. Soni, A., Dharmacharya, D., Pal, A., Srivastava, V.K., Shaw, R.N., Ghosh, A.: Design of a machine learning-based self-driving car. In: Bianchini, M., Simic, M., Ghosh, A., Shaw, R.N. (eds.) Machine Learning for Robotics Applications. SCI, vol. 960, pp. 139–151. Springer, Singapore (2021). https://doi.org/10.1007/978-981-16-0598-7_11
6. Ahmed, A., Islam, S., Chakrabarty, A.: Proposed identification and comparative analysis of potholes using image processing algorithms (2019)
7. Hasan, Z., Shampa, S.N., Shahidi, T.R., Siddique, S.: Proposed pothole and speed breaker detection using smartphone cameras and convolutional neural networks (2020)
8. Arjapure, S., Kalbande, D.R.: Proposed Road Pothole Detection Using Deep Learning Classifiers (2020)
9. Bucko, B., Lieskovská, E., Zábovská, K., Zábovský, M.: Computer vision based pothole detection under challenging conditions. Sensors 22, 8878 (2022). https://doi.org/10.3390/s22 228878
10. Mohan Prakash, B., Sriharipriya, K.C.: Enhanced pothole detection system using YOLOX algorithm. Auton. Intell. Syst. 2, 22 (2022). https://doi.org/10.1007/s43684-022-00037-z

Collating Weather Data and Grocery Cost Using Machine Learning Techniques

S. Sridevi[1], K. Hemalatha[2(✉)], and S. Gowthami[2]

[1] Vel Tech Rangarajan Dr. Sagunthala R&D Institute of Science and Technology, Chennai, India
[2] S. Bannari Amman Institute of Technology, Sathyamangalam, India
hemaa75@gmail.com

Abstract. Economic development is aided by farming. Farming is primarily defined by the utilization of family labours, which is limited in terms of land, water, and capital resources. Farmers must choose which agricultural goods to be produced based on various parameters which needs technical methods to make the best decision for cultivation. Machine learning algorithms shall be the best choice to solve above problem and predict the prices of agricultural goods based on the weather conditions. This paper suggests different regression models have been investigated to predict vegetable prices. Based on this predictions, vegetable prices are forecasted to aids farmers to plan their next crop and to avoid hyperinflation. In this work, weather data are collected using web scraping whereas the weather data is collected from the weather channel website for appropriate period. The dependency of weather data and the vegetable price is derived by graphically plotting both date for every five days. The data set is created by combining both the weather and vegetable data. The machine learning algorithms such as decision tree, random forest, linear regression are be applied on the weather-price dataset for testing and training. Here 80% of the data is utilized for training whereas 20% data is utilized for testing. The accuracy prediction of different models are calculated and compared. Decision Tree Regressor shows highest prediction accuracy of 92.17%

Keywords: Weather data · Random Forest · Decision Tree · Logistic regression · Linear regression

1 Introduction

Agriculture is the most important economic pillar in our country. Agriculture is the primary source of income for majority of families in India. Agriculture decides the country's GDP. To meet the demands of the region's inhabitants, more than half of the land is used for agriculture. To achieve the stringent criteria, agricultural techniques must be modernized. Our work intends to more effectively solve the problem of agricultural price forecast to assure farmers earnings. It leverages Machine Learning algorithms on various data to come up with superior solutions. Through this application, productivity can be enhanced by analyzing the anticipatory agricultural goods prices. A good vegetable price forecasting system can provide support to farmers with opportunities that

R. N. Shaw et al. (Eds.): ICACIS 2023, CCIS 1921, pp. 23–31, 2023.
https://doi.org/10.1007/978-3-031-45124-9_3

benefit the general public also. In general, rapid swinging of vegetable costs are usual. These cost changes are primarily due to the lack of prior knowledge about seasonally price changes which can also cause changes in demand and the market value of a crop. This leads loss of profit to farmers and also to public because of overprice. This is due to lack of technology analytics to help the formers to take decision which can give meaningful insights and make appropriate decisions. Generally, Machine learning algorithms are used to tackle prediction problems in a variety of industries, however only few studies have been reported in literature on price prediction for agricultural items, particularly vegetables. The main objective of this research to develop a systematic approach to understand the nature of the crop price-weather relationship and to predict the price based on weather data. To achieve the above objective machine learning prediction methodology has been chosen.

2 Literature Survey

Crop price prediction using random forest and decision tree regression was proposed by Brunda S. et al. [1] by using 330 different crop data sets across India to predict the price of the crops for the profit of the farmers using different machine learning algorithms like decision tree regressor and random forest regressor and the best accuracy was obtained in random forest regressor. However, the main draw-back is they didn't go for any other techniques like KNN which may give a better accuracy.

Prediction of vegetable price based on neural network and genetic algorithm was proposed by Changshou Luo et al. [2] working with the vegetable price that are collected from the market. They built four different prediction models namely neural network model, neural network model based on genetic algorithm, RBF neural network model and integrated prediction model. In which the integrated prediction model showed the best results.

Machine learning based future price prediction algorithm was proposed by Ishan Pandey et al. [3] by calculating the correlation coefficient on the basis of RNN algorithm, and then used Decision tree regression algorithm for the price prediction of commodities. However the number of data used by them are very limited.

Prediction of vegetable cost based on weather condition using FRNN was proposed by P. S. Keerthana et al. [4]. They created an application for the estimation of price of vegetables and an email has been sent to the user after the prediction.

Crop price forecasting system using supervised machine learning algorithms was reported by Rachana P. S. et al. [5] by designing a system of two roles called the Admin and the agriculture department in which the department shall take price prediction and profit prediction decisions. They used Naive Bayes algorithm for the prediction of price and KNN algorithm for the Profit Prediction.

Crop price prediction using supervised machine learning algorithms was suggested by Ranjani Dhanapal et al. [6]. In this paper they mainly focused the problems of the farmers that are faced after harvesting the crops. They collected the previous year data like weather, rainfall, etc. and they used the decision tree regressor for predicting the crop price.

Crop-yield and price forecasting using machine learning was reported by Sadiq A. Mulla et al. [7] by predicting the price of the crops by analyzing patterns of the past data.

They considered the parameters such as rainfall, market price, temperature, past yield, etc., on that particular land area. They used supervised machine learning algorithm such as decision tree algorithm to predict the price of next twelve months.

Crop Price Prediction System using Machine learning Algorithms was suggested by Sahithi B. et al. [8]. In their analysis price prediction of crops were achieved using different factors such as temperature, soil type, etc., they used an approach called as EDA for the analysis of data and used different machine learning techniques such as XGBoost, Linear regression, Decision Tree techniques to predict the price of the crops. Neural networks have been implemented for a better accuracy. Finally, XGBoost gave the best accuracy in predicting the price of the crops.

Crop Price Forecasting system using Supervised Machine Learning algorithms was proposed by Zhang D. et al. [9]. They found that, it will be easier for farmers to develop crops if we can predict the weather and water levels. The most important aspect of their idea is price prediction, which will improve yield if farmers earn more than they do now. This will also help the people to manage their expenses if the price is forecasted earlier, which means they would buy the vegetables sooner and consume later. This initiative may provide an almost exact price.

Though these works proposed various algorithms to predict the agricultural products, they have certain limitations such as minimum dataset utilization, effective weather prediction mechanism and need based analysis. The present study aims to address these issues and to formulate more efficient algorithm for vegetable price prediction based on weather data.

3 System Design and Implementation

The proposed model has data extraction, dependency graph of weather and vegetable price, data gathering, data cleaning and building a machine learning model. The block diagram of the proposed model has been given in Fig. 1.

The implementation is divided into the following modules:

- Data Extraction
- Dependency graph of weather and vegetable price
- Data Gathering
- Data Cleaning
- Building a machine learning model

3.1 Data Extraction

Web scraping, also known as web data mining or web harvesting, is the process of creating a program that can automatically gather, interpret, retrieve, and arrange data from the internet. In other words, rather than manually saving data from websites, web scraping software will load and extract data from many websites according to our specifications. Python is a widely used programming language for scraping the web. Web scraping can be done without the use of any third-party tools by using Python's basic programming language. Beautiful Soup is a Python package for reading HTML files and extracting

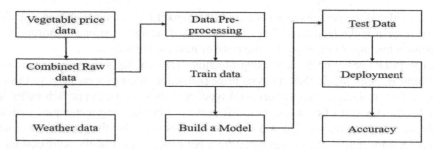

Fig. 1. System Architecture

data from them It can be used with requests since it requires an input to construct a soup object because it is incapable of fetching a web page on its own. This data extraction modification with Beautiful Soup is simple and effective. Tables 1 and 2 gives the extracted data.

Table 1. Extracted Weather Data

Day	Temperature	Description	Humidity
Day-1	37 °C	Mostly Sunny	Rain Chance 23%
Day-2	37 °C	Sunny	Rain Chance 2%
Day-3	36 °C	Sunny	Rain Chance 7%
Day-4	36 °C	Mostly Sunny	Rain Chance 7%
Day-5	36 °C	Sunny	Rain Chance 11%

Table 2. Extracted Vegetable Data.

Item	Price in Indian Rs
Garlic-Hill	115
Garlic Hill Peeled	90
Onion Big	30
Onion Big White	30
Onion Big Peeled	40
Onion Big White	30
Onion Big Peeled	40

The average weather data and vegetable price data are extracted and plotted using Python script. The relationship trend was observed. It was observed that vegetable price is indirectly based on temperature, because in general, the price of the vegetable depends upon its yield whereas the yield depends upon the temperature.

From Fig. 2 shows the average temperature for every five days and next part of the figure shows the price of selected vegetables (needy vegetables) for that period. From the figure, it is observed that some of the vegetables prices are decreasing and others are increasing as the temperature decreases.

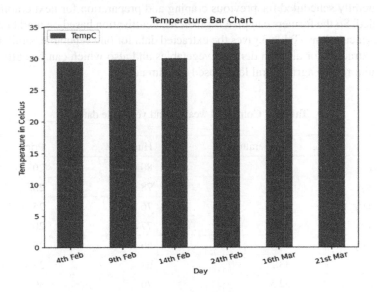

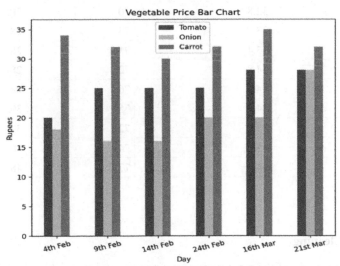

Fig. 2. Temperature and vegetable price Bar chart

3.2 Data Gathering

The average temperature, average humidity and corresponding rate of particular vegetable were extracted and tabulated for three months. The particular months January, February and March are considered particularly because during these months cultivation is generally scheduled for previous craping and preparation for next craping shall be scheduled. So the formers can plan for their next cultivation based on market demand and profit calculations. Table 3 gives the extracted data for one vegetable, similarly data has been extracted for all high demand vegetables and also which can be cultivated in the particular region agricultural land based on climate.

Table 3. Combined weather and vegetable data

Date	Temperature °C	Humidity	Price
4th February	29.5	80	20
9th February	29.8	78	25
14th February	30	76	25
19th February	31.2	77	20
24th February	32.4	66	25
1st March	33.2	68	25
6th March	32.5	70	30
11th March	32.8	70	30
16th March	33	74	28
21st March	33.4	71	28
26th March	34.8	72	28
31st March	34.4	76	28
5th April	34	75	30
10th April	33.6	72	32
15th April	35	74	36
20th April	34.2	77	48

3.3 Data Cleaning

Data cleaning is one of the most important processes in any machine learning project. Different statistical analysis and data visualization tools that can be used to investigate the data and to determine which data cleaning activities should be performed. Data cleaning are so crucial in any predictive model if they are overlooked, models shall be failed or indicated too optimistic success outcomes. In this work, all null values from our dataset were removed and verified whether all data are valid numbers.

3.4 Building Machine Learning Model

Exploratory data analysis (E.D.A)., is a critical stage in identifying, analyzing, and summarizing a variety of data sets, which frequently involves the use of various data visualization techniques. It enables a data analyst to spot patterns, identify abnormalities, test theories, and draw conclusions about the best strategy to monitor data sources for more precise findings. The data has been split as 80% of the data is for training and 20% of the data is for testing. Five different algorithms like decision tree regressor, random forest regressor, linear regression, logistic regression, and K-Neighbors, and found that the Decision Tree Regressor were applied to predict the price of vegetables.

The prediction has been done by following steps:

Step 1: Initialize the combined weather and grocery data set.
Step 2: Select all the rows of second column to the variable X, Which is an independent variable.
Step 3: Select all the rows of the last column to the variable y, which is dependent variable.
Step 4: Import the Machine learning module.
Step 5: Fit the values of X and y with the respected module.
Step 6: Get the accuracy of the module.

Here X and Y are weather date and vegetable price respectively.

4 Result and Discussion

Table 4 gives the accuracy of prediction of different models. The logistic regression shows very low prediction accuracy where as the highest accuracy was obtained in Decision Tree regressor. Compared to other algorithms decision trees requires less effort for data preparation during pre-processing. The high accuracy may be due to the advantages of decision tree such as it need no normalization and scaling of data, missing values in data has very less influence in decision making and very much intuitive. Hence the proposed Machine learning model serves as a good technological tool to educate farmers to decision about which crop shall be cultivated to make the best price at the time of harvesting based on weather condition. Because weather condition play vital role not only in cultivation but also to provide suitable "keeping quality" of various vegetables based on weather.

Table 4. Comparison of Models

Type of Algorithm	Accuracy
Linear Regression	89.56%
Decision Tree Regressor	97.22%
Random Forest Regressor	92.17%
K-Neighbors Regressor	86.37%
Logistic Regressor	85.19%

5 Conclusion

This work proposes estimation of vegetable prices based on weather data, which is powered by excellent machine learning techniques and also with a user-friendly interface. The previous year three months weather data and high demand vegetable data along with humidity level were considered as input data. All data were averaged for every five days in order to remove any other unexpected factors influences. The gathered training datasets give adequate forecasting of market price and demand. Different ML algorithms such as Decision trees, Random forest regressor, K-Neighbors, Linear regression, and Logistic regression were used to predict the vegetable prices. The Decision tree Regressor provides better accuracy compared to all other algorithms used here. Hence it helps the farmers to predict the vegetable rates in particular season and cultivate them accordingly to increase their profit. However, further analysis is need to get more accurate prediction by integrating weather prediction models and soil property.

References

1. Brunda, S., Nimish, L., Chiranthan, S., Khan, A.: Crop price prediction using random forest and decision tree regression. Int. Res. J. Eng. Technol. (IRJET) **7**(9), 235–237 (2020)
2. Luo, C., Wei, Q., Zhou, L.: Prediction of vegetable price based on neural network and genetic algorithm. IFIP AICT **7**, 672–681 (2011). Pandey, I., Sathish Kumar Reddy, M., Dharani Vamsidhar Reddy, M., Krishna Babu, K.: Machine learning based future priced prediction of the products. Int. Res. J. Eng. Technol. (IRJET), **8**(4), 865–871 (2021)
3. Keerthana, P.S., Keerthika, B., Shalini, R.: Prediction of vegetable cost based on weather condition using FRNN. Int. Res. J. Eng. Technol. (IRJET) **7**(3), 1608–1612 (2020)
4. Rachana, P.S., Rashmi, G., Shravani, D., Shruthi, N.: Crop yield prediction using machine learning approaches. Int. Res. J. Eng. Technol. (IRJET) **6**, 4805–4807 (2020)
5. Dhanapal, R., AjanRaj, A., Balavinayagapragathish, S., Balaji, J.: Crop price prediction using supervised machine learning algorithms. J. Softw. Eng. Simulat. **6**(1), 14–20 (2021)
6. Mulla, S.A.: Crop-yield and price forecasting using machine learning. Int. J. Analyt. Exp. Modal Anal. **7**(8), 1731–1737 (2020)
7. Das, S., et al.: Advance machine learning and artificial intelligence applications in service robot. In: Artificial Intelligence for Future Generation Robotics, pp. 83–91. Elsevier (2021). https://doi.org/10.1016/B978-0-323-85498-6.00002-2. ISBN 9780323854986
8. Gupta, V., et al.: A new era of automated market-makers (AMM) powered by non-fungible tokens - a review. Glob. J. Innov. Emerg. Technol. **1**(2), 1–7. https://doi.org/10.58260/j.iet.2202.0106
9. Ye, L., Li, Y., Liang, W., Song, Q., Liu, Y., Qin, X.: Vegetable price prediction based on PSO-BP neural network. In: International Conference on Intelligent Computation Technology and Automation. IEEE (2015). ISBN 978-1-4673-7644-0/15
10. Hemageetha, N., Nasira, G.M.: Radial basis function model for vegetable price prediction. In: International Conference on Pattern Recognition, Informatics and Mobile Engineering. IEEE (2013). ISBN 978-1-4673-5845-3/13
11. Ramesh, D., Khosla, E.: Seasonal ARIMA to forecast fruits and vegetable agricultural prices. In: IEEE International Symposium on Smart Electronic Systems. IEEE (2019). ISBN 978-1-7281-4655-3/19

12. Warnakulasooriya, H., Senarathna, J., Peiris, P., Fernando, S., Kasthurirathna, D.: Supermarket retail – based demand and price prediction of vegetables. In: International Conference on Advances in ICT for Emerging Regions. IEEE (2020). ISBN 978-1-7281-8655-9/20
13. Vohra, A., Pandey, N., Khatri, S.K.: Decision Making Support System for Prediction of Prices in Agricultural Commodity. IEEE (2019). ISBN 978-1-5386-9346-9/19

Integrating Scene and Text Recognition for Improved Scene Caption to Assist Visually Impaired

Jyoti Madake$^{(\boxtimes)}$, Mayank Jha, Nirmay Meshram, Narendra Muhal, Unmesh Naik, and Shripad Bhatlawande

Department of Electronics and Telecommunication, Vishwakarma Institute of Technology, Pune, Maharashtra, India
jyoti.madake@vit.edu

Abstract. The paper introduces an innovative real-time system designed to enhance the scene perception of visually impaired individuals. The proposed model leverages a deep learning approach, employing a CNN-LSTM encoder-decoder framework for efficient image captioning. This novel system integrates scene text information using optical character recognition (OCR) to generate meaningful scene captions as audible feedback for blind or visually impaired users. The proposed model is implemented on embedded processing unit, Jetson Nano equipped with monocular camera and mono-earphone. The model extracts scene features and text information to provide detailed descriptions of the environment. The LSTM-CNN model was trained on a Flickr 8K dataset and a custom dataset, specifically tailored to the Indian environment. Eight different CNN architectures, including VGG-16, EfficientNet-V2L, MobileNet-V2, Inception Resnet-V2, Resnet152-V2, EfficientNet-B7, Xception, and NASNet-Large, were tested to compare their scene caption performance with sigmoid and Tanh activation. Extensive evaluations were conducted using metrics such as BLUE, GLUE, METEOR, and RIBES, with VGG-16 and EfficientNet-V2L achieving the highest BLUE scores of 0.491 and 0.489, respectively. The proposed system presents a promising solution to provide visually impaired individuals with essential information about their surroundings through auditory perception for independent mobility and reduced risk for accident.

Keywords: Blind assistance · scene caption · OCR · CNN · LSTM

1 Introduction

A significant area of research that lies at the intersection of computer vision and natural language processing is image captioning. Automatically producing captions for scenes and photographs has arisen as a key interdisciplinary research subject in both academia and industry. Image captioning systems can be used for a variety of practical purposes, including image search, human-computer interaction, and assistance for persons who are visually impaired, by making it easier to organize and manage enormous amounts of often unstructured visual data.

R. N. Shaw et al. (Eds.): ICACIS 2023, CCIS 1921, pp. 32–44, 2023.
https://doi.org/10.1007/978-3-031-45124-9_4

Scene description can particularly be used to assist blind people, which is the aim of our model. Scene description can be of great help for blind people to become independent while going outdoors. Our system will help blind people exercise their freedom more effectively as they will no longer need to be completely dependent on other people's help to get an idea of the scenario around them. This was the main motivation behind the development of the model or system proposed in this paper.

This model is being implemented using deep learning models. Modern state-of-the-art models frequently base their structures on the encoder-decoder paradigm [1]. An encoder's objective is to turn an input image into a vector that represents the image's characteristics. A decoder's objective is to use those features to produce a string of words that describe an image. The most common deep convolutional neural networks used as encoders are CNN models [17]. Different CNN architectures include VGG, Resnet, Inception, MobileNet etc., all of which have been pre-trained on sizable picture datasets. Thus, compared to a model that was trained solely on an image captioning dataset, the entire image captioning model will contain more implicit information about items on an image. This enables the generation of captions that include things seen by both the encoder trained on a larger dataset as well as the total model during training.

The structure of the paper is as follows. Related works by various researchers are addressed in Sect. 2. The proposed method for the scene detection system is described in Sect. 3. In Sect. 4, the result of the proposed system is discussed. And a conclusion is made in Sect. 5.

2 Introduction

Image captioning has gained a lot of interest recently as a result of its expanding use cases. The various methods for captioning images, including retrieval-based, template-based, deep learning-based, and few sorts of evaluation techniques. There are image captioning techniques based on encoder-decoder frameworks, multimodal learning, and neural network-based retrieval and template methods in deep neural networks [2]. Template matching is described for finding and matching symbols in scene detection. It is done using the SURF algorithm with accuracy 91.67% [8]. Bag of Visual Words (BoVW), Histogram of Gradient Features (HOG), and Local Quinary Patterns (LQP), are used for scene classification in [3]. The Support Vector Machine (SVM) classifier is used for classification. To further develop the recognition system, objects' distinctive properties are extracted [4]. Uses RGB with depth data to find and locate objects inside a scene. For Image retrieving approach Remote Sensing (RS) and Content Based Image Retrieval (CBIR) is user [5, 6]. Other methods are ARGMM, MLIRM and MC-SVM [6].

In RNN-CNN architecture RNN is used for word generation by using Multimodal generation, the image and the generated text are combined for RNN to make predictions [7, 8]. ResNet50 is an established model of CNN, it is employed to take out images which serves as a source of data for the RNN model used to create captions [9]. CNN technique and SVM techniques are used for labeling of scenes. LSTM and RNN are used for sentence generation after extracting information from scenarios [10, 11]. Factorization of CNN model helps to get disentangled parameters of the network which results in faster training. But increases computational cost due to factorization [12]. Beam-Search algorithms with the CNN and RNN framework gives multiple captions for a targeted image [13]. An Approach where the image is passed through layers that include convolutional, flattening, pooling and connected layers [32]. The author [14] Used V3 CNN-model with LSTM, GRU and Bi-directional LSTM models. Bi-directional RNN can generate image features through sentences and vice-versa [15]. Their accuracy was 85.84%, 56.37% and 71.22 respectively with CNN as their image encoder [14]. In [16] the VGG16 based faster R-CNN network is used with a gaussian function to obtain the weighted distribution matrix which is then concatenated with the feature vector to get image caption.

Other methods such as RNN with CNN and LSTM with CNN are compared in [17] and [18]. And concludes that LSTM with CNN performs better. LSTM can have long- and short-term memorization but RNN has only short-term memorization [1, 19]. VGG19 and ResNet101 were utilized as image captioning encoders in [20].

SCA CNN is utilized for caption generation where SCA dynamically changes the context of sentence formation in multiple layer feature maps, recording the location and focus of visual attention [21]. J. Donahue et al. mentioned the comparison of LRCN Flow and LRCN RGB using Long-Term Recurrent Convolutional Networks (LRCN) for visual identification and description [22]. DeepSORT with a recursive Kalman filter is used for multi-object detection [23].

In another approach LSTM is fed a tag dependent weighted matrix of the parameters with the visual characteristics that SCN gathered from the image. Attention mechanism (bottom up) is used in image captioning [24, 25]. Consider the object and scene features from the input image for better scene recognition, they have used ImageNet and Places2 datasets.

Approaches for boosting image captioning with neural network architectures are discussed [26, 27]. First approach considers different attributes of LSTM such as Utilizing only attributes, feeding attributes first, inserting the picture first, inserting the image at each time step, and entering the attributes at each time step [26]. The visual representation at the highest levels of abstraction is considered in the deep hierarchical encoder-decoder network, and each of these levels is connected to a single LSTM. The middle layer is used in encoder-decoder applications to improve the top-most LSTM's decoding capabilities [27].

One method is to focus on the attentional regions, whose types are: Convolutional activation grids, object suggestions, and spatial transformers nets are used. The spatial transformer technique is the most successful [28]. Another strategy combines top-down and bottom-up attention methods to provide outstanding assessment metrics scores. The top-down technique employs task-specific context to forecast the regions of an image that should receive attention, the bottom-up approach collects regions of convolutional feature vectors [29]. The Jetson TX1 device from NVIDIA is used with the Deep learning Caffe network. ZF architecture for suggested deep detectors was used on Jetson [30]. Some experiments use LSTM and CNN on Raspberry pi. A paper compares performance of models on PC, Up Board and Raspberry pi, with Upboard performing better than RaspberryPi [6]. For embedded real time scene detection systems, a paper [31] uses FPGAs. SIFT keypoint detection with an 18-dimensional descriptor is used. MSCOCO, Flickr30k, Flickr8k, UIUC PASCAL, RSCID, and UCF01 are the datasets which were mentioned in the many papers [1, 13, 15, 19, 21, 22]. Evaluation metrics used were BLEU, METEOR, CIDEr, and PPL.

The literature review summarizes that of the many available deep learning approaches for scene recognition, combination of two neural networks - CNN and LSTM is most widely used these days. Most of the systems are trained on readily available datasets such as Flickr8K, Flickr30K, MSCOCO etc. So, this paper proposes a system trained on a region-specific dataset along with the available dataset Flickr8K so that the system can perform accurate scene detection in subcontinent conditions and environment.

3 Methodology

This paper proposes a system to detect scenes and give them as audio output to the blind people. The methodology is divided into three parts: Dataset and pre-processing, CNN-LSTM architecture, and OCR. The caption file is taken, and the filename and captions are separated. A vocabulary is then created from the available caption in the dataset, this vocabulary has the frequency at which each word is occurring in the caption's dataset. Punctuations, numeric values, and single character words are then removed from the caption to clean data before training the model.

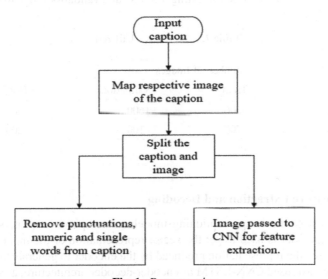

Fig. 1. Preprocessing

Figure 1 gives an overall flow of preprocessing being done in the model. Punctuations, numeric values, and single character words are then removed from the caption to clean data before training the model. Figure 1 gives an overall flow of preprocessing being done in the model.

3.1 Dataset

The CNN-LSTM model is trained on the dataset Flickr8K, another custom dataset is assembled in the Indian environment to make the model more robust to the sub-continent. Some of the images from the custom dataset are shown in Fig. 2.

Fig. 2. Custom Dataset

Flickr8K dataset has around 8090 images, the custom dataset created by authors has 600 images. These datasets are divided into training, testing and validation in the ratio 70:20:10 respectively, that is 70% training, 20% testing and 10% validation. Table 1 shows the number of images used for testing, training and validations in both the datasets.

Table 1. The Dataset Utilized

Dataset	Number Of Images		
	Train	Validation	Test
Flickr 8K	4800	1600	1600
Custom Dataset	700	100	200

3.2 Scene Feature Extraction and Decoding

These days most of the image captioning models are employed on encoder-decoder architectures. Encoder is used to get the vector representation of the input image. The decoder then uses the representation produced by the encoder to generate the output. In this system we have used CNN-LSTM as encoder-decoder architecture, as shown in fig 3.

The 8 models of CNN have been used in the proposed system. These models are used for feature extraction of the image. After that, a decoder produces output based on the representation the encoder produces. The decoder which we have used in LSTM. After encoding the data and having the feature extracted from these models, LSTM is used for decoding the data. After decoding the fitting of the model is done by using the training and testing data.

The general flow of the architecture is such that the input image is first passed into models, which maps the image data to a feature vector. This feature vector is then passed

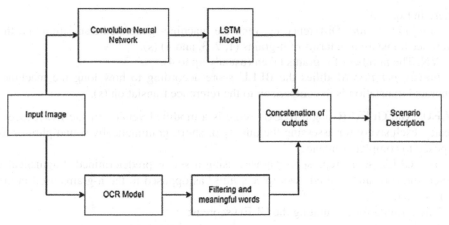

Fig. 3. Block Diagram of developed system

in the LSTM model, here sequential prediction on the feature vectors is done. A dense layer is then used to generate the final caption before displaying the output.

3.3 Scene Text Recognition

Optical Character Recognition is included in the proposed system to extract the text information present in the image input. This text information is vital in describing the scene present in the image. The OCR model is integrated with the Encoder-decoder framework to generate final captions.

Optical character recognition is implemented using one of the predefined models Keras based on Tensorflow. The input image is resized to 224 × 224; this gives better accuracy because the small irrelevant text in the image is blurred and only the big sized and important text is extracted. After this single- and double-character words are filtered out. Then the 5 text boxes with the largest area that is 5 largest words in the image are then taken and passed in a dictionary which is implemented using enchant library. Wrong or garbage words are eliminated by this process, followed by elimination of duplicates. The extracted words are then fused with the caption generated by the CNN-LSTM model to reach an optimum and meaningful caption for the input image.

3.4 Evaluation Metrics

BLEU. The measure BLEU (Bilingual Evaluation Understudy) is used to assess the accuracy of translations produced by software. It gauges how closely a translation created by a machine resembles one or more human-provided reference translations. The machine-generated translation is equal to the reference translation if the BLEU score is 1, which ranges from 0 to 1 (s).

The formula for calculating BLEU score is:

$$BLEU = brevity\_penalty * e^{(\Sigma log 2(precision\_ngram)/N)} \tag{1}$$

where in Eq. (1):

precision_ngram: Difference between the machine- generated translation and the reference translation in terms of n-grams (1, 2, 3, and 4) (s).

*N*N: The number of n-grams taken (usually up to 4).

brevity_penalty: Modifies the BLEU score according to how long the machine-generated translation is in comparison to the reference translation (s).

GLEU. The GLEU (Google-BLEU) score is a modified version of the BLEU score created exclusively for assessing the quality of short, grammatically sound phrases as opposed to complete sentences.

The GLEU score represents phrases using a set of predetermined, linguistically driven subword units called "wordpiece units" as opposed to the n-grams used in the BLEU score.

The formula for calculating the GLEU score is:

$$GLEU = Min(1, e\Sigma log2(pw)/M) * e(\alpha * |N - M|/M) \tag{2}$$

where in Eq. (2):

pw: Precision score of the wordpiece units between the machine-generated phrase and the reference phrase.

M: Number of wordpiece units in the machine-generated phrase.

N: Number of wordpiece units in the reference phrase.

α: Tunable parameter that controls the impact of the difference in length between the machine-generated phrase and the reference phrase on the GLEU score. Typically, alpha is set to 0.25.

METEOR. A metric called METEOR (Metric for Evaluation of Translation with Explicit Ordering) score is employed to assess the caliber of translations produced by automated means.

Compared to the BLEU score, which just considers the n-grams overlap, the METEOR score employs a more complicated method. It specifically considers the machine translation's quality in terms of word choice, word order, synonyms, and similarity to the reference translation (s). The METEOR score uses a stemming algorithm, which is one of its distinctive features.

The formula for calculating the METEOR score is:

$$METEOR = (1 - \alpha) * (P * R)/(\alpha * P + (1 - \alpha) * R) \tag{3}$$

where in Eq. (3):

P: precision score; *R*: recall score

α: Tunable parameter that controls the impact of precision and recall on the overall score. Typically, α is set to 0.5.

RIBES. Machine translation output quality is measured using the metric RIBES (Rank-based Intuitive Bilingual Evaluation Score). The RIBES score employs a rank-based methodology to assess how similar the word order in the machine-generated translation is to the word order in the reference translation, as opposed to the BLEU and METEOR scores, which concentrate on the overlap between machine-generated and reference translations (s).

The formula for calculating the RIBES score is:

$$RIBES = 1 - (d(R, M)/d(R, R\_avg)) \tag{4}$$

where in Eq. (4):

R: Reference translation(s).

M: Machine-generated translation.

R_avg: Average of the reference translations.

(R, M): Distance between the ranks of words in the reference translation(s) and the machine-generated translation.

(R, R_avg): Distance between the ranks of words in the reference translation(s) and the average of the reference translations.

4 Result and Testing

The training of the model was done on a custom dataset of 1000 images of Indian scenarios having five captions for each image. The testing was done by feeding random images having captions of those specific images.

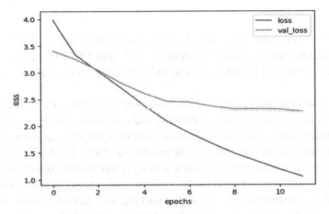

Fig. 4. Loss in training and validation.

The specifications used by the machine to train was Processor -AMD Rayzon 5 4600H with Radeon Graphics, 3 GHz processor. 64-bit OS, x64 based processor, with 8 GB Ram and Windows 11 Home Operating System.

Figure 4 shows the graph of loss in training and loss in validation vs the epochs. In Fig. 4 the epochs were set to 5. This was for training both the dataset -Flickr8K and custom dataset at once. This model showed good accuracy while trained with Flickr 8k and custom dataset.

Table 2. Comparisons of different CNN architectures and activation methods

Models	Activation Method	BLEU	BLEU 1	BLEU 2	BLEU 3	BLEU 4	GLEU	METEOR	RIBES
Efficient Net-B7	Sigmoid	0.453	0.398	0.202	0.1	0.038	0.232	0.379	0.315
	Tanh	0.445	0.341	0.151	0.06	0.038	0.191	0.311	0.223
Efficient Net-V2L	Sigmoid	0.489	0.37	0.198	0.138	0.075	0.236	0.346	0.306
	Tanh	0.434	0.362	0.188	0.104	0.025	0.219	0.332	0.255
Inception Resnet-V2	Sigmoid	0.179	0.133	0.055	0	0	0.078	0.106	0.117
	Tanh	0.194	0.146	0.055	0	0	0.084	0.113	0.117
MobileNet-V2	Sigmoid	0.405	0.294	0.136	0.076	0	0.162	0.285	0.242
	Tanh	0.349	0.31	0.17	0.101	0.038	0.19	0.308	0.257
NASNet-Large	Sigmoid	0.267	0.192	0.084	0.031	0	0.107	0.186	0.172
	Tanh	0.257	0.209	0.103	0.037	0	0.125	0.195	0.172
ResNet152-V2	Sigmoid	0.179	0.133	0.055	0	0	0.078	0.106	0.117
	Tanh	0.194	0.146	0.055	0	0	0.084	0.113	0.117
Xception	Sigmoid	0.42	0.281	0.118	0.061	0	0.147	0.259	0.141
	Tanh	0.442	0.279	0.145	0.1	0.057	0.171	0.255	0.246
VGG-16	Sigmoid	0.491	0.391	0.195	0.113	0.038	0.227	0.375	0.304
	Tanh	0.424	0.351	0.191	0.101	0.038	0.208	0.34	0.309

Table 2 above is a comparison of different evaluation metrics in different activation methods and architecture of CNN. EfficientNet-V2L and VGG-16 have the best BLEU score and GLEU score. EfficientNet-B7 and VGG-16 have the best METEOR and RIBES score.

Figure 5 shows captions generated for four images by our system. The first one is a SBI Atm, the second one is a view of parking and a building, the third one is an image of a medical store and the fourth image is in front of a burger king store. These are the results upon testing the custom dataset. The model was trained with 12 epochs and batch size of 16. In custom dataset the categories with a greater number of similar images give more accurate results as compared to the scenarios with fewer images. The categories in Fig. 5. That is classrooms, labs, buildings parking and shops had more images in the dataset, as a result the caption generated is up to the mark with the scenes in the images. Few scenarios such as outdoor sports activities had a limited number of images, so the accuracy in their caption was limited.

The average time taken by VGG-16, EfficientNet-B7 and EfficientNet-V2L were 21.48, 29.53 and 30.12 s respectively to generate the caption after feeding the input. Overall VGG-16 was the best and fastest amongst all the architectures. The images with text took more time comparatively for text recognition and integration with the generated caption.

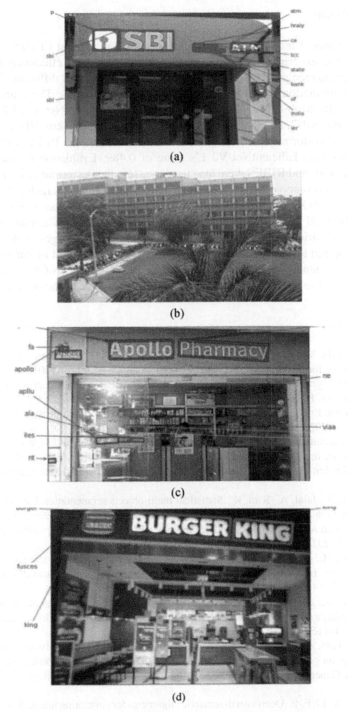

Fig. 5. Ground (a) Truth: - You are at SBI ATM. Caption Generated: - you are outside atm named atm. (b) Ground Truth: - There are bikes in front of building. Caption Generated: - there is parking in front of building. (c). Ground Truth: - You are at medical store. Caption Generated: - you are outside in store named pharmacy apollo. (d). Ground Truth: - You are at restaurant named Burger King Caption Generated: - you are at store named burger king.

5   Conclusion

The proposed model incorporates Scene Recognition and Optical Character Recognition (OCR). The experiments revealed that CNN models can be effectively trained on Indian datasets to recognize various scenarios. We evaluated eight different CNN architectures in combination with LSTM to generate image captions. These architectures include VGG-16, MobileNet-V2, ResNet152-V2, Inception ResNet V2, EfficientNet-V2 L, EfficientNet-B7, NASNet-Large, and Xception. Among them, VGG-16 demonstrated superior performance compared to the others, achieving a BLEU score of 0.49, slightly higher than EfficientNet-V2 L's score of 0.489. Evaluation metrics such as GLEU, METEOR, and RIBES were also used to assess the performance of the models.

This model consists of scene recognition as well as Optical Character Recognition. The integration of OCR significantly enhanced the overall performance of the model.

It was observed that CNN model can be trained enough for Indian dataset as well to recognize scenarios. Although approximately minimum 20 images of the same scenarios are required to train and get decent results. The dataset used in this paper is not augmented, augmentation can be done for improvising accuracy of the given model. Optical Character recognition improvised overall performance of the model.

References

1. Zakir Hossain, Md., Sohel, F., Fairuz Shiratuddin, M., Laga, H.: A comprehensive survey of deep learning for image captioning. ACM Comput. Surv. **51**(6), 1–36 (2018)
2. Sharma, H., Agrahari, M., Singh, S.K., Firoj, M., Mishra, R.K.: Image captioning: a comprehensive survey. In: 2020 International Conference on Power Electronics & IoT Applications in Renewable Energy and Its Control (PARC), pp. 325–328 (2020). https://doi.org/10.1109/PARC49193.2020.236619
3. Aziz, S., Kareem, Z., Khan, M.U., Imtiaz, M.A.: Embedded system design for visual scene classification. In: 2018 IEEE 9th Annual Information Technology, Electronics and Mobile Communication Conference (IEMCON) (2018). https://doi.org/10.1109/iemcon.2018.8614864
4. Rafique, A.A., Jalal, A., Kim, K.: Statistical multi-objects segmentation for indoor/outdoor scene detection and classification via depth images. In: 2020 17th International Bhurban Conference on Applied Sciences and Technology (IBCAST) (2020). https://doi.org/10.1109/ibcast47879.2020.9044576
5. Hoxha, G., Melgani, F., Demir, B.: Retrieving images with generated textual descriptions. In: 2019 IEEE International Geoscience and Remote Sensing Symposium (IGARSS 2019), pp. 5812–5815 (2019)
6. Chaudhuri, B., Demir, B., Chaudhuri, S., Bruzzone, L.: Multilabel remote sensing image retrieval using a semisupervised graph- theoretic method. IEEE Trans. Geosci. Remote Sens. **56**(2), 1144–1158 (2018)
7. Tanti, M., Gatt, A., Camilleri, K.: What is the role of recurrent neural networks (RNNs) in an image caption generator?" In: Proceedings of the 10th International Conference on Natural Language Generation, pp. 51–60. Association for Computational, Santiago de Compostela (2017)
8. Karpathy, A., Li, F.-F.: Deep visual-semantic alignments for generating image descriptions. In: Proceedings of the IEEE Conference on Computer Vision and Pattern Recognition (CVPR), pp. 3128–3137 (2015)

9. Calvin, R., Suresh, S.: Image captioning using convolutional neural networks and recurrent neural network. In: 2021 6th International Conference for Convergence in Technology (I2CT), pp. 1–4 (2021). https://doi.org/10.1109/I2CT51068.2021.9418001
10. Jia, X., Gavves, E., Fernando, B., Tuytelaars, T.: Guiding the long-short term memory model for image caption generation. In: Proceedings of the IEEE International Conference on Computer Vision (ICCV), pp. 2407–2415 (2015)
11. Kaur, M., Mohta, A.: A review of deep learning with recurrent neural network. In: 2019 International Conference on Smart Systems and Inventive Technology (ICSSIT) (2019). https://doi.org/10.1109/icssit46314.2019.8987
12. Szegedy, C., Vanhoucke, V., Ioffe, S., Shlens, J., Wojna, Z.: Rethinking the inception architecture for computer vision. In: 2016 IEEE Conference on Computer Vision and Pattern Recognition (CVPR) (2016). https://doi.org/10.1109/cvpr.2016.308
13. Hoxha, G., Melgani, F., Slaghenauffi, J.: A new CNN-RNN framework for remote sensing image captioning. In: 2020 Mediterranean and Middle-East Geoscience and Remote Sensing Symposium (M2GARSS), pp. 1–4 (2020)
14. Alzubi, J.A., et al.: Deep Image Captioning Using an Ensemble of CNN and LSTM Based Deep Neural Networks, pp. 5761–5769 (2021)
15. Chen, X., Zitnick, C.L.: Mind's eye: a recurrent visual representation for image caption generation. IEEE Conf. Comput. Vis. Pattern Recogn. (CVPR) 2015, 2422–2431 (2015)
16. Ding, S., Qu, S., Xi, Y., Sangaiah, A.K., Wan, S.: Image caption generation with high-level image features. Pattern Recogn. Lett. 123, 89–95 (2019), ISSN 0167-8655
17. Aneja, J., Deshpande, A., Schwing, A.G.: Convolutional image captioning. In: Proceedings of the IEEE Conference on Computer Vision and Pattern Recognition (CVPR), pp. 5561–5570 (2018)
18. Chohan, M., Khan, A., Mahar, M.S., Hassan, S., Ghafoor, A., Khan, M.: Image captioning using deep learning: a systematic literature review. Int. J. Adv. Comput. Sci. Appl. (2020)
19. Hrga, I., Ivašić-Kos, M.:Deep image captioning: an overview. In: 2019 42nd International Convention on Information and Communication Technology, Electronics and Microelectronics (MIPRO), pp. 995–1000 (2019)
20. Atliha, V., Šešok, D.: Comparison of VGG and ResNet used as encoders for image captioning. In: 2020 IEEE Open Conference of Electrical, Electronic and Information Sciences (eStream), pp. 1–4 (2020). https://doi.org/10.1109/eStream50540.2020.9108880
21. Chen, L., et al.: SCA-CNN: spatial and channel-wise attention in convolutional networks for image captioning. IEEE Conf. Comput. Vision Pattern Recogn. (CVPR) 2017, 6298–6306 (2017)
22. Donahue, J., et al.: Long-term recurrent convolutional networks for visual recognition and description. IEEE Trans. Pattern Anal. Mach. Intell. 39(4), 677–691 (2017)
23. Jadhav, A., Mukherjee, P., Kaushik, V., Lall, B.: Aerial multi-object tracking by detection using deep association networks. In: 2020 National Conference on Communications (NCC) (2020). https://doi.org/10.1109/ncc48643.2020.9056035
24. Gan, Z., et al.: Semantic compositional networks for visual captioning. In: Proceedings of the IEEE Conference on Computer Vision and Pattern Recognition (CVPR), pp. 5630–5639 (2017)
25. Sun, H., Meng, Z., Tao, P.Y., Ang, M.H.:Scene recognition and object detection in a unified convolutional neural network on a mobile manipulator. In: 2018 IEEE International Conference on Robotics and Automation (ICRA), pp. 5875–5881 (2018). https://doi.org/10.1109/ICRA.2018.8460535
26. Yao, T., Pan, Y., Li, Y., Qiu, Z., Mei, T.: Boosting image captioning with attributes. In: ICCV (2017)

27. Rennie, S.J., Marcheret, E., Mroueh, Y., Ross, J., Goel, V.: Self critical sequence training for image captioning. In: Proceedings of the IEEE Conference on Computer Vision and Pattern Recognition, pp. 7008–7024 (2017)
28. Pedersoli, M., Lucas, T., Schmid, C., Verbeek, J.: Areas of attention for image captioning. In: IEEE International Conference on Computer Vision (ICCV), pp. 1251–1259 (2017)
29. Anderson, P., et al.: Bottom-up and top-down attention for image captioning and visual question answering. arXiv preprint arXiv:1707.07998 (2017)
30. Mhalla, A., Chateau, T., Gazzah, S., Essoukri Ben Amara, N.: An embedded computer-vision system for multi-object detection in traffic surveillance. IEEE Trans. Intell. Transp. Syst. 1–13 (2018). https://doi.org/10.1109/tits.2018.2876614
31. Mukhopadhyay, M., Dey, A., Shaw, R.N., Ghosh, A.: Facial emotion recognition based on textural pattern and convolutional neural network. In: 2021 IEEE 4th International Conference on Computing, Power and Communication Technologies (GUCON), Kuala Lumpur, Malaysia, pp. 1–6 (2021). https://doi.org/10.1109/GUCON50781.2021.9573860
32. Tammina, S.: Transfer learning using VGG-16 with deep convolutional neural network for classifying images. Int. J. Sci. Res. Publ. 9(10) (2019)
33. Aneja, J., Deshpande, A., Alexander, S.: Convolutional image captioning. In: Proceedings of the IEEE Conference on Computer Vision and Pattern Recognition, Salt Lake City (2018)
34. Hsieh, H.-Y., Leu, J.-S., Huang, S.-A.: Implementing a real-time image captioning service for scene identification using embedded system. In: 2019 16th Annual IEEE International Conference on Sensing, Communication, and Networking (SECON) (2019). https://doi.org/10.1109/sahcn.2019.8824961
35. Dahiya, D., Issac, A., Dutta, M.K., Riha, K., Kriz, P.: Computer vision technique for scene captioning to provide assistance to visually impaired. In: 2018 41st International Conference on Telecommunications and Signal Processing (TSP) (2018). https://doi.org/10.1109/tsp.2018.8441428
36. Seong, H., Hyun, J., Chang, H., Lee, S., Woo, S., Kim, E.: Scene recognition via object-to-scene class conversion: end-to-end training. Int. Joint Conf. Neural Netw. (IJCNN) 2019, 1–6 (2019). https://doi.org/10.1109/IJCNN.2019.8852040
37. Staniūtė, R., Šešok, D.: A systematic literature review on image captioning. Appl. Sci. 9(10), 2024 (2019)
38. Gao, L., Guo, Z., Zhang, H., Xu, X., Shen, H.: Video captioning with attention-based LSTM and semantic consistency. IEEE Trans. Multim. 19(9), 2045–2055 (2017)
39. Dalal, N., Triggs, B.: Histograms of oriented gradients for human detection. In: 2005 IEEE Computer Society Conference on Computer Vision and Pattern Recognition (CVPR 2005), vol. 1, pp. 886–893 (2005)

An Analysis of Current Advancements: Elderly Fall Detection Systems Using Machine Learning Techniques

Rahul Modak[1], Ishani Roy[1], Enakshmi Ghosh[1], Santanu Chatterjee[1],
Koushik Majumder[1(✉)], Rabindra Nath Shaw[2], and Ankush Ghosh[2]

[1] Department of Computer Science and Engineering, Maulana Abul Kalam Azad University of
Technology, Nadia, West Bengal, India
koushikzone@yahoo.com
[2] University Center for Research and Development, Chandigarh University, Punjab, India

Abstract. According to the NPHCE (National Program for Health Care of the
Elderly), by 2025, 12% of India's population will be elderly, and the majority of
them will favor independent living. Among them 8–10% needs the highest level of
care. Therefore, the use of machine learning in AALS (Ambient Assisted Living
Systems) areas like fall detection has the potential to significantly affect society.
Falling is one of the most frequent accidents that can cause elderly individuals to
sustain severe injuries or even die. Therefore, early fall detection is essential to
minimizing the negative consequences of falls. The early detection and reporting
of human falls may result in lifesaving. There have been numerous suggested fall
monitoring systems. However, a large number of them identify a daily life activity
as a fall. This paper describes the most current advances in machine learning
(ML)-based fall detection and prevention systems. Recent works, ML algorithm,
datasets, and age groups are thoroughly studied. Additionally, it offers a detailed
analysis of current fall detection system trends as well as potential future directions
by addressing the existing issues. This summary can aid in understanding existing
systems and suggest new methodologies.

Keywords: Machine learning · Fall Detection · Fall Monitoring

1 Introduction

Thanks to recent improvements in medicine and health care, the average lifespan of a
person is now over 80 years. Therefore, it is anticipated that a greater proportion of
people will require additional care. For instance, according to studies by the NPHCE, by
2025, 12% of India's population will be elderly, with 8–10% needing the highest level
of care. Globally, the number of old persons living alone has been increasing [1]. The
World Health Organization (WHO) estimates that every year, 28% to 35% of people over
65 experience a fall. The percentage rises even more for those over 70, reaching 32–42%
[2]. To lessen the effects of falls, experts in the medical and technological fields have
been working for more than 20 years to improve treatment after falls and reduce response

time. One of the deadliest events that may happen to an aged person is a fall. The best choice is to employ a nurse or caretaker to keep a close eye on the elderly person's daily activities (activities of daily living, or ADL). Elderly people or their families will pay a high price for the caregiver option, and it will also be challenging for caretakers to constantly monitor and assist the elderly. A dependable, inexpensive, and intelligent fall detection system should also be considered to aid the elderly, particularly those who live alone or cannot afford to pay a substantial amount of money [3].

1.1 Fall Risk Factors

A fall occurs whenever someone struggles to maintain their balance and stands up straight. A young person has the stamina to right themselves when they lose their footing but when an elderly person does the same, it is much harder for him to do so because he is physically much weaker at that age. The fall could be caused by a variety of factors. Risk factors for falls refer to all potential contributing factors to falls [4]. In reality, the occurrence of falls is the result of a complex interplay between various factors. It is important to comprehend the potential risk factors behind elderly fall risks. With a deeper understanding of these risk factors, a more effective fall prevention system can be designed. Many factors in biology, behavior, demography, and the environment can cause falls (Fig. 1) displays a list of risk elements that have been discovered by research. A patient or elderly person falling might have many factors. The most frequent causes of falls include physiological problems and falls from the bed [2]. Behavior-related risk factors are connected to people's thoughts, feelings, and routine daily activities. Through strategic intervention, these factors can be under the person's control. For instance, if a person falls because they abuse drugs or alcohol excessively, this routine or behaviour is modifiable through strategic intervention. Environmental risk factors originate from a person's immediate surroundings. Cracked pathways, uneven surfaces, and inadequate lighting are some of the primary environmental risk factors. A person's physical condition, gender, and age are all biological risk factors. Several biological risk factors consist of chronic and acute diseases, diabetes, cardio-vascular ailments, eye impairments, balance issues, and high or low blood pressure. Age and gender are biological variables that cannot be changed, but diseases can be lessened or controlled with the right medical care, and physical health can also be enhanced [4].

1.2 Types of Falls Fall

Up until the 1990s, categorizing fall was a significant problem. The largest obstacle was a lack of agreement among researchers. The majority of the classification at that time was based on the causes of falls. Depending on the position preceding a fall, there were three (other categories of falls also shown in (Fig. 2) main categories of falls:

1. *Fall from Bed*

   - At the time of the fall, the person is lying in bed either sleeping or not.
   - From bed height to floor height, the body height decreases. The body typically experiences what feels like a free fall motion at that time.
   - The body is in a position on the floor that is close to the bed.

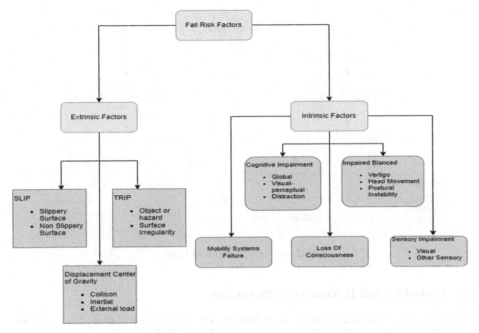

Fig. 1. Control Flow Model of Fall Risk Factors

- The entire procedure occurs in a series of smaller activities over the course of 1–3 s.

2. *Fall from Sitting*

- At the start of the fall, the person is sitting on a chair or another piece of furniture approximately at the same height.
- The head descends in a free fall fashion until its height is reduced to the floor.
- The body is lying close to the chair in this position.
- The falling process is divided into 1–3 s sub-actions.

3. *Fall from Walking or Standing.*

- When the fall begins, the person is either standing or walking.
- The head lowers itself to the floor while lying on it from a level that is equal to the person's height. It might move slightly while lying.
- Typically, the fall is unidirectional.

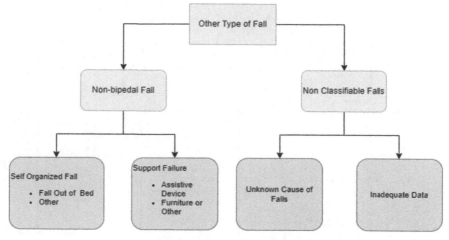

Fig. 2. Other Categories of Falls

1.3 Method for Fall Detection and Prevention

Researchers have created a variety of technologies to recognize and stop elderly people from falling. Different things have been done to deal with the problem of older people falling. These techniques combine machine learning, IoT devices, image software, etc. Fall prediction is the process of continuously monitoring an older person with wearable or non-wearable devices to determine whether they are likely to fall and how likely it is. However, the focus of fall prediction is on identifying risk factors of fall. It requires very precise and rapid prediction mechanisms. A precise prediction will greatly aid in protecting elderly people from the consequences of falls, even though it is not simple to achieve. Finding out that a senior has fallen is the first step in the fall detection process, after which an alarm signal is sent to alert medical personnel to the situation. Several situations, such as getting up from a chair, standing, bending down to pick something up, etc., could create the impression that you fell. The system must be able to distinguish between actual falls and normal daily activity and immediately alert the designated individuals or locations after making this determination. After a fall, assistance should be sent to elderly individuals as soon as possible to reduce any negative effects [1–3].

1.4 Detection of Fall

There are three basic kinds of fall detection techniques: wearable devices, camera-based devices, and ambiance devices.

In (Fig. 3), the classification of fall detection approaches is shown. In the wearable device strategy, individuals who are at risk of falling must wear some wearable devices or clothing. These devices gather data based on the movement or posture of the body, and a processing algorithm determines whether a fall has occurred or not. However, wearable technology appears to some users to be very intrusive and a burden. They do not bother to wear a device constantly. A problem with the device's placement is also present. Some activities, like sleeping and moving around, could move the device from

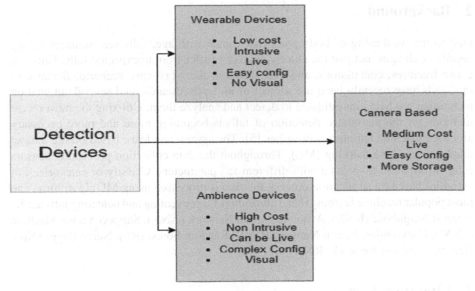

Fig. 3. Fall Detection Devices

its initial position, resulting in less precise results [2]. Some of these problems appear to be resolved by the camera-based strategy. The cameras are positioned in specific areas to enable passive, continuous monitoring of the elderly. Contrary to sensors, the camera allows for the evaluation and analysis of multiple features. When cameras were more expensive, these types of systems were initially less desirable. These devices can also record the data they collect for later analysis and use as a resource. Installing some sensors near the related people, such as on a wall, bed, floor, etc., is part of the ambience device approach. These sensors gather data, which is then used as input by an algorithm to determine whether or not there has been a fall. As a result, the caretakers are informed about the occurrence. Because no sensor needs to be worn, that person is unconcerned about any kind of overhead.

1.5 Fall Prevention

It is impossible to completely guarantee and achieve the goal of preventing falls in elderly people. It can be utilized as a task to ensure that the targeted individual is in a low-risk area. It is carried out by regularly checking on the status of recognized fall risk factors and conducting continuous monitoring. If the obtained values for those parameters fall within the acceptable range, the targeted individuals may be thought of as being in the safe zone. The following are some of the exercises that can be done to prevent falls:

- Check to see if they appear to be having trouble getting up from a chair or walking in general, or if they are holding onto walls or anything else while doing so.
- Discuss their medication.
- Talk about their present state of health.
- Maintain regular eye and eyewear examinations.

2 Background

Due to the weakening of body parts that comes with age, falls are common among people of all ages, not just the elderly, who can suffer from unexpected falls. Falls can cause fractures, concussions, and even death in the worst-case scenario. Because of this, falls have recently been the subject of in-depth research, and several automation techniques are being investigated to detect and analyze them. Utilizing the most recent methods for the automated detection of falls is becoming more and more necessary and uses machine learning approaches [5]. The system can learn based on the dataset thanks to machine learning (ML). Throughout the data collection procedure, sensors offer information associated with different fall parameters. Classify or categorize fall activities based on application criteria, the data is processed using ML algorithms. The most popular machine learning (ML) algorithms for preventing and detecting falls are K-Nearest Neighbour (KNN), Artificial Neural Network (ANN), Support Vector Machine (SVM), Convolution Neural Network (CNN) Random Forest (RF), Naive Bayes (NB), Recurrent Neural Network (RNN) etc.

3 Literature Survey

3.1 Related Works

Aactivity of human recognition has become a popular area of study as a result of the widespread use of technologies for human-computer interaction, behavior detection, and other related tasks. Regarding the detection of human falls using a variety of methods, a sizable number of reviews have been conducted.

3.1.1 Cell Phone-Based Approaches

It is simple to determine how likely it is that someone will fall with the aid of a smartphone and a accelerometer. In reality, using an accelerometer to track a person walking as an object is less expensive. In addition to the recommended effort, the authors defined gait symmetry and stability under acceleration data circumstances. The stability and symmetry of an Individual's gait might be examined using the suggested evaluation models. The suggested methodologies might accurately detect falls.

Shipkovenski et al. [3] proposed an elderly fall detection system. The primary objective of that system is to quickly summon medical help for a fallen senior citizen. The system detects falls during routine daily activities to keep track of human body movements. The proposed system makes use of a three-axis accelerometer, which is a feature of some smartwatches and contemporary smartphones. An accurate acceleration sensor is typically used in portable fall detection devices. A GPS module is present in the majority of smartphones, and it can be added to portable devices. In the absence of a GPS module (Fig. 4) on the smartwatch or portable device, it is possible to connect to the smartphone's GPS module. The mobile phone serves as both a tracking device and an Internet gateway in such a situation. Their system uses sensor nodes, which can be either wireless controllers with acceleration sensors or smartwatches. Mobile phones with integrated sensors and positioning modules can detect falls. The mobile phone serves as both an independent sensor node and a gateway with GPS. Two sensor nodes can be placed in two different algorithm operation cases at different locations, and 2 fall detection strategies can be combined while comparing the accelerometer data from the two sensors to achieve high reliability.

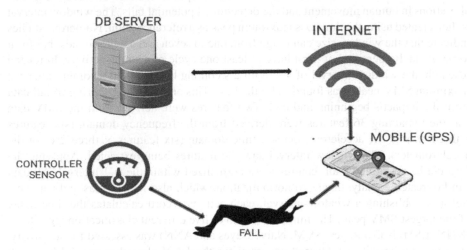

Fig. 4. Fall Sensing Using Smartphone

The proposed fall algorithm uses the data from each sensor node's accelerometer, and if someone falls, a database receives the fellers location information. Wi-Fi or Bluetooth are used to wirelessly connect the smartwatch to the smartphone. Separately, the smartphone is similarly connected to external controller with sensor. By relaying data through a single smart device, it functions as both an independent sensor node and a gateway. Falls are detected by using the sensors (external ISM6DS3, GY-521 on a Huawei smartphone, or bma on a nokia smartphone) and use the proper algorithm to post-process the input variables. When an occurrence has to be reported, the mobile device transmits the database its GPS coordinates. It is also optional to phone or text a caregiver for the elderly to inform him of the event's location. It analyzes the input data from an accelerometer using a powerful algorithm and notifies caregivers automatically of the location of the fall. The proposed system's accuracy in detecting falls can reach 100%, according to test results performed by seven volunteers 5 men and 2 women among the ages of 20 and 24, as well as two seniors, 65 and 72, were used in the experimental testing. The volunteers periodically mimicked spontaneous falls while wearing the devices on their wrists, chests, and thighs. The majority of the ADL data was gathered during the experiment by the more youthful volunteers, who attempted to emulate the motions of the adults and executed various falls and ADLs, with the elderly volunteers recording a much smaller portion of the ADLs.

Vallabh et al. [6] this study used the MobiFall dataset to identify and differentiate between fall activities and daily living activities. The dataset was collected using a phone that was kept in the user's pants pocket. The dataset includes standing, jogging, walking upstairs, walking down stairs, jumping, and sitting in a chair. The model was trained and validated on a sizable database. The use of feature selection techniques helped to reduce dimensionality. A fall detection classification system requires feature extraction because the chosen features will affect how accurate the system is. Data from a window interval is typically used for feature extraction. A set of values can be created in the window and then used to extract a special feature. The SMV explains alterations in human movement and the detection of potential falls. The window interval is then created using the threeaxis maximum peak as a reference point. Numerous studies indicate that the window size can range from one to seven and a half seconds, but for it to be uniquely identified, it must have at least one cycle of a single activity. In related research, the window interval of 4 s, with 2 s coming before and 2 s coming after the maximum SMV peak, was found to be the best. This enables the gathering of fall data from the impact's beginning and end. Two features were derived from the SMV data and the remaining 36 features were derived from the frequency domain (six features x three axes of the accelerometer) and time domain (six features × three axes of the accelerometer). The window interval saw the features being extracted. Applying the formula based on unity, all features were normalized within the 0–1 interval. All data can be treated equally, thanks to normalization, which also lessens bias and variance. Before establishing a window interval, each activity record calculates the time index of the largest SMV peak. The implementation of five different classification algorithms (KNN, LSM, Naive Bayes, SVM, Naive Bayes and ANN) was assessed for sensitivity, accuracy and specificity. Overall accuracy for the KNN algorithm was 87.5%, with sensitivity at 90.70% and specificity at 83.78%.

Despite the fact that research into the use of smartphones as fall-detection devices is still ongoing, there are some restrictions like

- It is questionable whether the quality of cell phones' internal sensors is sufficient to accurately detect falls. Smartphone accelerometer sensors can measure up to 2 g of dynamic range, but a fall detection device needs to measure dynamic ranges of 4 to 6 g (1 g = 9.8 m/s^2) [1, 3].
- When smartphones are used frequently, their short battery life (only a few hours) is a major concern. According to previous research, using three sensors simultaneously causes the battery consumption to increase by more than twofold. Although using the power-saver mode seems like a real solution, performance would be significantly decreased [2].
- Smartphones were not developed and designed to detect falls. Accuracy is compromised when used in real-time due to various compatibility and operational issues [2].
- Mobility sensor placement has a big effect on how to fall detectors operate.
- For smartphone-based fall detection systems to function accurately, they must be mounted or placed in an unusual location, usually on the wrist or chest [1, 6].

3.1.2 Ambience Devices Based Strategies

While using an ambience device, a variety of sensors are positioned throughout a person's residence, such as on the wall, the floor, the bed, etc., to track their movements. These sensors gather data, and an algorithm uses that data to figure out if there has been a fall or not. If those sensors identify a fall, the monitoring service alerts the caregiver.

Hussain et al. [4] in contrast to the most recent and cutting-edge methods, the proposed algorithm (Fig. 5) detects falls with high sensitivity, specificity, and precision. The proposed methodology employs a dataset accessible to the public for training and evaluation of the algorithm that will be used to determine whether an activity is falling or not. The proposed methodology starts with gathering the data that will be used in later steps after pre-processing. Collecting data from people in real time, especially from elderly people who are performing tasks, is a very difficult task. Numerous researchers have gathered information on fall activities and everyday activities. Various datasets are available, but the majority of them only include young participants performing activities. The system that detects elderly falls to be effective, the elderly's falls and daily activities must be included in the dataset. As a result, they chose the SisFall dataset, which includes participants of all ages.

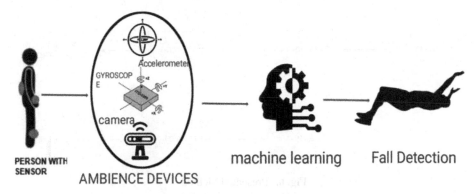

Fig. 5. Proposed Methodology

The SisFall dataset consists of more than four thousand files, of which more than seventeen hundred files contain fifteen different types of falls and two thousand seven files contain nineteen different ADL types performed by twenty young, adults ages nineteen to thirty and by 15 adults ages sixty to 75. Mounted at the participant's waist, a wearable device with 3 sensors for motion 1 gyroscope and 2 accelerometers is used to record all activities at a 200 Hz rate of sampling. The next step after data acquisition is pre-processing, which involves removing unwanted noise from a signal in order to improve the performance of machine learning classification algorithms. The frequency of a fourth-order low-pass infinite impulse response (IIR) cutoff point butter worth filter of 5 Hz was used for this methodology because it is simple and computationally affordable compared to other filters. Each characteristic is then extracted from the data of three sensors two accelerometers and one gyroscope along the three axes. For a single sensor, the size of a feature is [one (number of samples) × one (number of features) × three (number of axes)]. Each sensor's size is therefore [one (number of samples) × six (number of features) × three (number of axes)] for all six features and all three axes. For a single sample, = [one × eighteen]. As a result, they produce a final feature vector with dimensions [one × fifty-four] for all three sensors along with one sample on all three axes. Four machine learning classifiers are trained and tested using the extracted features.

SVM is the classifier that performs with the highest accuracy, at 99.98%, outperforming cutting-edge techniques. The proposed algorithm can be successfully applied to a fall detection system operating in real time.

Ayush Chandak, Nitin Chaturvedi, and Dhiraj [5]. Two methods for fall detection were presented (Fig. 6). In this paper, one is contact-based, and another is non-contact-based. For contact-based fall detection systems, use the UP-fall dataset. In this instance, the triaxial accelerometer's data was used to predict both falls and non-falls. Two three-axial accelerometer sensors were placed on the right wrist and pocket of the patient to resemble a watch and a mobile phone, respectively. The accelerometers are placed in close proximity to the person. Making it very institutional for automated detection to predict falls using them. For this, 1D CNN-based techniques and machine learning architectures were used. First, to capture the fall and non-fall parts accurately, The accelerometers' 3-axial data was condensed to 3 s.

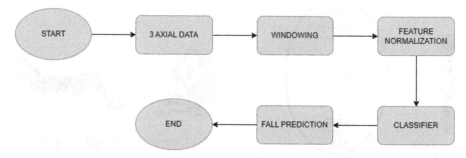

Fig. 6. Presented Method

To standardize the data, the mean was subtracted from the data points, and then the standard deviation was used to divide the data points by the difference. The normalized data was then extracted, and 1.5 s of continuous fixed arrays were added one by one in third-dimension order. Using the collected flow stacks, the classifier (ML models and oneD CNN) was used to forecast the arrival of fall. The dataset was split into two parts: 30% for testing and 70% for training, and In terms of every performance metric, the RF method outperformed every other machine learning technique. According to the results, the sequential data provided by the accelerometers can be significantly enhanced by ML techniques. They also tried the 1D CNN approach to boost the performance. Data streams are passed through 1D CNN after being transformed into 1D arrays and trained on numerous 1-dimensional layers. 500 training epochs were completed using a respectable gradient optimizer with a 10.4% learning rate. The accuracy achieved was 98.07%. In the noncontact-based fall detection method, predicting the fall and non-fall events used RGB camera recordings taken from the subject's frontal and lateral sides. Additionally, optical flow images were created using RGB images. Since optical flow images only record the motion between consecutive frames, they are useful for removing background noise. The camera recordings from the UP-Fall dataset were utilized as the data input. Videos were recorded at 18 frames per second from the subject's front and lateral sides. It involved 17 participants completing 11 tasks over the course of three trials. The images' resolution was decreased from 640 to 480 to 224, 240 to minimize computational costs. In addition, the recordings were condensed to 50 frames per recording because this is the minimum amount of time needed to distinguish between a fall and a non-fall event. The data set was further divided 80:20 into training and testing sets for VGG-16, DenseNet, and Xception architectures. The batch normalization method was used with ReLU as the e-learning rate was set at 10–6. 500 epochs were used to train the network. As can be seen, DenseNet performed better than other architectures, with accuracy rates of 99.85% for frontal camera recordings and 98.41% for lateral camera recordings.

Koichi Toda and Norihiko Shinomiya [7]. The main goal of the system shown in (Fig. 7) is to get rid of the need for the user to wear extra gadgets. Indoor footwear is tagged with passive sensor tags as a fall detection technique. The advantage of using battery-free sensors is that elderly individuals can engage in activities without restrictions or concern for damaging the sensors. Passive RFID tags necessitate no maintenance, so the suggested footwear can be worn continuously. To identify the activities, Using machine learning techniques, The system under consideration assessed RSSI values and sensor codes acquired from passive sensor tags. The inability of the footwear-based system to track upper-body activity is one of its drawbacks. As a result, not all types of daily activities are taken into account in this study. The suggested system keeps an eye on routine daily tasks (walking, standing, and falling). The proposed system makes use of passive RFID sensor tags made of RFMicron's Magnus S chip, which measures pressure in addition to RSSI.

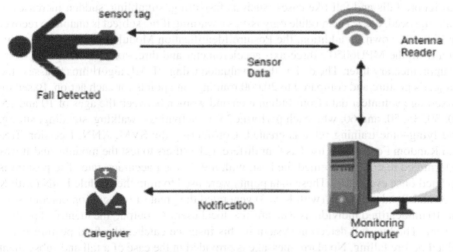

Fig. 7. Suggested System

These tags are used in the strategy to measure changes in during activity, the RSSI and pressure values by attaching them to indoor footwear. To characterize activities, feature extraction is crucial. When the classification system is trained on raw sensor data, it often has difficulty distinguishing between activities. In this study, a one-second sliding window method, which is equivalent to 10 samples, is used to recover several attributes from the RSSI values and Sensor Code of every tag. Features are taken from the raw data and used to classify the activities using machine learning. The experiment demonstrates how passive sensor tags with pressure features can perform better for classifying daily life activities. Two volunteers served as the subjects and naturally engaged in each activity. Subjects A and B engaged in the three activities of standing, walking, and falling for 600 and 300 s, respectively. Subjects A and B performed each activity 40 times and 20 times, respectively, with each trial lasting 5 s and varying the location and orientation. Additionally, according to their research, the proposed method for the random forest algorithm can generate F-measure scores of ninety % and ninety-four %, respectively.

Bhattacharjee, Pratik, and Suparna Biswas [8]. This research implements a fall and posture detection system using low-cost sensors and machine learning, which can assist those in need both indoors and outdoors. This sophisticated system can distinguish between falls that result in recovery and those that do not within a predetermined time-frame. If a fall occurs and no one recovers, a message is sent to a relative or caregiver with the location, time, and date of the fall. This function ensures real time support to prevent potentially critical delays. Additionally, a person's last known posture before a fall is also reported to determine his propensity to fall from a particular posture. This could help medical professionals take the necessary precautions to avoid falling in the future. The proposed SWA system includes a fall detection module that performs both fall detection and on-the-spot audible warning generation as a separate module. It uses the moving average filter to normalize the unprocessed live 3 axis accelerometer data. Min and max threshold values are used to detect the fall. Utilizing a method dependent on SVM to confirm the fall and analyzing the duration and threshold values, the module can ignore falls and fall like cases (such as fastsitting, stumbling, sudden increases in walkingspeed, etc.). The module only issues a warning if the subject is unable to recover on his or her own. In addition, the Posture Identification Module (PIM) combines live data from the MPU6050's three-axis accelerometer and three-axis gyroscope by using a supplementary filter. The data is then evaluated using RF ML algorithms to assess the subject's posture and compared to 20,000 training data points for each action. Based on mixed-age volunteer data from Indian men and women between the ages of 10 and 15, 20, 30, 35, 50, and 60, who each performed four activities—walking, standing, sitting, and lying—the training set was created. Considering the SVM, KNN, Decision Tree and Random Forest were used as four different classifiers to test the module, and It was determined that RF performed the best, with a 99% total accuracy rate. The posture is updated once every 20 s. These data points were used to train the module KNN (with K = 3) and Random Forest (with K = 3) generated the greatest recognition outcomes for the 10 unidentified individuals who are also local users As output, the identified posture is sent. The live fall detection system in this instance catches the final posture maintained before falling. No alarm message is provided in the case of a fall and subsequent recovery. However, if a person falls and is unable to get up, a message of alert is sent to a family member or caregiver, asking them to come to the distressed person's aid right away. Now, MPU data and its accurate analysis are what determine how accurate the entire system will be. If the sensor data leads to an incorrect identification, a false alarm may be triggered and prompting people to rush to the subject's location. A false alarm may be activated, causing people rush to the location of the subject.

Palmerini, et al. [9]. Developed and evaluated fall detection algorithms with characteristics derived from a multiphase fall model and a ML strategy by analyzing acceleration signals obtained from 143 actual falls by 40 subjects from the FARSEEING repository, which uses an inertial sensor. There was always at least a triaxial accelerometer in the inertial sensor. The sensor position was the subject's lower back, and the average fall risk for these subjects was calculated using the FRAT-up tool. They used 27.5-s windows with a one-second step, which provides a set of 26.5-s CFW (candidate fall windows) for additional analysis. One second is added to the CFW for the overlapping window. In this extra second, a peak search is conducted to make sure that there are always enough samples for CFW, thus introducing a new overlapping window technique is introduced. To assess the effectiveness of the classifiers, they used subject-based cross-validation. Five-fold cross-validation was chosen by them. To prevent dependencies that could reduce the generalizability of the findings, we avoided using dependent variables, subject-based cross-validation was used to limit the data (including the adl & fall) from a single subject to a single specific fold (among the five). This assures that while training with four of the five folds and testing with the fifth fold, the results will be the same, Data from participants in the testing fold are contained solely in the testing fold, therefore minimizing any overfitting. To account for individual differences in the number of falls and ADLs, the cross-validation was also stratified. Within each cross-validation fold, stratification was performed to ensure an even distribution of individuals with low/high falls and low/high ADLs. Based on the number of their ADLs compared to the median of the group, the subjects with ADLs were categorized as low or high, and the data for a subject (ADLs and, if available, falls) were arranged in a single fold and proportions of the two groups in each fold were balanced. Based on the number of falls, the remaining participants (fall without ADL) were separated into two groups (low/high number of falls) and stratify them into five subgroups, ensuring that the proportions of the two groups in each subgroup are equal and that each subject belongs to a single subgroup. They used a variety of classifiers to combine the data from all features. They used the fitting Matlab function for NB. The logistic regression Matlab functions are glmval and glmfit, and the standardized features for KNN are the fits knn Matlab function and its three closest neighbors. They chose 20 trees for random forests and using the TreeBagger function and the regression method, the area under the curve was calculated (AUC). A sensitivity higher than 80%, the vector support machine calculated a false alarm rate of 0.56 per hour and features from the multiphase fall model.

Badgujar, Sejal, and Anju S. Pillai [10] this research offers an elderly-wearable sensor-based fall detection system. The suggested technique leverages methods for ML to identify falls from a list of common activities. Due to pre-trained gait patterns, ml techniques are found to be superior to the threshold method because they produce fewer false alarms. The system identifies falls by classifying various actions as falls or non-falls and notifies a family member or other caregiver in the case of an urgent situation. To compute the features of the SisFall dataset, they use SVM and DT machine learning algorithms. SVM is an algorithm applicable to both regression and classification problems. To provide good separation, SVM identifies the hyperplane that is furthest from the closest training data point of any class. It may be possible to locate a hyperplane using a kernel function to determine the classification of a non-linear dataset. On each side of the plane, several sorts of data points are spread. The decision tree represents data as a tree, include nodes and edges. Trees consist mostly of the root node, internal nodes, and leaf nodes; however, actual datasets contain additional characteristics. The decision tree is a strategy for classifying data with a limited number of classifications. Once the training data for the tree has been prepared, decision rules are drawn and classification decisions are made using those rules. The popularity of decision tree classification models is due to how simple they are to interpret and how straightforwardly the outcomes can be comprehended. Decision makers can interpret the problem's solution thanks to the DT algorithm, which simplifies complex decision-making processes. Based on computed features, ml algorithms such as SVM and DT are used to identify falls. Sensitivity, specificity, accuracy, and confusion matrix are some of the criteria used to evaluate the models. The system uses the DT algorithm to achieve an accuracy of up to 96%. Compared to SVM, the DT is more accurate because it can precisely define and classify each attribute for each class. Additionally, SVM has a longer prediction time than a decision tree, which makes the system slower.

Syed, et al. [11] in this study, a fall detection and activity monitoring system that takes into account human motion was developed. The suggested plan adheres to a standard framework for deep learning solutions. First, windowed segments are extracted from the inertial sensor data from the IMU sensors used in the SisFall dataset. Next, data augmentation is conducted for minority classes, followed by feature extraction and classification. After the necessary data augmentation, raw sensor measurements must be appropriately processed prior to the IMU sensor data utilized for Fall and ADL detection. In this study, data pre-processing was divided into two steps: first, From the IMU recordings, uniform-sized windows are extracted, and then the data is improved. The extracted windows of the classes under consideration for noise augmentation were supplemented with white noise of Gaussian. With a standard deviation of 0.01, the noise was generated. The inclusion of noise simulates measurement noise that may be present while recording in IMU-based fall detection systems. A random number drawn at random from a uniform distribution between 0.8 and 1.2 multiplied the original extracted window for scale-based augmentation. This enables the inclusion of amplitude fluctuations across the same kind of activity or fall. The proposed CNN needs to be trained appropriately before it can be used for feature extraction. Added a totally connected layer with SoftMax output at the very end to act as the network's temporary intermediate output determining step. The SisFall dataset's windowed data was divided into three groups for training, validation, and testing. Using stochastic gradient descent with a learning rate of 0.01 and a batch size of 20, the network was tuned. The average recall score across all classes, also known as the UAR, was the additional chosen metric. Recall is considered because the system should accurately categorize as many positive samples for each class as possible. Early pausing was used in the design of the final network. After conducting data augmentation on the minority classes, the CNN network received data from the training set. During training, the validation set was used to monitor the performance of the network and select the top-performing instance. After training was complete, In lieu of the final fully linked classification layer, an XGB classification step was implemented. The CNN network layers were loaded using the weights of the CNN model with the highest performance, and the input samples were again passed through them to train the XGB stage. Using the XGB's input as the output of the CNN stage. Six types of falls were created as a result: Hard and soft in terms of impact, and forward, backward, and lateral in terms of direction. These include Lateral Hard Fall (LHF), Lateral Soft Fall (LSF) Forward Hard Fall (FHF), Forward Soft Fall (FSF), Backward Soft Fall (BSF), and Lateral Hard Fall (LHF) to more clearly demonstrate the falls' labeling procedure. According to the experiments, the gradient boosted CNN outperformed other methods of a similar nature, achieving an unweighted average recall of 88%.

Miawarni et al. [12] this paper uses SVM to define an FDS work. They used the eHomeSeniors dataset, which uses Omron D6T-8L-06 and Melexis MLX90640 sensors. Unlike other types of sensors like accelerometers, both sensors are affordable, they do not need to go through a laborious calibration process. Omron D6T-8L-06 can gauge an object's surface temperature. This sensor, which has an 8-channel sensor array, produces thermal images with a resolution of 1×8 pixels. This sensor is used to identify humans in the eHomeSeniors dataset. MEMS Thermal sensors are superior to traditional pyroelectric sensors in some ways. Based on the premise of detecting fluctuations in the human body's infrared light intensity, pyroelectric sensors can detect human movement. Nevertheless, if there is no movement, the signal for detecting will be lost. The Melexis MLX90640, which employs an infrared thermal sensor which is more sophisticated sensor than the OmronD6T-8L-06. This sensor is a 768-channel FIR (far infrared) sensor array that generates thermal pictures at 32×24 pixels and 16 frames per second (frames per second). This sensor can detect objects with temperatures ranging from $-$ 40 to 300 °C. Using SVM, they develop unique deep learning algorithm technique and apply them to this dataset (16,261 instances and 33 fall simulation attributes) in an effort to improve the sensor resolution's ability to distinguish human actions. To get the best results in capturing falling incidents, this dataset included more than 15 categories of falls. Additionally, they changed the gamma value without the need for normalization or standardization from the default value of 0.01 to 0.9. Additionally, Training and test data are separated 50:50, 60:40, 70:30, 80:20, and 90:10 respectively. Using a 90:10 data split, they were able to get 84.62% accuracy and 50.32 s of learning runtime.

3.1.3 Ambience Devices and Cell Phone-Based Approaches

Ramachandran, et al. [1] suggested a fall detection system that considers a subject's biological and physiological profile in addition to various wearable sensor node parameter readings. They conducted tests to see how detection accuracy varied when subjects were assigned to risk categories or not. They made use of the UMA ADL FALL Dataset, which includes information on almost 2 lakh incidents of falls and near-falls. To collect the data, about 17 people wear smartphones equipped with accelerometers, gyroscopes, and magnetometers on their wrists and chests. After data preprocessing, vector acceleration magnitude and angular velocity were employed as input characteristics. During the first phase, they tested the effectiveness of several algorithms for identifying and categorizing falls in forward, backward, and lateral directions and during typical activities such as bending, walking, jogging, sitting, and laying down. The likelihood of each component was used to get a normalized, weighted score for each topic. In the second stage, a risk category parameter was added to the sensor data previously collected. Based on their prior fall histories, The subjects were split into three groups: high-risk, medium-risk, and low-risk. These organizations gathered the fall data necessary to train the machine learning systems. The performance indicators were compared after the dataset was used to retrain several ML algorithms, this time with the inclusion of a parameter for risk category. They ran Naïve Bayes, kNN, ANN, and SVM classifiers. The kNN algorithm gives accuracy of 82.2%. For the second phase, It was discovered that including the risk category parameter into the feature set increased fall detection accuracy by 84.1%.

Chelli, Ali, and Matthias Pätzold [13] in this study, they develop a framework for machine learning that can identify daily activities and detect falls. Two public databases provided triaxial angular velocity and acceleration information. Six different types of activities are included in the first database: walking upstairs, walking, sitting, walking downstairs, lying and standing. This experiment involved Thirty participants in total. The participants' waists were fitted with a smartphone that was used to record their acceleration and angular velocity information. The gathered data were sampled at a rate of fifty Hz. These organizations gathered the fall data necessary to train the machine learning systems. Each data buffer includes the participant's tri axial acceleration and tri axial angular velocity as well as a label for the corresponding real-world activity based on ground truth. They got acceleration and angular velocity data for fall events from a public database in addition to the ADL data set; hence, the classification system includes acceleration and angular velocity signals in their raw form as inputs. In order to solve this issue, a collection of characteristics must be derived from the acceleration and angular velocity data, since the activity identification accuracy in this situation is relatively poor. For various activities, these features ought to fall into different value ranges. During the training phase, a considerable quantity of labelled data is presented to the classification algorithm. The value range for each feature for each activity must be learned by the classification algorithm. Using a updated acceleration and angular velocity data, the characteristics are extracted, which are then stored in a feature vector and sent to the classification method. The trained classification algorithm classifies this feature vector into one of seven activity types. The collected characteristics significantly influence the accuracy of this categorization. They extract time and frequency domain information from acceleration and angular velocity data and feed these features to four distinct classification methods, i.e., the ANN, KNN, QSVM, and EBT. According to their findings, the overall accuracy of the ANN, KNN, EBT and QSVM algorithms was 87.8%, 81.2%, 94.1%, and 93.2%, respectively. For the QSVM and EBT algorithms, respectively, without any false alarms, the fall detection accuracy reaches 97.2% and 99.1%. They improve the classification accuracy in a subsequent step by extracting features from the acceleration and angular velocity data's autocorrelation function and power spectral density. They were able to achieve overall accuracy of 91.8%, 85.8%, 97.7% and 96.1% for the ANN, KNN, EBT, and QSVM algorithms, respectively, by utilizing the proposed features. The QSVM and EBT algorithms' fall detection accuracy is 100% with no false alarms, which is the highest possible performance.

Wisesa, I. Wayan Wiprayoga, and Genggam Mahardika [14] made an algorithm that uses sensor data from an accelerometer and gyroscope built into a wearable device to tell the difference between a fall and other ADL. To analyses the sequence of time series data from sensors, they make use of LSTM as part of a RNN. The algorithm for AFDS was created using the UMA Fall Dataset. 746 samples of data from a variety of test subjects are included in the UMA Fall Dataset. Five different types of wireless sensor nodes were implanted in the subject's body during the experiment, one of which contained a smartphone and 4 sensor tags. Smartphone contains the sensors, which are also fastened to the wrist, ankle, waist and chest (for all 4 sensor tags). Utilizing the Bluetooth communication protocol, all 5-sensor nodes transmit triaxial accelerometer, triaxial gyroscope, and magnetometer data. Currently being tested are two different types of movement scenarios: ADL (Activity Daily Life) and falling. There are 12 sub-scenarios for the ADL scenario, including applauding, making a call, raising hands, sitting, opening a door, and standing up from a walking, chair, hopping, bending, when supine on a bed, jogging, going upstairs and going downstairs. There are three distinct types of falls: lateral, forward, and backward. From their respective official Internet pages, the dataset is freely downloadable. The data is stored in CSV files. Each CSV file, which can be recognized by its filename, contains a sample from a single subject, completing a single scenario. Each CSV file comprises (triaxial) accelerometer, gyroscope, and magnetometer data from the subject's body parts for all five recorded subject motions. Their experiment is divided into two scenarios. The first scenario uses their LSTM model to categorize the data from each tri-axial sensor accelerometer and gyroscope. This hypothetical situation aims to shed light on the characteristics of each sensor's data so that falls can be predicted. To comprehend the influence of merging all sensor data on categorization performance, in the second scenario, they made an effort to combine all sensor data so that it could be classified by the LSTM model. Utilizing data from X-axis accelerometers, their test shows that they were successful in classifying the UMA Fall Dataset.

3.2 Comparative Study

Researchers found that using a cell phone's inbuilt sensors, like a three-dimensional accelerometer and gyroscope, can be used as a straightforward system for predicting falls. Ramachandran et al. [1] suggested a cell phone-based fall detection system with risk categories based on an individual's health profile. For risk categorization, they chose 23 biological parameters that were most important and used their odds ratios to figure out how likely it was that a sample dataset would fall into each category. They discovered that ordinal logistic regression had higher fall detection accuracy. They assessed how well other algorithms performed with a risk category as an input feature vs without it. Found that KNN provides the most accurate results and that incorporating the risk category improves accuracy. Similarly, Hipkovenski et al. [3] as a prototype for a system to detect falls, they employed sensor nodes with a triaxial accelerometer, Bluetooth, GPS and Wi-Fi from a smartphone. Seven young people conducted the test using 10 pieces of hardware and a mobile software program that displays good accuracy. Compared to previous accelerometer-based algorithms used in other studies, this technique is superior, the proposed algorithm produces better results. Just like the 2 papers by Chelli, Ali, and Matthias Pätzold [13] and Vallabh et al. [6] used the publicly available dataset to study, with the aid of cell phone-based approaches to identify and make a distinction between fall and daily living activity. In this work [6], five different classification algorithms Naive Bayes, KNN, ANN, SVM, and LSM were implemented. They got highest accuracy of 87.5% using the K-Nearest Neighbors algorithm, with a sensitivity of 90.70% and a specificity of 83.78%. In the paper [1], they identify and differentiate fall from daily life activity using mobile phone-based techniques using risk categorization. Nonetheless, the subject's health profile that is utilized as input for risk classification might be expanded. However, in the paper [6] they only utilized five categorization strategies. Use of accelerometers and gyroscope sensors, solitary or in pairs, has been favored by researchers. In addition, a number of other sensors are installed close by the related individuals, such as on a floor, wall, bed, etc. These sensors collect data, and the algorithm uses that data as input to determine whether or not there has been a fall. This is called The Ambience Device Approach. In other studies, the desired sensors are connected externally. Hussain et al. [4] compare the most recent methods and sensor-based strategies. They made use of a collection of computationally effective features that were taken from a publicly accessible dataset. SVM is the classifier that performs with the highest accuracy, at 99.98%, outperforming state-of-the-art methods DT, LR, and KNN. Similarly, Koichi Toda and Norihiko Shinomiya [7] created a method that employs passive RFID sensor tags on footwear for fall detection. The advantage is that, due to the use of battery-less sensors and pressure features, for the dependent and independent persons, the created method can achieve an F-measure of 98% and 94%, respectively, using RF. In this paper, Ayush Chandak, Nitin Chaturvedi, and Dhiraj [5] primarily employed two methods: contact-based and non-contact-based. For contact-based sensors, 1D-CNN and machine learning algorithms were investigated. The proposed 1D-CNN outperformed the ML Contact methods, which provided an accuracy of 98.07%, for contact-based sensors. On the other hand, non-contact-based sensors use 16 layers of VGG-16, providing faster computation with good accuracy. To further improve the accuracy, DenseNet is proposed, and that gives 99.85% accuracy. Bhattacharjee, Pratik, and Suparna Biswas [8] designed and implemented a smart walking system using sensors in the 6050-microprocessor unit (MPU) combined with the low-cost ESP8266 microcontroller unit (MCU) and Wi-Fi connectivity. The system was randomly tested on 10 volunteers and achieved up to 98% detection accuracy. Data was utilized to train and test the suggested approach, which was built using KNN, SVM, RF, and DT classifiers, where RF was found to outperform the others with 98% accuracy. As a result of sensors' success and quick expansion, the IOT, and ML, etc., data was used to train and test the proposed algorithm. Palmerini et al. [9] analyzed acceleration signals obtained from an inertial sensor to detect the fall. SVM, along with features from the multiphase fall model, emerged as the most effective technique, achieving a sensitivity of over 80%, a false alarm rate of 0.56 per hour, and a 99.3% accuracy rate the method with the best fall detection performance requires less than one millisecond of total calculation time (0.7 ms). Even though two skilled assessors used visual inspection to identify falls, the fall reports did not always match the signal patterns precisely. Hence, it is probable that some falls were misidentified. Similarly, Badgujar, Sejal, and Anju S. Pillai [10] proposed a fall detection system based on ML. On the basis of computed characteristics, falls are detected using ML algorithms such as SVM and DT. Using a decision tree method, the system attains an accuracy of up to 96%. Then again, Syed et al. [11] proposed CNN and XGB fall detection system. An XGB is used for classification in the final stage after the CNN has been trained. From a sensor modalities standpoint, more sensor modalities might possibly enhance performance for the lowest identified classes but still, it achieves

88% accuracy in other hand SVM is used as a Deep Learning model in the fall detection system developed by Miawarni, Herti, et al. [12]. Their gamma-tuned SVM achieves an accuracy of 84.6% as a result. By utilizing an infrared heat sensor, with an AUC-ROC of 95.9%, its SVM exhibited its ability to handle multiclass classification. Also, the training and testing phases of their experiment had relatively brief runtimes, with 308.75 and 50.32. The optimal data split is also 90:10, both before and after changing the gamma to 0.9. Some researchers discovered that smartphones and ambient devices can work together fairly well, so they developed a novel approach for fall detection that uses smartphones as a master monitoring device and ambient device sensors as slave sensors. In the same way that Chelli, Ali, and Matthias Pätzold [13] and Ramachandran, Anita, et al. [1] used both smartphones and imu sensors, [13] in their paper, they developed a framework for machine learning that can identify daily activities and falls. Using acceleration and angular velocity information, they evaluated the effectiveness of four algorithms in detecting various human activities, including walking, climbing and descending stairs, sitting, lying and standing. Using data for angular velocity and acceleration, they evaluated the effectiveness of four algorithms in detecting various human activities, including walking, climbing and descending stairs, sitting, standing, and lying down. This shows that the ANN, KNN, EBT and QSVM algorithms achieved an overall accuracy of 87.8%, 81.2%, 94.1%, and 93.2% respectively. Just like that, Wisesa, I. Wayan Wiprayoga, and Genggam Mahardika [14] using data from the accelerometer and gyroscope sensors, a smartphone for monitoring and controlling the sensors through Bluetooth, and an algorithm for differentiating falls from other ADL. The Python-based keras framework is a high-level framework for deep learning, is being used to implement the LSTM networks. They designed simple RNN networks for the experiment with 1 layer of LSTM cells and hundred hidden neurons. Since their AFDS issue is regarded as a sequence classification problem, they imposed a fixed-length sequence input on the recommended LSTM. Based on the dataset's maximum number of sequences, 306 features are chosen as the input for the LSTM cell. Sequence data less than 306 used zero padding at the beginning of the sequence. The best accuracy for training was 86.63%, and the best accuracy for validation was 69.10% (Table 1).

Table 1. Comparative study

Author	Dataset	Method	Advantages	Disadvantages
Ramachandran, et al. [1]	TheUMA_ADL_FALL_Dataset	On a sample dataset, they utilized the odds ratios of 23 biological factors that they had narrowed down to assess the effectiveness of ordinal logistic regression and random forest. Regression analysis for predicting risk category	Generates accurate, simply understandable predictions. Large datasets can be handled effectively, and prediction accuracy is higher	The main disadvantage of random forest is that when there are many trees, it can become too slow and ineffective to provide forecasts in real-time

(*continued*)

Table 1. (*continued*)

Author	Dataset	Method	Advantages	Disadvantages
Shipkovenski, et al. [3]	The ADLs dataset	A fall detection system using sensor nodes with a triaxial accelerometer, a GPS module, Wi-Fi/Bluetooth modules, and a smartphone application	The suggested system's accuracy in fall detection can reach high accuracies, according to test results performed by seven young people using a mobile software application and ten hardware devices	It relies on volunteers
Hussain, et al. [4]	The SisFall dataset	SVM is the suggested algorithm's efficient choice for the real-time fall detection system	It performs effectively in high-dimensional spaces and uses a fair amount of memory	When the data set contains additional noise, such as when the target classes overlap and when there is null data, it does not operate very well
Ayush Chandak, Nitin Chaturvedi and Dhiraj [5]	The UP-Fall dataset (HAR-UP)	In this study, they described two techniques for fall detection that made use of smartphone accelerometer sensors and video camera recordings. These were carried out using DL and ML techniques. The application of 1D CNN and machine learning algorithms for contact-based sensors was examined	Having a 99.85% accuracy rate as opposed to the present state-of-the-art rating of 96.70%, the recommended non-contact-based strategy outperforms the existing designs. Moreover, contact-based accuracy is 98.30%	The CNN requires a lot of training data to effectively represent object location and orientation, which increases its complexity and resource dependability
Vallabh, et al. [6]	The MobiFall	The five categories of the following algorithms were used: k-NN, Naive Bayes, SVM, ANN and LSM. The maximum accuracy was attained by the KNN with k equal to five, which had an accuracy of 87.5%	k-NN, Navie Bayes, SVM, LSM, and ANN. The KNN with k equal to five had the highest accuracy, at 87.5%, when compared to the other categorization techniques	Unexpected outcomes occur when the k value is changed

(*continued*)

Table 1. (*continued*)

Author	Dataset	Method	Advantages	Disadvantages
Koichi Toda and Norihiko Shinomiya [7]	Real-life person-independent activity data	his study describes a fall detection system that attaches to indoor footwear and uses passive RFID sensor tags	The benefit of employing battery-free passive sensors is that older individuals may engage in activities without constraints or concern about harming the sensors	For detection, people must always wear modified RFID tag footwear. Use only Random Forest Algorithm
Bhattacharjee, Pratik, and Suparna Biswas [8]	The dataset was created using locals of various ages (between 10 and 70 years)	Smart healthcare is now a practical, approachable, and proactive solution that can ensure prompt assistance thanks to the success of sensors, the Internet of Things, machine learning, and other technologies. Micro Electro Mechanical System (MEMS)-based sensors are used in conjunction with knn, SVM, RF, and dt to detect falls	They suggested an SWA (Smart Walking Assistant), which utilizes KNN, SVM, RF, DT, and MEMS (Micro Electro Mechanical System)-based sensors to identify falls	The only issue is that installation is expensive and difficult. Also, it depends on human volunteers. Also requires decent connectivity for working
Luca Palmerini, Jochen Klenk, Clemens Becker [9]	FARSEEING repository	Detection of falls based on recorded acceleration impulses from a single wearable sensor. In terms of performance, the developed multi-phase model-based learning algorithms beat conventional feature-learning algorithms	They offered practical parameters those real-time systems, which are used in the real world, could use to detect falls. The SVM with multiphase features technique, which showed the most promising performance in fall detection, requires less than one millisecond for the entire calculation process (0.7 ms)	Fall reports did not always precisely match the signal patterns. It is therefore possible that some falls were misclassified. Unreported falls may potentially be included in the Daily life activity in addition to misreporting

(*continued*)

Table 1. (*continued*)

Author	Dataset	Method	Advantages	Disadvantages
SejalBadgujar, Anju S. Pillai [10]	The SisFall dataset	The suggested technique leverages machine learning algorithms to identify falls from a list of everyday activities. It has been shown that the threshold approach is inferior to machine learning since it produces more false alerts as a result of pre-trained walking patterns. DT are more accurate than SVMs	Because of the pre-trained gait patterns, it generates less false alerts. Compared to SVM, the decision tree is more accurate since it can properly Define each attribute and assign it to a class. With a 96% accuracy rate. Moreover, SVM's prediction time is longer than that of decision trees, making the system slower	By using a big dataset to train the models and by selecting the best features, the accuracy can be increased even more
Syed, Abbas Shah, et al. [11]	The SisFall dataset	By training the CNN, Maximize the unweighted average recall for the validation partition. When CNN has been educated, classification is done using the XGB final stage. Unweighted average recall achieved in experiments using the test set is 88%	The proposed approach outperforms the current designs with an accuracy of 88% when compared to XGB of the most recent technology methodologies already in use	For CNN's more complicated technique to operate, a vast dataset is required. From the perspective of the sensor modalities, more sensor modalities may aid in enhancing the performance of the lowest identified classes. These sensors' data can be combined and utilized as input for a deep learning network
HertiMiawarni [12]	The eHomeSeniors dataset	According to their findings, The TPR score for SVM is 84.6%, while the FPR score is 1.4%. Their gamma-tuned SVM achieves an accuracy rate of 84.62per cent as a result	Their results also show that SVM, with its gamma-tuned hyperparameter setup, can handle multiclass classification for a fall detection system	Change the hyperparameter settings of each DL model, as well as the kernels, to enhance the outcomes. By altering its extra mathematical properties, an SVM's capacity to manage numerous classes and data samples can be increased

(continued)

Table 1. (*continued*)

Author	Dataset	Method	Advantages	Disadvantages
Chelli, Ali, and Matthias Pätzold [13]	UCIHAR and Cogent Labs dataset	Classification accuracy improved by combining the algorithm with 328 features rather than 66 features. ANN, KNN, EBT, and QSVM algorithm are used to classify fall and activity from real-world acceleration data	Fall detection for QSVM and EBT reaches 100% with no false alarm which is the best achievable performance	The main flaw of the proposed SVM and EBT which become too slow and ineffective to provide real-time when there are several data points. It is also more challenging
Wisesa, I. Wayan Wiprayoga, and GenggamMahardika [14]	The UMA FALL ADL dataset	They successfully classified the UMA Fall Dataset using X-axis accelerometer data, and they also developed an algorithm using LSTM (as a variant of recurrent neural networks)	To distinguish between ADL and falls as part of automatic fall detection, which is quicker than the CNN System, using LSTM AFDS. Also, the experiment demonstrates that good categorization performance was obtained utilizing X-axis accelerometer data	Moreover, various adjustments must be made to increase categorization performance.as reducing signal noise during the preprocessing stage by use of an average filter Using the whole accelerometer (or gyroscope) value has another disadvantage

4   Observations and Findings

After a comprehensive literature study about fall detection and prediction, many findings have been made. After a thorough study, some limitations are found in existing models that can be used as future research domains; this is the research gap. Those loopholes are listed as follows:

- Camera-based methods are expensive and require a huge amount of data to store and process. This is a very complicated method of working and requires a more powerful GPU and CPU.
- Along with the benefits, camera-based systems have certain drawbacks, like privacy concerns and the inability to follow beyond the camera's field of view.
- Smartphones are not designed to work with wearable fall detection equipment. While smartphone accelerometer sensors can measure dynamic ranges of up to 2g, a fall detection device needs to measure dynamic ranges of four to six g (one $g = 9.8$ m/s^2).
- Since smartphones only have a limited amount of battery life, using their sensors, such as the accelerometer and gyroscope, draws more power.
- Battery consumption is a drawback of using mobile devices, but software optimization will also extend battery life.

- In this study, it was found that in a mobile-based approach, many algorithms are used, but KNN and SVM give the highest accuracy. Similarly, in the ambience-based approach, CNN and RNN have the highest accuracy.
- It's possible that not all falls require the assistance of emergency personnel. Similar problems can be resolved if they take proactive measures.
- For a medical professional, it might be hard to understand technical terms like power consumption, battery backup, response time, sensor installation, etc.
- A hybrid strategy that uses affordable wearable and ambient devices would be a good way to deal with the annoying factor.

5 Future Scope

Even though researchers have been studying the causes of elderly falls and ways to predict them for decades, some questions still haven't been answered. Concerns from a number of governments and reputable organizations, including the WHO, Researchers have become interested in this area because of the rise in fall incidents and their consequences. As technology advances, there are more and more smartphones and wearables available at a low price. As technology develops, more and more smartphones and wearables are becoming affordable. These days, using a smartphone to detect falls is incredibly affordable and accessible due to the fact that everyone has one. Therefore, use its built-in sensors like an accelerometer, gyroscope, magnetometer, and GPS for fall detection. However, there is one significant issue: smart phones are not intended to be used as fall-detection devices. Therefore, those sensors need to be calibrated. Cameras are frequently used for fall detection because it is an excellent strategy and provides high accuracy. However, the camera approach requires a lot of expensive resources and poses some privacy risks. Additionally, not all areas are visible to the camera. Therefore, use of the ambience device approach, which provides the highest accuracy while also being trustworthy and cost-effective, is recommended. A hybrid strategy with two-layer architecture might be developed in the future. The ambient devices in the middle layer and the smartwatch or smartphone on the edge have more potent machine learning algorithms that can detect real-time falls. Additionally, it can determine whether a person is indoors or outdoors and use that information to determine the fall data. While a person is inside rather than outdoors, information from IMU sensors is obtained to determine whether a fall has occurred. If the person is outside, data is collected from their smartphone. If a fall occurs, call for help and also contact emergency services.

References

1. Ramachandran, A., Adarsh, R., Pahwa, P., Anupama, K.R.: Machine learning-based techniques for fall detection in geriatric healthcare systems. In: 2018 9th International Conference on Information Technology in Medicine and Education (ITME), pp. 232–237. IEEE (2018)
2. Tanwar, R., Nandal, N., Zamani, M., Manaf, A.A.: Pathway of trends and technologies in fall detection: a systematic review. In: Healthcare, vol. 10, no. 1, p. 172. Multidisciplinary Digital Publishing Institute (2022)

3. Shipkovenski, G., Byalmarkova, P., Kalushkov, T., Valcheva, D., Petkov, E., Koleva, Z.: Accelerometer based fall detection and location tracking system of elderly. In: 2022 International Symposium on Multidisciplinary Studies and Innovative Technologies (ISMSIT), pp. 923–928. IEEE (2022)
4. Hussain, F., et al.: An efficient machine learning-based elderly fall detection algorithm. arXiv preprint arXiv:1911.11976 (2019)
5. Chandak, A., Chaturvedi, N.: Machine-learning-based human fall detection using contact-and noncontact-based sensors. Computat. Intell. Neurosci. (2022)
6. Vallabh, P., Malekian, R., Ye, N., Bogatinoska, D.C.: Fall detection using machine learning algorithms. In: 2016 24th International Conference on Software, Telecommunications and Computer Networks (SoftCOM), pp. 1–9. IEEE (2016)
7. Toda, K., Shinomiya, N.: Machine learning-based fall detection system for the elderly using passive RFID sensor tags. In: 2019 13th International Conference on Sensing Technology (ICST), pp. 1–6. IEEE (2019)
8. Bhattacharjee, P., Biswas, S.: Smart walking assistant (SWA) for elderly care using an intelligent realtime hybrid model. Evol. Syst. 13(2), 265–279 (2022)
9. Palmerini, L., Klenk, J., Becker, C., Chiari, L.: Accelerometer-based fall detection using machine learning: training and testing on real-world falls. Sensors 20(22), 6479 (2020)
10. Badgujar, S., Pillai, A.S.: Fall detection for elderly people using machine learning. In: 2020 11th International Conference on Computing, Communication and Networking Technologies (ICCCNT), pp. 1–4. IEEE (2020)
11. Tajammul, M., Shaw, R.N., Ghosh, A., Parveen, R.: Error detection algorithm for cloud outsourced big data. In: Bansal, J.C., Fung, L.C.C., Simic, M., Ghosh, A. (eds.) Advances in Applications of Data-Driven Computing. AISC, vol. 1319, pp. 105–116. Springer, Singapore (2021). https://doi.org/10.1007/978-981-33-6919-1_8
12. Miawarni, H., Sardjono, T.A., Setijadi, E., Gumelar, A.B., Purnomo, M.H.: Enhancing classification of elderly fall detection system using tuned RBF-SVM. In: 2022 IEEE International Conference on Imaging Systems and Techniques (IST), pp. 1–5. IEEE (2022)
13. Rajawat, A.S., et al.: Depression detection for elderly people using AI robotic systems leveraging the Nelder–Mead Method. In: Artificial Intelligence for Future Generation Robotics, pp. 55–70. Elsevier (2021). ISBN: 9780323854986. https://doi.org/10.1016/B978-0-323-85498-6.00006-X
14. Wisesa, I.W.W., Mahardika, G.: Fall detection algorithm based on accelerometer and gyroscope sensor data using Recurrent Neural Networks. IOP Conf. Ser. Earth Environ. Sci. 258(1), 012035 (2019). IOP Publishing

DLMEKL: Design of an Efficient Deep Learning Model for Analyzing the Effect of ECG and EEG Disturbances on Kidney, Lungs and Liver Functions

Sruthi Nair$^{(\boxtimes)}$ (iD)

Ramdeobaba College of Engineering and Management, Nagpur 44013, India
shrutiskmr@gmail.com, nairss1@rknec.edu

Abstract. Correlative analysisfor identification of body organ malfunction is a complex multidomain task, that involves collection and processing of correlative parameters for different organs. To perform this task, design of an efficient deep learning model for analyzing the effect of variations in Electrocardiograms (ECG) and Electroencephalograms (EEG) disturbances on kidney, lungs, and liver functions is discussed in this text. The proposed model integrates Generative Adversarial Networks (GANs) with Autoencoders and Long Short-Term Memory (LSTM) based Recurrent Neural Networks (RNN) for feature extraction and pattern recognition operations. The efficacy of the model is further enhanced by incorporating Vector Autoregressive Moving Average (VARMA) and Gated Recurrent Units (GRU) for accurate prediction of the impact of ECG and EEG disturbances on functioning of different organs. The proposed deep learning model provides a comprehensive analysis of the effects of ECG and EEG disturbances on vital organ functions. The integration of GANs with Autoencoders and LSTM-based RNNs enables efficient feature extraction and pattern recognition, leading to improved accuracy in predicting the effect of disturbances on organ functions. The VARMA GRU further enhances the accuracy of the model by capturing the complex interdependencies between the vital organs.

Keywords: Healthcare · EEG · ECG · Brain · Heart · Kidney · Liver · Lungs · Clinical · GAN · RNN · GRU · VARMA · Scenarios

1 Introduction

The human body is a complex system comprising numerous vital organs that work in tandem to maintain homeostasis. The kidneys, lungs, and liver are among the most critical organs in the body, performing a range of vital functions that are essential for the survival of the organism. The proper functioning of these organs is crucial for maintaining overall health and well-being. However, the functioning of these organs can be affected by a range of factors, including environmental factors, genetic factors, and diseases. The early detection and timely intervention of these factors are critical for preventing organ dysfunction and improving patient outcomes [1–3].

© The Author(s), under exclusive license to Springer Nature Switzerland AG 2023
R. N. Shaw et al. (Eds.): ICACIS 2023, CCIS 1921, pp. 70–84, 2023.
https://doi.org/10.1007/978-3-031-45124-9_6

One of the most common techniques used to monitor organ function is electrocardiography (ECG) and electroencephalography (EEG). ECG and EEG are non-invasive diagnostic tools [4–6] that enable the monitoring of the electrical activity of the heart and brain, respectively. These techniques are widely used in clinical practice for the diagnosis and monitoring of a range of diseases, including cardiovascular diseases, epilepsy, and sleep disorders. However, the impact of ECG and EEG disturbances on the functioning of vital organs such as the kidneys, lungs, and liver is not well understood when applied to real-time scenarios. Deep learning is a subset of machine learning that has shown significant promise in the analysis and prediction of complex biological systems [7–9]. Deep learning models are based on artificial neural networks that are designed to mimic the structure and function of the human brain. These models are capable of learning complex patterns and relationships in large datasets, making them ideal for the analysis of complex biological systems.

In recent years, several deep learning models have been proposed for the analysis and prediction of the impact of ECG and EEG disturbances on vital organ functions. However, these models have limitations, such as low accuracy, high computational complexity, and the inability to capture complex interdependencies between the vital organs. In this paper, we propose an efficient deep learning model that overcomes these limitations and provides accurate predictions of the impact of ECG and EEG disturbances on kidney, lung, and liver functions. The proposed deep learning model consists of two stages. In the first stage, we use a GAN with Autoencoders and LSTM-based RNNs for feature extraction and pattern recognition. The generator network of the GAN generates fake data that is intended to mimic the distribution of the real data, while the discriminator network tries to distinguish between the real and fake data. The generator network is based on a combination of Autoencoders and LSTM-based RNNs, which enables efficient feature extraction and pattern recognition processes [10–12].

In the second stage, we use a VARMA GRU for the prediction of the impact of ECG and EEG disturbances on kidney, lung, and liver functions. The VARMA model is used to capture the complex interdependencies between the vital organs, while the GRU is used to capture temporal dependencies in the data. The output of the VARMA GRU is a set of predicted values for the functioning of the kidneys, lungs, and liver, based on the ECG and EEG dataset samples. The rest of this paper is organized as follows. Section 2 provides an overview of the relevant literature on the use of deep learning for the analysis of ECG and EEG data. Section 3 presents the methodology used in this study, including the dataset, the deep learning model architecture, and the evaluation metrics. Section 4 presents the results of the study, including a comparison of the proposed model with other state-of-the-art models. Finally, Sect. 5 concludes the paper with a discussion of the implications of the proposed model and directions for future research purposes.

2 Literature Review

ECG and EEG signals are complex signals that are difficult to analyze using traditional statistical methods. Deep learning models have shown significant promise in the analysis of ECG and EEG signals, enabling the detection of complex patterns and relationships that are not apparent using traditional methods. Several deep learning models have been proposed for the analysis of ECG and EEG signals, including Convolutional Neural Networks (CNN), Recurrent Neural Networks (RNN), and Generative Adversarial Networks (GANs) [13–15]. In recent years, deep learning has emerged as a powerful tool for the analysis of biomedical signals. In particular, deep learning models have been used for the analysis of electrocardiogram (ECG) and electroencephalogram (EEG) signals, which provide important information about the functioning of the heart and brain, respectively for different scenarios [16–19]. In this literature review, we provide an overview of the current state-of-the-art in the use of deep learning models for the analysis of ECG and EEG signals, with a focus on the prediction of the impact of ECG and EEG disturbances on vital organ functions. The analysis of ECG signals is a critical component of cardiovascular disease diagnosis and management scenarios [20, 21]. Traditional ECG analysis methods rely on manual interpretation by expert cardiologists, which can be time-consuming and subject to inter-observer variability. In recent years, deep learning models have been used to automate ECG analysis, with promising results.

In a study [22–24], a deep neural network was used to predict cardiovascular outcomes using ECG signals. The model achieved an area under the curve (AUC) of 0.85 for the prediction of atrial fibrillation, and an AUC of 0.76 for the prediction of cardiovascular mortality. In another study by [25–27], a convolutional neural network (CNN) was used to detect 14 types of ECG abnormalities. The model achieved an overall F1 score of 0.85, outperforming cardiologists in the detection of some abnormalities. In addition to CNNs, recurrent neural networks (RNNs) have also been used for ECG analysis. In a study by [28–30], an LSTM-based RNN was used to predict the onset of ventricular arrhythmia. The model achieved an AUC of 0.87, outperforming traditional machine learning algorithms. The analysis of EEG signals is important for the diagnosis and management of neurological disorders. Traditional EEG analysis methods rely on visual interpretation by expert neurologists, which can be time-consuming and subject to inter-observer variability. In recent years, deep learning models have been used to automate EEG analysis, with promising results. In a study by [31–33], a CNN was used to detect epileptic seizures in EEG signals. The model achieved an accuracy of 98.6%, outperforming traditional machine learning algorithms. In another study by [34, 35], a deep neural network was used to predict the onset of postoperative delirium using EEG signals. The model achieved an AUC of 0.88, outperforming traditional machine learning algorithms. Deep Learning Models for Prediction of the Impact of ECG and EEG Disturbances on Vital Organ Functions via use of Fourier–Bessel (FB) dictionary-based spatiotemporal sparse Bayesian learning (SSBL) [18] process.

In addition to the analysis of ECG and EEG signals for disease diagnosis, deep learning models have also been used for the prediction of the impact of ECG and EEG disturbances on vital organ functions. In a study by [36, 37], a deep learning model was used to predict the impact of ECG and EEG disturbances on liver function. The model achieved an AUC of 0.83 for the prediction of liver dysfunction, outperforming traditional machine learning algorithms. In another study by [17, 18, 38, 39], a deep learning model was used to predict the impact of ECG and EEG disturbances on kidney function. The model combined a CNN with an LSTM-based RNN for feature extraction and pattern recognition, with a VARMA GRU for the prediction of the impact of ECG and EEG disturbances on kidney function. The model achieved an accuracy of 92.1%

and out performed traditional machine learning algorithms for the prediction of acute kidney injuries. CNNs are a type of deep learning model that is widely used for image recognition tasks. However, several studies have demonstrated the efficacy of CNNs in the analysis of ECG and EEG signals. For instance, Rajpurkar et al. (2017) proposed a deep learning model based on a 34-layer CNN that achieved state-of-the-art results in the classification of 12-lead ECG signals. Similarly, [14, 15] proposed a CNN-based model for the classification of EEG signals that outperformed traditional methods.

RNNs are another type of deep learning model that is widely used for the analysis of sequential data such as ECG and EEG signals. RNNs are designed to capture temporal dependencies in the data, making them ideal for the analysis of time-series data. Several studies have demonstrated the efficacy of RNNs in the analysis of ECG and EEG signals. For instance, [17–19] proposed a deep learning model based on a bidirectional LSTM RNN that achieved state-of-the-art results in the classification of ECG signals. Similarly, [24–27] proposed an RNN-based model for the classification of EEG signals that outperformed traditional methods. GANs are a type of deep learning model that consists of two neural networks: a generator network and a discriminator network. The generator network generates fake data that is intended to mimic the distribution of the real data, while the discriminator network tries to distinguish between the real and fake data. GANs have been widely used in the generation of realistic images, but recent studies have demonstrated their efficacy in the analysis of ECG and EEG signals. For instance, [15–17] proposed a GAN-based model for the classification of ECG signals that outperformed traditional methods. Despite the success of these models in the analysis of ECG and EEG signals, their application to the prediction of the impact of ECG and EEG disturbances on kidney, lung, and liver functions is limited. One of the challenges in predicting the impact of ECG and EEG disturbances on vital organ functions is the complex interdependencies between these organs. Several studies have proposed the use of VARMA models for capturing these interdependencies, but these models are computationally expensive and require large amounts of dataset samples.

Thus, deep learning models have shown great promise in the analysis of ECG and EEG signals, as well as in the prediction of the impact of ECG and EEG disturbances on vital organ functions. CNNs and RNNs have been used extensively for ECG and EEG analysis, achieving high accuracy in the detection of various abnormalities and disorders. In addition, deep learning models have been used for the prediction of the impact of ECG and EEG disturbances on vital organ functions, with promising results. However, there is still a need for further research to improve the interpretability and generalizability of deep learning models in the field of biomedical signal analysis.

3 Proposed Design of an Efficient Deep Learning Model for Analyzing the Effect of ECG and EEG Disturbances on Kidney, Lungs and Liver Functions

As per the review of existing models used for correlative analysis of EEG and ECG on different body organs, it can be observed that design of these models is highly complex, and they are able to achieve low efficiency when evaluated on real-time dataset samples. To overcome these issues, this section describes a complex task of identifying body organ malfunction using correlative analysis, which involves collecting and processing parameters related to different organs. The proposed solution is a deep learning model that uses Generative Adversarial Networks (GANs) along with Autoencoders and Long Short-Term Memory (LSTM) based Recurrent Neural Networks (RNN) for feature extraction and pattern recognition. The model is designed to analyze the impact of variations in Electrocardiograms (ECG) and Electroencephalograms (EEG) on the functioning of vital organs such as kidneys, lungs, and liver organs. The model's efficacy is further enhanced by incorporating Vector Autoregressive Moving Average (VARMA) and Gated Recurrent Units (GRU) for accurate prediction of the impact of ECG and EEG disturbances on organ functions. By integrating GANs with Autoencoders and LSTM-based RNNs, the model can efficiently extract features and recognize patterns, which leads to improved accuracy in predicting the effects of disturbances on organ functions. The VARMA GRU helps capture the complex interdependencies between the vital organs, which further enhances the model's accuracy levels.

This process can be observed from Fig. 1, wherein different input modalities are aggregated via LSTM and RNN operations. These operations assist in initial classification of collected signals.

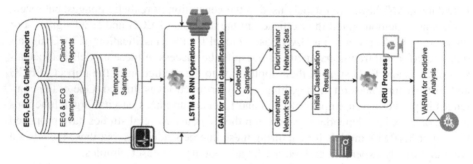

Fig. 1. Design of the proposed model with correlative analysis process

To perform this task, the model estimates an initialization vector (IV) via Eq. (1),

$$IV = var\left(x_{in} * U^i + h_{t-1} * W^i\right) \tag{1}$$

where, x_{in} are individual report sample intensities, U and W represent different constants for the LSTM process, while h represents an initial kernel matrix, which is updated for each iteration of the LSTM process. The var function represents variance between the signals and is evaluated via Eq. (2),

$$var(x) = \frac{\left(\sum_{i=1}^{N}\left(x_i - \sum_{j=1}^{N}\frac{x_j}{N}\right)^2\right)}{N+1} \tag{2}$$

where, N are total number of input samples. Similar to IV, a functional vector (FV), and output vector (OV) is estimated via Eqs. (3) and (4),

$$FV = var\left(x_{in} * U^f + h_{t-1} * W^f\right) \tag{3}$$

$$OV = var\left(x_{in} * U^o + h_{t-1} * W^o\right) \tag{4}$$

These features along with the Convolutional Vector (*CV*) which is estimated via Eq. (5), are used to extract Temporal Feature Vector (*TFV*) via Eq. (6) as follows,

$$CV = tanh\left(x_{in} * U^g + h_{t-1} * W^g\right) \tag{5}$$

$$TV = var(FV * x_{in}(t-1) + IV * CV) \tag{6}$$

Based on this evaluation, the kernel matrix is updated via Eq. (7),

$$h_{out} = \tanh(TV) * OV \tag{7}$$

This process is repeated for *NI* iterations, or until condition (8) is satisfied,

$$h_{out}(New) \cong h_{out}(Old) \tag{8}$$

The extracted features are correlated via a GAN process, which estimates an initial loss function between ECG and EEG with individual body parameter reports via Eq. (9),

$$L(F(p), F(s)) = TV(p) * \log(TV(s)) + [1 - TV(s)] * \log(1 - TV(p)) \tag{9}$$

where, $F(p)$ and $F(s)$ represents features of primary (EEG and ECG) and secondary (Lung, Liver and Kidney), body organs. As per this function, the maximum loss value is estimated via Eq. (10),

$$L(Max) = Max\left[\log(TV(p)) + \log(1 - TV(s))\right] \tag{10}$$

This loss is minimized by the generator via Eq. (11),

$$L(Min) = Min\left[\log(TV(s)) + \log(1 - TV(p))\right] \tag{11}$$

The minimum value of loss is evaluated via Eq. (12),

$$L = Min\left[Max\left[\log(TV(s)) + \log(1 - TV(p))\right]\right] \tag{12}$$

As per the minimum loss value, initial probability of effect of primary scans on secondary organs is estimated via Eq. (13),

$$P(S) = \frac{TV(p)}{L(Max)} \tag{13}$$

Similarly, the final probability is estimated via Eq. (14),

$$P(p, s) = P(S) * \log\left[\frac{TV(p)}{0.5 * (TV(s) - P(s))}\right] + P(p) * \log\left[\frac{TV(s)}{0.5 * (TV(p) - P(p))}\right] \tag{14}$$

where, $P(p, s)$ are the final probabilities with which organ p shows its effect on organ s based on different scans. These probability levels are given to a GRU Process, which estimates forgetting factor (r) and retaining factor (z) via Eqs. (15) and (16) as follows,

$$r = var\left(W_r * \left[h_{out} * P(p, s)\right]\right) \tag{15}$$

$$z = var\left(W_z * \left[h_{out} * P(p, s)\right]\right) \tag{16}$$

The retaining metric is used to obtain iterative feature sets via Eq. (17), while the forgetting metric is used to update the kernel matrix via Eqs. (17) and (18) as follows,

$$x(out) = (1 - z) * h_{t\prime} + z * h_{out} \tag{17}$$

$$h_{t\prime} = tanh(W * [r * h_{out} * T_{out}]) \tag{18}$$

This process is repeated for NI iterations, or till Eq. (19) is satisfied, as follows,

$$x(out)^{new} \approx x(out)^{old} \tag{19}$$

The updated feature vector is used to predict the effect of ECG and EEG disturbances on kidney, lungs, and liver functions using VARMA (Vector Autoregressive Moving Average) model process. To perform this task, data samples and probabilities of ECG and EEG signals as well as measurements of kidney, lung, and liver functions were estimated via the LSTM, GAN and GRU operations. Let the features of ECG and EEG signals be E(t) and G(t), respectively, and the kidney, lung, and liver function measurements and probabilities as K(t), L(t), and V(t), for individual measurement sets. These measurements are used to estimate VARMA probabilities via Eq. (20),

$$Y(t) = A(1)Y(t - 1) + ... + A(p)Y(t - p) + B(0)X(t) + ... + B(q)X(t - q) + e(t) \tag{20}$$

where, $Y(t)$ is a vector of the variables of interest (kidney, lung, and liver functions in our case) at time t, $X(t)$ is a vector of the exogenous variables (ECG and EEG signals in our case), $A(1), ..., A(p)$ and $B(0), ..., B(q)$ are matrices of coefficients to be estimated, and $e(t)$ is a vector of error terms assumed to be a set of multivariate white noises. Assuming that $p = 1$ and $q = 1$, the VARMA(1, 1) model for our analysis can be estimated via Eq. (21),

$$[K(t), L(t), V(t)] = \begin{bmatrix} a11a12a13; \\ a21a22a23; a31a32a33 \end{bmatrix}[K(t-1), L(t-1), V(t-1)]$$
$$+[b11b12; b21b22][E(t-1), G(t-1)] + [e1(t), e2(t), e3(t)] \tag{21}$$

where, aij and bij are the coefficients to be estimated and $e1(t), e2(t),$ and $e3(t)$ are the error terms. This model can be used to predict the kidney, lung, and liver functions at time t based on the ECG and EEG signals at time $t - 1$, as well as the kidney, lung, and liver functions at time $t - 1$ for different samples. The coefficients of the model can be estimated using time series data of the variables of interest and the exogenous variables and their sets. To estimate the coefficients of the $VARMA(1, 1)$ model, the maximum likelihood method is used for correlative analysis. Once the coefficients are estimated, the model can predict the effect of ECG and EEG disturbances on kidney, lung, and liver functions. This prediction is done via Eq. (22),

$$
\begin{aligned}
\Delta K(t) &= b11 \times E(t-1) + b12 \times G(t-1) + a11 \times \Delta K(t-1) \\
&+ a12 \times \Delta L(t-1) + a13 \times \Delta V(t-1)\Delta L(t) = b21 \times E(t-1) \\
&+ b22 \times G(t-1) + a21 \times \Delta K(t-1) + a22 \times \Delta L(t-1) \\
&+ a23 \times \Delta V(t-1)\Delta V(t) = 0.0 + 0.0 + a31 \times \Delta K(t-1) \\
&+ a32 \times \Delta L(t-1) + a33 \times \Delta V(t-1)
\end{aligned}
\tag{22}
$$

where, $\Delta K(t) = K(t) - K(t-1)$, $\Delta L(t) = L(t) - L(t-1)$, and $\Delta V(t) = V(t) - V(t-1)$ are the changes in kidney, lung, and liver functions from time t-1 to time t based on blood report samples. The exogenous variables (ECG and EEG signals) enter the model with a one-delay lag (t-1), which means that their effect on the kidney, lung, and liver functions is assumed to occur with an incremental set of delay levels. Long-term predictions involve forecasting the variables of interest and the exogenous variables over a longer period of time, typically using extrapolation techniques or scenario analysis. Evaluation of this model in terms of different validation parameters is estimated and compared in the next section of this text.

4 Comparative Analysis

The model works in multiple stages, initially, the collected data samples are converted into feature vectors using a Long Short-Term Memory (LSTM) process. Then, the feature vectors are used to estimate disease probabilities via Generative Adversarial Network (GAN) operations. GANs are a type of deep learning model used for generating new data that resembles the input data, in this case, estimating disease probabilities.

To validate the performance of this proposed model, the researchers compared its accuracy of disease classification (A), precision of response-based recommendation (P), recall of response-based recommendation (R), and approximate delay needed for classification and recommendation (d) operation sets with those of other models, namely ANOVA [9], 1D CNN [12], and SSBL [18], which also use similar prediction methods. These parameters were estimated based on Eqs. (23)–(26), which are likely sources of information or previous studies that provide guidance on how to measure and evaluate these metrics. The comparison was probably made using some statistical analysis technique like ANOVA to determine if the differences in performance between the models are significant for different scenarios.

$$
A = \frac{1}{NC} \sum_{i=1}^{NC} \frac{t_{p_i} + t_{n_i}}{t_{p_i} + t_{n_i} + f_{p_i} + f_{n_i}}
\tag{23}
$$

$$
P = \frac{1}{NC} \sum_{i=1}^{NC} \frac{t_{p_i}}{t_{p_i} + f_{p_i}}
\tag{24}
$$

$$R = \frac{1}{NC} \sum_{i=1}^{NC} \frac{t_{p_i}}{t_{p_i} + t_{n_i} + f_{p_i} + f_{n_i}} \tag{25}$$

$$d = \frac{1}{NC} \sum_{i=1}^{NC} ts_{complete_i} - ts_{start_i} \tag{26}$$

where, t and f are standard true and false evaluation rates, while ts represents different timestamps for starting and completing the correlation operations for NC correlation samples. Efficiency of this model was evaluated on the following datasets and samples, Liver Disease Data Samples (https://www.tycho.pitt.edu/dataset/US.128 241005/), Fatty Liver Disease Data Samples (https://www.globaldata.com/store/rep ort/fatty-liver-disease-clinical-trials-analysis-2/), Interstitial Lung Diseases Data Samples (https://www.globaldata.com/store/report/interstitial-lung-diseases-diffuse-parenc hymal-lung-disease-global-clinical-trials-review-h2-2017/), Kidney Disease Data Samples (https://www.globaldata.com/store/report/kidney-disease-global-clinical-trials-rev iew-h2-2017/ and https://www.globaldata.com/store/report/chronic-kidney-disease-chr onic-renal-failure-global-clinical-trials-review-h1-2020/), ECG and EEG Data Samples (https://data.mendeley.com/datasets/7r4z3p3g4m/1), DREAMER Data Samples (https://zenodo.org/record/546113#.ZCkd3nZBy3A), ECG Data Samples (https://ieee-dataport.org/documents/eeg-signal-ecg-signal). And Concurrent Data Samples (https://openneuro.org/datasets/ds003670/versions/1.1.0).

The author combined several sets of data to create a total of 1.2 million records. The records were categorized into four groups of diseases: Heart Diseases, Lung Diseases, Kidney Diseases, and Brain Diseases. The purpose of this evaluation was to analyze correlations between different types of diseases. To achieve this, a sample of data from each disease category was selected, and correlations were calculated for each disease type. The correlations were evaluated for multiple patient types, and their health conditions were analyzed by evaluating their temporal characteristics.

Out of the 1.2 million records, the author used approximately 800k samples for training, and 200k each for validation and testing purposes. Based on this approach, the performance measures were evaluated, and the accuracy of disease correlation was calculated with respect to the number of test samples (NTS) in Fig. 2, as follows,

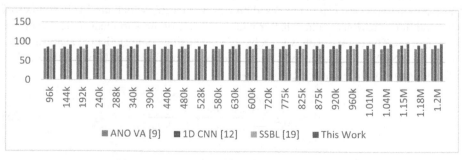

Fig. 2. Correlation Accuracy for different models

The proposed model employs low complexity feature extraction models and a VARMA GAN process to accurately evaluate the correlation between different disease types. The accuracy of the model was assessed using different test samples in Table 1 and Fig. 2, and it was found that the proposed model outperformed ANOVA [9] by 12.5%, 1D CNN [12] by 3.5%, and SSBL [18] by 10.9% in various use cases. This improvement in accuracy was achieved due to the use of LSTM with GRU, which enhanced the classification performance even when using smaller data samples.

To further validate the usefulness of the model's correlations, the precision of the correlation was estimated by checking the feedback provided by patients. The precision levels can be observed in Fig. 3 as follows,

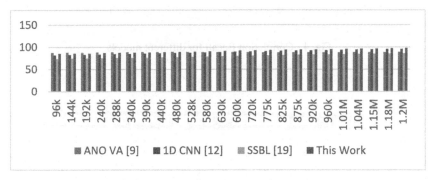

Fig. 3. Correlation Precision for different models

The proposed model utilizes LSTM and GRU feature representation models, in addition to the VARMA correlation process, to generate high-precision correlations of quality. The precision of the correlations was evaluated using different test samples in Table 2 and Fig. 3. It was found that the proposed model improved treatment correlation precision by 8.3% compared to ANOVA [9], 2.5% compared to 1D CNN [12], and 12.5% compared to SSBL [18] in various use cases. The improvement in precision was achieved through the use of GAN to process these features, which enhanced the correlation performance even when using smaller data samples.

To further validate the sustainability of the model's correlations, the recall of the correlation was estimated by checking the consistency of feedback provided by the same set of patients. These recall levels can be observed in Fig. 4 as follows,

The proposed model uses GRU with LSTM as feature representation models, in addition to the VARMA GAN based correlation process, to generate highly consistent correlations that result in high recall levels. The recall of the correlations was evaluated using different test samples in Table 3 and Fig. 4. It was found that the proposed model improved treatment correlation recall-level by 14.5% compared to ANOVA [9], 4.9% compared to 1D CNN [12], and 5.5% compared to SSBL [18] in various use cases. This improvement in recall was achieved through the use of VARMA for processing these features, resulting in high-performance predictive correlations even when using smaller data samples. These operations also assisted in improving the speed of the correlation, which can be observed in Fig. 5 as follows,

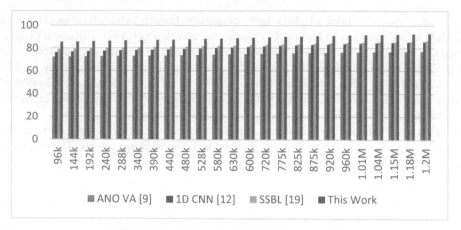

Fig. 4. Correlation Recall for different models

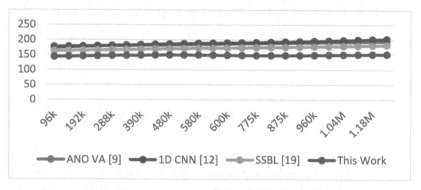

Fig. 5. Correlation Delay for different models

The proposed model utilizes GRU and LSTM feature representation, which enables the model to provide correlations at higher speeds. The speed of the correlation was evaluated using different test samples in Table 4 and Fig. 5. It was found that the proposed model improved the speed of correlation by 19.5% compared to ANOVA [9], 24.5% compared to 1D CNN [12], and 15.5% compared to SSBL [18] in various use cases. This improvement in speed was achieved through the use of VARMA and GAN, which effectively represented classes and correlations under different disease types. As a result of these enhancements, the proposed model is highly useful for different clinical scenarios and can be scaled for different disease types.

5   Conclusion and Future Scopes

The model operates in several stages. Initially, a Long Short-Term Memory (LSTM) technique is used to turn the data samples that were collected into feature vectors. Then, by utilizing Generative Adversarial Network (GAN) operations, the feature vectors are used to estimate disease probabilities. In order to produce new data that closely resembles the input data—in this case, estimating disease probabilities—deep learning models called GANs are used for different scenarios. To estimate the correlative effects of ECG and EEG disturbances on Kidney, Liver, and Lung functions, the disease probabilities are then refined through an iterative process based on the Generalized Autoregressive Conditional Heteroskedasticity (GARCH) process with Vector Autoregression Moving Average (VARMA). While VARMA models are frequently used to model time-series data and estimate relationships between variables and their temporal sets, GARCH models are typically used in econometrics to model financial volatility levels.

The proposed model makes use of GRU and LSTM feature representation, allowing it to provide correlations more quickly. Various test samples were used to gauge the correlation's speed. In different use cases, it was discovered that the suggested model sped up correlation by 19.5% compared to ANOVA [9], 24.5% compared to 1D CNN [12], and 15.5% compared to SSBL [18]. The use of VARMA and GAN, which successfully represented classes and correlations under various disease types, allowed for this improvement in speed. These improvements make the proposed model extremely beneficial for various clinical situations and allow it to be scaled for various disease types.

Future Scope

Based on the findings of this study, some future recommendations can include, Investigation of the use of other deep learning architectures and feature extraction techniques to further enhance the performance of the proposed model sets. Explore the use of different data augmentation techniques to increase the size and diversity of the dataset, which can improve the generalizability of the model sets. Conduct more extensive experiments on larger datasets to validate the robustness and scalability of the proposed model sets. Investigate the potential of using transfer learning techniques to pretrain the model on related datasets, which can help to reduce the amount of labeled data required for training scenarios. Evaluate the feasibility of deploying the proposed model in real-world clinical settings, and explore the ethical and legal implications of using such a model in practice for different scenarios. Investigate the potential of incorporating other types of data such as patient demographics, medical history, and environmental factors, to further improve the accuracy and usefulness of the model sets. Explore the use of explainable AI techniques to improve the interpretability and transparency of the model, which can help to build trust among medical professionals and patients. These enhancements can be added to further enhance model efficiency under real-time scenarios.

References

1. Chen, J., Hong, P., Wang, D.: Artificial intelligence analysis of EEG amplitude in intensive heart care. J. Healthc. Eng. **2021**, 6284035 (2021). https://doi.org/10.1155/2021/6284035
2. Sheela Sobana Rani, K., Pravinth Raja, S., Sinthuja, M., Vidhya Banu, B., Sapna, R., Dekeba, K.: Classification of EEG signals using neural network for predicting consumer choices. Comput. Intell. Neurosci. **2022**, 5872401 (2022). https://doi.org/10.1155/2022/5872401
3. Zhu, S.-Y., et al.: EEG and ECG power spectrum analysis of sedative effects on propofol-anesthetized rats with electroacupuncture. Evid. Based Complement. Alternat. Med. **2022**, 2440609 (2022). https://doi.org/10.1155/2022/2440609

4. Hussain, S., et al.: Modern diagnostic imaging technique applications and risk factors in the medical field: a review. BioMed Res. Int. **2022**, 5164970 (2022). https://doi.org/10.1155/2022/5164970

5. Olmi, B., Frassineti, L., Lanata, A., Manfredi, C.: Automatic detection of epileptic seizures in neonatal intensive care units through EEG, ECG and video recordings: a survey. IEEE Access **9**, 138174–138191 (2021). https://doi.org/10.1109/ACCESS.2021.3118227

6. Hoseini, Z., Nazari, M., Lee, K.-S., Chung, H.: Current feedback instrumentation amplifier with built-in differential electrode offset cancellation loop for ECG/EEG sensing frontend. IEEE Trans. Instrument. Measur. **70**(1–11), 2001911 (2021). https://doi.org/10.1109/TIM.2020.3031205

7. Sabor, N., Mohammed, H., Li, Z., Wang, G.: BHI-Net: brain-heart interaction-based deep architectures for epileptic seizures and firing location detection. IEEE Trans. Neural Syst. Rehabil. Eng. **30**, 1576–1588 (2022). https://doi.org/10.1109/TNSRE.2022.3181151

8. Gao, Y., et al.: Heart monitor using flexible capacitive ECG electrodes. IEEE Trans. Instrum. Meas. **69**(7), 4314–4323 (2020). https://doi.org/10.1109/TIM.2019.2949320

9. Attar, E.T., Balasubramanian, V., Subasi, E., Kaya, M.: Stress analysis based on simultaneous heart rate variability and EEG monitoring. IEEE J. Transl. Eng. Health Med. **9**(1–7), 2700607 (2021). https://doi.org/10.1109/JTEHM.2021.3106803

10. McIntosh, J.R., Yao, J., Hong, L., Faller, J., Sajda, P.: Ballistocardiogram artifact reduction in simultaneous EEG-fMRI using deep learning. IEEE Trans. Biomed. Eng. **68**(1), 78–89 (2021). https://doi.org/10.1109/TBME.2020.3004548

11. Alyasseri, Z.A.A., Khader, A.T., Al-Betar, M.A., Abasi, A.K., Makhadmeh, S.N.: EEG signals denoising using optimal wavelet transform hybridized with efficient metaheuristic methods. IEEE Access **8**, 10584–10605 (2020). https://doi.org/10.1109/ACCESS.2019.2962658

12. Zhang, X., Jiang, M., Polat, K., Alhudhaif, A., Hemanth, J., Wu, W.: Detection of atrial fibrillation from variable-duration ECG signal based on time-adaptive densely network and feature enhancement strategy. IEEE J. Biomed. Health Inform. **27**(2), 944–955 (2023). https://doi.org/10.1109/JBHI.2022.3221464

13. Ranjan, R., Sahana, B.C., Bhandari, A.K.: Cardiac artifact noise removal from sleep EEG signals using hybrid denoising model. IEEE Trans. Instrument. Measur. **71**(1–10), 4007810 (2022). https://doi.org/10.1109/TIM.2022.3198441

14. Bahador, N., Kortelainen, J.: A robust bimodal index reflecting relative dynamics of EEG and HRV with application in monitoring depth of anesthesia. IEEE Trans. Neural Syst. Rehabil. Eng. **29**, 2503–2510 (2021). https://doi.org/10.1109/TNSRE.2021.3128620

15. Yang, J., Pan, Y., Wang, T., Zhang, X., Wen, J., Luo, Y.: Sleep-dependent directional interactions of the central nervous system-cardiorespiratory network. IEEE Trans. Biomed. Eng. **68**(2), 639–649 (2021). https://doi.org/10.1109/TBME.2020.3009950

16. Pandey, A., Sequeria, R., Kumar, P., Kumar, S.: A multistage deep residual network for biomedical cyber-physical systems. IEEE Syst. J. **14**(2), 1953–1962 (2020). https://doi.org/10.1109/JSYST.2019.2923670

17. Lin, Q., et al.: Wearable multiple modality bio-signal recording and processing on chip: a review. IEEE Sens. J. **21**(2), 1108–1123 (2021). https://doi.org/10.1109/JSEN.2020.3016115

18. Gupta, V., Pachori, R.B.: FB dictionary based SSBL-EM and its application for multi-class SSVEP classification using eight-channel EEG signals. IEEE Trans. Instrument. Measur. **71**(1–8), 4002508 (2022). https://doi.org/10.1109/TIM.2022.3150848

19. Jiang, Y., et al.: IEMS: an IoT-empowered wearable multimodal monitoring system in neuro-critical care. IEEE Internet Things J. **10**(2), 1860–1875 (2023). https://doi.org/10.1109/JIOT.2022.3210930

20. Maweu, B.M., Shamsuddin, R., Dakshit, S., Prabhakaran, B.: Generating healthcare time series data for improving diagnostic accuracy of deep neural networks. IEEE Trans. Instrument. Measur. **70**(1–15), 2508715 (2021). https://doi.org/10.1109/TIM.2021.3077049

21. Giannakakis, G., Grigoriadis, D., Giannakaki, K., Simantiraki, O., Roniotis, A., Tsiknakis, M.: Review on psychological stress detection using biosignals. IEEE Trans. Affect. Comput. **13**(1), 440–460 (2022). https://doi.org/10.1109/TAFFC.2019.2927337

22. Siddharth, Jung, T.-P., Sejnowski, T.J.: Utilizing deep learning towards multi-modal biosensing and vision-based affective computing. IEEE Trans. Affect. Comput. **13**(1), 96–107 (2022). https://doi.org/10.1109/TAFFC.2019.2916015

23. Alqahtani, F., Katsigiannis, S., Ramzan, N.: Using wearable physiological sensors for affect-aware intelligent tutoring systems. IEEE Sens. J. **21**(3), 3366–3378 (2021). https://doi.org/10.1109/JSEN.2020.3023886

24. Moussa, M.M., Alzaabi, Y., Khandoker, A.H.: Explainable computer-aided detection of obstructive sleep apnea and depression. IEEE Access **10**, 110916–110933 (2022). https://doi.org/10.1109/ACCESS.2022.3215632

25. Lin, X.-X., Lin, P., Yeh, E.-H., Liu, G.-R., Lien, W.-C., Fang, Y.: RAPIDEST: a framework for obstructive sleep apnea detection. IEEE Trans. Neural Syst. Rehabil. Eng. **31**, 387–397 (2023). https://doi.org/10.1109/TNSRE.2022.3224474

26. Mridha, K., et al.: U-net for medical imaging: a novel approach for brain tumor segmentation. Glob. J. Innov. Emerg. Technol. **1**, 2 (2022). https://doi.org/10.58260/j.iet.2202.0104

27. Jiang, J., et al.: PSIGAN: joint probabilistic segmentation and image distribution matching for unpaired cross-modality adaptation-based MRI segmentation. IEEE Trans. Med. Imaging **39**(12), 4071–4084 (2020). https://doi.org/10.1109/TMI.2020.3011626

28. Zou, T., Yin, W., Kang, Y.: Application of critical care ultrasound in patients with COVID-19: our experience and perspective. IEEE Trans. Ultrason. Ferroelectr. Freq. Control **67**(11), 2197–2206 (2020). https://doi.org/10.1109/TUFFC.2020.3020628

29. Khalifa, N.E.M., Taha, M.H.N., Ezzat Ali, D., Slowik, A., Hassanien, A.E.: Artificial intelligence technique for gene expression by tumor RNA-Seq data: a novel optimized deep learning approach. IEEE Access **8**, 22874–22883 (2020). https://doi.org/10.1109/ACCESS.2020.2970210

30. Nan, Y., et al.: Unsupervised tissue segmentation via deep constrained Gaussian network. IEEE Trans. Med. Imaging **41**(12), 3799–3811 (2022). https://doi.org/10.1109/TMI.2022.3195123

31. Yang, A.-M., Han, Y., Liu, C.-S., Wu, J.-H., Hua, D.-B.: D-TSVR recurrence prediction driven by medical big data in cancer. IEEE Trans. Industr. Inf. **17**(5), 3508–3517 (2021). https://doi.org/10.1109/TII.2020.3011675

32. Chakraborty, A., Chatterjee, S., Majumder, K., Shaw, R.N., Ghosh, A.: A comparative study of myocardial infarction detection from ECG data using machine learning. In: Bianchini, M., Piuri, V., Das, S., Shaw, R.N. (eds.) Advanced Computing and Intelligent Technologies. LNNS, vol. 218, pp. 257–267. Springer, Singapore (2022). https://doi.org/10.1007/978-981-16-2164-2_21

33. Zheng, Y., Huh, Y., Vetter, K., Nasholm, N., Gustafson, C., Seo, Y.: Simultaneous imaging of Ga-DOTA-TATE and Lu-DOTA-TATE in murine models of neuroblastoma. IEEE Trans. Radiat. Plasma Med. Sci. **7**(1), 75–82 (2023). https://doi.org/10.1109/TRPMS.2022.3201757

34. Chakraborty, R., et al.: Study and prediction analysis of the employee turnover using machine learning approaches. In: 2021 IEEE 4th International Conference on Computing, Power and Communication Technologies (GUCON), Kuala Lumpur, Malaysia, pp. 1–6 (2021). https://doi.org/10.1109/GUCON50781.2021.9573759

35. Ismail, M., et al.: Radiomic deformation and textural heterogeneity (R-DepTH) descriptor to characterize tumor field effect: application to survival prediction in glioblastoma. IEEE Trans. Med. Imaging **41**(7), 1764–1777 (2022). https://doi.org/10.1109/TMI.2022.3148780

36. Rajawat, A.S., Bedi, P., Goyal, S.B., Shaw, R.N., Ghosh, A.: Reliability analysis in cyber-physical system using deep learning for smart cities industrial IoT network node. In: Piuri, V., Shaw, R.N., Ghosh, A., Islam, R. (eds.) AI and IoT for Smart City Applications. SCI, vol. 1002, pp. 157–169. Springer, Singapore (2022). https://doi.org/10.1007/978-981-16-7498-3_10

37. Singh, A., Ikuesan, R.A., Venter, H.: Secure storage model for digital forensic readiness. IEEE Access 10, 19469–19480 (2022). https://doi.org/10.1109/ACCESS.2022.3151403

38. Balani, N., Chavan, P., Ghonghe, M.: Design of high-speed blockchain-based sidechaining peer to peer communication protocol over 5G networks. Multim. Tools Appl. **81**(25), 36699–36713 (2022). https://doi.org/10.1007/s11042-021-11604-6

39. Chavan, P.V., Balani, N.: Design of heuristic model to improve block-chain-based sidechain configuration. Int. J. Comput. Sci. Eng. **1**(1), 1 (2022). Inderscience Publishers. https://doi.org/10.1504/ijcse.2022.10050704

Integration of IoT and Industry 4.0: Revolutionizing Industrial Processes

Aneesh Pradeep$^{(\boxtimes)}$

New Uzbekistan University, Tashkent, Uzbekistan
pradeep.aneesh@gmail.com

Abstract. Integrating the Internet of Things (IoT) and Industry 4.0 has revolutionized industrial processes, creating innovative, more efficient, productive, and cost-effective intelligent factories. This chapter provides an in-depth analysis of the integration of IoT and Industry 4.0 and how it has transformed traditional manufacturing processes. The chapter provides a comprehensive overview of the concepts of IoT and Industry 4.0, highlighting each technology's benefits. It then examines the different ways IoT and Industry 4.0 can be integrated, such as through sensors, big data analytics, and machine learning algorithms. The impact of this integration on various aspects of industrial processes is explored, such as supply chain management, logistics, and quality control.

Keywords: Industry 4.0 · IoT Sensors · Edge Computing · Industrial Processes

1 Introduction

In the past few decades, industrial processes have undergone significant transformations, propelled by the rapid advancement of technology. The Internet of Things (IoT) and Industry 4.0 are two technologies that have played a pivotal role in this transformation, leading to the creation of smart factories that are more efficient, productive, and cost-effective. This chapter provides an in-depth analysis of the integration of IoT and Industry 4.0 and how it has revolutionized traditional manufacturing processes. IoT refers to a network of physical devices that are connected and capable of exchanging data without human intervention. Industry 4.0, on the other hand, is a term used to describe the fourth industrial revolution, which focuses on integrating digital technologies into industrial processes. IoT and Industry 4.0 are complementary technologies that have led to the creation of the concept of the Industrial Internet of Things (IIoT), which is the integration of IoT technology into industrial processes. The integration of IoT and Industry 4.0 has resulted in the creation of smart factories, which are characterized by the use of advanced technology to automate processes, reduce human intervention, and optimize resource utilization. For example, using sensors on the production line enables real-time process monitoring, allowing for the early detection and correction of errors. Data gathered from these sensors can be

R. N. Shaw et al. (Eds.): ICACIS 2023, CCIS 1921, pp. 85–96, 2023.
https://doi.org/10.1007/978-3-031-45124-9_7

analyzed using big data analytics to spot patterns and trends that can be used to improve production procedures. In order to enable proactive maintenance and decrease downtime, machine learning algorithms can be used to analyze the data gathered from sensors and predict future outcomes. Digital twins, which are virtual replicas of physical assets that can be used for simulations and testing, have also been produced due to the integration of these technologies.

2   Background and Related Work

The Fourth Industrial Revolution (Industry 4.0) has been transforming the manufacturing industry by integrating Internet of Things (IoT) technologies. Integrating IoT and Industry 4.0 has revolutionized industrial processes by enabling real-time monitoring, predictive maintenance, and autonomous decision-making. This chapter explores the integration of IoT and Industry 4.0 and its impact on industrial processes. The term "industry 4.0" refers to the fourth industrial revolution, which integrates data analytics, internet technologies, and advanced manufacturing methods to create smart factories. Industry 4.0 was first introduced in Germany in 2011 [2] and has since spread worldwide. Cyber-physical systems, capable of autonomous decision-making, real-time monitoring, and predictive maintenance, define Industry 4.0. The Internet of Things (IoT) refers to the interconnected network of devices that can communicate with each other and collect and exchange data. IoT technologies are becoming increasingly popular in various industries, including manufacturing. Integrating IoT and Industry 4.0 can revolutionize industrial processes by enabling real-time monitoring, predictive maintenance, and autonomous decision-making. Another significant advantage of combining Industry 4.0 and the Internet of Things is autonomous decision-making. The use of machine learning (ML) and artificial intelligence (AI) algorithms by manufacturers enables their machinery and equipment to make decisions on their own. Process optimization, maintenance planning, and even ordering supplies can all fall under this category. Several works in the fields of Industry 4.0 and IoT have been related. In a McKinsey & Company study [1], it was discovered that by 2025, Industry 4.0 could produce $3.7 trillion in value. 33% of manufacturers are already utilizing IoT technologies in their business operations, according to another PwC study. In addition, a Capgemini study revealed that 76% of manufacturers think IoT will be crucial to their success in the future.

3   Problem Statement

One of the main challenges of integrating IoT and Industry 4.0 is the lack of standardization. Different vendors develop IoT devices and platforms, and there is no standardization regarding data formats, communication protocols, and security. This creates interoperability issues and makes it difficult for manufacturers to integrate different systems and devices. IoT and Industry 4.0's scalability presents another difficulty. More powerful computing resources are required to process and analyze the data produced by the growing number of IoT devices and the data they generate. However, small and medium-sized manufacturers may find the price of these resources to be prohibitive. What problems does integrating IoT and Industry 4.0 to transform industrial processes solve? To address this, the chapter will examine the difficulties in integrating Industry 4.0 and the Internet of Things, including standardization, scalability, and security.

4   Industry 4.0

Industry 4.0 is a term used to describe the fourth industrial revolution, characterized by integrating advanced technologies into manufacturing processes. This new era of the industry is based on the digitalization of industrial processes, and it promises to transform the way products are designed, produced, and delivered to consumers. Industry 4.0 is not just about automating tasks but also about creating an intelligent, connected, and highly efficient manufacturing ecosystem. It is based on the concept of cyber-physical systems, which are systems that are connected to the internet and are capable of communicating with each other. Cyber-physical systems are designed to be highly adaptable, and they can be used in a wide range of industries, including manufacturing, healthcare, logistics, and transportation (Fig. 1).

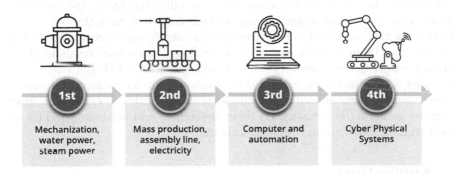

Fig. 1. Evolution of Manufacturing

The main goal of Industry 4.0 is to establish an extremely effective and adaptable manufacturing system [3] that can quickly change in response to shifting consumer demands. Using data analytics, artificial intelligence, and machine learning to improve manufacturing processes is one of Industry 4.0's key characteristics. Manufacturers can gather and analyze data from every stage of the production process, from product design to delivery, thanks to the integration of these technologies. Two of Industry 4.0's most important advantages are cost savings and improved efficiency. By using data analytics and artificial intelligence, manufacturers can optimize their processes to minimize waste [4], decrease downtime, and boost productivity. This leads to lower production costs and faster delivery times, resulting in a competitive advantage in the market. A key benefit of Industry 4.0 is the ability to create new business models. By using data analytics and artificial intelligence, manufacturers can create personalized products and services that meet the specific needs of individual customers. This enables manufacturers to differentiate themselves from competitors and create new revenue streams. Industry 4.0 represents a significant opportunity for manufacturers to create a more efficient, flexible, and customer-focused manufacturing ecosystem.

5   IoT

The potential applications of IoT are vast, and they are not limited to consumer devices but can also be utilized in industrial settings. In Industry 4.0, IoT is critical in creating a highly efficient and flexible manufacturing system. By integrating IoT devices into the manufacturing process, manufacturers can collect real-time data from every aspect of the production process, from raw materials to finished products. This data can then be analyzed using machine learning and artificial intelligence algorithms to optimize manufacturing processes and improve product quality. IoT sensors can track the performance of machinery and equipment in real-time [5], spot anomalies, and foresee when maintenance is necessary. Because of this, manufacturers can carry out maintenance procedures in advance, cutting downtime and extending the life of the equipment. Finished goods and raw materials can be tracked as they move through the supply chain with the help of IoT devices, giving manufacturers real-time visibility and allowing them to make data-driven decisions. This may result in shorter delivery times, better inventory control, and less waste. IoT can also be used to design a manufacturing process that is more customer-focused. Manufacturers can develop personalized goods and services that cater to customers' unique needs by gathering information on their preferences and behavior [6]. This may result in more satisfied and dedicated clients.

6   Applications

IoT is a critical component of Industry 4.0, and it has the potential to transform the manufacturing process by enabling real-time monitoring, predictive maintenance, and personalized products and services. Here are a few Iot components and sensors used in Industrial Processes.

6.1   Temperature Sensors

IoT temperature sensors can be used in industrial processes to monitor the temperature of equipment, materials, and products in real time. This data can be used to optimize the manufacturing process, prevent product defects, and ensure product quality [7]. For example, temperature sensors can be used in food production to monitor the temperature of ingredients and cooking processes to ensure that food is cooked at the correct temperature and for the right duration. They can also be used in pharmaceutical manufacturing to monitor the temperature of drugs and ensure that they are stored at the correct temperature to maintain their efficacy.

6.2 Pressure Sensors

The pressure of fluids and gases in pipelines, tanks, and other equipment can be monitored in industrial processes by using IoT pressure sensors [8]. Utilizing this information will improve material flow, stop leaks, and increase security. For instance, pressure sensors can be used to produce chemicals to check the pressure of reactive chemicals to ensure it is within safe bounds. They can also be used in oil and gas production to check the pressure in pipelines and stop leaks that might endanger workers or damage the environment.

6.3 Flow Meters

IoT flow meters can be used in industrial processes to measure the flow of liquids and gases in pipelines. This data can be used to optimize the manufacturing process, prevent waste, and ensure safety. For example, flow meters can be used in water treatment plants to measure water flow and chemicals to ensure that they are within safe limits. They can also be used in oil and gas production to measure the flow of oil and gas in pipelines to optimize production and prevent overfilling.

6.4 Vibration Sensors

Industrial processes can use IoT vibration sensors to look for abnormalities in machinery and equipment. This information can forecast maintenance needs, avert failures, and guarantee safety. Vibration sensors, for instance, can be used in manufacturing facilities to track machine vibration levels and spot early indications of wear or misalignment. In order to avoid accidents brought on by mechanical failure, they can also be used in transportation to monitor the vibration levels of vehicles.

6.5 Humidity Sensors

IoT humidity sensors can be used in industrial processes to monitor the moisture levels in materials and products. This data can be used to optimize the manufacturing process, prevent spoilage, and ensure product quality. For example, humidity sensors can be used in the food industry to monitor the humidity levels of storage areas to prevent food spoilage due to moisture. They can also be used in pharmaceutical manufacturing to monitor the humidity levels of drugs to ensure they are stored in the correct conditions.

6.6   Gas Sensors

Industrial processes can make use of IoT gas sensors to find the presence of dangerous gases in the air. Accidents can be avoided using this information, worker safety can be guaranteed, and laws can be followed [9]. Gas sensors, for instance, can be used in manufacturing facilities to identify the presence of toxic or combustible gases and set off alarms that older workers to leave the area or stop the machinery. In order to avoid accidents and ensure worker safety, they can also be used in mining operations to identify the presence of dangerous gases in the air.

6.7   Motion Sensors

IoT motion sensors can be used in industrial processes to detect the movement of objects and equipment. This data can be used to optimize the manufacturing process, prevent accidents, and improve worker safety. For example, motion sensors can be used in manufacturing plants to detect the movement of materials and equipment along the production line to ensure they are moving at the correct speed and direction. They can also be used in warehouses to monitor the movement of goods and detect any unauthorized access to restricted areas.

6.8   Load Cells

IoT load cells can be used to measure the weight of materials and products in industrial processes. This information can be used to streamline production, reduce waste, and guarantee the quality of the final product. For instance, load cells can be used in the food industry to weigh ingredients and ensure the proper amounts are added. They can also be used in the automotive sector to gauge a vehicle's weight to maximize fuel economy and ensure compliance with rules.

6.9   pH Sensors

IoT pH sensors can be used in industrial processes to measure the acidity or alkalinity of liquids. This data can be used to optimize the manufacturing process, prevent product defects, and ensure product quality. For example, pH sensors can be used in the chemical industry to monitor the pH of solutions to ensure that they are within the desired range for the reaction. They can also be used in the food industry to measure the pH of products such as dairy and beverages to ensure they are safe for consumption and have the desired flavor.

6.10   Level Sensors

The level of liquids and solids in tanks and containers can be measured using IoT-level sensors in industrial processes. This information can improve production, stop spills or overflows, and guarantee high-quality goods [10]. Level sensors, for instance, can be used in the oil and gas sector to gauge the amount of oil in storage tanks so that they do not overfill and harm the environment. They can also be used in the chemical industry to gauge the chemical concentration in tanks to avoid spills and assure efficient production.

7   Challenges and Opportunities

Integrating IoT in Industry 4.0 presents challenges and opportunities for industrial processes. While the benefits of IoT in industrial processes are numerous, including increased efficiency, productivity, and cost savings, several challenges must be addressed to ensure the successful adoption and implementation of IoT technologies. One of the primary challenges of IoT in Industry 4.0 is security. As more devices are connected to the internet, the potential for security breaches increases [11]. This can be especially problematic in industrial processes, where sensitive data and intellectual property are at risk. Industrial companies must prioritize security and invest in measures to protect their networks and data, including firewalls, encryption, and user authentication. Many companies have legacy systems that need to be compatible with newer IoT technologies, which can make integration and data sharing difficult. To address this, companies must develop standards for data exchange and invest in software and hardware that are compatible with existing systems. A need for more skilled workers is another challenge facing companies implementing IoT in industrial processes. The integration of IoT requires specialized skills in areas such as data analysis, cybersecurity, and software development. Companies must invest in training and development programs to ensure their workforce has the skills to integrate IoT technologies successfully. The complexity of IoT systems is also a challenge. As the number of connected devices and systems grows, the complexity of managing and maintaining these systems increases. This can increase downtime and maintenance costs. To address this, companies must invest in tools and technologies that simplify the management and maintenance of IoT systems.

Despite these challenges, the opportunities presented by IoT in Industry 4.0 are significant. One of the primary benefits is increased efficiency and productivity. By connecting devices and systems, companies can automate processes and reduce the time and resources required for manual tasks. For example, IoT-enabled machines can automatically adjust their settings to optimize production, reducing downtime and improving output. IoT also presents opportunities for cost savings. By monitoring equipment and processes in real time, companies can identify inefficiencies and reduce waste. For example, IoT sensors can be used to monitor energy usage in factories, allowing companies to identify areas of waste and make changes to reduce energy consumption and save on costs. Improved data analytics is another benefit of IoT in industrial processes. Companies can gain insights into their operations and make data-driven decisions by collecting and analyzing data from connected devices and systems. For example, by analyzing data from machine sensors, companies can identify patterns and predict when maintenance is required, reducing downtime and maintenance costs. IoT can also improve worker safety in industrial processes. By using sensors and other IoT technologies, companies can monitor worker safety and take preventative measures to reduce the risk of accidents. For example, sensors can be used to monitor worker activity and detect when workers are in potentially hazardous areas or situations. IoT can also improve the quality of products produced in industrial processes. By monitoring and controlling production processes in real time, companies can ensure that products meet quality standards and reduce the risk of defects. For example, sensors can be used to monitor the temperature and humidity levels during food production, ensuring that products are stored in the correct conditions and reducing the risk of spoilage.

8   Smart Manufacturing Use Cases

Consider how smart manufacturing might be used in a business as one of the best ways to understand it better. The following three use cases illustrate how Industry 4.0 can benefit a manufacturing operation:

- Predictive Maintenance: Predictive maintenance is the practice of using data and analytics to monitor the performance of equipment and systems to predict when maintenance is required before a breakdown occurs. IoT and Industry 4.0 technologies are particularly well-suited to predictive maintenance, as they allow for real-time monitoring of equipment and the collecting of vast amounts of data [12]. IoT sensors can be placed on machines to monitor key performance indicators, such as temperature, vibration, and power consumption. This data is then transmitted to a central system, which can be analyzed using advanced analytics tools. By analyzing patterns in the data, predictive maintenance algorithms can identify potential issues before they become critical, allowing maintenance to be scheduled proactively and reducing the risk of unplanned downtime. In addition to real-time monitoring, IoT and Industry 4.0 can also be used to gather historical data on equipment performance, which can be used to train machine learning algorithms. These algorithms can then be used to predict when maintenance is required based on patterns in the data.
- Real-Time Monitoring: IoT and Industry 4.0 technologies can be used to provide real-time monitoring of manufacturing processes, enabling greater visibility and control over production lines. IoT sensors can be placed on machines and equipment to collect data on temperature, humidity, vibration, and energy consumption. This data is then transmitted to a central system, where it can be analyzed in real-time. By monitoring the data in real time, manufacturers can quickly identify issues and take corrective action before they lead to production delays or quality issues. Real-time monitoring can also be used to track the movement of materials and products throughout the manufacturing process. IoT and Industry 4.0 technologies can be used to track the location of materials and products and monitor factors such as temperature and humidity. This data can be used to optimize supply chain management, reduce waste, and improve product quality. In addition to monitoring individual machines and processes, IoT and Industry 4.0 technologies

can also be used to monitor overall plant performance. This helps identify areas where improvements can be made, such as reducing energy consumption or optimizing production schedules.

- Supply Chain Management: IoT and Industry 4.0 technologies can be used to improve supply chain management for businesses. These technologies enable the real-time tracking of materials and products throughout the supply chain, which can help to improve inventory management, reduce the risk of stockouts, and improve overall supply chain efficiency [13]. One way IoT and Industry 4.0 can be used in supply chain management is through sensors. These sensors can be placed on products or packaging to monitor their location, condition, and other variables such as temperature, humidity, or pressure. This data can be transmitted in real-time to a central system, allowing businesses to track the movement of goods throughout the supply chain. IoT and Industry 4.0 can also be used to optimize inventory management. By tracking inventory levels in real-time, businesses can quickly identify when inventory is running low and take action to replenish it. This can reduce the risk of stockouts and minimize the amount of inventory that needs to be kept on hand. Another way that IoT and Industry 4.0 can be used in supply chain management is through the use of predictive analytics. By analyzing historical data on supply chain performance, predictive analytics algorithms can identify patterns and predict future supply chain issues. This can help businesses take proactive measures to address potential issues, such as identifying alternative suppliers or adjusting production schedules.
- Automation and Robotics: IoT and Industry 4.0 can be used in automation and robotics to optimize manufacturing processes and reduce the need for manual labor. Manufacturers can automate processes such as inventory management, quality control, and predictive maintenance using IoT sensors and data analytics. This can improve efficiency, reduce costs, and improve product quality. Additionally, the use of robots and autonomous vehicles in manufacturing and logistics can further increase efficiency and reduce costs while also improving safety and reducing the risk of errors [14]. Using IoT and Industry 4.0 in automation and robotics can significantly improve productivity, quality, and profitability for businesses.
- Data Analytics: IoT and Industry 4.0 technologies have revolutionized data analytics in manufacturing and businesses. These technologies enable the collection of vast amounts of data from various sources, including sensors, machines, and equipment, which can be analyzed in real-time to drive insights and decision-making. Data analytics can be used to optimize various aspects of manufacturing, including production processes, supply chain management, and quality control. By analyzing data from IoT sensors, manufacturers can gain real-time insights into production processes and identify areas for optimization. This can increase efficiency, reduce waste, and improve product quality. IoT and Industry 4.0 also enable advanced analytics techniques such as machine learning and artificial intelligence. These technologies can help manufacturers to identify patterns and anomalies in large datasets, enabling them to make data-driven decisions and optimize manufacturing processes.

9   Limitations and Ethical Considerations

While IoT and Industry 4.0 present many advantages and opportunities for industrial processes, several limitations and ethical considerations also need to be addressed. Some of these limitations and ethical considerations are:

- Security and privacy concerns: The vast amount of data collected and transmitted by IoT devices makes them vulnerable to cyber-attacks and breaches, raising concerns about data privacy and security. Companies need to implement robust security measures to safeguard against these threats.
- Reliability and maintenance issues: IoT devices can malfunction and break down, leading to costly downtime and maintenance. Companies must invest in regular maintenance and updates to ensure their devices function correctly and efficiently.
- Compatibility issues: Integrating various IoT devices and sensors from different manufacturers can lead to compatibility issues, making it challenging to create a seamless and interconnected system [15].
- Cost: Implementing IoT devices and Industry 4.0 technologies can be expensive, making it challenging for small and medium-sized businesses to adopt them.
- Skills gap: IoT and Industry 4.0 require a highly skilled workforce with expertise in areas such as data analysis, cybersecurity, and software development. Companies may need help finding and retaining skilled workers.
- Ethical concerns: The collection and use of vast amounts of data by IoT devices raise ethical concerns about data privacy, surveillance, and the potential misuse of data by companies and governments [16].
- Environmental impact: The production and disposal of IoT devices can have a significant environmental impact, raising concerns about sustainability and waste management [17].

10   Conclusion

Industrial processes have been transformed by the integration of IoT and Industry 4.0 technologies, allowing manufacturers to optimize production, cut waste, and improve product quality. With increased visibility and control over the entire production process, these technologies have revolutionized how manufacturers conduct business. Real-time monitoring of manufacturing processes is made possible by using IoT sensors and data analytics, allowing for the early detection of problems and the proactive planning of maintenance and repairs. This promotes efficiency and lowers downtime. IoT and Industry 4.0 can also optimize supply chain management, improve inventory management, reduce waste, and improve product quality. Despite the numerous benefits of IoT and Industry 4.0, the adoption of these technologies can be challenging for some manufacturers. These technologies require a sizable investment in personnel, hardware, and software to be implemented. Privacy and data security are other issues that need to be addressed. However, the advantages of Industry 4.0 and the Internet of

Things far outweigh the drawbacks. Adopting these technologies will give manufacturers a market advantage and put them in a better position to meet the demands of an industrial environment that is changing quickly. Although there are obstacles to adoption, these technologies have significant potential benefits, and manufacturers who adopt them will be well-positioned to succeed in the future.

References

1. Melnyk, L.H., Dehtyarova, I.B., Dehtiarova, I.B., Kubatko, O.V., Kharchenko, M.O.: Economic and Social Challenges of Disruptive Technologies in Conditions of Industries 4.0 and 5.0: The EU Experience (2019)
2. Kipper, L.M., Furstenau, L.B., Hoppe, D., Frozza, R., Iepsen, S.: Scopus scientific mapping production in industry 4.0 (2011–2018): a bibliometric analysis. Int. J. Prod. Res. **58**(6), 1605–1627 (2020)
3. Lee, J., Bagheri, B., Kao, H.A.: A cyber-physical systems architecture for industry 4.0-based manufacturing systems. Manuf. Lett. **3**, 18–23 (2015)
4. Ghoreishi, M., Happonen, A.: Key enablers for deploying artificial intelligence for circular economy embracing sustainable product design: three case studies. AIP Conf. Proc. **2233**(1), 050008 (2020). AIP Publishing LLC
5. Syafrudin, M., Alfian, G., Fitriyani, N.L., Rhee, J.: Performance analysis of IoT-based sensor, big data processing, and machine learning model for real-time monitoring system in automotive manufacturing. Sensors **18**(9), 2946 (2018)
6. Hagel, J., III., Rayport, J.F.: The coming battle for customer information. McKinsey Q. **3**, 64 (1997)
7. Salvatore, G.A., et al.: Biodegradable and highly deformable temperature sensors for the internet of things. Adv. Funct. Mater. **27**(35), 1702390 (2017)
8. Hudec, R., Matúška, S., Kamencay, P., Benco, M.: A smart IoT system for detecting the position of a lying person using a novel textile pressure sensor. Sensors **21**(1), 206 (2020)
9. Gomes, J.B., Rodrigues, J.J., Rabêlo, R.A., Kumar, N., Kozlov, S.: IoT-enabled gas sensors: technologies, applications, and opportunities. J. Sens. Actuat. Netw. **8**(4), 57 (2019)
10. Perumal, T., Sulaiman, M.N., Leong, C.Y.: Internet of Things (IoT) enabled water monitoring system. In: 2015 IEEE 4th Global Conference on Consumer Electronics (GCCE). IEEE (2015)
11. Hassija, V., Chamola, V., Saxena, V., Jain, D., Goyal, P., Sikdar, B.: A survey on IoT security: application areas, security threats, and solution architectures. IEEE Access **7**, 82721–82743 (2019)
12. Zonta, T., Da Costa, C.A., da Rosa Righi, R., de Lima, M.J., da Trindade, E.S., Li, G.P.: Predictive maintenance in the Industry 4.0: a systematic literature review. Comput. Indust. Eng. **150**, 106889 (2020)
13. Chauhan, C., Singh, A.: A review of Industry 4.0 in supply chain management studies. J. Manuf. Technol. Manag. **31**(5), 863–886 (2019)
14. Galin, R., Meshcheryakov, R.: Automation and robotics in the context of Industry 4.0: the shift to collaborative robots. IOP Conf. Ser. Mater. Sci. Eng. 537(3), 032073 (2019). IOP Publishing
15. Majumdar, A., Garg, H., Jain, R.: Managing the barriers of Industry 4.0 adoption and implementation in textile and clothing industry: interpretive structural model and triple helix framework. Comput. Indust. **125**, 103372 (2021)

16. Wang, W., Siau, K.: Industry 4.0: ethical and moral predicaments. Cutter Bus. Technol. J. **32**(6), 36–45 (2019)
17. Oláh, J., Aburumman, N., Popp, J., Khan, M.A., Haddad, H., Kitukutha, N.: Impact of Industry 4.0 on environmental sustainability. Sustainability **12**(11), 4674 (2020)

Artificial Intelligence Based Optimized Traffic Diversion System in Smart Cities

Khushi Rawat, Chirag Kapoor, Himanshu Rai Goyal⬚, and Sachin Sharma(✉) ⬚

Department of Computer Science and Engineering, Graphic Era Deemed to be University,
Dehradun 248002, India
sachin.cse@geu.ac.in

Abstract. In smart cities, an AI-based optimized traffic diversion system uses artificial intelligence algorithms to enhance traffic flow and lessen congestion. This technique uses information from numerous sources, including GPS and traffic sensor data, to create a model of the traffic network. With the aim of minimizing trip time, fuel consumption, and emissions, algorithms like reinforcement learning and graph neural networks are used to decide the optimum routing decisions for vehicles depending on the current traffic conditions. Although this technology has the ability to completely transform the way we manage traffic, it is crucial to think about the moral ramifications and potential negative effects of employing AI to manage a vital infrastructure.

Keywords: Sensor · Reinforcement · graph · neural network

1 Introduction

An AI-based optimised traffic diversion system is a smart city technology that employs artificial intelligence algorithms to improve traffic flow and reduce congestion. Such a system's objective is to provide real-time routing recommendations for moving cars depending on the flow of traffic in order to cut down on travel time, fuel consumption, and enhance air quality. AI is being used more and more in smart cities to enhance different areas of urban life, including transportation. A model of the traffic network can be created using a variety of data sources, including traffic sensors, GPS devices, and information about the road infrastructure, in AI-based optimised traffic diversion systems in smart cities. This model enables the system to identify the most effective routing strategy for each vehicle using methods like reinforcement learning, graph neural networks, multi-agent systems, or optimisation. By directing traffic away from collisions or road closures, an AI-based optimised traffic diversion system in smart cities can also contribute to increased road safety. The system can also lower the danger of secondary accidents and assist keep traffic flowing effectively and safely by continuously monitoring road conditions and changing traffic flow. Additionally, a gadget like this can help improve urban air quality by reducing pollutants. The device can aid in reducing fuel consumption and emissions by cutting down on travel time and the length of time cars are left idle in traffic. An AI-based optimised traffic diversion system can also offer helpful information into traffic patterns and road usage in addition to these advantages. City planners and decision-makers can utilise this in-formation to guide data-driven decisions on how to enhance transportation infrastructure and lessen congestion in the future. However, it's crucial to take into account the possible negative effects of utilising AI to manage a vital infrastructure like traffic. Because there are moral concerns with the employment of AI, such as justice and accountability, it is imperative that the technology be developed and used in a responsible and transparent manner. By easing traffic congestion, enhancing air quality, and enhancing the safety and efficiency of our roadways, this technology has the potential to revolutionise the way we manage traffic in urban areas. But it's crucial to make sure the technology is reliable and morally sound, and to carefully assess any potential repercussions of utilising AI to manage such a vital infrastructure. Traffic is a major is-sue in cities, as it impacts the quality of the air, lengthens travel times, and compromises road safety. Current traffic management systems frequently rely on out-of-date data and are ill-equipped to deal with changing traffic patterns. The goal of this effort is to develop an artificial intelligence (AI)-based optimised traffic diversion system that utilises AI algorithms to enhance traffic flow and lessen congestion in smart cities. This problem statement emphasises the need for a more sophisticated and dynamic traffic management solution in smart cities, one that con-siders current traffic circumstances in real-time and makes use of the most recent developments in artificial intelligence. The technology aims to cut down on travel time, fuel use, and air quality while also enhancing road safety and offering insightful data on traffic trends.

2 Literature Review

A number of authors had recognised that the only the rerouting of vehicle traffic will result in better traffic flow. Yet, recommending better routes for each vehicle based solely on traffic data falls far short of meeting the standards of effective transportation admin-istration. For effective traffic management, context-aware and multi-objective rerouting algorithms will be essential. Yet, the majority of methods cannot meet the stringent stan-dards of traffic management systems since they are deterministic and several cars may choose to use the same route, diminishing traffic efficiency overall. As a result, we pro-mote an effective strategy based on Pareto-efficiency known as Better Safe Than Sorry (BSTS). Our methodology lowers the likelihood of mishaps, and simulation results show that it achieves a better balance between speed and safety than cutting-edge methods [1]. Peter et al. show that vehicle numbers are rising globally, which causes traffic, air pollution, and de-lays in reaching destinations. The roads now have more traffic, espe-cially at the lights. The efficiency, aggression, and financial growth of a country have all been badly impacted by traffic congestion. As a result, traffic congestion control has drawn major academic attention, and in recent decades, several research projects in this area have produced a sizable number of solutions to this problem. Long traffic line-ups are created at the street junctions as a result of the traffic volume shifting over time. The Intelligent Transport System thus provides a solution to these associated problems. It has amazing potential and capacity to create safe, intelligent, and effective transportation systems. In a smart city, ITS offers driving and accessing services for easily taking part in transportation systems. By employing time estimation and another route diversion in a planned manner, traffic congestion may be properly handled. For this purpose, we first identify the nearby route and calculate the numbers for the density of traffic congestion. The closest path was found using the Swarm method, and the traffic density was calculated using the densities and distance measure algorithms [2]. According to earlier reports, they had discussed their study of The Real-Time Route Diversion System (RTRDS) is a tool created for Florida State University's SunGuide Automatic Transportation Management System ATMS. To create the best route alternatives based on the traffic data that is currently available in real-time and in the past, and to disseminate these plans in real-time, a modular, driver-based framework called RTRDS was created. When a route diversion is required, operators have the option of selecting an existing historical route diversion or having the system construct a new one. The user interface enables operators to instantly alter previously developed and current route diversion plans before implementing them with already installed gear (such as dynamic message signs, etc.) [3]. Several studies suggested that the majority of individuals are now able to buy several automobiles for personal commuting because to improvements in economic conditions and rising standards of life. The growing number of cars, particularly large and four-wheeled vehicles, on the roads results in frequent traffic congestion and lengthier commuting times, especially in populated regions. Unfortunately, restricting the usage of automobiles won't be able to solve these issues. In-stead, a strategy for effective traffic management may be useful in this situation. Due to the rising usage of two- and four-wheel vehicles, metropolitan communities today are more likely to have traffic-related is-sues. These kinds of issues are addressed by smart traffic management systems, which are employed in smart cities and are viewed as more of a need than just a required. This study suggests the iSMART smart traffic management system. It uses data analytics, image processing, GPS, and IOT sensors. The iSMART system is not only easy to set up and use, but it also outperforms many other traditional traffic management systems that make comparable claims in terms of effectiveness. It provides a journey planner that utilizes real-time traffic information processing and takes into account various traffic circumstances. The study also covered in detail the various traffic control systems now in use and their typical characteristics [4]. Using specialized signal timing systems on detour routes during highway events is a workable traffic management tactic. Estimating a route variation in event scenarios is necessary for the creation of such designs. The construction of specific signal timing plans for highway events is aided by this work, which employs a data analytic approach to assist in the computation of the diverting rate during events. First, a technique is created that uses information from the highway mainline detector coupled with event data to predict the rate of traffic diversion brought on by occurrences. The diversion prediction approach combines predictive data analytics, cluster analysis, and cumulative volume analysis. Three predictive data analysis methods—multilayer perceptron's, linear regression, and support vector machine models—are examined to anticipate detour as a result of event characteristics. Second, an approach is put out for developing special signal plans that would manage the surge in traffic on the diversion routes without affecting the intersection's functionality as a whole. The study of the developed approach shows that delays on additional routes can be significantly reduced [5]. A substantial body of literature on deep reinforcement learning has grown over time (DRL). It has demonstrated significant potential for ATSC appli-cations at single-intersection. Cooperative learning amongst inter systems is a fiercely discussed research subject in the area of transit system multi-agent systems. For the dynamic densities approach to junctions, this study suggests a mixed reward function mod-el based on distributed control theory. Underscoring the importance of emergency vehicles (EMV) and maximising the traffic efficiency of social vehicles, it solves the issue of sparse reward caused by the vague guidance connection between the inter-Deep Reinforcement Learning (MDRL) state and compensation function of the urban road network scenario. On the opposing hand, this work suggests using the multi-agent A2C (MA2C) technique to model common experience MA2C (SEMA2C) amongst agents. An agent with a set of associated job objectives is used to represent each junction in the transportation network. With the present agent acting as the main body of self-learning, the SMEA2C technique leverages the principle of significance sample to learn from of the experienced data of the agents located at nearby inter-sections. The results of the experiments show that the suggested SEMA2C performs better and offers more benefits than other algorithms for multi-agent traffic signal control jobs [6]. Most early studies as well as current studies focus on artificial intelligence (AI) technology in transportation systems has given rise to a novel idea known as the "Internet of Vehicles" (IoV). Due to the huge need, as well as the rise in the number of different applications for vehicle communication, The IoV has indeed been connected to a IoT era and has become a hot research is-sue. AI also offers special ways to improve IoV system performance and quality of services (QoS). As one application of machine learning in IoV systems, several deep learning network principles will be addressed in this study. in addition to researching how neural networks (NNs) work and the different kinds of NNs they can be, together with deep learning methods that help in processing enormous volumes of raw data Also, this paper examines the categorization and clustering methods applied in attributive analysis and briefly examines how they might enhance the functionality of IoV application systems [7]. Finding the best signal timing approach for the chal-lenge of widespread traffic signal management is tough, according to research by X. Wang et al. (TSC). The solution to this issue is multi-agent learning (MARL), which shows promise. In term of scaling up to complex situations and modelling every agent's behaviour in relation to the actions of other agents, there is still space for development. Collaborative double Q-learning (Co-DQL), a novel MARL with a number of unique properties, is suggested in this study. To solve the overestimation issue that classic inde-pendent Q-learning suffers from while preserving exploration, it uses an applications functionality-independent double Q-learning approach based on the UCB policy and the double estimation methods. It aids agents in creating a more effective cooperative strat-egy by modeling agency interactions with mean-field approximation. We present a new incentive allocation technique as well as a regional and state-sharing strategy to enhance the stability and robustness of the learning process. We also examine the proposed algo-rithm's convergence properties. Co-DQL is evaluated with TSC utilizing various road traffic scenarios. The findings demonstrate that in a number of traffic measures, Co-DQL surpasses even the most complex decentralised MARL algorithms [8].

3 Proposed Methodology

Unmanned aerial vehicles (UAVs), which include drones, are, can be used for traffic prediction by collecting real-time data from various sources. Unmanned aerial vehicles (UAVs), sometimes known as drones, are aircraft that are flown without a human pilot present. Military operations, delivery services, and aerial photography are just a few of the many uses for UAVs. UAVs have also been investigated in recent years for their possible application in traffic control and forecasting. The capacity to collect real-time data from numerous sources, including traffic cameras, road sensors, and GPS data, is the main benefit of employing UAVs for traffic prediction.

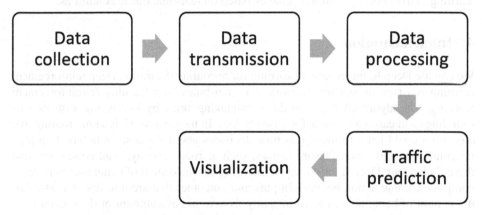

Fig. 1. Data flow for the traffic prediction.

Predictions regarding traffic patterns and congestion can then be made using this data after it has been processed and analysed. UAVs can be fitted with sophisticated sensors and cameras to collect data on the state of the roads, including information on accidents, road closures, and weather conditions. As seen in Fig. 1, this information can subsequently be used to enhance traffic pre-diction algorithms and produce more precise predictions. Collaboration between a number of parties, including governmental organisations, tech firms, and private contractors, is likely necessary for the functioning of UAVs for traffic prediction. Governmental organisations like the Department of Transportation would be in charge of policing UAV use and making sure that it complies with security and privacy standards. Companies in the technology industry might create and manage UAVs as well as the hardware and software required for data collecting, processing, and analysis. To ensure a secure and effective operation, private contractors could be recruited to operate the UAVs, particularly during the data collection phase. Ultimately, the specific roles and responsibilities of each stakeholder would depend on the specific implementation and regulatory environment. From Fig. 1 we can see that how the data will be used

- Data Collection: The UAVs would be equipped with sensors such as cameras, LIDAR, and GPS for real-time data collection about traffic conditions.

- Data Transmission: The collected data would be transmitted in real-time to a central server for processing.
- Data Processing: The data would be processed to extract relevant in-formation about traffic patterns and congestion.
- Traffic Prediction: The processed data would be used to make predictions about traffic patterns and congestion using machine learning algorithms.
- Visualization: The predicted traffic information would be visualized in real-time to help drivers and traffic management authorities make informed decisions.

We will collect data about the traffic condition and then we will use the data to re-route the traffic. We can implement this by the use of artificial intelligence and machine learning to dynamically re-route vehicles based on real-time traffic conditions.

4   Implementation

We can use Deep Reinforcement Learning for re-routing the traffic. Deep reinforcement learning is a type of machine learning that com-bines deep learning & reinforcement learning. The algorithm picks up decision-making skills by interacting with its sur-roundings and earning rewards for wise choices. In the context of dynamic routing, the algorithm could learn to make real-time decisions about the best route based on traf-fic conditions and other relevant factors, such as road capacity, road conditions, and driver behaviour. Deep Reinforcement Learning has the benefit of being able to manage complicated, interaction between in-puts and outcomes that are non-linear. It also has the benefit of being able to learn instantly from a massive amount of data. Because it makes it possible to design extremely sophisticated and adaptive routing systems, deep reinforcement learning is in fact a promising method for dynamic routing. In order to choose the ideal route, the algorithm may learn from a vast quantity of data, including real-time traffic situations, road capacity, road conditions, and driver behaviour. Training an artificial neural network to make decisions depending on the inputs it receives is the key to Deep Reinforcement Learning. The neural network is trained using supervised learning and reinforcement learning. The system learns during training to link particular inputs, like traffic conditions, with particular actions, like rerouting a vehicle.

This will work as:

- Real-time Data Collection: Gather current traffic information from a variety of devices, including GPS, road sensors, and traffic cameras.
- Data Processing: Utilize the information gathered to extrapolate pertinent details regarding traffic conditions, including congestion, road closures, and accidents.
- Predictive Modeling: To predict traffic patterns and congestion, use machine learning techniques.
- Dynamic Routing: Vehicles should be dynamically rerouted in real-time to avoid crowded regions and reduce delays based on the anticipated traffic patterns and congestion.
- Continuous Monitoring: To ensure the most effective route, continuously monitor traffic conditions and adjust the routing in real-time.

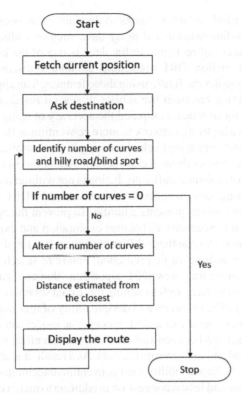

Fig. 2. Flowchart of proposed methodology.

After training, the system can be used in real-world situations to dynamically reroute vehicles in response to shifting traffic conditions. This can serve to lessen traffic congestion, increase traffic safety, and increase the overall effectiveness of the transportation system. Figure 2 shows the proposed methodology's flowchart.

Algorithm

Step 1: Start

Step 2: Fetch the current position of the vehicle

Step 3: Ask the destination

Step 4: Identify number of curves and hilly road/blind spot

Step 5: If number of curves = 0 then go to step 9 else go to step 6

Step 6: Alter for number of curves

Step 7: Distance estimated from the closest

Step 8: Display the route

Step 9: Stop

5   Result Analysis and Discussion

A potential method for predicting real-time traffic, Deep Reinforcement Learning (DRL), has produced impressive results in recent studies. DRL is a branch of machine learning that combines deep learning and reinforcement learning. Agents can learn and make judgements based on tri-al and error thanks to deep neural networks. The capacity of DRL can handle high-dimensional and noisy data, such as traffic sensor data, video footage, and other sources of real-time traffic data, is one of the key benefits of utilising DRL for traffic prediction. DRL algorithms are able to discover useful aspects in unprocessed data and predict the future using those features. The application of DRL for real-time traffic prediction has been the subject of several research, with encouraging results. One research, for instance, compared the accuracy of using a DRL algorithm to forecast traffic flow on a highway network to more convention-al time-series forecasting techniques. Another study optimised vehicle routing in a transportation network using a DRL algorithm, and the results showed considerable reductions in trip time and congestion. The use of DRL for real-time traffic prediction is not without its difficulties, though. Large amounts of training data are necessary to make sure the DRL agent learns reliable and transferable policies, which presents a hurdle. To prevent the agent from becoming stuck in local optima, it is necessary to balance exploration and exploitation during the decision-making process. Despite these difficulties, there is a lot of research being done on the use of DRL for real-time traffic prediction. Future re-search in this field is anticipated to concentrate on creating new DRL algorithms that can manage more intricate and dynamic traffic conditions as well as adding more data sources to improve prediction accuracy and reliability. The accuracy and dependability of real-time traffic predictions are increased as a result of the use of a DRL model. The model can understand the intricate patterns and interactions between various variables that affect traffic flow by using a vast amount of historical and real-time traffic data. As a result, it is able to forecast events with greater accuracy and dependability than conventional techniques. DRL models can help optimise traffic flow and lessen congestion in addition to increasing traffic prediction accuracy. The model, for instance, can pinpoint lo-cations where traffic is most likely to clog up and offer suggestions for alternate routes or modes of transportation. This may shorten travel times and enhance traffic flow generally. Improved safety is a side effect of using DRL for traffic prediction. On the basis of past accident da-ta and current traffic circumstances, the model can assist in identifying regions where accidents are likely to happen. The danger of accidents can be reduced by using this data to alert drivers and offer detours. Keep in mind that a variety of factors, such as the quantity and quality of the data, the DRL method employed, the parameters, and the complexity of the traffic network, all affect how efficient DRL models are at predicting traffic. Unpredictable factors like the weather, accidents, and road closures may also have an impact on the model's accuracy and dependability. One of DRL's main advantages for real-time traffic prediction is its capacity to manage irregular and changing traffic situations. DRL algorithms are capable of responding appropriately to unanticipated events like accidents or road closures based on the available information. Due to the frequent unpredictability and rapid changes in traffic conditions in metropolitan settings, DRL is very helpful for managing traffic. Additionally, ethical and legal considerations including data privacy, bias, and accountability must be carefully considered before deploying DRL models for real-world traffic prediction.

The use of DRL models for traffic prediction should be transparent and explainable, and should not perpetuate existing biases or discriminate against certain groups of people. DRL has the ability to dramatically in-crease traffic management's efficacy and efficiency

Table 1. Comparative analysis of different techniques for optimized traffic diversion system in smart cities.

Reference	Technique	Automatic System	Monitoring	Visibility	Hilly Road/ Blind spot
[9]	Current signal plan selection systems	X	✓	X	X
[10]	Deep Reinforcement Learning	✓	✓	X	X
[11]	AI-based	✓	✓	✓	X
[12]	Energy Efficient Optimized Path Discovery	✓	✓	✓	X
[13]	Improved Visibility On Curve Hilly Road Using Internet-of-Things	X	✓	✓	✓
Proposed Methodology	Deep learning and ANN	✓	✓	✓	✓

overall. It reduces the environmental impact of transportation. With ongoing research and development, DRL could revolutionize the way we approach traffic pre-diction and management and contribute to a more sustainable and equitable transportation system. Table 1 depicts the comparative analysis of different techniques for optimized traffic diversion system in smart cities.

6   Challenges

While there are many potential benefits of an Artificial Intelligence (AI) based Optimized Traffic Diversion System (OTDS) in smart cities, there are also several challenges that need to be addressed. Here are some of the main challenges associated with AI-based OTDS [Fig. 3]:

- Data Quality: The effectiveness of AI-based OTDS depends on the quality and accuracy of the data it uses to make decisions. If the da-ta is incomplete, inconsistent, or inaccurate, the system's ability to optimize traffic flow will be compromised.
- Privacy Concerns: Collecting and analyzing data about individuals' movements can raise privacy concerns. Therefore, it is important to ensure that the data is collected and used in compliance with privacy regulations.
- Cybersecurity: AI-based OTDS may be susceptible to cyberattacks that damage its capacity to optimize traffic flow, result in mishaps, or jeopardize data security.
- Public Acceptance: Public acceptability is necessary for AI-based OTDS to be successful. Therefore, it is crucial to interact with the public to allay any worries they might have over how the system would affect their daily life.

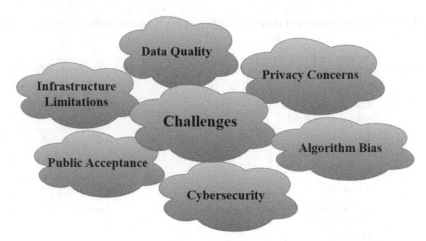

Fig. 3. Challenges.

- Infrastructure Limitations: The effectiveness of AI-based OTDS can also be limited by the availability of infrastructure such as sensors, cameras, and communication networks. Therefore, a significant in-vestment in infrastructure may be required to ensure the system operates optimally [14].
- Algorithm Bias: The algorithms used in AI-based OTDS must be de-signed to be fair and unbiased. Otherwise, certain groups of people may be unfairly disadvantaged.

7 Future Perspectives

The Optimized Traffic Diversion System (OTDS), which is powered by artificial intel-ligence (AI), has the power to completely transform traffic management in smart cities. In order to guide traffic to less congested routes, the system can analyze traffic trends and predict traffic congestion in real-time. Here are a few potential uses for AI-based OTDS in smart cities in the future [Fig. 4]:

- Better Air Quality: The AI-based OTDS can aid in lowering air pollution in smart cities by reducing traffic congestion and enhancing travel times. This can significantly affect the environment and enhance residents' general health and well-being.
- Efficient Use of Resources: The AI-based OTDS can assist smart cities in maxi-mizing the utilization of resources like infrastructure and fuel. The technology can assist reduce fuel consumption and improve the life of infrastructure by easing traffic congestion and reducing travel times.
- Enhanced Safety: The AI-based OTDS can contribute to increased road safety by spotting possible dangers and directing traffic accordingly. By doing so, accidents may be avoided, thus saving lives [15].
- Reduced Traffic Congestion: Smart cities can lessen traffic congestion on their high-ways by utilizing AI-based OTDS. By rerouting traffic to less congested routes, the system can dynamically change traffic flow, thereby easing traffic congestion.

Fig. 4. Future perspective.

- Improved Travel Time: By determining the quickest routes and re-routing traffic accordingly, the AI-based OTDS can assist commuters in getting to their destinations more quickly. As a result, com-mute times can be shortened and citizens' productivity can increase.

8   Conclusion

Real-time traffic prediction involves estimating the present and future levels of traffic on roads and transportation networks using data and algorithms. The goal is to improve the transportation system so that it is safer on the roads, more efficient, and predictable. Machine learning algorithms, like neural networks and reinforcement learning, are used to assess the data needed for real-time traffic prediction. Although real-time traffic prediction has numerous advantages, it also has drawbacks, including protecting drivers' privacy and assuring the quality and dependability of the data. Real-time traffic forecasting is a fascinating field of study and development despite these obstacles, and it has a lot of promise to enhance the transportation system. Smart cities could benefit immensely from improved traffic flow and less congestion thanks to an AI-based optimised traffic diversion system. The system can forecast and respond to traffic patterns in a way that conventional traffic management systems cannot by using real-time data and machine learning techniques. To find the most effective routes for vehicles, the AI system can analyse traffic data from numerous sources, including traffic cameras, GPS devices, and social media. Additionally, it can spot potential congestion hot spots and reroute traffic accordingly. The system can al-so continuously refine its recommendations by learning from its own performance over time. In smart cities, shorter travel times, increased safety, and lower emissions could all be achieved by using an AI-based optimised traffic diversion system. But putting such a system into place would cost a lot in terms of infrastructure, data collection, and machine learning know-how. The system would also need to be properly planned to prevent it from escalating already-existing disparities in access to transit.

References

1. De Souza, A.M., Braun, T., Botega, L.C., Cabral, R., Garcia, I.C., Villas, L.A.: Better safe than sorry: a vehicular traffic re-routing based on traffic conditions and public safety issues. J. Internet Serv. Appl. **10**, 1–18 (2019)
2. Peter, M.N., Rani, M.P.: Traffic management for smart cities using traffic density and swarm algorithm to inform diversion route. Int. J. Eng. Adv. Technol. **3**, 3166–3171 (2020)
3. Aved, A., et al.: A real-time route diversion management system. In: 2007 IEEE Intelligent Transportation Systems Conference, pp. 1131–1136. IEEE (2007)
4. Gade, D.: ICT based smart traffic management system "iSMART" for smart cities. Int. J. Recent Technol. Eng. **8**(3), 1000–1006 (2019)
5. Tariq, M.T., Saha, R., Hadi, M.: Data and modeling support of the management of diversion routes during freeway incidents. Transp. Res. Rec. **2676**(6), 437–452 (2022)
6. Wang, Z., Yang, K., Li, L., Lu, Y., Tao, Y.: Traffic signal priority control based on shared experience multi-agent deep reinforcement learning. IET Intell. Transp. Syst. (2022)
7. Elmoiz Alatabani, L., Sayed Ali, E., Mokhtar, R.A., Saeed, R.A., Alhumyani, H., Kamrul Hasan, M.: Deep and reinforcement learning technologies on internet of vehicle (IoV) applications: current issues and future trends. J. Adv. Transp.(2022)
8. Wang, X., Ke, L., Qiao, Z., Chai, X.: Large-scale traffic signal control using a novel multiagent reinforcement learning. IEEE Trans. Cybernet. **51**(1), 174–187 (2020)
9. Bielli, M., Ambrosino, G., Boero, M., Mastretta, M.: Artificial intelligence techniques for urban traffic control. Transp. Res. Part A: Gen. **25**(5), 319–325 (1991)
10. Huang, X., Yuan, T., Qiao, G., Ren, Y.: Deep reinforcement learning for multimedia traffic control in software defined networking. IEEE Netw. **32**(6), 35–41 (2018)
11. Zhang, H., Jiang, M., Liu, X., Long, K., Leung, V.C.: AI-aided traffic control scheme for M2M communications in the internet of vehicles. In: ICC 2022-IEEE International Conference on Communications, pp. 5053–5057. IEEE (2022)
12. Rawat, R., Rajawat, A.S., Mahor, V., Shaw, R.N., Ghosh, A.: Surveillance robot in cyber intelligence for vulnerability detection. In: Bianchini, M., Simic, M., Ghosh, A., Shaw, R.N. (eds.) Machine Learning for Robotics Applications. SCI, vol. 960, pp. 107–123. Springer, Singapore (2021). https://doi.org/10.1007/978-981-16-0598-7_9
13. Soni, A., Dharmacharya, D., Pal, A., Srivastava, V.K., Shaw, R.N., Ghosh, A.: Design of a machine learning-based self-driving car. In: Bianchini, M., Simic, M., Ghosh, A., Shaw, R.N. (eds.) Machine Learning for Robotics Applications. SCI, vol. 960, pp. 139–151. Springer, Singapore (2021). https://doi.org/10.1007/978-981-16-0598-7_11
14. Biswas, S., Bianchini, M., Shaw, R.N., Ghosh, A.: Prediction of traffic movement for autonomous vehicles. In: Bianchini, M., Simic, M., Ghosh, A., Shaw, R.N. (eds.) Machine Learning for Robotics Applications. SCI, vol. 960, pp. 153–168. Springer, Singapore (2021). https://doi.org/10.1007/978-981-16-0598-7_12
15. Gupta, A., Ghanshala, K., Joshi, R.C.: Machine learning classifier approach with Gaussian process, ensemble boosted trees, SVM, and linear regression for 5g signal coverage mapping. Int. J. Interact. Multim. Artif. Intell. **6**(6), 156 (2021). https://doi.org/10.9781/ijimai.2021.03.004

Understanding Career Trajectories of IT Professionals - A Machine Learning Approach

Yaswanthram Ponnada[✉], B. A. Sabarish, T. Srehari, D. Lathika, and S. Sneha Latha

Amrita School of Computing, Amrita Vishwa Vidyapeetham, Coimbatore 641112, India
yaswanthramponnada@gmail.com

Abstract. Because of high job transitions in the software industry, career trajectory prediction has become increasingly important. It has an impact on the industry's economy in terms of the cost and time involved in replacing qualified human resources. Analyzing an individual's career trajectory patterns clarifies the skills acquired and the various factors that contribute to each job transition. Identifying the right candidate is difficult with so much Human resource available across the globe. Online hiring and networking platforms generate huge volume of relevant and frequently updated profile of professionals. By identifying and analyzing patterns of learning and predicting career transitions can improve industry stability. Hiring and learning platforms based on social networking presented a challenge of more open opportunities for industries and individuals to choose the right opportunity. Huge volume of data from professional networking sites like Glassdoor and Linkedin are used to forecast patterns and the impact of career trends on the shift. This paper tries to identify the relative moving pattern among the IT professional and supporting the individual and industry for better decision making. Proposed methodology is verified over the dataset collected from the linkedin platform and shows 80% accurate prediction of career transition.

Keywords: Recommendation system · Career Trajectory · Machine Learning

1 Introduction

In modern days, Indian economy is aligned towards the IT sector companies. The economy of the IT sector mainly depends on the cost incurred in maintaining the knowledgeable workforce and producing quality competent products in the global market. The major cost incurred in the IT sector is the training cost of employees which is increased by the rate of employee turnover between companies. As an individual in IT sector career trajectory is set to be changing positively in a

R. N. Shaw et al. (Eds.): ICACIS 2023, CCIS 1921, pp. 109–119, 2023.
https://doi.org/10.1007/978-3-031-45124-9_9

shorter period while comparing to other fields which serves as a motivation for this study. Linkedin has approximately 740 million active users worldwide, making it well-known. Linkedin has evolved into a platform for learning and sharing information. It facilitates the exchange of knowledge and values. This makes learning from Influencers more adaptable against the new opportunities in the field. Linkedin contains a variety of content such as blog posts, job postings, articles, and other industry-related information that assists working professionals in upskilling. As a result of career planning, employees may learn new skills and take on new challenges. A career path enables an individual to develop, broaden, and pursue diverse interests in a supportive environment for growth of professionals in turn to the field. This paper organized as Sect. 2 describes about the related works and identifying the research gaps and open problems from the literature, Sect. 3 gives the overview of the problem statement and proposed methodology, Sect. 4 analyses the results followed by the conclusion and future enhancements.

2   Section 2

2.1   Related Work

In this section, few similar career prediction works carried out earlier has been discussed to identify the research gaps. A Fuzzy based clustering algorithm approach, which uses similar career interests to predict the users career. In this model, Khousa used a reciprocated weighted approach to interact with the person outside the clusters and then interests are identified and recommended to the user to improve career growth [1]. The career trajectories of multiple individuals are mentioned as a time series to depict the relevance of each position/experience as more relevant roles could have a higher significance when it comes to determining an individual's career. Further a similarity score could be generated using a feature matrix to identify career similarities [2]. Measurement of similarity based on intervals, each profile in the database is studied in a 5, 10 and 15 years gap depends on nature. When a graduate has a similar profile to an alumnus his career trajectory is predicted considering alumnus profile as reference [3]. Fauser analyzes the relationship between cumulative labor market income and 10-year career sequences that can be classified into several career patterns. Typical career sequences are compared, which include continuous full-time employment, to stepping stone career patterns (promotion in the same domain), using propensity score matching. The overall data used in this research work was obtained from the German SOEP waves 1994 to 2017 [4]. Space-Time Factor Graph Model mainly focuses on presuming career paths in the academic networking site and how the postulated Space-Time Factor Graph Model (STFGM) incorporates temporal and spatial correlation accomplishes the complex and novel task of inferring temporal locations. The dataset used in this work is made up of two well-known academic networks: MAG and AMiner [5]. Massoni suggests the use of the Drifting Markov Model(DMM) for career path analysis for graduates. Instead of transforming the categorical variables into quantitative via factorial analysis An associated non-homogeneous Markov chain is generated for every career trajectory of professionals. DMM which represents a wide class of non-homogeneous Markov models characterized by an initial and a final transition matrix linked together by a linear or a polynomial deterministic function is used for career path analysis [6].

Feature extraction and feature based prediction are also widely used methods to predict the movement pattern in trajectories. Latent states for skill evaluation is a series of stochastic, binary-valued latent states that are used to characterize whether or not a user masters a skill at each point in their career. Each skill or the feature is assigned a weight using which the skill gap could be identified from the dataset. This model is also used to find skill gap and plan career trajectory. Based on this skill gap career trajectories and suggestions recommendations provided to the user [7]. Brockmann works on what career competencies the underrepresented groups of students need to master for future careers as IT professionals and how diversity inclusion can help computer science students plan their future careers. Support Vector Machine (SVM) is selected to perform the classification of the job ads in the training phase and K-means Clustering is used in the testing phase [8]. Arakelyan discusses the relative importance of musical performances in specific venues and their impact on career trajectories and how to jointly characterize influential artists and venues. Link mining is performed using matrix factorization and node similarity to get the desired model after performing SVD on the dataset. Dataset is collectively formed from Songkick which is a concert-discovery platform that aims to link fans to artists' events and Discogs which is a music database that contains cross-referenced discographies of artists and labels [9]. Lops proposed a user graph constructed based on the connections of an individual as well their profile to assert a person's interests and recommend research papers. The model extracts the connections and interests using Linkedin API and vector space retrieval model is used for initial representation of data, further Natural Language Processing based text processing is performed and predictions of interests done using a rank list approach [10]. Researchers created an application that would help high school students to recommend a career option based on their area of interest and based on their score background study. All the data used in this work was collected using online forms. Various regression algorithms are used to forecast and to identify the relationship effect between variables. Later, Adaptive boosting was implemented on the algorithm to improve the accuracy of prediction [11]. Paparrizos proposes a method for predicting an employee's next job transition with the help of all previous job shifts along with data linked with individuals and organizations. To test the model, a larger proportion of job shifts and corresponding meta-data was retrieved from five million employee profiles which are publicly available in the web. Decision table/naive Bayes hybrid classifier (DTNB) achieved highest accuracy when implemented on the collected dataset [12].

The rank and heuristic (RnkHEU) technique was introduced as a hybrid feature selection method. This new method generates an array of candidate features by their scores and then it ranks candidate features. Later, it uses a heuristic method to obtain the results of the study. The findings of the experiments reveal that the four key evaluation factors perform similarly in predicting student's performance. When compared to the forward search method, the heuristic search strategy can greatly enhance prediction accuracy [13]. Researchers focuses on parsing resumes and identify best resumes by scoring them using their features and ranking all the resumes. It aims to investigate the link between employee development, work time and workspace flexibility as relevant characteristics of sustainable Human Resource Management. Further, binary logistic regression models are often used to quantify the impact of both employee and individual mobility on work engagement [14]. Skill2vec is a recruitment technique that uses machine learning methods to enhance the search strategy to find people with the relevant skills. It converts skills into a new vector space with calculation properties and displays all skill relations. To show the performance of our strategy, the research was manually reviewed by specialists from a recruitment firm [15]. An application to predict the resume with best fit for a provided job description, this mainly focuses on parsing resumes and identifying best resumes by scoring them using their features and ranking all the resumes. The resulting score is the criteria for comparison of different career paths a user is taken and order it in the order of how easy it is for the user to reach the next step of their career [16].

3   Section 3

3.1   Problem Statement

Consider career trajectory $TR_c = \{TR_1, TR_2, ... TR_n\}$ where each TR_i represents job position held by the individual to reach current job TR_n. Career trajectory can be represented as a weighted graph , whereas weight of each transition represents the score (knowledge earned to shift between the jobs). This paper tries to learn from the graphs generated by the individuals in the IT companies to predict the probable job shift paradigm of employees, and also suggest a better job opportunity based on the score.

3.2   Proposed Methodology

Dataset Creation. Linkedin is a social networking site for professional where each node is represented by a job title and relationship is represents job shift paradigm by the professionals. Dataset consists 26 attributes (skillsets, job titles etc.,) extracted from the linkedin network. Figure 1 shows the extraction model of data from linkedin. It is extracted in various levels as shown in Fig. 1 and integrated as single dataset. Model consists of three phases: Dataset generation; Trajectory representation; Trajectory prediction.

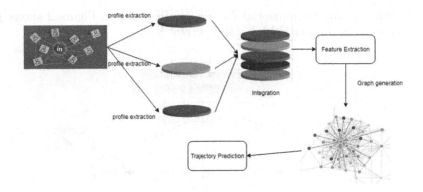

Fig. 1. Trajectory prediction methodology)

Data Preprocessing. Dataset is generated from Linkedin network using beautiful soup and selenium. Profiles are extracted using PhantomBuster in multiples of 100. Because of the limitation of software only 100 profiles can be extracted in a single execution. During the preprocessing steps data deemed redundant and unnecessary for the model are removed and data cleaning is performed. The following roles are used as search queries to retrieve the user profiles from Linkedin. Roles extracted in the sample are given below Table 1.

Graph Representation. In graph representation of Career trajectory TR_c is given by TR_c^9, each node in the graph represents a job title or shift (TR_i). Shifting between careers can be influenced by various factors including knowledge or skillset, experience etc. Some node may remain unvisited in a career trajectory

Table 1. Sample list of job titles

Software-Engineer	SDE	Software Developer
Systems-Analyst	ML engineer	cloud security engineer
sap developer	java developer	Senior Programmer
Data Analyst	IT Support Specialist	Network Architect
Embedded engineer	GET (Graduate Engineer Trainee)	Sales Manager
Cyber Security consultant	systems engineer	data engineer
python developer	Solutions architect	Devops
Tester	site reliability engineer	SWE
UX developer	Web Developer	salesforce developer
IT Analyst	Data scientist	Cloud developer

of an individual, due to influential factors specified above. Figure 2 shows job transition between a entry level job and current job.

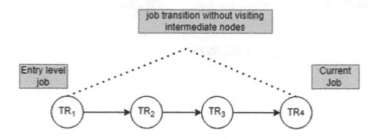

Fig. 2. Job transition between nodes

Markov Chain Representation. In the markov chain representation, each state could represent different jobs and probability that a job shift can be done from a current position to next. By this, we can model the probabilities of job transactions among them at a point of time. The challenge involved is there could be multiple positions from a particular state for each profile or unique trajectory; this option requires one to compute a unique state transition diagram for each profile.

Figure 3 represents the graph where vertices are the different job titles in an individual's career and edges e between (TR_i, TR_j) represent the weight w generated using the feature vector score indicative of the skills, education, experiences needed to make the transition from on job profile to other. Every individual is created career trajectory graph as generated above. In the next level include weight in the graph for each edge which represents the transition score needed for transition from one job profile to another.

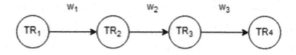

Fig. 3. Graph representing nodes as job titles

Here each unique job title is represented with a vertex TR_i and the edge between two vertices is represented by e_{ij}. An individual's career trajectory consists of a few job titles and an individual's features such as skill-set, education and experience. For multiple professional's individual career trajectories are generated as weighed directed graph. Collection of individual trajectories are generated as T=$\{TR_{c1}, TR_{c2}, ... TR_{cn}\}$ where each TR_c represents individual trajectory. Sample individual career trajectory TR_c is given below in Fig. 4.

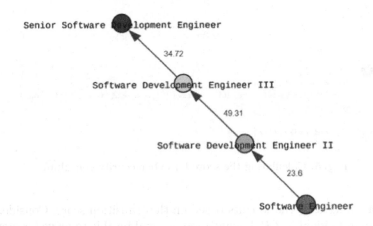

Fig. 4. Sample individual career trajectory

Weight Generation (Score Calculation). Multiple factors that contribute to an individual's career trajectory, the module aims at identifying the key influencing factors. The key features that were extracted from the dataset are the skill set of a person, educational qualification and years of experience. These features are drawn out from columns "Degree", "Skills" and "jobDateRange2" respectively. The features extracted from the profile are used to generate a feature vector score S.

The Skills column is compared to the must have skills dataset [15] to bring about a score that denotes skill level on a scale of five for each job title that a person has specified in his linkedIn profile. The Degree column is processed to group different school degrees that are same but have been addressed differently and given a score on scale of five depending on the total credits of the degree. The jobDateRange2 column describes the work experience of a person and it is processed to analyze and identify their influence on job shifts, time period duration and finally given a score on a scale of five. A combined feature vector is formed using the above vectors which is in turn used as the weights in the career trajectory graph. Calculation of final score(x) is done as below [16]:

$$x = 20^*E_x + 30^*W_x + 50^*S_x$$
$$E_x\text{-Educational Qualification,} \quad W_x\text{-Work Experience,} \quad S_x\text{-Skill set} \tag{1}$$

Figure 5 shows the implementation, where the job title "cybersecurity consultant" is used with an educational experience score of 2.86, work experience score of 2.5 and skill score of 1 then the final transition score is 37.2.

Trajectory Prediction. Considering the global environment of career opportunities across the globe has opened up multiple options available for every individual. As shown in above figure, career trajectory is generated for every

```
[ ]  def cummulative_score(a,b,c):
         return ((a/5)*30) +  ((b/5)*20) + ((c/5)*50)


 ●   weights=[]
     for e in score_exp:
         weights.append(cummulative_score(e,score_edu,final_skill_score))
     weights


 ●   [37.22222222222222]
```

Fig. 5. Calculating the score for cybersecurity consultant

individual along with the weights based on the transition score. Consider a scenario of an individual in TR_i having a score x, will be able to move for more than one job opportunities as shown in figure below. An individual in TR_3, having a transition score of 30 is having options for three job positions in his career trajectory TR_4, TR_5, TR_6. Hence, extracted paths are compared and checked for existence of intermediate vertices from the list of vertices. The paths are explored and the paths with most intermediate vertices are slightly most likely to be further explored. The most optimal successors are identified by tracing the outgoing edges from the most recent job and the weights are extracted and ranked. A list of job transitions are suggested and arranged in the ascending order of scope in Fig. 6.

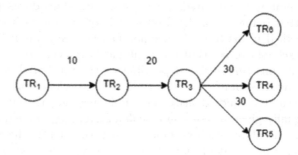

Fig. 6. List of suggested job transitions

4   Section 4

4.1   Results

From the complete career trajectory graph T={$TR_{c1}, TR_{c2}, ... TR_{cn}$}, available job options are selected by comparing the previous nodes and similarity between the other sub-graphs. From the options available for individual is ranked according to the transition score. If more than one options available for same score, the

jobs	weight
Senior Software Engineer	25.72
Python Developer	27.08
SDE II	37.72
Software Development Engineer II	37.72
Software Development Engineer III	39.40
Software Development Engineer	41.40
Software Engineer	43.72
Software Engineer at Instagram	54.28
Senior Software Development Engineer	78.84
SAP Developer	81.68
Senior Programmer	84.52

Fig. 7. Job recommendations according to their respective weights

trajectory will be predicted by comparing the traversed path during previous career of an individual. The given profile is evaluated once a feature vector score is generated which further acts as a metric for comparison against the list of existing ranked list of roles.

Graph prediction helps the individual based on the score, professional can identify the jobs where the immediate transfer is possible. In another case the graph also suggests the paths, skills or score has to attained for the dream job transition from current position. The roles with a transition score lesser than the current profile score will be considered more easily transferable to while the jobs with a higher weightage indicate that one needs to work on their skills or experience.

Figure 7 shows possible job opportunities along with the scores expected for each of the job profiles. It helps the individual to decide the job shift and expected score if individual wants to shift to some other job options. From the diagram its evident that if professional in software engineering can make an easy transition to Senior software engineer (score=25.72) where as to Senior Programmer (Score=84.52), professional needs to improve the score by adding extra skillset and expertise.

4.2   Conclusion

Career trajectory is analyzed using the weighted graph representation. Graph representation is chosen over normal text or csv representation. Analysis is done to identify, predict and recommend possible job opportunities based on the weight value. Weight value plays a vital role in deciding the role, which job opportunity to shift. Recommendation and prediction system is tested over the data set for the prediction of next possible job opportunity and skills needed to be added to the profile for better opportunities. Work can be extended to identifying patterns of job shift paradigms, which can be used by IT sector to predict the human resource requirement and knowledge management within the industry.

References

1. Khousa, E.A., Atif, Y.: Social network analysis to influence career development. J. Ambient. Intell. Human Comput. **9**, 601–616 (2018)
2. Xu, Y., Li, Z., Gupta, A., Bugdayci, A., Bhasin, A.: Modeling professional similarity by mining professional career trajectories. In: Proceedings of the ACM SIGKDD International Conference on Knowledge Discovery and Data Mining (2014). https://doi.org/10.1145/2623330.2623368
3. Li, L., Zheng, J., Peltsverger, S., Zhang, C.: Career Trajectory Analysis of Information Technology Alumni: A LinkedIn Perspective, pp. 2–6 (2016). https://doi.org/10.1145/2978192.2978221
4. Fauser, S.: Career trajectories and cumulative wages: the case of temporary employment. Res. Soc. Stratific. Mobil. **69**, 100529 (2020). https://doi.org/10.1016/j.rssm.2020.100529
5. Wu, K., Tang, J., Zhang, C.: Where Have You Been? Inferring Career Trajectory from Academic Social Network, pp. 3592–3598 (2018). https://doi.org/10.24963/ijcai.2018/499
6. Massoni, S., Olteanu, M., Rousset, P.: Career-path analysis using drifting Markov models (DMM) and self-organizing maps. In: MASHS, 2010, Lille. ffhal-00443530 (2010)
7. Ghosh, A., Woolf, B., Zilberstein, S., Lan, A.: Skill-Based Career Path Modeling and Recommendation, pp. 1156–1165 (2020). https://doi.org/10.1109/BigData50022.2020.9377992
8. Brockmann, P., Schuhbauer, H., Hinze, A.: Diversity as an Advantage: An Analysis of Career Competencies for IT Students, pp. 209–216 (2019). https://doi.org/10.33965/celda2019_201911L026
9. Arakelyan, S., Morstatter, F., Martin, M., Ferrara, E., Galstyan, A.: Mining and Forecasting Career Trajectories of Music Artists (2018). https://doi.org/10.1145/3209542.3209554
10. Lops, P., de Gemmis, M., Semeraro, G., Narducci, F., Musto, C.: Leveraging the linked in social network data for extracting content-based user profiles. In: Proceedings of the 5th ACM Conference on Recommender Systems (RecSys 2011), pp. 293–296 (2011). https://doi.org/10.1145/2043932.2043986
11. Chaudhary, D., Prajapati, H., Rathod, R., Patel, P., Gurjwar, R.: Student future prediction using machine larning. In: International Journal of Scientific Research in Computer Science, Engineering and Information Technology, pp. 1104–1108 (2019). https://doi.org/10.32628/CSEIT1952300
12. Paparrizos, I., Cambazoglu, B., Gionis, A.: Machine Learned Job Recommendation, pp. 325–328 (2011). https://doi.org/10.1145/2043932.2043994

13. Xiao, W., Ji, P., Hu, J.: "RnkHEU: A Hybrid Feature Selection Method for Predicting Students' Performance". Sci. Program. **2021**, 1670593:1–1670593:16 (2021)
14. Davidescu, A., Apostu, S., Paul, A., Casuneanu, I.: Work flexibility, job satisfaction, and job performance among Romanian employees-implications for sustainable human resource management. Sustainability **12**, 6086 (2020). https://doi.org/10.3390/su12156086
15. Le, V.-D., Vo, M.-Q., Dang, Q.-A.: Skill2vec: Machine Learning Approaches for Determining the Relevant Skill from Job Description (2017)
16. Amin, S., Jayakar, N., Kiruthika, M., Gurjar, A.: Best fit resume predictor. Int. J. Eng. Technol. **06**, 2395 (2020)

A Review on Machine Learning Based Security in Edge Computing Environment

Ishani Roy[1], Rahul Modak[1], Enakshmi Ghosh[1], Sk Nooralam Rahaman[1], Santanu Chatterjee[1], Koushik Majumder[1(✉)], Rabindra Nath Shaw[2], and Ankush Ghosh[2]

[1] Department of Computer Science and Engineering, Maulana Abul Kalam Azad University of Technology, Nadia, West Bengal, India
koushikzone@yahoo.com
[2] University Center for Research and Development, Chandigarh University, Punjab, India

Abstract. One of the major breakthrough technologies that can revolutionize different enterprises and institutions aiming to overcome the existing constraints of conventional cloud-based networks is Edge Computing (EC). Large number of sensors can be connected through it and it can also deliver services as per user requirement at the device end. Security is a big challenge despite the fact that EC offers end-to-end connection, accelerates operations, and minimizes data transmission latency. Due to the augmentation in uses of Edge Devices and generation of significant amount of confidential information at the IoT devices (hardware including machines, appliances, gadgets and other sensors) as well as in the cloud in our daily lives, it is important that static and mobile data are protected with utmost priority. The many forms of threats that the intrusion detection systems as well as the Edge network face are covered in detail in this article. The remaining section of the article covers the implementation difficulties for present Edge network security techniques as well as discusses potential future research scopes.

Keywords: Security · Intrusion Detection · Machine Learning · Edge Computing

1 Introduction

We are submerged in a sea of data as a result of way the modern world operates these days, where continuously new technologies are getting invented and various applications are being developed to meet our daily needs. One of the largest developments in technology over the last few decades has been cloud computing, which enables the transmission of computing resources through the Internet. At that time, PCs and other end-user gadgets constituted the majority of the devices that accessed cloud services. Shifting our focus to the present day, the number of digital devices using cloud services has multiplied dramatically. Smartphones, fitness trackers, embedded technology and Internet of Things (IoT) appliances that transfer data to be analysed online may be found in secluded areas and dangerous operational situations almost anywhere in the world and are constantly

R. N. Shaw et al. (Eds.): ICACIS 2023, CCIS 1921, pp. 120–137, 2023.
https://doi.org/10.1007/978-3-031-45124-9_10

growing. The establishment of smart infrastructure that makes a significant contribution to daily data generation is often achieved by further connecting cameras and other sensors to the Internet. The storage of the enormous amounts of data in a cloud platform is frequently outsourced.

The conventional computing approach, which is mainly based on centralized data centers and the World Wide Web, is not ideally fit for transporting floods of real-world data that are constantly expanding. Such attempts may be thwarted by bandwidth restrictions, latency problems, and unforeseen network interruptions often resulting in a slow response time as well as introducing privacy and security concerns.

This is where edge computing enters the picture. Thanks to edge computing, earlier devices that depended heavily on the cloud can now process some of their own data, which often leads to drastically lowering the amount of data delivered to the cloud. A layer that connects a device to the cloud is called the Edge. As EC removes a fraction of the storage and computing capability from the main data center and brings processing capacity closer towards the data origin as feasible, it is able to provide improved data protection than cloud computing. Additionally it facilitates plenty of attractive features e.g. reduces the amount of bandwidth consumption, minimizing the use of network resources, enabling low latency during data transfer and decreasing cloud expenses following which improvement in Quality of Service (QoS) can be obtained. According to recent statistics, large businesses have invested a lot in EC to boost their operational effectiveness, accelerate their workflows, and ensure unmatched availability. Of course, there are corresponding drawbacks to every new technology that must be overcome. Similarly, EC faces little difficulties such as additional hardware and software requirements, accidental misinterpretation and destruction of important data in an irrecoverable way also data breaches due to implementation of poor security strategies. The security restriction which is the subject of this article, is one of the aforementioned difficulties that is of particular significance with regard to its effect on the value of Edge Computing.

2 Edge Computing Architecture

Before further discussing on this matter, it is important to first understand the basic architectural representation as well as workflow of EC.

The EC architecture, illustrated in the above Fig. 1 is composed of three layers. First layer is referred as EDL or Edge device layer, next one is called as ESL or Edge server layer with the last one is called as CSL, abbreviated form of Cloud server layer. These are only a handful of the fundamental components that comprise the edge ecosystem.

Cloud. This public or private cloud serves as a repository for workloads that utilize containers, such as applications and machine learning models. The software required to coordinate and manage the various edge nodes is also stored and run on these clouds. Workloads at the edge, such as local and device workloads, will be able to communicate with workloads on these clouds. The cloud might be a source or destination for any data that the other nodes require.

Edge Device. An edge device is a piece of machinery specifically designed for certain tasks and well equipped with built-in processing power. A factory floor assembly line,

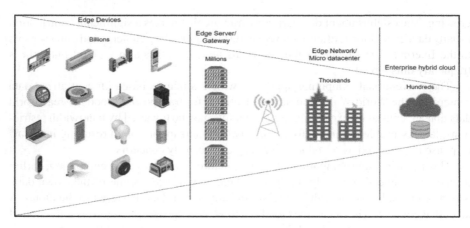

Fig. 1. Architecture of Edge Computing.

an ATM, an intelligent camera or an automobile are examples of edge devices. It is used at EDL to perform various interesting tasks e.g. sensing, actuating, and regulating operations. Typically, an edge device has reduced computing capabilities. Even though the capability of edge devices could increase, they are now the exception rather than the usual standard.

Each sublayer of the ESL can have a wide range of processing capabilities. ESL is made up of Edge servers and Edge gateways.

Edge Server. An edge server is usually a general-purpose IT computer that is often placed in remote operations facility, such as a company, commercial shops, hotel, distribution center or banking institutions. An industrial PC is commonly used to build edge servers. The majority of the time, it is used to operate shared services and business application workloads.

Edge Gateway. An edge server that can serve business application operations and shared services as well as provides network services including protocol translation, termination of networks, tunneling, firewall protection or establishing wireless connection is generally referred as an edge gateway. Edge gateways are conventionally separated from edge devices, even though some edge devices can perform limited gateway operations or handle network functions.

The security of EC is significantly impacted by the heterogeneous features of the underlying software and hardware. It is multi perimetered thanks to the segmented Edge layers, which speeds up a number of attacks. One method to secure the data transmission is to create a boundary that is difficult to breach at each segmented Edge layer. 91% of the data sent from Edge Devices is unencrypted, according to a recent research. Therefore, encrypting and decrypting data while it is in flight as well as in the EDL and CSL levels may help to reduce attacks. Given that EC will inevitably be attacked, one appealing possibility is to protect EC by implementing the appropriate machine learning technologies (Singh et al.) [1].

3 Security Threats in Edge Computing

The primary security concerns (Xiao et al.) [2] and difficulties affecting the EC network have been discussed in this section for better understanding.

3.1 Distributed Denial of Service (DDoS)

In a DoS attack, the antagonist employs techniques to deliberately reduce the system or network resource's availability and connectivity. Flooding of superfluous requests is directed towards the server of the resource which is under attack, limiting access for authorized devices. In a DDoS attack (Zhang et al.) [3], a number of devices serve as attack platforms, greatly enhancing the attacker's ability to launch a successful attack. Due to their diverse firmware, lack of computing resources for security monitoring and higher percentage of nodes lacking mutual authentication, edge servers are more susceptible to DDoS attacks than cloud servers are. Protocol exploit, Flooding, amplification and malformed packet attacks are the several types of DDoS attacks that can be identified till date.

3.2 Eavesdropping

Eavesdropping, often known as sniffing or snooping, is the act of intercepting a sent packet transmitted within a network. Devices that use radio waves for identification (RFID) are vulnerable to this kind of to attack. As the attacker acquires access to sensitive data like node configuration and identifiers, the confidentiality of systems degrades.

3.3 Spoofing

This type of attack (Wang et al.) [4] involves a spoofing node impersonating a genuine Edge network device using a fake identity, such as a RFID tag or medium access control (MAC) address. Once access is gained to the system, DDoS and MITM attacks are feasible in a continuous fashion.

3.4 Malware Injection

The system is subjected to this attack by the injection of malicious code or applications. The attacker misleads the EC into thinking that the newly implemented service is a part of the system as a whole. The attacker's code is then implemented after a legalized user request is forwarded to this utility. Privacy exposure, power drain, and performance degradation are all effects of malware (Narudin et al.) [5] such as Trojans, Rootkits, worms and viruses.

3.5 Jamming

Through the deployment of false signals, cyber attackers shut down connectivity in the Edge network. The attacker tampers with the wireless sensor nodes' radio frequency leading to jamming (Han et al.) [6] or delaying transmission. In the course of unsuccessful communication attempts, this reduces the nodes' bandwidth and memory resources.

3.6 Man-in-the-Middle Attack

A bunch of system devices exchanging keys creates a secure communication channel. An MITM attack involves the invader intercepting the signals and individually exchanging keys with a number of few devices. The hacker takes charge of the channel used for communication by authorized network nodes and uses jamming signals to record, eavesdrop on or otherwise modifying the exchanged information between the network's edge devices. Numerous methods, such as port stealing, dynamic host configuration protocol (DHCP) spoofing, address resolution protocol (ARP) cache positioning, domain name system (DNS) and session hijacking are available to carry out this attack.

3.7 Routing Attacks

Attacks against routing (Sardar et al. and Singh et al.) [7, 8] such as the selective forwarding attack, wormhole attack, Sybil attack and sinkhole attack (Banerjee and Majumder) [9] involve rogue nodes interfering with routing operations which can then be exploited to launch a DDoS attack. In a Sybil attack, the attacking node exploits the network's routing mechanism (Sardar and Majumder) [10] to get access to node's private information or divide the network by claiming numerous false identities. Through the use of the routing metric, a Sinkhole attack aims to direct traffic from a particular area onto the malicious node. This gives the node the appearance of being authentic to the other nodes.

3.8 Phishing

Phishing is the practice of obtaining private or confidential information from a user while posing as a reliable or genuine source. Typosquatting, which involves utilizing repeated or imperceptible spelling errors, and cybersquatting, which utilizes already registered domain names for fraudulent reasons, are two methods that make it simpler to deceive users.

4 Literature Survey

Because different research publications implement different data sets and evaluation settings, the goal of this format is to evaluate the effectiveness of the classification algorithms employed inside a single study rather than between studies. These examples show the variety of techniques that can be used for attack detection but also attack prevention.

Chen et al. proposed a model [11] that actively extracts attack features from massively heterogeneous wireless devices networked together utilizing the deep learning framework. Proposed model is implemented on Mobile Edge Computing devices (abbreviated as MEC) running on Android OS to learn the attack features. The open MEC environment includes jamming threats and eavesdropping. Without manually labelling the data utilized for the learning process, the suggested model's learning process is active for the characteristics of harmful attacks. To implement the active procedure for actively detecting anomalous threats, unsupervised learning is used. A series of unsupervised networks are combined in this deep belief network (e.g., restricted Boltzmann machines, RBMs). The evaluation of the suggested model is done using ten different datasets from the MEC environment. This architecture makes it simple to include additional input features to meet the demands of complex attack circumstances.

Lee et al. [12] suggest the IMPACT model, which is a simple machine learning-based IDS framework (IMPersonation Attack deteCTion using deep auto-encoder and feature abstraction). In order to deploy and operate on devices with limited resources, approach is based on linear Support Vector Machines with gradient-based deep feature learning (SVM). To do this, mutual information (MI), a stacked autoencoder (SAE) and C4.8 wrapper are used to extract and select features from a larger set of features. The Aegean Wi-Fi Intrusion Dataset (AWID) is used to train the IMPACT to recognize impersonation attacks. Using of SAE and MI made deployment and running on devices with inadequate resources possible. It was done by limiting the number of features through feature extraction and feature selection. Further, their success in terms of both efficiency and performance was evaluated.

This study by Wang et al. [13] was done on ACM KDD CUP'99 dataset for mainly botnet detection and intrusion detection. Different ML algorithms were compared to find out which models were able to detect attacks better than the others. Supervised and unsupervised. Here the supervised ML algorithms were Support Vector Machine (SVM), Random Forest, Logistic Regression (LR) and Decision Tree. Unsupervised ML algorithms deployed were K-means, K-Dimensional Tree (KD tree), DBSCAN. These ML models were implemented in various test case scenarios. It is observed that on the network traffic analysis challenge, SVM and K-means scored best when training in partnership with the cloud. In the use case of real-time response, KD Tree and Random Forest both performed better.

The effectiveness of seven machine learning classifiers e.g. Decision Tree, Random Forest, MLP, AdaBoost, KNN, Naive Bayes and lastly Random Forest was investigated in this study by Alrowaily et al. [14], using a number of IDS experiments. The authors employed the CICIDS2017 public intrusion detection dataset, which contains sophisticated and popular attacks. It was required to calculate a number of performance metrics such as recall, precision, accuracy and F1-score as well as training and prediction times, for the purpose of assessing the chosen algorithms. Nevertheless, all of the chosen machine learning classifiers, with the exception of KNN, trained their models in a respectable amount of time.

This study (Verma and Ranga) [15] explores the potential of machine learning classification models for defending the Internet of Things (IoT) from denial-of-service (DoS) attacks. The two classification algorithm types, ensembles and single classifiers that might simplify the creation of anomaly-based intrusion detection systems (IDSs) are thoroughly examined. In order to assess the performance of classifiers accuracy, sensitivity, specificity, FPR, and AUC are the measures that are taken. To compare classifier performance, the UNSWNB15, CIDDS-001 and NSL-KDD datasets are used. The performance evaluation of supervised ML algorithms is the focus of this article in particular. However, evaluation of the performance of unsupervised ML systems for IoT intrusion detection is still yet to be done.

In CyberLearning modelling, (Sarker) [16] a binary classification model is offered for identifying anomalies as well as a multi-class classification model for different categories of cyberattacks. The top ten machine learning classification approaches including naive Bayes, stochastic gradient descent, logistic regression, K-nearest neighbours, support vector machines (SVM), decision trees, random forests, adapted boosts, eXtreme boosts, and linear discriminant analysis are initially employed to build the security model. The security model based on artificial neural networks is then introduced, taking into account several hidden layers. Using the two most widely used security datasets UNSW-NB15 and NSL-KDD, a series of experiments are conducted to evaluate the efficacy of these learning-based security models. When binary classification is taken into account, the RF model produces superior results for detecting cyber abnormalities.

The real-time lightweight (Kumar and Subba) [17] phishing attack detection model using machine learning suggested here is based on an analysis of Uniform Resource Locators (URLs). In the beginning, the proposed method extracts from the corpus of URL strings a number of very unique and unrelated attributes. Following the collection of these traits, transforming the URL strings into the appropriate numeric feature vectors and then later using them to train a variety of machine learning-based classifier models in order to detect harmful phishing URLs are done. Using the UNB dataset and the Kaggle two well-known datasets, the effectiveness of the suggested security framework was assessed. The proposed security framework is then examined with existing security frameworks of a similar kind. The suggested framework has significantly reduced processing overhead and model training time compared to the framework proposed in by Khan et al. [18].

Using three supervised machine-learning algorithms, a novel analysis of integrity attacks against network intrusion detection systems (Apruzzese et al.) [19] throughout the training and testing phase is described. It contains Multi-layer Perceptron, K-Nearest Neighbor and Random Forest. The authors consider probable types of evasion, poisoning, and intrusion attacks against spam, malware, and networks. This study uses publicly available datasets of network traffic monitored in a centralized setting with hundreds of servers some of which are affected with malware to perform a number of performance evaluations based on several parameters, such as Precision, Accuracy, F1-score and Recall. The effectiveness of the attacks prior to and after retraining is compared in adversarial Attacks at Test-time. The attack's diminished severity following retraining supports the effectiveness of adversarial retraining.

Li et al. [20] offer a system for adaptive intrusion detection (IDS) utilizing RF and AdaBoost on two distinct datasets, the NSL-KDD dataset and the KDD99 dataset. By assessing the importance of each variable, RF is used to select the best subset of flow features. Then, using the selected attributes as input, AdaBoost, a hybrid clustering-based ensemble method, would classify traffic into several attack types. The many evaluation metrics that are used are precision (P), accuracy (AC), F-score (F), recall (R) and false positive rate (FPR). The choice of algorithms for feature selection and traffic classification have an interdependent relationship; therefore, the authors placed more emphasis on the performance of their combination.

Intrusion Detection Tree ("IntruDTree") is introduced by Sarker et al. [21]. Before creating a tree-based generalized intrusion detection model constructed according to the selected key features, it first takes into account the grading of security features in accordance with their relevance. The performance of the IntruDTree model was assessed by running tests on the openly available Kaggle incursion dataset and measuring the recall, accuracy, fscore, precision and ROC scores. The results of the IntruDTree model were compared with a number of commonly used machine learning algorithms, such as the logistic regression, naive Bayes classifier, support vector machines and k-nearest neighbour, in order to assess the effectiveness of the resultant security model. Key features are used to help in reducing the computing complexity of the resulting data-driven security model. The described model has a high accuracy and little amount of false alarm rate for attack detection.

In this study, Ho et al. [22] provide a novel intrusion detection technique that creates an RGB image from network data flow that can be identified using cutting-edge deep learning models. In this approach, an overlapping and windowing technique is suggested to transform the fluctuating input size for an image of a standard size. A decision tree algorithm is presented to find out the significant characteristics of the datasets. The final step is to classify the generated image using a Vision Transform (ViT) classifier. In datasets, using the ViT classifier produced results that are commendable in terms of precision and accuracy.

5 Comparative Study

This section contains comparative analysis which is derived from the advantages and disadvantages found in various security studies suggested by the researchers. In this engine [11], this architecture makes it simple to include additional input features to meet the demands of complex attack circumstances, which meets the dynamic attack detection in an EC environment. This is further supported by addition of the unsupervised learning module. It comes handy in case of developing active feature learning function. It's detection accuracy is 12.61%, 5.76%, 3.20%, 2.61% greater than the algorithms based on respectively support vector machines as well as softmax regression, also decision tree as well as random forests which clearly proves its efficacy as a security system. In the downside, in MEC environment managing streaming data and using it to do model's training becomes the most important problem. As the suggested model needs to be trained using streaming data which is time consuming, it is not feasible for the model to be taught online and then to be used in real-time applications. Training data sets in a parallel fashion can be a solution to it. The evaluation [12] results demonstrated that using the MI values of the features could be used to eliminate unnecessary information, reducing the model's complexity without lowering performance while outperforming other models. When compared to DEMISe models, the IMPACT showed superior performance, including significantly lower FAR. In contrast to its rival DEMISe, DETEReD and D-FES algorithms, IMPACT gave its new benchmark results in the AWID dataset without employing any temporal characteristics. However, the effective deployment of a SAE for the extraction of abstract features using other deep neural networks can be further discovered. While flooding and injection attacks are also included in the AWID dataset, this study exclusively focuses on impersonation attacks. Both of these and more recent attack types discovered in wireless IoT networks have not yet been evaluated by IMPACT. In order to demonstrate IMPACT's value and effectiveness, it must be trained and evaluated on additional datasets.

[13] Due to its light weight and quick responsiveness, RF has the ability to provide entirely on-device training at the edge and is easily adaptable to online learning. Network traffic data can be analysed for anomaly detection and intrusion detection using both K-means and DBSCAN as they can perform well on low-dimensional datasets that are appropriate for edge devices. The system must be able to respond or make judgments quickly without sacrificing accuracy. Due to its simplicity, KD trees have a quick computation time and are simple to implement at the edge in real time response scenario. A prominent use case for anomaly detection involves time-series data and with the help of TinyML, it is discovered that DNN is more practical to execute at the edge than LR. However, in a real-time response scenario DT/RF delivers great accuracy but with an extended computation duration. Generally, in EC environment memory space is not adequate. As a result, its high computational complexity, memory requirements makes LR and DNN unable to be trained entirely on-device for time-series data analysis. In addition, SVM performs well when analyzing network traffic data, however it is not sufficiently lightweight to train entirely on a device because to its relatively high computational cost and memory footprint. Despite the training and projecting times [14], the K-Nearest Neighbors (KNN) classifier was shown to be the top performer according to each of the four evaluation metrics. Hence, it can be concluded that KNN is suitable for implementing in EC environment as it can handle large datasets quite well which can be further advantageous for detecting new attack types. The second-best performance was attained by the MLP, which also maintained a stable modest training and prediction time. However, when compared to using of all features following the data cleaning process, the Random Forest classifier-based feature selection did not help the classifiers perform better due to overfitting issues. Here subsampling plays a crucial role which needs to be handled carefully. Based on the evaluation measures, there is no discernible difference between the Naive Bayes and QDA classifiers' performances. Despite their limited training and prediction time, both had the worst overall performances.

With regard to specificity (91.6%) and accuracy (94.94%) [15], it has been found that RF performs better than other classifiers. Sensitivity-wise, GBM performs best (99.53%). XGB performs best in terms of the AUC statistic, getting a score of 98.76%. As a result of the sampling effect, it has been found that all of the classifiers in use perform better with 10f validation than with hold-out validation. From a comparison standpoint, CART excels in terms of accuracy (96.74%). The highest specificity average (97.5%) is attained by AB. Sensitivity-wise, RF and XGB perform best, obtaining 97.31% performance measure. The classifier that performs the best in terms of AUC is XGB, which achieves 98.77%. As a conclusion, XGB works well when training data consists of large number of observations and feature numbers are less than that. The performance evaluation of supervised ML algorithms is the focus of this article in particular. Nevertheless, evaluation of the performance of unsupervised ML systems for IoT intrusion detection is still yet to be done. It is necessary as the intruders are introducing new attack types and without first labelling them, training supervised ML algorithms are not possible. Besides when there are many input features, ensemble-based classification techniques are vulnerable to over-fitting which leads to generation of poor results in case of new data sample [16]. When binary classification is considered, the RF model produces superior results for detecting cyber abnormalities. It is because of the creation of a set of logical rules based on the chosen security attributes that take into account a number of decision trees generated in the forest and deliver a result based on the popularity of those trees. The dataset UNSW-NB15 is utilized in the scenario for detecting Multi-Attacks and the RF model is again shown to be the most successful with an accuracy of 83%. In NSL-KDD dataset, RF, KNN, XGBoost, SVM and DT shows the highest accuracy of 99%. From before mentioned discussions regarding different ML techniques, it can be drawn as conclusion that this security models may result in different results for different datasets depending on the quality and characteristics of the data. Hence, feature selection, refining dataset plays major role here. Deep learning algorithms typically work well with big data sets but EC is generally resource constrained. As a result, sometimes algorithms may not produce satisfactory results. Collecting higher-dimensional, up to date security data in the context of Internet of Things (IoT) and further test algorithms based on this can be beneficial for getting a better perspective in case of run time implementation. RF loses a lot of important information while minimizing the features, resulting into poor outcome. Thus, the quantity of features is important in this context.

Comparing the suggested framework [17] to the one proposed in [18], a considerable reduction in features is used. As a result, the suggested framework has significantly reduced processing overhead and model training time than other ones that are already in use. The Random Forest-based classifier model generates the best results on the Kaggle datasets, UNB multi-class and UNB binary class, with accuracy levels of 95.07%, 97.75%, and 99.72% respectively. However, other than the phishing attack another kind of attacks were not considered in the dataset. UNB binary class dataset provided better accuracy than the other two datasets, again proving that security models that are based on ML are extremely dependent on the quality as well as with the characteristics of the data, which also can produce non identical outcomes for different datasets. So feature extraction, fine tuning datasets play a major role here. [19] The effectiveness of the attacks prior to and after retraining is compared in adversarial Attacks at Test-time. The attack's diminished severity following retraining supports the effectiveness of adversarial retraining. The feature removal technique, which adopts a set without features linked to duration in order to reduce the impacts of evasion attacks, will not entirely prohibit evasion attacks. By simply deleting features that have a negligible influence on the detector's decision-making, the performance reduction can be mitigated. The issue with this method is that it frequently has an impact on the detector's performance in situations where adversarial attacks are not present.

The findings of the evaluation [20] confirm that the proposed system is the best option for obtaining improved accuracy and lower overhead with little investment of time. The choice of algorithms for feature selection and traffic classification have an interdependent relationship; therefore, the authors placed more emphasis on the performance of their combination. The chosen approaches produce remarkable Precision, Recall, F-score, and FPR values of 94.48%, 92.62%, 91.02% and 0.54%, respectively. These values outperform all other combination choices in every parameter. Without prior training, the suggested system lacks the generalization ability to identify different attacks. It proves to be a major setback as this approach cannot automatically detect new types of attack, which is crucial in EC environment. In addition, the fine-grained classification process that takes more time than a single method requires the preliminary clustering technique to classify data into normal and attack classes making it not suitable for implementing in real time scenario. The ensemble algorithm AdaBoost requires the construction of a predetermined number of trees (NTs), which further extends the processing time. By taking into account the crucial features [21], IntruDTree reduces model variance and over-fitting problems while also generalizing the security model. As a result, the model can improve prediction outcomes for hypothetical test cases. Key features also help in reducing the computing complexity of the resulting data-driven security model. Using huge datasets with more security feature dimensions in IoT security services, the IntruDTree model may be further assessed. [22] outperformed all other methods (BP, CNN, SVM, DBN, and DBN-KELM) in terms of accuracy and precision, with the exception of the accuracy in the CIC IDS2017 dataset. On the CICIDS2017 dataset, the proposed technique had an accuracy of 98.5%, and on the UNSW-NB15 dataset, it had an accuracy of 96.3%. Even while the accuracy performance of their suggested strategy in the CIC-IDS2017 dataset is inferior to the SVM model by only 0.4%, it still outperformed all other methods. They also conducted multi-class classification tests using the balanced UNSW-NB15 and CIC IDS2017 datasets. The generated image collection had a very serious imbalance in the CIC IDS2017 dataset. More than a majority of network traffic types (>75%) are composed of benign and DoS attack kinds. Nine classes made up the CIC IDS2017's multi-class classification: Heartbleed, PortScan, Benign, Bot, DoS, DDoS and Infiltration Webattack. 20,000 test samples are used to perform the multi-class classification using the suggested approach and the ViT classifier. On the CIC IDS2017 dataset, the suggested model had 100% accuracy for both the Patator attack and the DDoS attack. Suggested approach, which employs the ViT classifier, also had accuracy that was 5.6% better than the DBN-KELM model [23], which comes in second. The top F1-scores on the UNSW-NB15 dataset were acquired when compared to results obtained across other cutting-edge methods like bi-directional long short term memory and convolutional neural network. When compared to other attack types like DoS and Heartbleed, the CIC IDS 2017 dataset contained far less PortScan attack flows. This tiny amount of data results in very small training and test set sizes for the PortScan attack, which results in mediocre training and testing accuracies. The most common misclassifications has been found involves misclassification of DoS as Benign and vice versa. Because there are very few attack packets at the commencement and termination of a DoS attack, it is easy for them to be misconstrued for benign packet flows. The UNSW-NB-15 uses a nine-class classification system: Unknown, Benign, Shellcode, DoS, Exploits, Fuzzers, Generic, Worms and Reconnaissance. The accuracy of the ViT classifier-based strategy that was suggested in this case was nearly 11% greater than that of the CNN-BiLSTM model, the second-best approach. More than 80% of the UNSW-NB15 dataset's requests are still benign and generic, despite their efforts to balance the dataset before classification. Worms, Shellcode, and Unknown (Analysis and Back-door) attack types are among the tiny percentage of attack types in the sample, which has a significant negative impact on their accuracy (Table 1).

Table 1. Comparative studies in a brief

Refs.	Advantage	Disadvantage
[11]	1. Simple to include additional input features to meet the demands of complex attack circumstances 2. Addition of the unsupervised learning module comes handy in case of developing active feature learning function	1. Managing streaming data and using it to do model training is the most important problem 2. The suggested model needs to be trained using streaming data, which is time consuming. Hence, implementation in real time scenario is not possible
[12]	1. Using of SAE and MI made several things possible. Direct deployment and operation on devices with adequate resources was made possible by the ability to reduce the amount of features through feature extraction and selection. Further assessing their success in terms of both efficiency and performance 2. The evaluation findings showed that employing the feature's MI values could eliminate unnecessary information, reducing the model's complexity without lowering performance while outperforming other models	1. This study exclusively focuses on impersonation assaults. Both of these and more recent attack types discovered in wireless IoT networks have not yet been evaluated by IMPACT 2. In order to demonstrate IMPACT's value and effectiveness, it must be trained and evaluated on additional datasets
[13]	1. Due to its light weight and quick responsiveness, RF has the ability to provide entirely on-device training at the edge and is easily adaptable to online learning 2. Network traffic data can be analyzed for anomaly detection and intrusion detection using both K-means and DBSCAN as they can perform well on low-dimensional datasets that are appropriate for edge devices	1. In a real-time response scenario, DT/RF delivers great accuracy but with a longer computation time 2. Due to its high computational complexity, memory requirements, and near-perfect accuracy, LR and DNN cannot be trained entirely on-device for time-series data analysis

(*continued*)

Table 1. (*continued*)

Refs.	Advantage	Disadvantage
[14]	1. The K-Nearest Neighbors (KNN) classifier was demonstrated to be the top performer based on all four performance metrics, despite the training and projection times 2. The second-best performance was attained by the MLP, which also maintained a stable modest training and prediction time	1. Random Forest classifier-based feature selection had no positive impact on the performance of the classifiers 2. Based on the evaluation measures, there is no discernible difference between the QDA classifier and Naive Bayes's performances as both performed equally worst
[15]	1. In terms of accuracy and specificity, it has been found that RF performs better than other classifiers. Sensitivity-wise, GBM performs best. XGB performs best in terms of the AUC statistic 2. As a result of the sampling effect, it has been found that all of the classifiers in use perform better with 10f validation than with hold-out validation. From a comparison standpoint, CART excels in terms of accuracy. The highest specificity average is attained by AB. Sensitivity-wise, RF and XGB perform best, obtaining 97.31% performance measure	1. The performance evaluation of supervised ML algorithms is the focus of this article in particular. However, evaluation of the performance of unsupervised ML systems for IoT intrusion detection is still yet to be done 2. When there are many input features, ensemble-based classification techniques are vulnerable to over-fitting which leads to generation of poor results in case of new data sample
[16]	1. When binary classification is considered, the RF model produces superior results for detecting cyber abnormalities. It is a result of the developing a set of logical rules based on the chosen security characteristics. It considers several decision trees generated in the forest and deliver an outcome on basis of the majority of those trees 2. The dataset UNSW-NB15 is utilized in the scenario of detecting Multi-Attacks, and the RF model is again shown to be the most successful	1. Machine learning-based security models may yield different results for various datasets depending on the quantity, quality, and characteristics of the data 2. Deep learning algorithms typically work well with big data sets but EC is generally resource constrained 3. RF loses a lot of important information while minimizing the features, resulting into poor outcome

(*continued*)

Table 1. (*continued*)

Refs.	Advantage	Disadvantage
[17]	1. Comparing the suggested framework to the one proposed in [18], a considerable reduction in features is used. Hence, the suggested framework has significantly reduced processing overhead and model training time than other ones that are already in use 2. For the UNB multi-class, Kaggle and UNB binary class datasets the Random Forest-based classifier model outperforms the competition	1. Other than the phishing attack, another type of attacks were not considered in the dataset 2. The UNB binary class dataset demonstrated greater accuracy than the other two datasets, demonstrating once more how ML based security models might produce different outcomes for different datasets depending on the type and quality of the data
[19]	1. This article's extensive collection of unique experiments and creative approach to dealing with adversarial attack-related problems may lead the direction for machine learning-based powerful cyber detection systems 2. The effectiveness of the attacks prior to and after retraining is compared in adversarial Attacks at Test-time. The attack's diminished severity following retraining supports the effectiveness of adversarial retraining	1. The feature removal technique, which adopts a set without features linked to duration in order to reduce the impacts of evasion attacks, will not entirely prohibit evasion attacks 2. By simply deleting features that have a negligible influence on the detector's decision-making, frequently has an impact on the detector's performance in situations where adversarial attacks are not present
[20]	1. The findings of the evaluation confirm that the proposed system is the best option for obtaining improved accuracy and lower overhead with little investment of time 2. The choice of algorithms for feature selection and traffic classification have an interdependent relationship; therefore, the authors placed more emphasis on the performance of their combination. The chosen approaches produce remarkable Precision, Recall, F-score, and FPR values which outperform all other combination choices in every parameter	1. Without prior training, the suggested system lacks the generalization ability to identify different attacks 2. The ensemble algorithm AdaBoost requires the construction of a predetermined number of trees (NTs), which extends the processing time
[21]	1. By take into consideration the crucial features, it reduces model over-fitting and variance problems while also generalizing the security model. As a result, the model can improve prediction outcomes for hypothetical test cases 2. Key features help in reducing the computing complexity of the resulting data-driven security model	1. To have a better understanding, the IntruDTree model needs to be further evaluated utilizing huge datasets and more dimensions of security characteristics in IoT security services

(*continued*)

Table 1. (*continued*)

Refs.	Advantage	Disadvantage
[22]	1. ViT requires less training time and offers a higher precision rate on a large dataset. It is a much required characteristics for edge computing & IoT as they continually generate a large mass of data every passing second. These data need to be processed accurately in a very short span of time 2. The CIC IDS2017 suggested technique scored 100% accuracy for the Patator and DDoS object classes in multi-class categorization	For the PortScan attack in the CIC IDS 2017 dataset, the minimal amount of data leads to extremely short training and test set sizes. It leads to unsatisfactory training and testing accuracy. It has been discovered that misclassifying DoS as benign or vice versa is the most frequent mistake. It is simple for them to be mistaken for benign packet flows since there are so few attack packets during the beginning and end of a DoS attack. Shellcode, Unknown (Analysis and Back-door) and Worm attack types are among the extremely small fraction of attack types in the sample in the UNSW-NB15 dataset, which has a major negative effect on their accuracy.

6 Future Scope

Edge computing security system implementation using machine learning is still in its infancy stage. Researchers are still working on this domain to develop robust security systems, which will be able to detect and resolve all the major security threats. However, most of the methodologies are suffering from some fundamental drawbacks. To ease the whole process, here a study has been presented based on some recent works done by the researchers. It goes into great detail about potential Edge security and privacy threats. The effectiveness of classifiers used in research articles is then examined which should be helpful throughout the design process of an architecture.

1. Machine learning-based security models may generate different results for different datasets because they are highly dependent on the nature and quality of the data. Through the removal of unnecessary or redundant features, feature selection and extraction approaches in the preprocessing phase are used to decrease the number of input variables [19]. The list of features is then reduced to those that are most important [21] to the machine learning model. This objective determines the most beneficial group of attributes that may be applied to create effective models of the phenomenon under study.
2. It can be clearly seen from the previous discussions in majority of the existing methodologies [13, 15, 16, 18, 19] Random Forest has proven to be an effective classifier in this scenario. Mostly because of its numerous impressive features such as simple to implement, quick and simple training and automatic determination of feature importance and interaction. Another notable thing is being lightweight makes it ideal for online training.

3. Another notable ML method is XGBoost [15, 16]. XGB works well when training data consists of large number of observations. In addition, less number of features adds to its advantage. Gathering more recent security data with higher dimensions in the context of the Internet of Things (IoT) and further test algorithms based on this can be beneficial for getting a better perspective in case of run time implementation. All these aspects of XGB are going to be valuable when the various new types of security threats as well as latency in EC is concerned.

Considering the weaknesses in the security comparisons building a robust security system in EC will be future agenda, comprising all the ML techniques mentioned earlier. After that, further evaluating its performance by testing its efficacy in different security attacks is going to be another goal.

7 Conclusion

Early edge computing initiatives aimed to lower the price of bandwidth, which was used to transfer raw data from the point of creation to either a business data center or the cloud. The notion is being advanced more recently thanks to the growth of real-time applications that demand little latency. Due to 5G's ability to speed up computing for these cutting-edge low-latency use cases and applications, edge computing is closely related to the current global implementation of the 5G wireless standard. However, there are still some existing problems that need to be resolved. The network is subjected to fresh attacks every day, the majority of which cannot be captured for behavior analysis. Therefore, it is necessary to train the Edge Devices to dynamically recognize security flaws. The memory in edge devices is minimal. Data parallelism tasks are generally not supported by edge devices and their delayed execution could compromise network security.

This research marks the beginning towards using ML techniques on edge devices to address various edge security challenges. It is strongly believed that this research paves a promising road and can serve as a reference manual for academics and enterprise in the development of related applications. This article can prove to be beneficial in future, as it will help researchers in taking all the technical and practical aspects of overcoming these security challenges into account while designing a security model.

References

1. Singh, S., Sulthana, R., Shewale, T., Chamola, V., Benslimane, A., Sikdar, B.: Machine-learning-assisted security and privacy provisioning for edge computing: a survey. IEEE Internet Things J. **9**, 236–260 (2022)
2. Xiao, Y., Jia, Y., Liu, C., Cheng, X., Yu, J., Lv, W.: Edge computing security: state of the art and challenges. Proc. IEEE **107**, 1608–1631 (2019)
3. Zhang, H., Hao, J., Li, X.: A method for deploying distributed denial of service attack defense strategies on edge servers using reinforcement learning. IEEE Access **8**, 78482–78491 (2020)
4. Wang, N., Jiao, L., Wang, P., Li, W., Zeng, K.: Machine learning-based spoofing attack detection in mmWave 60 GHz IEEE 802.11 ad networks. In: IEEE INFOCOM 2020-IEEE Conference on Computer Communications, pp. 2579–2588 (2020)

5. Narudin, F.A., Feizollah, A., Anuar, N.B., Gani, A.: Evaluation of machine learning classifiers for mobile malware detection. Soft. Comput. **20**, 343–357 (2016)
6. Han, G., Xiao, L., Poor, H.V.: Two-dimensional anti-jamming communication based on deep reinforcement learning. In: 2017 IEEE International Conference on Acoustics, Speech and Signal Processing (ICASSP), pp. 2087–2091 (2017)
7. Sardar, A.R., Sahoo, R.R., Singh, M., Sarkar, S., Singh, J.K., Majumder, K.: Intelligent intrusion detection system in wireless sensor network. In: Satapathy, S.C., Biswal, B.N., Udgata, S.K., Mandal, J.K. (eds.) Proceedings of the 3rd International Conference on Frontiers of Intelligent Computing: Theory and Applications (FICTA) 2014. AISC, vol. 328, pp. 707–712. Springer, Cham (2015). https://doi.org/10.1007/978-3-319-12012-6_78
8. Singh, M., Sardar, A.R., Sahoo, R.R., Majumder, K., Ray, S., Sarkar, S.K.: Lightweight trust model for clustered WSN. In: Satapathy, S.C., Biswal, B.N., Udgata, S.K., Mandal, J.K. (eds.) Proceedings of the 3rd International Conference on Frontiers of Intelligent Computing: Theory and Applications (FICTA) 2014. AISC, vol. 328, pp. 765–773. Springer, Cham (2015). https://doi.org/10.1007/978-3-319-12012-6_85
9. Banerjee, S., Majumder, K.: A comparative study on wormhole attack prevention schemes in mobile ad-hoc network. In: Thampi, S.M., Zomaya, A.Y., Strufe, T., Alcaraz Calero, J.M., Thomas, T. (eds.) SNDS 2012. CCIS, vol. 335, pp. 372–384. Springer, Heidelberg (2012). https://doi.org/10.1007/978-3-642-34135-9_37
10. Sardar, M., Majumder, K.: A new trust based secure routing scheme in MANET. In: Proceedings of the International Conference on Frontiers of Intelligent Computing: Theory and Applications (FICTA) 2013, pp. 321–328. Springer, Cham (2014). https://doi.org/10.1007/978-3-319-02931-3_36
11. Chen, Y., Zhang, Y., Maharjan, S., Alam, M., Wu, T.: Deep learning for secure mobile edge computing in cyber-physical transportation systems. IEEE Netw. **33**(4), 36–41 (2019)
12. Lee, S.J., et al.: IMPACT: Impersonation attack detection via edge computing using deep autoencoder and feature abstraction. IEEE Access **8**, 65520–65529 (2020)
13. Kumar, A., Das, S., Tyagi, V., Shaw, R.N., Ghosh, A.: Analysis of classifier algorithms to detect anti-money laundering. In: Bansal, J.C., Paprzycki, M., Bianchini, M., Das, S. (eds.) Computationally Intelligent Systems and their Applications. SCI, vol. 950, pp. 143–152. Springer, Singapore (2021). https://doi.org/10.1007/978-981-16-0407-2_11
14. Malsa, N., Vyas, V., Gautam, J., Shaw, R.N., Ghosh, A.: Framework and smart contract for blockchain enabled certificate verification system using robotics. In: Bianchini, M., Simic, M., Ghosh, A., Shaw, R.N. (eds.) Machine Learning for Robotics Applications. SCI, vol. 960, pp. 125–138. Springer, Singapore (2021). https://doi.org/10.1007/978-981-16-0598-7_10
15. Verma, A., Ranga, V.: Machine learning based intrusion detection systems for IoT applications. Wireless Pers. Commun. **111**(4), 2287–2310 (2020)
16. Sarker, I.H.: Cyberlearning: effectiveness analysis of machine learning security modeling to detect cyber-anomalies and multi-attacks. Internet of Things **14**, 100393 (2021)
17. Kumar, Y., Subba, B.: A lightweight machine learning based security framework for detecting phishing attacks. In: 2021 International Conference on COMmunication Systems & NETworkS (COMSNETS), pp. 184–188 (2021)
18. Khan, H.M.J., Niyaz, Q., Devabhaktuni, V.K., Guo, S., Shaikh, U.: Identifying generic features for malicious URL detection system. In: 2019 IEEE 10th Annual Ubiquitous Computing, Electronics & Mobile Communication Conference (UEMCON), pp. 0347–0352 (2019)
19. Apruzzese, G., Colajanni, M., Ferretti, L., Marchetti, M.: Addressing adversarial attacks against security systems based on machine learning. In: 2019 11th International Conference on Cyber Conflict (CyCon), vol. 900, pp. 1–18 (2019)
20. Li, J., Zhao, Z., Li, R.: Machine learning-based IDS for software-defined 5G network. IET Networks **7**(2), 53–60 (2018)

21. Sarker, I.H., Abushark, Y.B., Alsolami, F., Khan, A.I.: Intrudtree: a machine learning based cyber security intrusion detection model. Symmetry **12**(5), 754 (2020)
22. Ho, C.M.K., Yow, K.C., Zhu, Z., Aravamuthan, S.: Network intrusion detection via flow-to-image conversion and vision transformer classification. IEEE Access **10**, 97780–97793 (2022)
23. Wang, Z., Zeng, Y., Liu, Y., Li, D.: Deep belief network integrating improved kernel-based extreme learning machine for network intrusion detection. IEEE Access **9**, 16062–16091 (2021)

Ransomware Taxonomy and Detection Techniques Based on Machine Learning: A Review

Akram Al-banaa$^{(\boxtimes)}$ (iD), Subrata Sahana(iD), Jabir Ali(iD), and Sanjoy Das(iD)

Department of Computer Science and Engineering, Sharda University, Greater Noida, Uttar Pradesh 201306, India
akramalbanaa2016@gmail.com

Abstract. Malicious software continues to be one of the most dangerous dangers in the digital world, despite the significant progress that has been made in computer security systems and the continued expansion of those systems. Ransomware detection is of the utmost relevance in view of the sophisticated technological position that the world has acquired in the present day. Because there are so many unique varieties of emerging malware, researchers in this field often depend on techniques that are based on machine learning rather than strategies that are based on signatures. On the other hand, adopting signature-based tactics will not be successful since there is a continuous influx of new malicious software. The primary purpose of this chapter is to identify the several techniques of machine learning that have been shown to be the most successful in analyzing and identifying ransomware in recent years. In addition, the study that was conducted here is frequently useful as a basis for future research on the analysis and detection of ransomware using machine learning methods.

Keywords: Ransomware Analysis · Ransomware Detection · Machine Learning

1 Introduction

Despite considerable advancements in cyber security systems and their ongoing growth, malicious software remains one of the most potent threats in the cyber world [1]. Malware is the abbreviation for malicious software, which is a malicious piece of code that is dangerous [2]. Malware is continually emerging and presents a significant danger to computer systems and networks. Disruptions, including distributed data breaches and denial-of-service attacks, are becoming more widespread and difficult to predict [3]. In recent years, millions of new types of malware, such as computer viruses and other potentially harmful software, have been developed and released into the wild. Approximately a million threats are produced every day, according to this estimate [4]. Ransomware is one of the most dangerous malwares, which takes control of a device and prevents the victim from accessing the data until some sort of ransom is paid [5]. They have two options for doing so: locker ransomware and crypto-ransomware. Users are compelled to pay a ransom in both situations in order to recover access to that data or device [6].

© The Author(s), under exclusive license to Springer Nature Switzerland AG 2023
R. N. Shaw et al. (Eds.): ICACIS 2023, CCIS 1921, pp. 138–160, 2023.
https://doi.org/10.1007/978-3-031-45124-9_11

Antivirus programs play an essential role in defense. They maintain hashes and signatures of known ransomware samples; it is a fast and user-friendly way of detecting it. Hackers do everything they can to trick antiviruses by rewriting code, using polymorphic code, or developing new variants. To combat the proliferation of new malware, new techniques for identifying it and preventing the dangers posed by it are being developed. However, owing to the continually evolving nature of ransomware features, the technique of recognizing ransomware has become much more difficult as ransomware families have proliferated at an alarming rate [7]. One of the key objectives of malware analysis is to gather new characteristics that may be utilized to bolster security requirements and make escape as tough as possible. Machine learning in simple work is an obvious candidate for assisting in such a knowledge extraction process [1]. It is just difficult to manually analyze and comprehend this huge sea of malware. Luckily for the malware analyst, relatively few of these malwares are actually innovative. Writing software is a difficult problem, regardless of whether the software is benign or malevolent. As a result, malware authors frequently reuse code and coding patterns while building new malware. As a result, there are intrinsic patterns and similarities among connected malware, which malware researchers can exploit. To leverage this intrinsic resemblance and shared patterns across viruses, the anti-malware business has resorted to machine learning, a field of study focused on "training" computers to detect concepts. Machine learning is one of the most intriguing technologies that one has ever encountered. This "learning" takes place through the discovery of suggestive patterns in a group of items representing the subject getting discussed or through the exploration of parallels among things. While people utilize patterns in learning as well, such as using sound, color, form, and smell to distinguish objects, computers can reveal patterns in massive amounts of data that could be meaningless to humans, such as detecting patterns in a collection of malware's bit sequences. As a result, machine learning is an ideal fit for malware analysis since it can train and find patterns quicker than humans in the ever-growing corpus of malware. In this chapter we are going to compare the recent studies that used machine learning to detect ransomware in recent years. The five main sections of this chapter are as follows: In the second section, we will explain ransomware behavior and the steps of the ransomware lifecycle. The third section will describe the techniques used to analyze and detect ransomware. Section four contains the recent studies in ransomware detection using machine learning as well as a comparison table to compare these studies. In Sect. 5, this chapter is concluded.

2   Ransomware Behavior

Ransomware is a type of malware whose specific goal is to force victims to pay a ransom in order to regain full access to their computers. Sometimes, these ransom payments are in bitcoin; other times, they are through prepaid cards. Ransomware is a type of malware that is different from the usual virus or worm because it generally does not spread to other computers through e-mail. Instead, it can enter your computer via a vulnerability in your operating system or by exploiting security flaws on websites you visit.

There are two ways to reach their goals: locker ransomware and crypto-ransomware. The first kind locks the victim's computer to prevent them from using it. The second one is more forceful and difficult to break down. The victims are unable to access their personal data since it is encrypted. Data encryption is computationally difficult to break if the ransomware is written well. As seen in Fig. 1, the lifecycle of ransomware consists mostly of seven parts, creation, campaign, infection, command and control, search, encryption, and extortion [8, 9].

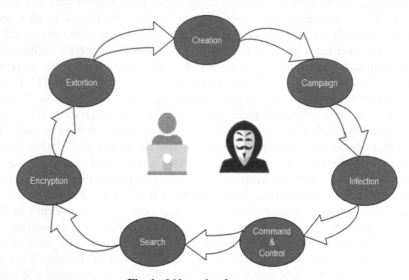

Fig. 1. Life cycle of ransomware

2.1 Creation

The main goal of the creator is to create ransomware using programming techniques. The development step also includes boosting codes to improve the ransomware's strength at the conclusion of each cycle. The professional will conduct research on the current security system, such as Windows, Mac, and Linux. In order to create proper ransomware, it is important for the creator to have a clear understanding of how data is transferred and stored so that they can exploit this flaw. The best step is to understand how the file transfer process works because this will help them create ransomware that will not be discovered until it has already infected the target system.

2.2 Campaign

The success of the campaign will be determined by how successfully the human psychology of dread and insatiability is exploited on a more widespread scale through an effective "viral marketing" strategy. Some types of ransomware are also able to circumvent security firewalls by taking advantage of vulnerabilities in widely used apps and platforms, such as Adobe Flash Player. This allows them to encrypt data without being detected. The first two categories of objectives are simpler to accomplish, and as a result, they have a greater percentage of accomplishment; nevertheless, the third category of goals is far more difficult to accomplish.

2.3 Infection

In this step, the ransomware is introduced to the victim's system and starts the installation process. In the infection step, the ransomware has the potential to propagate to other interconnected systems or devices by exploiting network shares or other security loopholes. The rapid propagation of ransomware can result in the infection of numerous systems, thereby increasing the scope of the attack and rendering containment efforts more challenging.

2.4 Command and Control

After the installation process is complete, the ransomware communicates with the command-and-control center in order to collect the encryption key for the encryption process [8]. In the C&C step, the ransomware has the capability to transmit data to the attackers, which may include the infection's status, the encrypted file formats, or other confidential information that can be leveraged for ransom collection or additional offensive maneuvers.

2.5 Search

The malware will scan through the network and gather any and all sensitive data that can be used to blackmail the organization or individual. The search step is significant importance in the lifecycle of ransomware since it allows the identification of high-value targets for encryption or damage by the malware. After the identification of its targets, the ransomware proceeds to the subsequent stage of its lifecycle.

2.6 Encryption

The contemporary ransomware known as WannaCry and others like it use hybrid encryption techniques, which combine symmetric and asymmetric encryption methods [10]. The files are encrypted using symmetric encryption (such as AES), which is fast and does not need a connection to the internet; nonetheless, the executable of the ransomware includes the public key of a remote command and control server that is lurking on the dark web.

2.7 Extortion

After the backup copies are removed and the encryption is finished, the user is given instructions on how to restore their data and pressured into paying. In most cases, a corporation will be granted a few days to complete the payment before the sum increases.

3 Ransomware Analysis and Detection

3.1 Ransomware Analysis

The goal of ransomware analysis is to obtain a better understanding of how ransomware works. Depending on this knowledge, defense measures to avoid any possible infections can be developed. Malware analysis is divided into static, dynamic, memory, and hybrid analyses [11].

Static Analysis. Static analysis examines the portable executable file without running it [7, 12]. A byte or source code could be the object of static analysis [13]. A PE file needs to be decompressed first using disassembler and memory dumper tools [14]. After the executable has been extracted and decrypted, the detection characteristics utilized in static analysis, including such Windows API calls, byte n-grams, strings, opcodes, and control flow graphs, may be retrieved.

PE Header. The Microsoft Windows operating systems have established the PE file format for executables, dynamically linked libraries (DLL), and object files.

Opcode. The opcode is a fundamental unit of machine language instructions that communicates to the hardware the specific operation to be executed by the instruction. The design of each processor regulator is characterized by its unique arrangement of opcodes. An operation code (opcode) is typically followed by additional information such as location and values, as needed [15].

N-Gram. It is a way of estimating that has been built on a sample of text. An N-gram analysis is such a language model, which is concerned with determining the probability distribution across word sequences [16]. Several studies have been conducted during the last ten years to spot unusual ransomware based on binary code content.

Strings. The presence of malicious code can be reliably indicated by the presence of strings. The presence of significant semantic information within strings enables the deduction of an attacker's objectives and motives [12]. The sentence "This application cannot be launched in DOS mode" is suggestive of a malevolent file when detected beyond the typical PE header, a feature frequently observed in droppers and installers (Fig. 2).

Dynamic Analysis. The term "dynamic analysis" refers to an umbrella term that encompasses a number of distinct approaches, the most common of which are function call analysis, function parameter analysis, instruction tracing, and information flow tracking. In dynamic analysis, dangerous software is run in a safe environment so that the live activity of harmful files may be seen without the risk of the software causing damage to the system. The application programming interface (API) and system calls are extensively used in malware dynamic analysis, in addition to the file system, the Windows registry, and network characteristics [17, 18].

API Calls. One of the dynamic approaches is to examine API calls, which are code commands that instruct systems to conduct certain actions. Instead of attempting to reverse engineer a protectively packed file, we apply an analysis based on API calls to determine what a certain file may be supposed to achieve. We can tell if a file is dangerous by its API calls, some of which are common for specific forms of malware. A significant number of attackers rely on the features offered by the Microsoft Cryptographic API in order to finish the execution of their malware. These capabilities include random number generators and AES encryption [19]. The characteristic of API calls is an important static measure that is used to detect harmful behaviors [20–22].

Function Call. The function call is a pre-existing method that can be utilized to compose distinct methods for various objects. The method is invoked by passing the object that

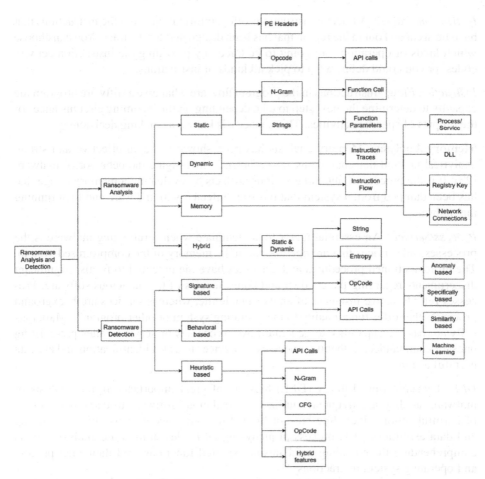

Fig. 2. Ransomware analysis and detection

has been newly acquircd as the parameter. The aforementioned statement pertains to the possessor of the function, denoting the entity to which the function belongs. The phrase "object methods" encompasses all functions present in programming languages. The utilization of the 'call ()' method enables the binding of a function to a particular object within the program.

Function Perimeters. A parameter is a value that you provide to a function so that it may use that value to accomplish something else. Functions can accept parameters, which are simply variables that you give to the function. Whenever we execute the method, the values of these parameters are specified; the parameters of these values are not given values while the function is being executed. These parameters are identical to variables in every other respect. In the definition of the function, the parameters are stated between the pair of parentheses, with commas separating each parameter. When we make a call to the function, we provide the variables in the exact same manner as before.

Instruction Traces. A trace of instructions offers information about the instructions that have been carried out in the region that has been designated for the trace. You can choose which kinds of operations are going to be traced by providing the instruction activity codes, or you could define a (*) to pick all kinds of instructions.

Instruction Flow. Instructions in the program flow are what give a software program the capacity to determine the next step to take depending on the incoming circumstances or the outputs of specific activities. This capacity is known as making decisions.

Memory Analysis. Memory analysis has been shown to be an effective and strong analytical method that may be used to efficiently investigate the behavior of malware [23]. It is the process of obtaining various artifacts by evaluating a memory image that has been dumped from a system that has been infected with malware and then running the malware.

Process/Service. An essential factor to contemplate when scrutinizing malware is the processes and services that are operational in the memory of the compromised system. The aforementioned procedures and amenities have the potential to furnish significant discernments regarding the conduct and competencies of the malicious software. Processes refer to active instances of an executable file, whereas services are background processes that offer functionality to the operating system or other programs. Malicious software has the capability to generate novel processes or services, alter pre-existing ones, or commandeer authentic processes or services to avoid identification and execute harmful actions.

DLL. Dynamic Link Library (DLL) files are of great importance in the analysis of malware, as they are frequently utilized by malicious software to carry out a range of harmful actions, including but not limited to code injection, evasion, persistence, and data exfiltration. The process of analyzing DLL files in malware analysis entails comprehending their loading mechanism, exported functions, and their inter-process and operating system interactions.

Registry Key. Registry keys are a crucial component in the analysis of malware due to their frequent utilization by malicious software for the purposes of persistence, evasion, and other nefarious actions. The process of scrutinizing registry keys in malware memory analysis entails the careful examination of the stored values and data within the registry as well as comprehending their application by the malware.

Network Connection. The analysis of malware necessitates the consideration of network connections, which are frequently utilized by malware to engage in malevolent activities such as communication with command and control (C&C) servers and data exfiltration. The process of scrutinizing network connections in malware analysis entails the identification of the network traffic produced by the malware and comprehending its mode of communication with other systems and servers.

Hybrid Analysis. Hybrid is a technique for trying to analyze files that combines the analysis of runtime data with the assessment of memory dumps in order to identify each of the prospective implementation paths, even for the sneakiest ransomware. This allows hybrid analysis to uncover all of the potential execution paths [24, 25]. Each and every piece of information that is received by the hybrid analysis engines is promptly examined and incorporated into the findings that are created by the malware analysis.

3.2 Ransomware Detection

The technique of detecting ransomware is the machinery that has to be put into place in order to uncover and identify the harmful actions that are taking place inside the files that are being investigated. Therefore, malicious software has been identified on the basis of two primary features, which are signatures and behaviors, employing three different techniques for malware detection: signature-based, behavioral-based, and heuristic-based, respectively.

Signature Based. It is the most straightforward and efficient method of identifying known forms of malware. The process of checking input files for previously determined viral signatures, which is known as signature detection, is how viruses are found and removed. A malware signature is a series of bytes that are exclusive to the infection and do not appear in regular files. After doing an investigation of the infection, a malware specialist would often extract a signature like this [26]. The extraction of manual signatures may sometimes be a laborious and time-consuming task [27]. However, in order to hasten the process of signature extraction, certain automated signature extraction systems have been created and tested effectively in recent years. Due to the ease with which it may be implemented and the fact that it has the capacity to produce a low number of false alarms, or instances in which it incorrectly identifies regular files as malicious software, signature detection is a popular approach on the PC platform. However, signature detection does have a drawback in that it is unable to identify newly discovered viruses since those viruses' signatures have not yet been compiled.

Behavioral Based. The utilization of behavioral-based ransomware detection is a security measure employed by software to detect and avert ransomware attacks through the examination of the behavior of software and applications that are operational on a computer or network.

Anomaly-Based. The primary objective is to investigate the behavior of both known and new ransomware. A variety of criteria, including the source or destination address of ransomware, the sorts of attachments, and other countable statistical characteristics, are included in the behavioral variable [28]. This method has the benefit of being able to identify existing cases of malware in addition to brand new ones that are unknown, and it concentrates on the behavior of the computer in order to discover unknown attacks.

Specifically Based. Is an offshoot of anomaly-based identification that makes an effort to address the often-increased prevalence of false positives that is associated with the former method. Specification based detection is dependent upon feasible solution, which are documents which outline exact functionality that is anticipated for safety software. This includes monitoring software execution and then identifying deviations in its conduct first from its description instead of determining the existence of particular known attacks. This is done instead of recognizing the presence of cyberattack trends. The above method seems to be very comparable to anomaly detection; however, rather than relying on machine learning approaches, it is predicated on individually evolved requirements that encapsulate the valid behavior of the system. The main difference between the two methods is that anomaly detection relies on machine learning techniques. This method has the benefit of being able to detect known as well as unidentified occurrences of ransomware. Additionally, this same threshold of false-positive would be lesser, whereas the threshold of false-negative is significant. Additionally, this method isn't as efficient as behavior pattern identification in automatically detecting threats, particularly network needling and denial of service attacks.

Similarity-Based. The similarity measure is the foundation of similarity-based approaches. A function known as a similarity measure is one that assigns an integer value to a set of episodes, with the understanding that a larger value implies a greater degree of similarity between the two sequences. By way of conversion, it is sometimes stated as a value between 0 and 1: 0 denotes a low similarity, while 1 denotes a great similarity.

Machine Learning. To give computers "the possibility of learning without being explicitly programmed," a set of methods known collectively as "machine learning" is applied to them." An algorithm for machine learning will find and then codify the underlying principles that are revealed by the data that it examines. Using this data, the algorithm has the ability to "learn" about the qualities of data that it's never encountered before and provide accurate results [29]. In the process of detecting ransomware, a sample that was not analyzed previously may stand in for a newly created file. It is not out of the question that the hidden characteristic is harmful software [30, 31]. The following methods are used in machine learning: supervised learning, unsupervised learning, and semi-supervised learning [32].

Supervised learning used in situations in which the data as well as the appropriate responses for each item are accessible. The purpose of this exercise is to adjust the model so that it can correctly predict the properties of new objects. The following are the two steps that make up supervised learning: Training a model and fitting a model to the data that is currently available for training Utilizing the trained model to analyze newly collected data in order to provide predictions. The algorithms employed in the peer-reviewed studies are as following in Table 1.

Unsupervised learning: The only thing that is provided in this kind of test is a data set, rather than the actual solutions to the job. The purpose of this endeavor is to determine the patterns in the data or the rule that governs the formation of data [33]. Clustering is a good illustration of this concept. The process of clustering involves dividing a data set into several groups that each contain items that are quite similar to one another [33, 34]. An additional challenge is representation learning, which entails constructing an effective feature set for objects by using their low-level descriptions. Because cybersecurity vendors have access to huge datasets that were not previously classified, and because the expense of manually classifying these datasets by specialists is significant, unsupervised machine learning may be an effective method for threat identification. The mechanical classification of samples is an activity that may be optimized via clustering [35].

Semi-supervised learning is a machine learning approach that involves training a model using both labeled and unlabeled data. This technique is particularly useful when labeled data is scarce or expensive to obtain, as it allows the model to learn from a larger pool of data. By leveraging the relationships between labeled and unlabeled data, semi-supervised learning can improve the accuracy and efficiency of machine learning models. The integration of labeled and unlabeled data in machine learning is a technique aimed at improving the accuracy of predictive models.

Reinforcement learning is an independent learning paradigm that does not depend on either supervised or unsupervised learning. Furthermore, the algorithms employed in this context are instructed to autonomously react to their environment. The entity is experiencing rapid expansion and generating multiple algorithms for learning. The algorithms under consideration find practical use in various fields such as robotics, games, and other related domains.

Heuristic Based. In order to determine how a program is behaving while it is being executed, these approaches rely heavily on machine learning and data mining techniques. The Hidden Markov Model approaches have been the most prominent ones used up to this point [36].

Table 1. Compression between ML algorithms used in recent studies

Ref	DT	RF	SVM	LR	J48	AdaBoost	KNN	NB	MLP	NN
[37]		✓		✓						
[38]		✓	✓	✓	✓	✓				
[39]		✓				✓				
[40]						✓		✓		
[41]		✓								
[42]										
[43]		✓	✓	✓			✓	✓		
[9]	✓	✓	✓	✓		✓	✓			
[44]	✓							✓		
[45]	✓	✓				✓				
[46]		✓	✓	✓						
[47]		✓	✓	✓	✓	✓				
[48]		✓	✓							
[49]	✓	✓		✓			✓			
[50]	✓	✓				✓		✓	✓	
[51]	✓	✓	✓				✓			
[7]		✓	✓				✓	✓	✓	
[52]		✓	✓	✓						
[53]	✓	✓		✓				✓		✓
[54]	✓									

DT: Decision tree, RF: Random forest, LR: Logistic regression, K-NN: K-nearest neighbor, NB: Naïve bayes, MLP: Multilayer perceptron, NN: Neural networks.

4 Literature Survey

Hwang et al. [37] suggested a model with two stages, a Markov model, and a random forest algorithm. To begin, they have amassed a total of 3048 samples, of which 1909 are ransomware and 1139 are normal. The Cuckoo Sandbox was used in order to get API sequences. The Markov chain model was used to identify ransomware in the first stage since it has a low false positive rate (FPR). In the subsequent stage, the random forest approach was used to analyze the remaining data. This model achieves an overall accuracy score of 97.28%, with an FPR of 4.83% and a FNR of 1.47%.

In [38] Poudyal et al. proposed a model that is first used hybrid strategy in order to do reverse engineering on both ransomware and benign samples. The second step is to extract the binary features and characteristics of the code by doing an analysis of it on three different levels. NLP is used to produce a feature database, which is then sent to the machine learning classification for further processing. Discovering remarkable linkages and patterns at several levels may be accomplished with the help of the FP-growth algorithm's association rules component. It is possible to think of the pattern database as a feature database for the machine learning classifier since it contains all of the found patterns. The supervised machine learning classifiers have been used by the machine learning classifier component in order to train, test, and verify the model and arrive at a conclusion about whether or not a binary under evaluation is malicious software or a benign program.

Khammas [39] proposed an approach based on the random forest technique. The dataset that has been used contains 840 ransomware infections and 840 benign infections. The first stage is preprocessing, which includes feature extraction to extract the features from raw bytes, frequent pattern mining, and normalization. The second stage is feature selection, which has been done using gain ratio. The last stage in this proposed work is the classification process using the random forest algorithm. This work achieved an accuracy of 97%, a FPR of 0.04, and a FNR of 0.002.

In [40] Khan et al. proposed DNAact-Ran, an engine for the digital sequencing of DNA, used for the detection of ransomware using machine learning. Multi-Objective Grey Wolf Optimization and Binary Cuckoo Search are used in the first step of the DNAact-Ran process, which is the selection of essential features from the pre-processed data. After that, the digital DNA sequence for the specified features is constructed by applying the design constraints of the DNA sequence and the k-mer frequency vector. The experiment result showed 87.9% accuracy in detecting ransomware attacks.

In [41] a pre-encryption detection algorithm has been proposed to detect crypto ransomware before the encryption process occurs by Azween et al. The PDEA algorithm operates on two levels of detection. At the first level, it looks for any matches with the known ransomware signature. At the second level, it uses the learning algorithm (random forest) to detect unknown ransomware, which uses a machine learning approach to train the model. RF trains the prediction model using API data and machine learning. RF is analyzed using traditional and atypical criteria to determine PEDA functioning. Based on the data, RF detected crypto ransomware before encryption and performed well with a significant net benefit.

Faris et al. [42] proposed a technique for the detection of Android ransomware that is based on metaheuristics and machine learning. First extracted the raw sequences of the application's API calls and permissions. After that, a hybrid of the Salp Swarm Algorithm (SSA) and the Kernel Extreme Learning Machine (KELM) is modeled. The SSA is used to search for the best subset of features, and the KELM hyperparameters are optimized using the results of the SSA's search. In the meantime, the KELM algorithm is being applied for the purpose of identifying and classifying the applications as either benign or ransomware. The work that has been presented demonstrates an accuracy of 98% and a ratio of 2% for the rate of false positives.

A model that is used to distinguish between ransomware and benign, as well as ransomware and other malware, has been proposed by Bae et al. [43]. Windows Native API has been extracted as a feature for the classification process that has been done using Random Forest, Logistic Regression, Naïve Bayes, Stochastic Gradient Descent, K-NN, and SVM.

Dynamic Pre-encryption Boundary definition has been implemented by Al-Rimy et al. [9] to detect crypto-ransomware before the encryption process. The aTF-IDF approach that was suggested was used in the process of extracting the features from inside the pre-encryption. Seven machine learning algorithms have been used in the classification process.

Zuhair et al. [44] presented a hybrid machine learning technique that categorizes different ransomware variants into groups by studying static and dynamic features. The proposed approach follows four layers of characteristic extraction and has a 97% accuracy rate. FaizanUllah et al. [45] proposed a machine learning model that uses decision tree, random forest and AdaBoost for classification of ransomware at runtime. API calls have been used as a feature, and after that, the dataset has been divided into training and testing. This model has an accuracy of 95%.

Jethva et al. [46] All introduced ransomware classification models, which add an extra set of features to the field of current features, hence strengthening the approach. Using machine learning methods such as SVM, logistic regression, and random forest, they conduct an analysis of the newly developed feature model. The suggested technique enables distinguishing between encryption that is caused by the client and encryption that is induced by ransomware.

Poudyal et al. [47] suggested a technique for multi-level profiling of ransomware that captures the specific characteristics of the ransomware at the dynamic link library, function call, and assembly levels. The sophisticated static and dynamic methods of evaluating behavioral chains using AI are included in the hybrid multi-level analysis approach. In addition, association rule mining, natural language processing methods, and machine learning classifiers are included in the process of constructing a validation and detection model for ransomware. Experimented with several samples of crypto-ransomware.

Usharani et al. [48] proposed the model for detecting ransomware attacks through network traffic. URLs, IP addresses, web pages, and file extensions were used as features for classification that was done using the random forest algorithm. Ahmed et al. [49] suggested a machine learning approach that uses 6 supervised algorithms to detect ransomware on mobile phones by analyzing the network traffic.

A model for detection of ransomware that was proposed by Azeez et al. [50] works in two stages. The first stage is done using CNN, and the second stage is done using machine learning classification algorithms. Bastian [51] suggested an approach for improving antivirus signatures for ransomware detection using machine learning classification after extracting features as DLL files and API calls from the portable executable.

Almomani et al. [7] proposed a SMOTE-tBPSO-SVM model when it used SVM to classify with the SMOTH, and the BPSO was included in order to maximize the SVM's cost coefficient efficiency. In comparison to more conventional machine learning algorithms, the performance of the SMOTE-tBPSO-SVM technique that was suggested was better, with an accuracy of 97.5%.

Zahoora et al. [52] suggested CSPE-R to identify new ransomware threats. It changes the dynamic feature space at the base into a more stable and core semantic feature space using the CAE. Next, it searches semantic spaces at different levels to discover robust features. This work gets 93% accuracy with a 0.01 false-positive rate.

Masum et al. [53] provide a methodology based on feature selection that employs many machine learning techniques, including neural network-based designs. The findings reveal that RF classifiers are more accurate than other approaches, with 99% accuracy. In [54] Talabani et al. used Rule-Based algorithms to classify Bitcoin ransomware attacks using Bitcoin transaction data. The Bitcoin dataset included 61,004 addresses and 10 descriptive and decision characteristics. Partial decision tree (PART) classification outperformed Decision Table classification has 96.01% accuracy (Table 2).

Table 2. Comparison the methodologies and result between the resent studies

Paper	ML Approach	Description	Accuracy	Limitations
Hwang et al. [37] 2020	Markov model, scikit-learn, Keras, LR, RF, NLP	This model detected ransomware using Markov chain model as first stage and random forest algorithm in the second stage	97.3%	The proposed model is not very diverse and adaptable as the results show a high false negative rate and this is disastrous for the systems, so it is preferable to keep the FNR as lower as possible

(*continued*)

Table 2. (*continued*)

Paper	ML Approach	Description	Accuracy	Limitations
Poudyal et al. [38] **2020**	NLP, LR, SVM, RF, J48, Adaboost	In this model ransomware has been detected using static and dynamic analysis with machine learning with the help of AI	99.17% 99.54% 98.99% 99.26% 98.71%	The proposed system shown good results when using a very small data set, as the system takes a long time to detect ransomware and this is impractical when implementing this system in real time
Khammas [39] **2020**	WEKA GUI, Ada Boost M1, Bagging, Rotation Forest, RF	Here static analysis used to extract the features from raw byte next using random forest algorithm for classification purposes	97.74%	This system achieved high results when the number of features is less than 100, but the higher the number of features, the lower the accuracy rate
Khan et al. [40] **2020**	Naïve Bayes, Decision Stump, AdaBoost	In this work Digital DNA sequencing used with machine learning for ransomware detection	87.9%	In this research, the accuracy was not at the required level, as they were relatively low
Azween et al. [41] **2020**	Pre-encryption detection algorithm, RF	This model is focused on detection ransomware before the encryption process done	99%	NA
Faris et al. [42] **2020**	Salp Swarm, Kernel Extreme Learning Machine,	Within the context of the diversification technique that has been suggested, the Salp Swarm Method is put to use in order to concurrently optimize the hyper - parameters of the KELM and choose the features to be used	98.4%	NA

(*continued*)

Table 2. (*continued*)

Paper	ML Approach	Description	Accuracy	Limitations
Bae et al. [43] **2020**	RF, LR, Naïve Bayes, Stochastic Gradient Descent, K-NN, SVM	This model uses Windows Native API for detection ransomware	98.65%	The data set that was used was quite limited, and because of this, applying it in real time would not be powerful
Al-Rimy et al. [9] **2020**	RF, DT, SVM, AdaBoost, LR, MLP, K-NN	The DPBD approach that has been presented was successful in defining the limit of the pre-encryption process of crypto-ransomware assaults with such a good degree of accuracy	94%	This model was focusing only on crypto-ransomware
Zuhair et al. [44] **2020**	DT, Naïve Bayes	It has been shown by experimentation and justification through analysis that this ransomware streaming analytics methodology is superior to other anti-ransomware solutions	97%	Only the currently recognized ransomware families may be categorized using this suggested methodology
FaizanUllah et al. [45] **2020**	DT, RF, AdaBoost	The detection was carried out by the model while it was being executed, and it involved scanning API calls, registry activities, the network, and the file system	99.56%	NA
Jethva et al. [46] **2020**	SVM LR, RF	The suggested technique enables distinguish between encryption that is caused by the client and encryption that is induced by ransomware	95%	NA

(*continued*)

Table 2. (*continued*)

Paper	ML Approach	Description	Accuracy	Limitations
Poudyal et al. [47] **2021**	LR, SVM, RF, J48, AdaBoost, Neural network, (NLP)	The model detecting ransomware attacks through network traffic	99.63% 99.72% 98.99% 99.54% 99.17%	Due to the dynamic nature of malware, some samples did not go well with dynamic analysis For behavioral chaining with first phase manual chaining few crypto-ransomware families (six families) were only considered
Usharani et al. [48] **2021**	SVM, RF, GBTA		98.45%	This work they take only crypto-ransomware without taking locky ransomware
Ahmed et al. [49] **2021**	RF, k-NN, MLP, DT, LR, eXtreme Gradient Boosting	Detection ransomware on mobile phones by analyzing network traffic and using 6 ML algorithms	97.02% 98.16% 91.64% 99.30% 99.20%	The features used in this research are not precise enough to distinguish between ransomware and benign software
Azeez et al. [50] **2021**	RF, Naïve Bayes, AdaBoost, DT, Gradient boosting, MLP, CNN Model	This approach used CNN model in the first stage after that used ML algorithms	99.24% 32.53% 98.06% 98.29% 98.06%	Experts are required to identify and classify both benign and harmful ransomware in order to fulfill the requirements of the conceptual methodology. In the environment of the actual world, it is possible that certain harmful software may not be detected

(continued)

Table 2. (*continued*)

Paper	ML Approach	Description	Accuracy	Limitations
Bastian [51] 2021	SVM, DT, RF, K-NN	approach for improving antivirus signature for detection ransomware using machine learning classification after extraction a feature as DLL files and API calls	94%	This technique is capable of identifying malicious content that have the same kinds of MD5 and hexadecimal dumps, however it is unable to identify malicious programs that have different types of MD5 and hexadecimal dumps
Almomani et al. [7] 2021	SVM, Naïve Bayes, K-NN, MLP, RF	The findings demonstrated the benefits of the suggested method's capacity to identify ransomware in an effective manner	97.5%	This model's justification lies on its ability to converge smoothly across several model training
Zahoora et al. [52] 2022	RF, SVM, LR	This work changes the dynamic feature space at the base into a more stable and core semantic feature space	93%	In This work the accuracy is low
Masum et al. [53] 2022	DT, RF, Naïve Bayes, LR, Neural Network	This study utilized the variance inflation factor technique to eliminate features with low variance and high correlation from the dataset	99%	NA
Talabani et al. [54] 2022	DT	This work proposed to classify Bitcoin ransomware attacks using Bitcoin transaction data	96.01%	Only two models have been used in this work

In the following Table 3, we will give the different kinds of datasets that were used in each study, along with the total quantity of ransomware and benign software, as well as the source of these files. There are a few websites, such as virustotal, virusshare, and the Zoo, that provide malicious datasets to researchers. The popular types are Portable Executable PE for Windows operating systems and Android Package Kit APK for Android operating systems. PE is a type of format that is used in Windows (both x86 and x64) APK is the file format that programs on the Android OS utilize to store their data. The Android Platform is an integrated development environment (IDE) for producing Android applications, and it is used to assemble APK files.

Following that, a listing of the various sorts of features that have been retrieved in each paper, together with the total number of features, will be shown.

Table 3. The datasets, sources, and the features used in each study.

Ref	Dataset	Ransomware	Benign	Source	NO. of Features	Type of features
[37]	PE files	2,507	3,886	VirusShare http://en.sof tonic.com/	303	API call
[38]	PE files	550	554	VirusTotal Windows 10 OS Open-Source Apps	NA	DLL, Function call
[39]	PE files	840	840	VirusTotal Windows 10 OS	NA	Byte level
[40]	Real-time dataset	582	942	https://github. com/PSJoshi	26	NA
[41]	PE files	904	942	TheZoo VirusTotal	NA	API Calls
[42]	APK files	500	500	Google Play HelDroid project, RansomProper project VirusTotal		API Calls, Android Permission
[43]	PE files	1900	300	VirusTotal Windows 7 OS		Native API
[9]	PE files	39,378	16,057	VirusShare, https://www.inf ormer.com/	21	API Calls
[44]	PE files	35,000	500	VirusTotal VirusShare	NA	NA

(continued)

Table 3. (*continued*)

Ref	Dataset	Ransomware	Benign	Source	NO. of Features	Type of features
[45]	PE files	35,369	43,191	VirusTotal	14	API Calls
[46]	PE files	666		VirusTotal	400	API Calls, Registry key, Command line, Directories, Strings
[47]	PE files	550	540	VirusTotal Windows 7/10 OS Open-Source Apps	NA	DLL, Function Call
[48]	Network Traffic	40,000	25,000	http://www.mal ware-traffic/, analysis.net		URL IP Addresses, Web pages
[49]	APK files	353,288	250,000	Canadian Institute for Cybersecurity, Google Play store	85	Network flow, Network traffic
[50]	PE files	19,611		Virus share	55	File header
[51]	PE files	483	180	NA	NA	DLL, API Calls
[7]	APK files	500	9,653	RansomProper Project Koodous, VirusTotal, Google Play	32	API Calls, Permissions
[52]	PE files	582	942	[49]	NA	Opcode
[53]	PE files	138,047		GitHub	12	File Header
[54]	Bitcoin transactions	61,004		NA	NA	NA

5 Conclusion

As a result of the proliferation of the Internet and the fast development of related technologies, an ever-increasing number of apps are being downloaded and installed on various terminals, including mobile phones and personal computers. On the other hand, this development was followed by a rise in the number of ransomware attacks on the system. As a result of this, a significant number of studies are being put into the process of identifying apps that have been corrupted by ransomware. The likelihood of successfully detecting ransomware has significantly increased with the emergence of techniques based on AI, such as machine learning. This chapter gives a complete assessment of existing methodologies for detecting ransomware, with an emphasis on the use of machine learning. The review was accomplished by conducting literature research and collecting relevant secondary sources. The primary goal of this investigation is to provide a comprehensive analysis and detection of ransomware using machine learning.

References

1. Ucci, D., Aniello, L., Baldoni, R.: Survey of machine learning techniques for malware analysis. Comput. Secur. **81**, 123–147 (2019). https://doi.org/10.1016/j.cose.2018.11.001
2. Raghuraman, C., Suresh, S., Shivshankar, S., Chapaneri, R.: Static and dynamic malware analysis using machine learning. Adv. Intell. Syst. Comput. (2020). https://doi.org/10.1007/978-981-15-0029-9_62
3. Kilgallon, S., De La Rosa, L., Cavazos, J.: Improving the effectiveness and efficiency of dynamic malware analysis with machine learning. In: Proceedings - 2017 Resilience Week, RWS 2017 (2017). https://doi.org/10.1109/RWEEK.2017.8088644
4. Babaagba, K.O., Adesanya, S.O.: A study on the effect of feature selection on malware analysis using machine learning. ACM Int. Conf. Proc. Ser. (2019). https://doi.org/10.1145/3318396.3318448
5. Aurangzeb, S., Bin Rais, R.N., Aleem, M., Islam, M.A., Iqbal, M.A.: On the classification of Microsoft-Windows ransomware using hardware profile. PeerJ Comput. Sci. **7**, e361 (2021). https://doi.org/10.7717/peerj-cs.361
6. Sgandurra, D., Muñoz-González, L., Mohsen, R., Lupu, E.C.: Automated dynamic analysis of ransomware: benefits, limitations and use for detection. arXiv preprint http://arxiv.org/abs/1609.03020 (2016)
7. Almomani, I., et al.: Android ransomware detection based on a hybrid evolutionary approach in the context of highly imbalanced data. IEEE Access **9**, 57674–57691 (2021). https://doi.org/10.1109/ACCESS.2021.3071450
8. Kok, S.H., Abdullah, A., Jhanjhi, N.Z., Supramaniam, M.: Ransomware, Threat and Detection Techniques: A Review (2019)
9. Al-Rimy, B.A.S., et al.: A pseudo feedback-based annotated TF-IDF technique for dynamic crypto-ransomware pre-encryption boundary delineation and features extraction. IEEE Access **8**, 140586–140598 (2020). https://doi.org/10.1109/ACCESS.2020.3012674
10. Mos, M.A., Chowdhury, M.M.: The growing influence of ransomware. IEEE Int. Conf. Electro Inf. Technol. (2020). https://doi.org/10.1109/EIT48999.2020.9208254
11. Sihwail, R., Omar, K., Ariffin, K.A.Z.: A survey on malware analysis techniques: static, dynamic, hybrid and memory analysis. Int. J. Adv. Sci. Eng. Inf. Technol. **8**(4–2), 1662 (2018). https://doi.org/10.18517/ijaseit.8.4-2.6827
12. Ye, Y., Li, T., Adjeroh, D., Iyengar, S.S.: A survey on malware detection using data mining techniques. ACM Comput. Surv. **50**(3), 1–40 (2017). https://doi.org/10.1145/3073559
13. Christodorescu, M., Jha, S.: Static analysis of executables to detect malicious patterns. In: Proceedings of the 12th USENIX Security Symposium (2003)
14. Saini, A., Gandotra, E., Bansal, D., Sofat, S.: Classification of PE files using static analysis. ACM Int. Conf. Proc. Ser. (2014). https://doi.org/10.1145/2659651.2659679

15. Santos, I., Brezo, F., Ugarte-Pedrero, X., Bringas, P.G.: Opcode sequences as representation of executables for data-mining-based unknown malware detection. Inf. Sci. (N. Y.) **231**, 64–82 (2013). https://doi.org/10.1016/j.ins.2011.08.020

16. Abou-Assaleh, T., Cercone, N., Kešelj, V., Sweidan, R.: N-gram-based detection of new malicious code. Proc. Int. Comput. Softw. Appl. Conf. (2004). https://doi.org/10.1109/cmpsac.2004.1342667

17. Darabian, H., Dehghantanha, A., Hashemi, S., Homayoun, S., Choo, K.K.R.: An opcode-based technique for polymorphic Internet of Things malware detection. In: Concurrency and Computation: Practice and Experience. John Wiley and Sons Ltd. (2020). https://doi.org/10.1002/cpe.5173

18. Kamal, A., et al.: A user-friendly model for ransomware analysis using sandboxing. Comput. Mater. Cont. **67**(3), 3833–3846 (2021). https://doi.org/10.32604/cmc.2021.015941

19. Moussaileb, R., Cuppens, N., Lanet, J.L., Le Bouder, H.: A survey on windows-based ransomware taxonomy and detection mechanisms: case closed? ACM Comput. Surv. **54**(6), 1–36 (2021). https://doi.org/10.1145/3453153

20. Ma, Z., Ge, H., Liu, Y., Zhao, M., Ma, J.: A combination method for android malware detection based on control flow graphs and machine learning algorithms. IEEE Access **7**, 21235–21245 (2019). https://doi.org/10.1109/ACCESS.2019.2896003

21. Almomani, I., Alenezi, M.: Android application security scanning process. In: Telecommunication Systems - Principles and Applications of Wireless-Optical Technologies (2019). https://doi.org/10.5772/intechopen.86661

22. Almomani, I., Khayer, A.: Android applications scanning: the guide. In: 2019 International Conference on Computer and Information Sciences (ICCIS 2019) (2019). https://doi.org/10.1109/ICCISci.2019.8716380

23. Rathnayaka, C., Jamdagni, A.: An efficient approach for advanced malware analysis using memory forensic technique. In: 2017 IEEE Trustcom/BigDataSE/ICESS, pp. 1145–1150. IEEE (2017). https://doi.org/10.1109/Trustcom/BigDataSE/ICESS.2017.365

24. Damodaran, A., Di Troia, F., Visaggio, C.A., Austin, T.H., Stamp, M.: A comparison of static, dynamic, and hybrid analysis for malware detection. J. Comput. Virol. Hacking Techniq. **13**(1), 1–12 (2017). https://doi.org/10.1007/s11416-015-0261-z

25. Choudhary, M., Kishore, B.: HAAMD: hybrid analysis for android malware detection. In: 2018 International Conference on Computer Communication and Informatics (ICCCI 2018) (2018). https://doi.org/10.1109/ICCCI.2018.8441295

26. Chaumette, S., Ly, O., Tabary, R.: Automated extraction of polymorphic virus signatures using abstract interpretation. In: Proceedings - 2011 5th International Conference on Network and System Security (NSS 2011) (2011). https://doi.org/10.1109/ICNSS.2011.6059958

27. Kephart, J.O., Arnold, W.C.: Automatic extraction of computer virus signatures. Virus Bulletin Ltd (1994)

28. Arabo, A., Dijoux, R., Poulain, T., Chevalier, G.: Detecting ransomware using process behavior analysis. Proc. Comput. Sci. (2020). https://doi.org/10.1016/j.procs.2020.02.249

29. Kaspersky Research. Machine Learning Methods for Malware Detection (2020)

30. Singh, J., Singh, J.: A survey on machine learning-based malware detection in executable files. J. Syst. Architect. **112**, 101861 (2021). https://doi.org/10.1016/j.sysarc.2020.101861

31. Dion, Y.L., Brohi, S.N.: An experimental study to evaluate the performance of machine learning algorithms in ransomware detection. J. Eng. Sci. Technol. **15**(2) (2020)

32. Khammas, B.M.: Comparative analysis of various machine learning algorithms for ransomware detection. Telkomnika (Telecommun. Comput. Electron. Control) **20**(1), 43 (2022). https://doi.org/10.12928/TELKOMNIKA.v20i1.18812

33. Rizvi, S.K.J., Aslam, W., Shahzad, M., Saleem, S., Fraz, M.M.: PROUD-MAL: static analysis-based progressive framework for deep unsupervised malware classification of windows

portable executable. Complex Intell. Syst. **8**(1), 673–685 (2022). https://doi.org/10.1007/s40 747-021-00560-1

34. Cortial, K., Pachot, A.: Sodinokibi intrusion detection based on logs clustering and random forest. ACM Int. Conf. Proc. Ser. (2021). https://doi.org/10.1145/3469213.3469221
35. Scheibmeir, J.A., Malaiya, Y.K.: Social media analytics of the Internet of Things. Discov. Internet of Things **1**(1) (2021). https://doi.org/10.1007/s43926-021-00016-5
36. Alqurashi, S., Batarfi, O.: A comparison of malware detection techniques based on hidden Markov model. J. Inf. Secur. **7**(3), 215–223 (2016). https://doi.org/10.4236/jis.2016.73017
37. Hwang, J., Kim, J., Lee, S., Kim, K.: Two-stage ransomware detection using dynamic analysis and machine learning techniques. Wirel. Pers. Commun. **112**(4), 2597–2609 (2020). https:// doi.org/10.1007/s11277-020-07166-9
38. Poudyal, S., Dasgupta, D.: AI-powered ransomware detection framework. In: 2020 IEEE Symposium Series on Computational Intelligence (SSCI 2020) (2020). https://doi.org/10. 1109/SSCI47803.2020.9308387
39. Khammas, B.M.: Ransomware detection using random forest technique. ICT Express **6**(4), 325–331 (2020). https://doi.org/10.1016/j.icte.2020.11.001
40. Khan, F., Ncube, C., Ramasamy, L.K., Kadry, S., Nam, Y.: A digital DNA sequencing engine for ransomware detection using machine learning. IEEE Access **8**, 119710–119719 (2020). https://doi.org/10.1109/ACCESS.2020.3003785
41. Rajawat, A.S., Rawat, R., Shaw, R.N., Ghosh, A.: Cyber physical system fraud analysis by mobile robot. In: Bianchini, M., Simic, M., Ghosh, A., Shaw, R.N. (eds.) Machine Learning for Robotics Applications. SCI, vol. 960, pp. 47–61. Springer, Singapore (2021). https://doi. org/10.1007/978-981-16-0598-7_4
42. Faris, H., Habib, M., Almomani, I., Eshtay, M., Aljarah, I.: Optimizing extreme learning machines using chains of salps for efficient android ransomware detection. Appl. Sci. (Switzerland) **10**(11), 3706 (2020). https://doi.org/10.3390/app10113706
43. Il Bae, S., Bin Lee, G., Im, E.G.: Ransomware detection using machine learning algorithms. In: Concurrency and Computation: Practice and Experience (2020). https://doi.org/10.1002/ cpe.5422
44. Zuhair, H., Selamat, A., Krejcar, O.: A multi-tier streaming analytics model of 0-day ransomware detection using machine learning. Appl. Sci. (Switzerland) **10**(9), 3210 (2020). https://doi.org/10.3390/app10093210
45. Ullah, F., et al.: Modified decision tree technique for ransomware detection at runtime through API calls. Sci. Prog. **2020**, 1–10 (2020). https://doi.org/10.1155/2020/8845833
46. Jethva, B., Traoré, I., Ghaleb, A., Ganame, K., Ahmed, S.: Multilayer ransomware detection using grouped registry key operations, file entropy and file signature monitoring. J. Comput. Secur. **28**(3), 337–373 (2020). https://doi.org/10.3233/JCS-191346
47. Poudyal, S., Dasgupta, D.: Analysis of crypto-ransomware using ML-based multi-level profiling. IEEE Access **9**, 122532–122547 (2021). https://doi.org/10.1109/ACCESS.2021.310 9260
48. Usharani, S., Bala, P.M., Mary, M.M.J.: Dynamic analysis on crypto-ransomware by using machine learning: gandcrab ransomware. J. Phys: Conf. Ser. (2021). https://doi.org/10.1088/ 1742-6596/1717/1/012024
49. Ahmed, O., Al-Dabbagh, O.: Ransomware detection system based on machine learning. J. Educ. Sci. **30**(5), 86–102 (2021). https://doi.org/10.33899/edusj.2021.130760.1173
50. Tajammul, M., Shaw, R.N., Ghosh, A., Parveen, R.: Error detection algorithm for cloud outsourced big data. In: Bansal, J.C., Fung, L.C.C., Simic, M., Ghosh, A. (eds.) Advances in Applications of Data-Driven Computing. AISC, vol. 1319, pp. 105–116. Springer, Singapore (2021). https://doi.org/10.1007/978-981-33-6919-1_8

51. Bastian, A.: Improving antivirus signature for detection ransomware attacks with machine learning. Smart Comp: Jurnalnya Orang Pintar Komputer **10**(1), 30–34 (2021). https://doi.org/10.30591/smartcomp.v10i1.2190

52. Zahoora, U., Khan, A., Rajarajan, M., Khan, S.H., Asam, M., Jamal, T.: Ransomware detection using deep learning based unsupervised feature extraction and a cost sensitive Pareto Ensemble classifier. Sci. Rep. **12**(1) (2022). https://doi.org/10.1038/s41598-022-19443-7

53. Masum, M., et al.: IEEE 12th annual computing and communication workshop and conference. CCWC **2022**, 2022 (2022). https://doi.org/10.1109/CCWC54503.2022.9720869

54. Talabani, H.S., Abdulhadi, H.M.T.: Bitcoin ransomware detection employing rule-based algorithms. Sci. J. Univ. Zakho **10**(1), 5–10 (2022). https://doi.org/10.25271/sjuoz.2022.10.1.865

Analysis and Design of Document Similarity Using BiLSTM and BERT

Chintan Gaur[1]([✉]), Ashwini Kumar[1], and Sanjoy Das[2]

[1] Graphic Era Deemed to be University, Dehradun, India
gaurchintan@gmail.com
[2] Indira Gandhi National Tribal University, RCM, Amarkantak, India

Abstract. In this paper, we propose a deep learning-based approach to measure document similarity using bidirectional encoder representations (BERTs) from transformers and its implementation as an application programming interface (API). BERT has recently shown significant improvements in natural language processing and is widely used in various applications such as question answering and text classification. We trained and refined a BERT model on a large corpus of documents to measure document similarity. The proposed API receives two text arguments and returns the degree of similarity between them. On several benchmark datasets, we demonstrated that our approach outperforms conventional state-of-the-art similarity measures. Our experimental results show that the proposed method of measuring document similarity using BERT and API is effective and efficient, and that API implementations can be used in a variety of real-world scenarios is visible.

Keywords: Natural Language Processing · Semantic Textual Similarity · Bidirectional Encoder Representations from Transformers · Machine Learning · Deep Learning

1 Introduction

BERT (Bidirectional Encoder Representations from Transformers) is a Google-developed pre-trained language model. It has been trained on massive volumes of text data and can understand the context and meaning of words in a phrase. BERT has demonstrated cutting-edge performance in a variety of natural language processing (NLP) tasks such as text classification, question answering, and language translation. It is one of the most used NLP models due to its capacity to handle jobs that need a thorough comprehension of language.

Measuring similarity between documents is a fundamental problem in natural language processing and has many practical applications such as plagiarism detection, document retrieval, and content-based recommendation systems. Traditional approaches to document similarity rely on lexical and structural features, which are often inadequate to capture the underlying semantic similarity between documents. Recently, deep learning-based approaches, especially those based on pre-trained language models such

R. N. Shaw et al. (Eds.): ICACIS 2023, CCIS 1921, pp. 161–167, 2023.
https://doi.org/10.1007/978-3-031-45124-9_12

as [12] Bidirectional Encoder Representation (BERT) from Transformers, have shown significant improvements in natural language processing tasks.

In this article, we propose a deep learning-based approach to measure document similarity using BERT and implement it as an application programming interface (API). We trained a BERT model on a large corpus of documents and refined it to measure document similarity. The proposed API takes two text arguments and returns the similarity value between them. We evaluated the model on several benchmark datasets and showed that our approach outperforms conventional state-of-the-art similarity measures.

Additionally, we have implemented the model as an API for easy integration with other applications. This API can be used in a variety of scenarios such as plagiarism detection, document searching, and content-based recommendation systems. We have also developed an easy-to-use web-based interface for the API. This gives non-technical users access to document similarity measurement functionality.

The proposed approach using BERT and API is an effective and efficient way to measure document similarity, and the API implementation can be used in various real-world scenarios.

The rest of this paper is structured as follows. In Sect. 2, we discussed related work. Our proposed BERT Model architecture is described below Sect. 3. Section 4 goes over our experiments and findings. The paper is completed in Sect. 5.

2 Related Work

Measuring document similarity is a long-standing problem in natural language processing and has received a great deal of attention in literature. Traditional approaches to document similarity are based on lexical and structural features such as word frequencies, n-grams, and parse trees. However, these methods often fail to capture basic semantic similarities between documents and perform poorly in real-world scenarios.

Many natural language processing (NLP) applications, such as sentiment analysis, machine translation, and information retrieval, rely on word embeddings. The Global Vectors for Word Representation (GloVe) model, introduced by [4] Pennington et al., is one of the most widely used methods for generating word embeddings (2014).

The distributional hypothesis, which states that words that appear in similar contexts tend to have similar meanings, underpins the GloVe model. GloVe learns word embeddings by factoring a co-occurrence matrix, which represents the frequency of word pairs in a corpus. The resulting word vectors capture both syntactic and semantic information and have been shown in several benchmark tasks to outperform other methods such as skip-gram and continuous bag-of-words (CBOW) [13] (Mikolov et al., 2013).

Several changes to the GloVe model have been proposed in order to improve its performance or adapt it to specific tasks. To improve sentiment analysis, [14] Zhang et al. (2019) proposed a multi-task learning framework that combines GloVe with a convolutional neural network (CNN). [15] Zhang and Yang (2018) proposed a regularisation method that encourages semantically related word embeddings to be close in the embedding space, improving the quality of word similarity measures.

The authors suggest a Siamese Recurrent Architecture (SRA) for learning sentence similarity in their paper "Siamese Recurrent Architectures for Learning Sentence Similarity" [16] (Mueller and Thyagarajan, 2016). The SRA is a neural network model that computes a similarity score between two input words. The authors show that the SRA beats numerous baselines on benchmark datasets for sentence similarity after training it on a large dataset of sentence pairs with similarity labels. Since then, the SRA has been modified for document similarity tasks, with promising results.

The authors present a deep neural network model for encoding sentences into fixed-length vectors in their paper "Universal Sentence Encoder" [17] (Cer et al., 2018). The Universal Sentence Encoder (USE) is trained on a huge corpus of literature using a supervised learning objective and can capture both semantic and syntactic information in sentences. The authors assess the USE on numerous downstream NLP tasks, including document similarity, and find that it outperforms several baselines. Since then, the USE has been utilised as a pre-trained model for numerous NLP tasks, yielding state-of-the-art results in several cases.

3 Methodology

3.1 Dataset

We will use the [3] SNLI (Stanford Natural Language Inference) dataset for training and evaluating our model. The dataset consists of approximately 570k sentence pairs, with each pair labeled as either entailment, contradiction, or neutral. For this project we took 200k sentence pairs to feed our model.

3.2 Preprocessing

We will preprocess the dataset by performing the following steps:

1. Remove any non-alphabetic characters, such as numbers and punctuation marks.
2. Drop all the NaN entries from the train data.
3. Tokenize the text into words and sub words using the BERT tokenizer.
4. Add special tokens, such as [CLS] and [SEP], to mark the beginning and end of sentences.

3.3 Proposed Model

The model architecture (Fig. 2) is made up of three input layers: input ids, attention masks, and token type ids, which are followed by the TFBertMainLayer from the TensorFlow implementation of the BERT model. This layer's output is routed to a 256-unit bidirectional layer, which is then routed to a batch normalisation layer. The batch normalisation layer's outputs are then fed into a global average pooling layer and a global max pooling layer, which are then concatenated to produce a 512-dimensional output. To predict the three classes of the SNLI dataset, a dropout layer is applied to the concatenated output, followed by a dense layer with three units. The model has a total of 110,403,331 parameters, of which only 920,579 are trainable. Figure 1 shows the model architecture graphically. Also, the model implementation is referenced from here. [1].

We created an API using the Flask Python library to make the document similarity model available to other applications. Flask is a lightweight web framework that enables developers to create RESTful APIs quickly and with minimal overhead. Flask was chosen due to its ease of use and flexibility in handling HTTP requests and responses [18].

We used ngrok, a tool that creates secure tunnels to expose local web servers to the internet, to make the API public. External applications can now interact with our API without us having to deploy our model to a remote server or configure firewall settings.

The API accepts two text arguments and returns a similarity score. The input text is pre-processed using the same tokenization and encoding techniques that were used during training and testing. The pre-processed text is then run through the trained BERT model to determine the degree of similarity between the two documents.

External applications can send HTTP requests to the API to obtain similarity scores once the API endpoint is operational. The response is a JSON object that contains the similarity score between the two input documents.

Overall, the API makes it easy for developers to incorporate our document similarity model into their own applications.

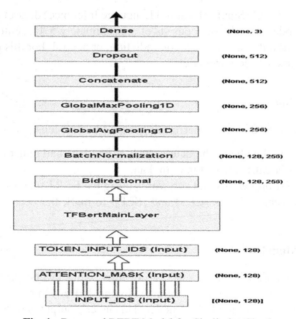

Fig. 1. Proposed BERT Model for Similarity Check

```
Layer (type)                    Output Shape           Param #
=================================================================
input_ids (InputLayer)          [(None, 128)]          0

attention_masks (InputLayer)    [(None, 128)]          0

token_type_ids (InputLayer)     [(None, 128)]          0

bert (TFBertMainLayer)          TFBaseModelOutputWi    109482240
                                thPoolingAndCrossAt
                                tentions(last_hidde
                                n_state=(None, 128,
                                768),
                                 pooler_output=(Non
                                e, 768),
                                 past_key_values=No
                                ne, hidden_states=N
                                one, attentions=Non
                                e, cross_attentions
                                =None)

bidirectional (Bidirectional)   (None, 128, 256)       918528

batch_normalization (BatchNorm  (None, 128, 256)       1024
alization)

global_average_pooling1d (Glob  (None, 256)            0
alAveragePooling1D)

global_max_pooling1d (GlobalMa  (None, 256)            0
xPooling1D)

concatenate (Concatenate)       (None, 512)            0

dropout_37 (Dropout)            (None, 512)            0

dense (Dense)                   (None, 3)              1539

=================================================================
Total params: 110,403,331
Trainable params: 920,579
Non-trainable params: 109,482,752
```

Fig. 2. Details of our BERT model.

4 Experiments and Results

As shown in Table, we compare our performance on the 10k validation data for the benchmark dataset using the proposed model to the other models Table 1.

Table 1. Comparison of our proposed model with machine learning methods

Models	Accuracy (%)
Unlexicalized features	50.4
100D LSTM encoders	77.6
300D Tree-based CNN encoders	82.1
300D SPINN-PI encoders	83.2
100D LSTMs w/word-by-word attention	83.5
100D DF-LSTM	84.6
Our Proposed Model	**88.53**

4.1 Training and Validation Loss

With a batch size of 64, we trained the model on 20k sentence pairs for 10 epochs and achieved an accuracy of 83.4%. However, we wanted to improve the model's accuracy even further, so we fine-tuned it with 200k sentence pairs and achieved an accuracy of 88.53% in only 3 epochs. This improvement in accuracy demonstrates the effectiveness of our semantic similarity simulation (Fig. 3).

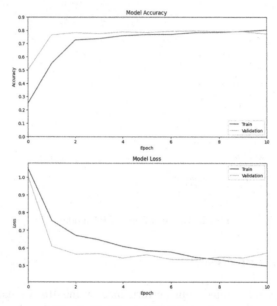

Fig. 3. Training and Validation loss

5 Conclusion

Finally, this paper presented a novel approach for detecting semantic similarity using the pre-trained BERT model. Fine-tuning BERT on the SNLI dataset significantly improves the model's accuracy for semantic similarity detection, according to the results of the experiments.We achieved an accuracy of 83.4% in 10 epochs with a batch size of 64, and with further fine-tuning on 200k sentence pairs, we achieved an accuracy of 88.53% in just 3 epochs.

Our model can now be used in a variety of applications thanks to the use of the Flask library for API Endpoint Creation and ngrok for secure tunnelling. Because of its high accuracy and ability to detect semantic similarity, the model is useful for a variety of natural language processing tasks.

Overall, the proposed approach yielded promising results and has the potential to be improved further with additional fine-tuning and the use of larger datasets. The application of BERT for semantic similarity detection lays a solid foundation for future research in this field.

In this study, we presented how to put together an API for document similarity using the BERT with BiLSTM; however, in future work, we can expand our model to check document similarity with multiple languages so that this model can be utilised across a broad spectrum.

References

1. BERT Model Reference. https://colab.research.google.com/github/keras-team/keras-io/blob/master/examples/nlp/ipynb/semantic_similarity_with_bert.ipynb#scrollTo=Y43ctXNkK56zI
2. Hugging Face Library. https://huggingface.co/keras-io/bert-semantic-similarity
3. Data for Training and Testing. https://nlp.stanford.edu/projects/snli/
4. Pennington, J., Socher, R., Manning, C.D.: GloVe: global vectors for word representation (2014)
5. Mutinda, F.W., Yada, S., Wakamiya, S., Aramiki, E.: Semantic Textual Similarity in Japanese Clinical Domain Texts Using BERT
6. Zheng, L.: Performance Analysis of RESTful APIs: A Systematic Mapping Study
7. Zhang, J., Jagadish, H.V.R.: API Design Patterns and Best Practices: A Survey
8. Ostendorff, M., Ruas, T., Blume, T., Rehm, B.G.G.: Aspect-Based Document Similarity for Research Papers
9. Xia, C., He, T., Li, W., Qin, Z., Zou, Z.: Similarity Analysis of Law Documents Based on Word2vec
10. Ramadhanti, N.R., Mariyah, S.: Document Similarity Detection Using Indonesian Language Word2vec Model
11. Vitale, T., Tasso, C.: The State of the Art in API Usability Evaluation
12. Devlin, J., Chang, M.-W., Lee, K., Toutanova, K.: BERT: Pre-training of Deep Bidirectional Transformers for Language Understanding
13. Mikolov, T., Chen, K., Corrado, G., Dean, J.: Efficient estimation of word representations in vector space (2013)
14. Zhang, H., Lan, Y., Yu, N.: Multi-task learning for sentiment analysis using convolutional neural networks and Global Vectors (2019)
15. Zhang, Y., Yang, Q.: Regularizing matrix factorization with user and item embeddings for recommendation (2018)
16. Mueller, T.: Siamese Recurrent Architectures for Learning Sentence Similarity (2016)
17. Cer, D., et al.: Universal sentence encoder for English. In: Proceedings of the 2018 Conference on Empirical Methods in Natural Language Processing: System Demonstrations, pp. 169–174. Association for Computational Linguistics, Brussels, Belgium (2018)
18. Baid, D., Goel, P.M., Bhardwaj, P., Singh, A., Tyagi, V.: Comparative analysis of serverless solutions from public cloud providers. In: Bhattacharya, M., Kharb, L., Chahal, D. (eds.) ICICCT 2021. CCIS, vol. 1417, pp. 63–75. Springer, Cham (2021). https://doi.org/10.1007/978-3-030-88378-2_6

Customer Churn Analysis for Live Stream E-Commerce Platforms by Using Decision Tree Method

Aoxia Shi[1] , Chia Yean Lim[1(✉)] , and Sau Loong Ang[2]

[1] Universiti Sains Malaysia, Gelugor, Penang, Malaysia
summershi99@student.usm.my, cylim@usm.my
[2] Tunku Abdul Rahman University of Management and Technology, Penang Branch,
Tanjung Bungah, Malaysia
angsl@tarc.edu.my

Abstract. The popularity of online live stream sales as a successful business model has increased due to its effectiveness in promoting sales quickly. This growth has been further accelerated by the COVID-19 pandemic, which has restricted physical store visits and forced consumers to rely more heavily on online shopping. However, with the increasing number of retail companies entering the industry, achieving profitability has become increasingly challenging, especially for small- and medium-sized companies without sufficient industry experience. One of the main problems that retailers face is the inability to retain customers and predict customer churn effectively, which is crucial for developing an effective marketing strategy. The objective of this paper is to propose a classification model that can accurately classify customers into churners and non-churners groups. To achieve this goal, Naive Bayes (NB), Decision Tree (DT), and K-nearest neighbor (KNN) algorithms are used to build prediction models using customer data from an existing E-commerce company. The research findings showed that the Decision Tree algorithm with an accuracy of 93.6% outperformed the other classification models. Additionally, it is discovered that the algorithm achieved its highest accuracy when the depth of the Decision Tree is set to 14.

Keywords: Classification · Decision Tree · K-nearest neighbor · Livestream · Naive Bayes · Online Sales

1 Introduction

The COVID-19 pandemic, which began in early 2020, has rapidly spread across the globe and caused an ongoing health crisis. As a result of COVID-19 lockdowns and travel restrictions, physical retail stores have experienced a significant decline in sales during the pandemic period. In contrast, the pandemic has accelerated the growth of E-commerce, leading to a massive increase in online sales. For instance, in the US, E-commerce sales surged by $219 billion in 2020–2021 due to the pandemic [1]. Similarly, Chinese E-commerce sales were predicted to reach $1 trillion in 2020, an increase from

© The Author(s), under exclusive license to Springer Nature Switzerland AG 2023
R. N. Shaw et al. (Eds.): ICACIS 2023, CCIS 1921, pp. 168–178, 2023.
https://doi.org/10.1007/978-3-031-45124-9_13

$862 billion in 2019 [2]. Statistics of retail E-commerce sales worldwide [3] showed that E-commerce sales will increase rapidly in coming years, and it was expected to reach 8 trillion by 2026.

Live streaming E-commerce emerged as a new business model that gained popularity in China and many other countries during the COVID-19 pandemic. During China's Black Friday, also known as the annual Single's Day Global Shopping Festival of Taobao in 2020, live streams contributed to $6 billion in sales, nearly double the amount from the previous year [4]. In December 2020, Walmart launched live shopping events on TikTok, while Amazon launched a live platform for influencers to promote products and support customer chats. Unlike traditional E-commerce, live streaming E-commerce was a new business able where celebrities, influencers, or retailers manage to sell their products or services via online video streaming. During these live streams, presenters demonstrated and discussed offerings, and answered audiences' questions in real time. Despite the growing popularity of live stream purchases, competition between E-commerce giants and large retail companies was becoming increasingly fierce. Many startups and new entrants into the live-streaming E-commerce industry, faced difficulties in attracting and retaining customers due to a lack of resources and relevant technology, compared to leading companies.

Retaining customers is crucial for the survival and success of any business. Research showed that a new customer's acquisition cost was often higher than retaining an existing one [5]. Furthermore, predicting customer churn was 16 times less expensive than acquiring new customers [6], and reducing the customer churn rate by just 5% can increase the average profit margin of a business by over 25% [7]. Therefore, small businesses need to leverage their current customer base and avoid losing them to ensure long-term success.

The objective of the research is to compare various classification models and propose the best model to classify customers for a China well-known E-commerce company. In this paper, Sect. 2 will cover the overview of related technology and previous studies done by other researchers. Section 3 will discuss the dataset, data pre-processing, evaluation measures, and modeling. Section 4 will discuss model implementation and results. Finally, the discussion and conclusion are written in Sect. 5.

2 Literature Review

2.1 Overview of E-Commerce and Real-Time Streaming Technology

E-commerce refers to the products or services buying and selling activities over the internet [8]. With the existence of rapidly evolving, highly adaptable, and affordable information technologies in E-business, companies are required to innovate their business models to meet changing customer needs [9]. Data mining, the latest technology in this field, supported E-commerce's transformation by enabling companies to interpret external data, learn from it, and use those insights to achieve specific goals and tasks through flexible adaptation [10]. By using data mining techniques, businesses can better understand their target audiences and improve their chances of eliciting a response. Businesses can turn their data into actionable insights by utilizing the appropriate analytics and data science technologies. The rapid growth of real-time streaming technology and analytics has resulted in numerous companies and organizations adopting or considering the implementation of this technology.

Real-time streaming analytics has several noteworthy characteristics, including its ability to: 1) analyze and act on real-time data, 2) analyze and mitigate potential risks, 3) analyze customer behavior to identify novel business opportunities and revenue streams, and 4) process tens of millions of events per second to facilitate highly responsive and proactive decision-making. As shown in Fig. 1, there are five steps in the streaming architecture to enable stream analytics.

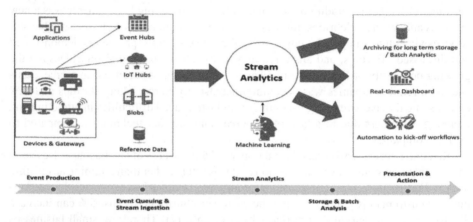

Fig. 1. Streaming architecture

2.2 Data Mining

The customer churn prediction is conducted to distinguish churners from non-churners. Although most churn prediction techniques were concentrated in industries such as telecommunication, banking, and insurance, there was limited research on customer churn prediction in E-commerce. This literature review will primarily focus on KNN, DT, and NB algorithms which are believed to be suitable models for E-commerce customers' churn prediction.

K-Nearest Neighbor (KNN)

The KNN algorithm is a widely used machine learning method that is both efficient and simple. It can make predictions even when the existing knowledge about the data distribution is unknown. It is particularly well-suited to situations where the entire training data is available. It functions by calculating the distance between the input data and the k closest objects in the dataset, where k represents the number of neighbors and can be adjusted to improve model performance. While a larger value of k can reduce the impact of noise, it can also result in fewer distinct boundaries between classes. Euclidean and Manhattan distances are the most commonly used methods for calculating distance. The distance, d, between two points (a and b) is calculated using the formula (1).

$$d(a, b) = \sqrt{\sum_{i=0}^{n} (a_i - b_i)^2} \tag{1}$$

From the literature study, KNN was adopted by Sjarif et al. [11] and Pamina et al. [12] to create a customer churn prediction model for obtaining telco customer churn data and traits that highly influence customer churn. Meanwhile, Imron and Prasetiyo [13] from German, and Miao and Wang [14] from China used the KNN algorithm to predict customer churn on credit services. All prediction models in the above research achieved high accuracy of above 70% (97.78% [11], 75.4% [12], 82.5% [13], 90.32% [14]).

Decision Tree (DT)
The DT classifier is a recursive algorithm that divides the dataset into smaller sets based on certain tests performed at each node on the tree. The root node of the tree is located at the top of the tree, and each node of the decision tree is partitioned recursively until the new points have been classified with the fullest purity. The DT is a tree that has three key properties: Firstly, an attribute is represented by an inner node. Secondly, a test on the attribute of the parent node is represented by an edge. Finally, one of the classes is represented by a leaf. The decision tree construction process follows a top-down strategy and is based on the training data.

From the literature study, Saini et al. [15] compared the performance of variants of decision trees and analyzed a large customer dataset for churn. The researchers found that the exhaustive Chi-Squared Automatic Interaction Detection (CHAID) technique was more efficient and accurate than others for predicting customer churn, with an accuracy of 87.8%. Scriney et al. [16] used two decision trees with the Classification and Regression Tree (CART) algorithm to predict customer churn for insurance data and bridge the gap between available information in application databases and required dataset types for calculating customer lifetime values. Both decision tree methods (Entropy and Gini split) showed very small differences in accuracy, with an overall accuracy of 88.7%.

Naive Bayes (NB)
Naïve Bayes (NB) classification is a supervised learning model that assumes each feature is independent and equally important. It is based on Bayes' Theorem of probability, which simplifies prediction by assuming each feature is independent and equally essential. The theorem breaks down conditional probability into its constituent parts to make predictions as shown in Eq. (2).

$$p(C_k|x) = \frac{p(C_k)p(x|C_k)}{p(x)} \tag{2}$$

where C is a class whose probability value will be calculated since it is affected by the value that is assigned to feature x.

Several studies employed the Naive Bayes (NB) classification algorithm to predict customer churn. Petkovski et al. [17] analyzed multiple machine learning algorithms including C4.5 DT, KNN, and NB, and found that NB achieved an accuracy of over 85%, while KNN and DT achieved an accuracy of 90%. Amin et al. [18] proposed a novel approach called CCP based on estimating the classifier's certainty using the distance factor. They implemented NB in MATLAB for their study. Yulianti and Saifudin [19] explored the use of feature selection to improve customer churn prediction using NB and found that Sequential Backward Selection (SBS) was the best-performing model.

2.3 Summary of Recent Years' Customer Churn Prediction

The summary of recent years' customer churn prediction research findings is shown in Table 1.

Table 1. Summary of recent years' customer churn prediction

Reference	Type of Data	Algorithm Used	Prediction Performance
Kraljević and Gotovac [20], 2010	Telecom company data	Neural Network Log. Regression Decision Tree	85.7% 83.6% 90.9%
Shaaban et al. [21], 2012	Mobile service provider data	Neural Network SVM Decision Tree	83.7% 83.7% 77.9%
Kirui et al. [22], 2013	Telecomm company data	Naïve Bayes Bayesian Network Decision Tree	88% 70% 51%
Merchie and Ernst [23], 2022	Online gambling company data	Recurrent Neural Network	83.7%

3 Research Method

The purpose of this research is to explore and propose the best classification model to predict customer churn for an E-commerce company, focused on the livestream business model.

3.1 DataSet

The data is mainly from an E-commerce company's internal database which consists of more than 5600 records. Table 2 shows the dataset details of the customer attributes and there are 19 columns of attributes.

Table 2. Attributes from Dataset

No	Variable	Data Type	Description
1	Customer_ID	Categorical	Unique customer ID
2	Discount_Amount	Numerical	Average cashback in the last month
3	Tenure	Numerical	Tenure for using the platform (months)
4	Preferred_LoginDevice	Categorical	Customer's preferred login device
5	City_Tier	Categorical	City tiers
6	Dist_WarehouseToHome	Numerical	The distance from the warehouse to the customer's home
7	Age_Group	Categorical	The customer's age (eg. 2:20–29)
8	Marital_Status	Categorical	Marital status of the customer
9	Gender_Customer	Categorical	Customer's gender
10	HourSpend_OnApp	Numerical	Total hours spent on apps
11	Preferred_OrderCat	Categorical	Customer's preferred order category in last month
12	Satisfaction_Score	Numerical	Customer's score on satisfactory service
13	NumberOf_StreamerFollowed	Numerical	Total number of streamers followed by customer
14	Complaint	Categorical	The complaint raised in the previous month
15	OrderAmount_HikeFromlastYear	Numerical	Previous year's order's increment percentage
16	Coupon_Utilized	Numerical	The sum of coupons has been utilized in the previous month
17	Order_Count	Numerical	Total orders placed in the previous month
18	Recency	Numerical	Total days since the last order
19	Churn	Categorical	Churn flag (1 represents customer loss)

3.2 Data Pre-processing

The first crucial step is to verify the data quality of the dataset since data is seldom perfect. This stage aids in comprehending the data and preparing it for further analysis. Initially, missing value analysis was conducted to eliminate any missing values from the dataset. After eliminating the null values, the dataset now consists of 3774 rows and 19 columns, making it ready for model building in the next phase.

The selection of attributes is the second step, and it involves using a correlation heatmap. A correlation heatmap is a graphical representation of a correlation matrix. It shows the correlation between different variables. The correlation between two variables can be measured using the correlation coefficient from -1 to $+1$. Correlated features have a significant impact on the classification accuracy of machine learning algorithms. It is recommended to consider the features that have a high correlation with the class. If the features' number is too large in comparison to the training sample size, reducing the number of features is advantageous.

The output of the correlation heatmap showed that the attributes that are highly related to customer churn are Tenure, Preferred Login Device, City Tier, Warehouse To Home, Marital Status, Age Group, Day Since Last Order, Number of Streamer Followed, Satisfaction Score, and Complaint. Consequently, such features will be chosen for building the classification model.

3.3 Modeling

The modeling phase is the most critical part of this project since it is directly related to the primary objective. To classify the customers, classifiers such as KNN, DT, and NB will be employed. The KNN algorithm will be executed with different numbers of neighbors, while the DT algorithm will be executed with different numbers of tree depths. The NB algorithm will be executed with various types of probability models. The cleansed dataset will be split into a training set (70%) and a validation set (30%) to evaluate the quality of the model. After constructing each classification model, the testing set will be used to assess its performance.

3.4 Evaluation Measures

This research used a confusion matrix or also known as an error matrix, which has a specific table layout to visualize the performance of the prediction model. The confusion matrix provides additional insight to interpret the predictive model's performance. The matrix can tell the correctness of the class's prediction outcome, and the types of errors that occurred during the prediction. In addition, the quality of a classification model is generally described in terms of precision, recall, and accuracy. The calculation formulae for the three metrics are shown in Table 3.

Table 3. Calculation formula of precision, recall, and accuracy

Metric	Calculation Formula
Precision	Total number of correct positive predictions (TP)/the total number of positive predictions (TP + FP)
Recall	Total number of correct positive predictions (TP)/total number of positives (P)
Accuracy	A total number of correct predictions (TP + TN)/the total number of datasets (P + N)

4 Model Evaluation and Result

4.1 KNN

To achieve optimal results from the KNN algorithm, various numbers of neighbors are employed. The relationship between the accuracy score and the value of K is depicted in Fig. 2. Notably, the highest accuracy score is obtained when K equals 2. Consequently, the KNN algorithm is executed using K = 2.

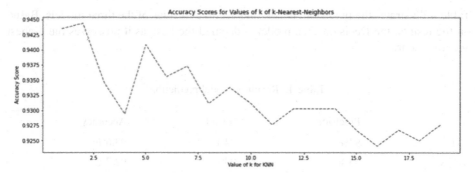

Fig. 2. Number of neighbors vs. accuracy score

4.2 Decision Tree

To obtain optimal outcomes from the Decision Tree algorithm, diverse depth values are utilized during execution. The accuracy and depth of the tree are correlated, as displayed in Fig. 3. Notably, the highest accuracy score is achieved when the depth is 14. Consequently, the DT algorithm is executed using a depth value of 14.

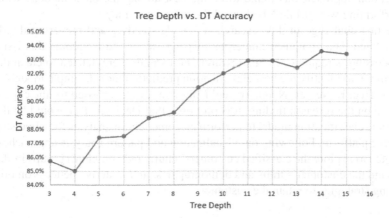

Fig. 3. Tree Depth vs. Decision Tree Accuracy

4.3 Naive Bayes

To achieve optimal outcomes from the Naïve Bayes algorithm, three types of probability models are employed during execution, namely Gaussian, Multinomial, and Bernoulli. Interestingly, these three models generate the same level of accuracy. Therefore, the Naïve Bayes algorithm is executed using the Gaussian model.

4.4 Comparison of Models

Table 4 illustrates the precision, recall, and accuracy values of the three models. Based on the results, the Decision Tree model is deemed the best, as it possesses the highest accuracy score.

Table 4. Result of model prediction

	Precision	Recall	Accuracy
DT	94%	94%	93.6%
KNN	93%	93%	92.7%
NB	84%	85%	85.4%

5 Discussion and Conclusion

In business, predicting customer churn using machine learning is crucial. This paper explores a classification problem in which various machine-learning algorithms are utilized to determine the optimal model for customer churn prediction. The Decision Tree classification approach was found to be the best among the other models, with KNN also performing well, while NB showed the lowest accuracy.

The first challenge in this research was understanding and preparing the data, as the structured data contained numerous missing values. To overcome this issue, data pre-processing is required. In this research, null values were deleted to clean the data. Furthermore, to identify the best classification prediction model, simple models such as Decision Tree, K-Nearest Neighbor, and Naïve Bayes were chosen for the experiment.

Based on the research finding, it is proposed that Decision Tree would be the most appropriate classification model to perform customer churn analysis for a live-stream E-commerce platform. Following on, visualization and pattern analysis approaches could be adopted to explore the classified customers' churn and non-churn groups in-depth, to understand the customer's traits and demographics, and to derive better promotion and marketing strategies to retain the customers.

References

1. Berthene, A.: Coronavirus pandemic adds $219 billion to US e-commerce sales in 2020–2021. Digital Commer. **360** (2022). https://www.digitalcommerce360.com/article/corona virus-impact-online-retail/

2. Greenwald, M.: Live streaming E-commerce is the rage in China. Is the U.S. next? (2020). Webpage: https://www.forbes.com/sites/michellegreenwald/2020/12/10/live-stream ing-e-commerce-is-the-rage-in-china-is-the-us-next/?sh=23e56cc16535. Accessed 15 Mar 2022

3. Chevalier, S.: Global retail e-commerce sales 2014–2026. Webpage: https://www.statista.com/statistics/379046/worldwide-retail-e-commerce-sales/#:~:text=In%202021%2C%20r etail%20e%2Dcommerce,8.1%20trillion%20dollars%20by%202026. Accessed 15 Mar 2022

4. Hallanan, L.: Live streaming drives $6 billion USD in sales during the 11.11 global shopping festival (2020). Webpage: https://www.forbes.com/sites/laurenhallanan/2020/11/16/live-str eaming-drives-6-billion-usd-in-sales-during-the-1111-global-shopping-festival/?sh=5607af 5d21e5. Accessed 15 Mar 2022

5. Berson, A., Smith, S., Thearling, K.: Building Data Mining Applications for CRM. McGrawHill, New York (2002)

6. Borja, B., Bernardino, C., Alex, C., Ricard, G., David, M.M.: The architecture of a churn prediction system based on stream mining. Front. Artif. Intell. Appl. **256**, 157–166 (2013)

7. Nie, G., Rowe, W., Zhang, L., Tian, Y., Shi, Y.: Credit card churn forecasting by logistic regression and decision tree. Expert. Syst. Appl. **38**, 15273–15285 (2011)

8. Holsapple, C.W., Singh, M.: Electronic commerce: from a definitional taxonomy toward a knowledge-management view. J. Organ. Comput. Electron. Commer. **10**(3), 149–170 (2000)

9. Gielens, K., Steenkamp, J.B.E.: Branding in the era of digital (dis) intermediation. Int. J. Res. Mark. **36**(3), 367–384 (2019)

10. Kaplan, A.M., Haenlein, M.: Siri, Siri, in my hand: who's the fairest in the land? On the interpretations, illustrations, and implications of artificial intelligence. Bus. Horiz. **62**(1), 15–25 (2019)

11. Sjarif, N., et al.: A customer churn prediction using Pearson correlation function and K nearest neighbor algorithm for telecommunication industry. Int. J. Adv. Soft Comput. Appl. **11**(2), 46–59 (2019)

12. Pamina, J., Raja, B., SathyaBama, S., Sruthi, M.S., VJ, A.: An effective classifier for predicting churn in telecommunication. J. Adv. Res. Dyn. Control Syst. **11**, 221–229 (2019)

13. Imron, M.A., Prasetiyo, B.: Improving algorithm accuracy k-nearest neighbor using Z-score normalization and particle swarm optimization to predict customer churn. J. Soft Comput. Explor. **1**(1), 56–62 (2020)

14. Miao, X., Wang, H.: Customer churn prediction on credit card services using random forest method. In: Proceedings of the 2022 7th International Conference on Financial Innovation and Economic Development (ICFIED 2022), pp. 649–656. Atlantis Press, Paris, France (2022)

15. Saini, N., Monika, Garg, K.: Churn prediction in telecommunication industry using decision tree. Int. J. Eng. Res. Technol. **6**, 439–443 (2017)

16. Gupta, V., et al.: A new era of automated market-makers (AMM) powered by non-fungible tokens-a review. Global J. Innov. Emerg. Technol. **1**(2), 1–7 (2023). https://doi.org/10.58260/j.iet.2202.0106

17. Petkovski, A.J., Stojkoska, B.L.R., Trivodaliev, K.V., Kalajdziski, S.A.: Analysis of churn prediction: a case study on telecommunication services in Macedonia. In: 2016 24th Telecommunications Forum (TELFOR), pp. 1–4. IEEE (2016)

18. Amin, A., Al-Obeidat, F., Shah, B., Adnan, A., Loo, J., Anwar, S.: Customer churn prediction in telecommunication industry using data certainty. J. Bus. Res. **94**, 290–301 (2019)
19. Yulianti, Y., Saifudin, A.: Sequential feature selection in customer churn prediction based on Naive Bayes. IOP Conf. Ser. Mater. Sci. Eng. **879**(1), 012090 (2020)
20. Kraljević, G., Gotovac, S.: Modeling data mining applications for prediction of prepaid churn in telecommunication services. Automatika **51**(3), 275–283 (2010)
21. Shaaban, E., Helmy, Y., Khedr, A., Nasr, M.: A proposed churn prediction model. Int. J. Eng. Res. Appl. **2**(4), 693–697 (2012)
22. Kirui, C., Hong, L., Cheruiyot, W., Kirui, H.: Predicting customer churn in mobile telephony industry using probabilistic classifiers in data mining. Int. J. Comput. Sci. Issues (IJCSI) **10**(2 Part 1), 165 (2013)
23. Merchie, F., Ernst, D.: Churn prediction in online gambling. arXiv:2201.02463 (2022)

Estimation of Reliability, BER, BLER and Throughput During the Coexistence of 4G LTE and 5G NR

Jayanta Kumar Ray[1($\boxtimes$)], Rabindranath Bera[1], Sanjib Sil[2], Quazi Mohmmad Alfred[3], Safiul Alam Mondal[4], and Malay Pit[5]

[1] Sikkim Manipal Institute of Technology, Sikkim Manipal University, Gangtok, Sikkim, India
jayantakumar.ray@gmail.com
[2] Calcutta Institute of Engineering and Management, Kolkata, India
[3] Aliah University, Kolkata, India
[4] Gobindapur Sephali Memorial Polytechnic, Gobindapur, West Bengal, India
[5] Santiniketan Medical College, Bolpur, India

Abstract. The real world deals with the process of advancement of the sharing of uniform spectrum by both 4G LTE and 5G NR. This uniform spectrum gives rise to the problem of interference. Hence the process of cognition is utilized for minimizing the interference and improves the spectral efficiency. The Dynamic Spectrum Sharing (DSS) is the applicable technique for decreasing interference. Due to the same spectrum sharing made by both 4G LTE and 5G NR, there will be the origin of the problem of interference which gives challenges for various innovations in future. The problem of interference creates the minimization of reliability. For minimizing the interference, the oscillator frequency is kept stable whereas the range of oscillator frequencies for 5G NR has maximum and minimum value. The analysis specifies that for same or approximate value of frequencies for both 4G LTE and 5G NR, the reliability of the signal becomes negligible. Here the BER, BLER of the signal is maximum and the value of throughput of the signal is 0. For the purpose of maximizing the reliability and throughput, the oscillator frequencies for 5G NR is varying from maximum value to minimum value. It has been realized that if the frequency difference between 4G LTE and 5G NR is very high, then the reliability and throughput of the signal becomes maximum safeties.

Keywords: 4G LTE · 5G NR · DRiVE · ESS · 3GPP · V-2X · DSS

1 Introduction

The 5G communication system, which was already in use in 2020, is the current generation of communication technology. Initially, 5G devices were launched in some developed countries. Now it had gained a large popularity in the real world. The technologies while shifting from 4G LTE to 5G NR [1], the users avail huge opportunities such as massive capacity, high data rate, ultra high reliability etc. In future, these opportunities will transform the real world into smart world. Hence 5G communication system is

© The Author(s), under exclusive license to Springer Nature Switzerland AG 2023
R. N. Shaw et al. (Eds.): ICACIS 2023, CCIS 1921, pp. 179–195, 2023.
https://doi.org/10.1007/978-3-031-45124-9_14

much more superior than the 4G communication system. The smart world specifies the application of intelligence in various platforms such as factories, hospitals, institutions, transport etc.

The conversion from wired to wireless system is still going on and applicable to specific devices. After few years, the wireless system will be applicable in most of the devices. It will be more advantageous for the users to operate most of the devices in wireless mode. In future, the upcoming environment will be the wireless environment. This situation will maximize the utility of radio spectrum [2]. Due to the creation of wireless environment, the use of radio spectrum is much higher in comparison to the availability of radio spectrum. Hence the requirements of radio spectrum in different devices are not fulfilled. The spectrum sharing approach, which divides a small amount of spectrum across numerous users, is used to meet the requirements. The wireless networks' spectral efficiency is assessed.

Through the use of dynamic spectrum access [3], primary and secondary users can share the same spectrum. It is a method in which the spectrum resources and identical frequencies for 4G LTE and 5G NR are dynamically distributed based on user demand. Three models—Exclusive usage Model, Open Sharing Model, and Hierarchical Access Model—are used to categorise dynamic spectrum access.

There are two different kinds of spectrum bands: licenced and unlicensed. The licenced spectrum bands are applicable in the dynamic exclusive model while preserving the current policy for spectrum control, but the addition of flexibility results in an increase in spectrum efficiency. The two strategies are spectrum property rights and dynamic spectrum allocation. When it comes to spectrum property rights, licenced users are the only ones permitted to buy, apply for, and use the spectrum in accordance with their demands. The dynamic spectrum system was developed by the DRiVE (Dynamic Radio for Internet Protocol Services in Vehicular Environments) [4] initiative in Europe.

When dynamic spectrum is assigned, spectrum efficiency is increased because the spatial and temporal traffic statistics of varied services are taken into account. The spectrum is shared among peer users under the open sharing paradigm in order to manage the spectral region. In this approach, radio band (Wi-Fi), an unlicensed Industrial, Scientific, and Medical (ISM) [5] radio spectrum wireless system, offers benefits to users.

Here the spectrum sharing which involves in centralized distributed system had been evaluated. The hierarchical access model specifies the presence of structure in hierarchical format in which there will be the presence of both primary and secondary users. The primary users are licensed users and the secondary users are unlicensed users. Here the secondary users can get a scope to access licensed spectrum without causing disturbance to the primary users.

There are two approaches for the spectrum sharing between primary (licensed) users and secondary (unlicensed) users. These approaches are spectrum underlay and spectrum overlay [6]. In the spectrum underlay, there are various restrictions for the unlicensed users when the power is emitted. The utilization of spectrum for the unlicensed users will be possible when the frequency during signal transmission is expanded over Ultra Wide Band (UWB) having less power. Hence massive data rate will be evaluated by the unlicensed users within small range. In the spectrum overlay, different rules and regulations for the unlicensed (secondary) users are not applied in reference to the transmitted power. Here the location for the signal transmission is specified. The Spectrum overlay facilitates the unlicensed or secondary users to utilize the spatial and temporal white space which is used for identification and exploitation.

The 5G technology is much more advanced in contrast to 4G technologies. When 4G is shifted to 5G, lot of facilities for the users have been increased and users can able to fulfill their requirements. The requirements include application of spectrum asset, utilization of bands for social demand, improvement in smartness in devices, rural development etc. In case of 5G, the applicable frequency bands are mid band and high band. In 5G NR, the mid band frequency is Sub-6 GHz whereas the high band frequencies are ranging from 28 GHz to 40 GHz. To capture New Radio (NR) in wide area, the execution of NR in lower frequency band is mandatory.

A reputable global company named Ericsson introduced Ericsson Spectrum Sharing (ESS) [7], allowing users to simultaneously use 4G LTE and 5G NR on the same carrier frequencies. At the millisecond level, time frequency resources are allotted to various objects, and the ESS carries out the assignment. While various LTE devices use LTE cells, NR devices use 5G cells. The ESS software enables dynamic access to dynamic spectrum allocation on an equal frequency band for both 4G LTE and 5G NR. The transition from 4G to 5G is made possible by giving 4G less of a priority as 5G is introduced in the same frequency range. The performance decrease can be attributed to the spectrum mismatch between 4G LTE and 5G NR. This issue is resolved by ESS because it provides both 4G LTE and 5G NR to the entire carrier bandwidth, improving system performance. The ESS offers the chance to switch from 4G LTE to 5G NR in a seamless, simple, orderly, and quick way. The network's performance is improved by installing ESS. The ESS is isolated, simple, effective, and affordable. The ESS will eventually enable every user to utilise 5G anywhere and produce quick responses.

Following Third Generation Partnership Project (3GPP), withdrawal of 4G LTE V2X is not mandatory while the 5G NR V2X [8] was launched. Here 4G LTE V2X is coexisting with 5G NR V2X. 4G LTE V2X constitute the vehicular protection and security techniques and 5G NR V2X constitute the vehicular movement technique. This development includes ultra connectivity and intelligence phenomenon. The choice of Radio Access Technology (RAT) is decided following the requirements in V2X communication system. By using a 4G LTE or 5G NR communication infrastructure, the phenomenon of transmission and reception between two cars is made possible. Release 16 highlights the benefits of having 4G LTE and 5G NR simultaneously. For the resource management of Side Link, one device is present beside another. Two Radio Access Technologies (RAT) are said to be participating in coexistence, which is referred to as cross-RAT.

Here the two radio access technologies are 4G LTE and 5G NR. When 4G LTE is coexisting with 5G NR, then various problems are generated. Due to this coexistence, there arises a modern phrase called Co-channel coexistence where both NR and LTE are in the equal frequency or time. This situation gives rise to signal interference.

Co-channel cohabitation is not agreed upon by Release 16. The transmission of the 4G LTE V2X and 5G NR V2X signals at the same or nearly adjacent times and frequencies [9] is what causes the interference. It is necessary for two RATs to be used or executed simultaneously. The dependability of signal transmission and reception will decline as a result of interference. As a result, vehicles are unable to transmit and receive data and information correctly.

Work Arrangement:

In this paper, the Reliability and the throughput are evaluated. In Article 2, the System Vue 2020 developed by Keysight Technologies is utilized to design the circuit in software mode for software simulation. The simulation diagram is specified in Fig. 1. Side by side, the Article 2 mention the simulation procedure by specifying essential parameters defined in Table 1. The frequency of 4G LTE is fixed at 1.901 GHz but for 5G NR, the variation is from 1.892 GHz to 1.908 GHz. Article 3 defines the examination outcome of the software simulation. In order to analyze Reliability, at first Bit Error Rate (BER), Block Error Rate (BLER) is evaluated. The values of BER, BLER, Throughput, Reliability etc. are specified in Table 2. The variation of and Reliability, BLER, throughput and throughput fraction with frequency are given from Figs. 6, 7, 8 and 9.

2 Plan and Progress of the Coexistence of 4G LTE and 5G NR

2.1 Simulation Diagram

Keysight Technologies developed software called SystemVue 2020 and it is the reliable software for simulation purpose. This software provides assistance to develop the coexistence of two communication technologies. Figure 1 illustrates the simulation diagram. Here spectrum analyzers are attached at both 4G LTE and 5G NR in which the spectrum for both cases can be evaluated. Usually the spectrum sharing is of two types i.e. horizontal spectrum sharing and vertical spectrum sharing. In this phenomenon, the horizontal spectrum sharing is utilized. Here the frequency of the oscillator for 5G NR is shifting periodically where as the oscillator frequency for 4G LTE is stable.

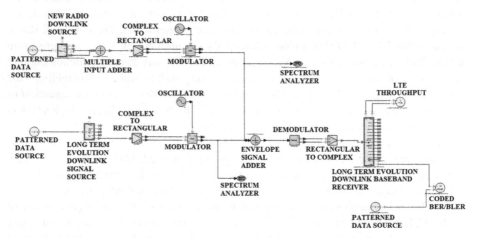

Fig. 1. Simulation Diagram for the coexistence of 4G LTE and 5G NR

2.2 Test Progress

The origin of the signal for two communication technologies may be in audio or video format.

4G LTE: The signals are originating from patterned data source which is attached with the 4G LTE downlink signal source. The signals from this source are flowing towards Complex to Rectangular system in which the signals are being resolved into real and imaginary parts. Later on, the signals are being transmitted to the modulator. The modulator has two portions i.e. In–phase and Quadrature. The real part is joined with the In-phase part and the imaginary part is joined with the Quadrature part. An oscillator is attached with the modulator. With the help of modulator, the modulated signal is produced and its spectrum can be observed utilizing spectrum analyzer (denoted by purple color).

5G NR: The signals are originating from patterned data source which is attached with the 5G NR downlink signal source. The signals from this source are flowing towards Complex to Rectangular system where the signals are being resolved into real and imaginary parts. Later on, the signals are being transmitted to the modulator. The modulator has two portions i.e. In-phase and Quadrature. The real part is joined with the In-phase part and the imaginary part is joined with the Quadrature part. An oscillator is attached with the modulator. With the help of modulator, the modulated signal is produced and its spectrum can be observed utilizing spectrum analyzer (denoted by green color). The oscillator frequency varies from 1.892 GHz to 1.908 GHz.

The modulated signals have been achieved from these communication technologies. These signals are being summed utilizing envelope signal adder. The added signals are flowing to the demodulator in which the signals are being demodulated. The demodulated signals are transferred towards rectangular to complex which changes the signal from the rectangular form to complex form. These complex signals are flowing towards the 4G LTE Downlink Baseband Receiver. From the receiver, the throughput is connected from which the throughput can be evaluated. On the other hand, the Coded BER/BLER is also connected with the raw bits part of the receiver from which the BER/BLER can also be estimated.

3 Test Outcome

There will be the problem of interference when the frequency of the two oscillators (4G LTE and 5G NR) are more or less same. Due to the problem of interference, various type of errors such as BER, BLER will be created. This situation specifies the minimization of reliability and maximization of Errors. To increase the reliability, BER/BLER must be reduced and increase in throughput is mandatory. To fulfil this target, the frequency of the oscillator in case 5G NR must be changed so that there will a certain difference between the oscillator frequencies which specifies that the oscillator frequency for 4G LTE should be fixed (1.901 GHz) whereas for 5G NR, the oscillator frequencies should be ranging from 1.892 GHz to 1.908 GHz. With the change in oscillator frequencies for 5G NR, the Bit Error Rate (BER), Block Error Rate (BLER) and throughput can be evaluated. The Reliability related to BER can also be evaluated. The combination of two spectrums (4G LTE, 5G NR) is specified from Figs. 2, 3, 4 and 5. The parameters for 4G and 5G are specified in Table 1. The oscillator frequencies for both 4G LTE and 5G NR are denoted by f_1 and f_2. The Transit Time Interval (TTI) is fixed at 8 μs.

The Reliability of the signal is expressed by

$$\text{Reliability}(R) = 1 - \text{BER}$$

Table 1. Parameters for 4G LTE and 5G NR

Serial No.	Parameters	4G LTE	5G NR
1	Transmission	LTE Downlink	NR Downlink
2	Oscillator Frequency	1.901 GHz	1.892 to 1.908 GHz
3	Power of oscillator	17 dBm	−41 dBm
4	Sample Rate	20 MHz	20 MHz
5	Cyclic Prefix	Normal	Normal
6	Source Bandwidth	5 MHz	50 MHz
7	Modulator	In-phase/Quadrature (I/Q)	In-phase/Quadrature (I/Q)
8	Demodulator	In-phase/Quadrature (I/Q)	
9	Receiver	LTE Downlink Baseband receiver	
10	Carrier Frequency	1.901 GHz	1.901 GHz
11	Multiple Input Adder	Not Applicable	Applicable
12	Transit Time Interval (TTI)	8 μs	

3.1 Different Situations

The color of the two spectrums are denoted by purple (4G LTE) and green (5G NR). From Figs. 2, 3, 4 and 5, the y axis specifies the power of the spectrum whereas the x axis specifies the frequency. The power for 4G LTE is denoted as S1_Power whereas the power for 5G NR is denoted as S2_Power.

Situation 1: $f_2 = 1.901$ *GHz,* $f_1 = 1.901$ *GHz,*

Here the frequencies of the oscillator for both cases are same. Hence the problem of interference will be probable. In this situation, there will be the absence of reliability and throughput. The value of BER and BLER is maximum. The test of the spectrum is specified in Fig. 2. The output of BER is 0.224282560706401 whereas for BLER is 1. Here the throughput of the signal is 0.

Situation 2: $f_2 = 1.892$ *GHz,* $f_1 = 1.901$ *GHz*

Here the frequencies of the oscillator for both cases are not same. Their frequency difference (4G LTE and 5G NR) is very huge. Hence the problem of interference will not

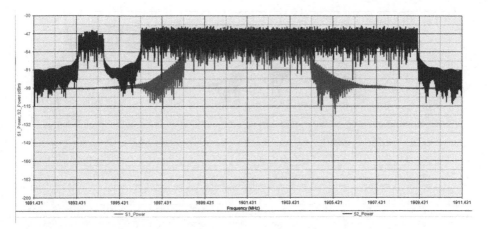

Fig. 2. Test of the spectrum during the coexistence of 4G LTE and 5G NR. ($f_1 = 1.901$ GHz, $f_2 = 1.901$ GHz)

be probable. In this situation, there will be the presence of high reliability and throughput will be 246.9 Mbps. The output of BER is 0.0000310327and BLER is 0.09. The test of the spectrum is specified in Fig. 3.

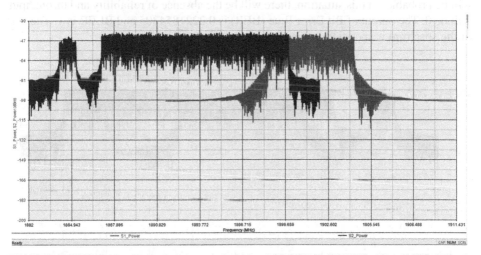

Fig. 3. Test of the spectrum during the coexistence of 4G LTE and 5G NR. ($f_1 = 1.901$ GHz, $f_2 = 1.892$ GHz)

Situation 3: $f_2 = 1.908$ GHz, $f_1 = 1.901$ GHz

Here the frequencies of the oscillator for both cases are also not same. Their frequency difference (4G LTE and 5G NR) is very huge as in situation 2. Hence the problem of interference will not be probable. In this situation, there will be the presence of high reliability and throughput will be 246.9 Mbps. The output of BER is 0.0000310327 and BLER is 0.09. The test of the spectrum is specified in Fig. 4.

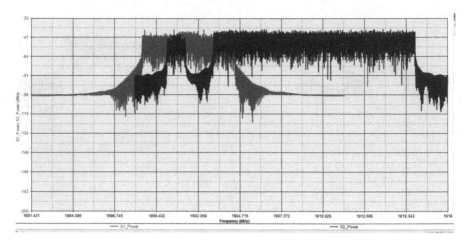

Fig. 4. Test of the spectrum during the coexistence of 4G LTE and 5G NR. (f₁ = 1.901 GHz, f₂ = 1.908 GHz)

Situation 4: $f_2 = 1.902$ GHz, $f_1 = 1.901$ GHz,

Here the frequencies of the oscillator for both cases are not same. Their frequency difference (4G LTE and 5G NR) is not very huge. Hence the problem of interference will be probable. In this situation, there will be the absence of reliability and throughput will be 0. The output of Bit Error Rate (BER) is 0.2221854305 and BLER is 1. The test of the spectrum is specified in Fig. 5.

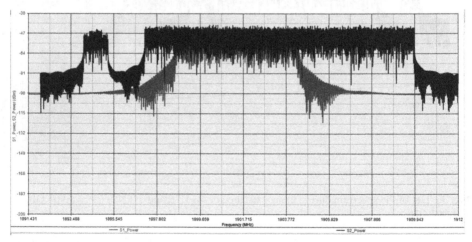

Fig. 5. Test of the spectrum during the coexistence of 4G LTE and 5G NR. (f₁ = 1.901 GHz, f₂ = 1.902 GHz)

3.2   Variation of BER, BLER, Reliability, Throughput and Throughput Fraction with Frequency

The range of oscillator frequency for 5G NR is varying from 1.892 GHz to 1.908 GHz. The variation of frequencies specifies the value of BER, BLER, throughput and throughput fraction in the coexistence scenario mentioned in Table 2. According to Table 2, the variation of throughput and reliability are opposite to BER, BLER. From Table 2, variation of different parameters like BER, BLER, throughput, throughput fraction with different oscillator frequencies of 5G NR are specified.

Table 2. Different Parameters (BER, Reliability, BLER, Throughput, Throughput Fraction) with Frequency

Frequency (GHz)	BER	Reliability	BLER	Throughput (Mbps)	Throughput Fraction
1.892	0.0000310327	0.9999689673	0.09	246.9	90.828
1.8921	0.0000241956	0.9999758044	0.09	246.9	90.828
1.8922	0.0000231956	0.9999768044	0.09	246.9	90.828
1.8923	0.0000345182	0.9999654818	0.1	244.1	89.809
1.8924	0.0000156297	0.9999843703	0.09	246.9	90.828
1.8925	0.0000314528	0.9999685472	0.09	246.9	90.828
1.8926	0.0000321960	0.9999678040	0.09	246.9	90.828
1.8927	0.0000143894	0.9999856106	0.09	246.9	90.828
1.8928	0.0000347321	0.9999652679	0.09	246.9	90.828
1.8929	0.0000256719	0.9999743281	0.1	244.1	89.809
1.893	0.00003451	0.9999654900	0.09	246.9	90.828
1.8931	0.00026674	0.9997332597	0.1	244.1	89.809
1.8932	0.000025679	0.9999743210	0.09	246.9	90.828
1.8933	0.000441501	0.9995584989	0.1	244.1	89.809
1.8934	0.000015349	0.9999846510	0.11	241.3	88.79
1.8935	0.0000183959	0.9999816041	0.11	241.9	88.981
1.8936	0.001048565	0.9989514349	0.14	233	85.732
1.8937	0.000913135	0.9990868653	0.12	239.1	87.962
1.8938	0.001131347	0.9988686534	0.16	227.5	83.694
1.8939	0.001030169	0.9989698308	0.16	227.5	83.694
1.894	0.001508462	0.9984915379	0.23	208.1	76.56
1.8941	0.009115158	0.9908848418	0.36	172.6	63.503
1.8942	0.019637601	0.9803623988	0.44	150.4	55.35
1.8943	0.012325239	0.9876747609	0.47	142.7	52.483

(continued)

Table 2. (*continued*)

Frequency (GHz)	BER	Reliability	BLER	Throughput (Mbps)	Throughput Fraction
1.8944	0.022130243	0.9778697572	0.64	94.52	34.776
1.8945	0.037132082	0.9628679176	0.79	52.97	19.489
1.8946	0.055675129	0.9443248712	0.89	27.85	10.063
1.8947	0.068736203	0.9312637969	0.89	25.79	9.489
1.8948	0.08781273	0.9121872701	0.96	9	3.311
1.8949	0.098142016	0.9018579838	0.96	9	3.311
1.895	0.111957322	0.8880426784	0.99	2.25	0.828
1.8951	0.129939294	0.8700607064	1	0	0
1.8952	0.136157101	0.8638428992	1	0	0
1.8953	0.142798013	0.8572019868	1	0	0
1.8954	0.15481972	0.8451802796	1	0	0
1.8955	0.164339588	0.8356604121	1	0	0
1.8956	0.175321928	0.8246780721	1	0	0
1.8957	0.175229948	0.8247700515	1	0	0
1.8958	0.186543414	0.8134565857	1	0	0
1.8959	0.194472038	0.8055279617	1	0	0
1.896	0.200800221	0.7991997792	1	0	0
1.8961	0.208462104	0.7915378955	1	0	0
1.8962	0.210458057	0.7895419426	1	0	0
1.8963	0.215020235	0.7849797645	1	0	0
1.8964	0.217108168	0.7828918322	1	0	0
1.8965	0.226995953	0.7730040471	1	0	0
1.8966	0.223086829	0.7769131714	1	0	0
1.8967	0.221274834	0.7787251656	1	0	0
1.8968	0.226140545	0.7738594555	1	0	0
1.8969	0.223463944	0.7765360559	1	0	0
1.897	0.223804268	0.7761957322	1	0	0
1.8971	0.222461369	0.7775386313	1	0	0
1.8972	0.225174761	0.7748252391	1	0	0
1.8973	0.222415379	0.7775846210	1	0	0
1.8974	0.222213024	0.7777869757	1	0	0

(*continued*)

Table 2. (*continued*)

Frequency (GHz)	BER	Reliability	BLER	Throughput (Mbps)	Throughput Fraction
1.8975	0.223353569	0.7766464312	1	0	0
1.8976	0.225910596	0.7740894040	1	0	0
1.8977	0.228771155	0.7712288447	1	0	0
1.8978	0.230123252	0.7698767476	1	0	0
1.8979	0.227575423	0.7724245769	1	0	0
1.898	0.226867182	0.7731328182	1	0	0
1.8981	0.221210449	0.7787895511	1	0	0
1.8982	0.224852833	0.7751471670	1	0	0
1.8983	0.223243194	0.7767568065	1	0	0
1.8984	0.22223142	0.7777685798	1	0	0
1.8985	0.220327447	0.7796725533	1	0	0
1.8986	0.224503311	0.7754966887	1	0	0
1.8987	0.226020971	0.7739790287	1	0	0
1.8988	0.22129323	0.7787067697	1	0	0
1.8989	0.226453274	0.7735467255	1	0	0
1.899	0.222838484	0.7771615158	1	0	0
1.8991	0.221688742	0.7783112583	1	0	0
1.8992	0.22379507	0.7762049301	1	0	0
1.8993	0.224567697	0.7754323032	1	0	0
1.8994	0.221330022	0.7786699779	1	0	0
1.8995	0.226545254	0.7734547461	1	0	0
1.8996	0.226223326	0.7737766740	1	0	0
1.8997	0.228283664	0.7717163355	1	0	0
1.8998	0.228440029	0.7715599706	1	0	0
1.8999	0.225928992	0.7740710081	1	0	0
1.9	0.224181383	0.7758186166	1	0	0
1.9001	0.227777778	0.7722222222	1	0	0
1.9002	0.228274467	0.7717255335	1	0	0
1.9003	0.226434879	0.7735651214	1	0	0
1.9004	0.226140545	0.7738594555	1	0	0
1.9005	0.224604489	0.7753955114	1	0	0
1.9006	0.227051141	0.7729488595	1	0	0
1.9007	0.226434879	0.7735651214	1	0	0

(*continued*)

Table 2. (*continued*)

Frequency (GHz)	BER	Reliability	BLER	Throughput (Mbps)	Throughput Fraction
1.9008	0.225257542	0.7747424577	1	0	0
1.9009	0.2261313466	0.7738686534	1	0	0
1.901	0.2242825607	0.7757174393	1	0	0
1.9011	0.2270051508	0.7729948492	1	0	0
1.9012	0.2223877851	0.7776122149	1	0	0
1.9013	0.2230132450	0.7769867550	1	0	0
1.9014	0.2217807211	0.7782192789	1	0	0
1.9015	0.2257358352	0.7742641648	1	0	0
1.9016	0.2253679176	0.7746320824	1	0	0
1.9017	0.2266280353	0.7733719647	1	0	0
1.9018	0.2224245769	0.7775754231	1	0	0
1.9019	0.2248712288	0.7751287712	1	0	0
1.902	0.2221854305	0.7778145695	1	0	0
1.9021	0.2279341428	0.7720658572	1	0	0
1.9022	0.2247332597	0.7752667403	1	0	0
1.9023	0.2241997792	0.7758002208	1	0	0
1.9024	0.2295529801	0.7704470199	1	0	0
1.9025	0.2277869757	0.7722130243	1	0	0
1.9026	0.2258738043	0.7741261957	1	0	0
1.9027	0.2237306843	0.7762693157	1	0	0
1.9028	0.2248436350	0.7751563650	1	0	0
1.9029	0.2241169978	0.7758830022	1	0	0
1.903	0.2252575423	0.7747424577	1	0	0
1.9031	0.2217899191	0.7782100809	1	0	0
1.9032	0.2284584253	0.7715415747	1	0	0
1.9033	0.2222958057	0.7777041943	1	0	0
1.9034	0.2212196468	0.7787803532	1	0	0
1.9035	0.2225625460	0.7774374540	1	0	0
1.9036	0.2151030169	0.7848969831	1	0	0
1.9037	0.2116721854	0.7883278146	1	0	0
1.9038	0.2059326711	0.7940673289	1	0	0
1.9039	0.2055463576	0.7944536424	1	0	0

(*continued*)

Table 2. (*continued*)

Frequency (GHz)	BER	Reliability	BLER	Throughput (Mbps)	Throughput Fraction
1.904	0.1941409124	0.8058590876	1	0	0
1.9041	0.1896707138	0.8103292862	1	0	0
1.9042	0.1809050773	0.8190949227	1	0	0
1.9043	0.1755886681	0.8244113319	1	0	0
1.9044	0.1664367182	0.8335632818	1	0	0
1.9045	0.1570732156	0.8429267844	1	0	0
1.9046	0.1551692421	0.8448307579	1	0	0
1.9047	0.1400570272	0.8599429728	1	0	0
1.9048	0.1363226637	0.8636773363	1	0	0
1.9049	0.1232431935	0.8767568065	0.99	2.25	0.828
1.905	0.1028421634	0.8971578366	0.95	11.25	4.139
1.9051	0.0810430464	0.9189569536	0.97	6.75	2.483
1.9052	0.0751103753	0.9248896247	0.93	16.79	6.177
1.9053	0.0611662987	0.9388337013	0.88	29.6	10.89
1.9054	0.0638980868	0.9361019132	0.83	44.49	16.369
1.9055	0.0554175865	0.9445824135	0.86	34.1	12.546
1.9056	0.0376655629	0.9623344371	0.65	91.75	33.756
1.9057	0.0246872701	0.9753127299	0.51	130.5	48.024
1.9058	0.0186626196	0.9813373804	0.48	138.8	51.082
1.9059	0.0153421634	0.9846578366	0.5	133.8	49.235
1.906	0.0103108904	0.9896891096	0.28	194.2	71.464
1.9061	0.0116813834	0.9883186166	0.36	172.1	63.311
1.9062	0.0068340692	0.9931659308	0.26	200.3	73.694
1.9063	0.0066317145	0.9933682855	0.26	199.8	73.503
1.9064	0.0097406181	0.9902593819	0.26	200.8	73.885
1.9065	0.0038447388	0.9961552612	0.16	227.5	83.694
1.9066	0.0008462104	0.9991537896	0.15	230.3	84.713
1.9067	0.0003127299	0.9996872701	0.13	235.8	86.751
1.9068	0.0001839588	0.9998160412	0.13	235.8	86.751
1.9069	0.0000758120	0.9999241880	0.1	244.1	89.809
1.907	0.0010301692	0.9989698308	0.12	238.6	87.77
1.9071	0.0000275938	0.9999724062	0.11	241.3	88.79
1.9072	0.0000156820	0.9999843180	0.09	246.9	90.828

(*continued*)

Table 2. (*continued*)

Frequency (GHz)	BER	Reliability	BLER	Throughput (Mbps)	Throughput Fraction
1.9073	0.0000267480	0.9999732520	0.1	244.1	89.809
1.9074	0.0000235980	0.9999764020	0.09	246.9	90.828
1.9075	0.0000243120	0.9999756880	0.09	246.9	90.828
1.9076	0.0000278910	0.9999721090	0.1	244.1	89.809
1.9077	0.0000367240	0.9999632760	0.09	246.9	90.828
1.9078	0.0000143780	0.9999856220	0.09	246.9	90.828
1.9079	0.0000227130	0.9999772870	0.09	246.9	90.828
1.908	0.0000157810	0.9999842190	0.09	246.9	90.828

It has been estimated that the region with maximum throughput and minimum BER, BLER denotes the used portion which specifies the absence of interference and will be applicable for future purposes and rest of the region will be unused portion having interference. The reliability of the signal can be evaluated from the value of BER also given in Table 2. The different values specified in Table 2 help us to create various charts given from Figs. 6, 7, 8 and 9. The used portion specifies the reliability of the signal. Here the difference between oscillator frequencies for 5G NR and 4G LTE is very large. But in the unused portion, the frequencies for 5G NR and 4G LTE are equal or mild difference. When the oscillator frequencies for 5G NR are varying from 1.892 GHz to 1.908 GHz, the maximum value of throughput obtained is 246.9 Mbps and the throughput fraction is 90.828. The minimum value of BER obtained is 0.0000157810, BLER is 0.09. Hence the reliability evaluated will be 0.9999842190. Different chart shows the variation of Reliability with frequency (Fig. 6), BLER with frequency (Fig. 7), Throughput with frequency (Fig. 8), Throughput Fraction with frequency (Fig. 9).

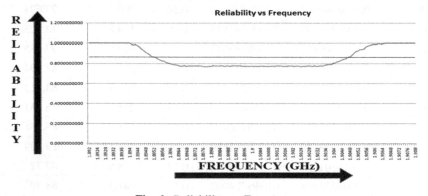

Fig. 6. Reliability vs. Frequency

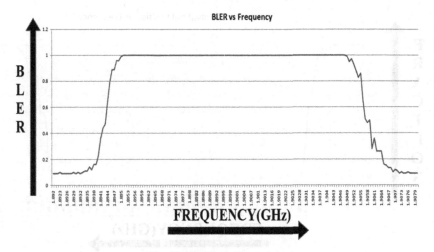

Fig. 7. BLER vs. Frequency

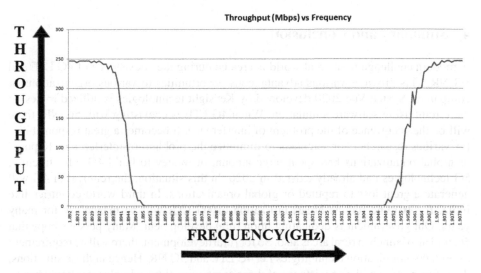

Fig. 8. Throughput vs. Frequency

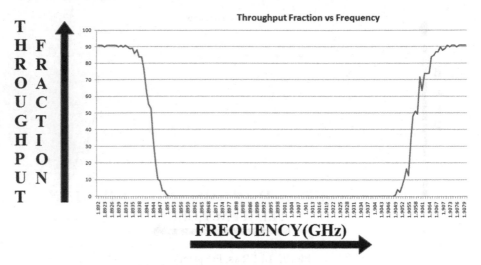

Fig. 9. Throughput Fraction vs. Frequency

4 Summary and Conclusion

A modern challenge in the real world is created during the coexistence of 4G LTE and 5G NR. This provides various advantageous opportunities to various organizations or companies. SystemVue 2020 developed by Keysight technologies is utilized to design the circuit using software simulation. When 4G LTE is coexisting with 5G NR, there will be the occurrence of the problem of interference. It becomes a great responsibility for various researchers or scientists to minimize the problem of interference. Reputed or global organizations had spent large amount of money to build 4G infrastructure. 5G technologies had already existed in 2020. In this situation, the removal of 4G will generate a great loss to reputed or global organizations. In third world countries like India, for extreme remote areas, utilization of 4G LTE will be mandatory for many years. Our government is dedicating upon rural development. Many persons hope that 5G will also launch in rural areas also. So for rural development, there will be requirement of both communication technologies i.e. 4G LTE and 5G NR. Hence in these situations, the infrastructure of the coexistence of these communication technologies should have a great demand. This coexistence creates the problem of interference. When the frequency of communication technologies (5G NR and 4G LTE) are more or less same, then the problem of interference will be originated. It has been realized that with the increase in frequency for both 4G LTE and 5G NR, there will be the decrease in BER, BLER and increase in throughput. With the help of Table 2, the hardware infrastructure regarding the coexistence of both communication technologies (4G LTE and 5G NR) can be developed.

Acknowledgement. The authors initiated to expect financial aid from Sikkim Manipal University to develop the advanced infrastructure in physical platform for Dr. TMA PAI Grant towards achieving 'Center of Excellence' in '5G IoT'.

References

1. Hajlaoui, E., Zaier, A., Khlifi, A., Ghodhbane, J., Hamed, M.B., Sbita, L.: 4G and 5G technologies: a comparative study. In: 2020 5th International Conference on Advanced Technologies for Signal and Image Processing (ATSIP), pp. 1–6 (2020). https://doi.org/10.1109/ATSIP49331. 2020.9231605

2. Barb, G., Otesteanu, M.: 4G/5G: a comparative study and overview on what to expect from 5G. In: 2020 43rd International Conference on Telecommunications and Signal Processing (TSP), pp. 37–40 (2020). https://doi.org/10.1109/TSP49548.2020.9163402

3. Jayaweera, S.K.: Cognitive radios and dynamic spectrum sharing. In: Signal Processing for Cognitive Radios, pp. 42–63. Wiley (2015). https://doi.org/10.1002/9781118824818.ch3

4. Bhattarai, S., Park, J.J., Gao, B., Bian, K., Lehr, W.: An overview of dynamic spectrum sharing: ongoing initiatives, challenges, and a roadmap for future research. IEEE Trans. Cogn. Commun. Networking 2(2), 110–128 (2016). https://doi.org/10.1109/TCCN.2016.2592921

5. Xu, L., Paila, T., Hansmann, W., Frank, M.: IPv6 based infrastructure for wireless IP in multi-radio environments with quality of service support. In: Proceedings LCN 2001. 26th Annual IEEE Conference on Local Computer Networks, pp. 278–286 (2001). https://doi.org/10.1109/LCN.2001.990797

6. Blasco-Serrano, R., Lv, J., Thobaben, R., Jorswieck, E., Kliks, A., Skoglund, M.: Comparison of underlay and overlay spectrum sharing strategies in MISO cognitive channels. In: 2012 7th International ICST Conference on Cognitive Radio Oriented Wireless Networks and Communications (CROWNCOM), pp. 224–229 (2012). https://doi.org/10.4108/icst.crowncom.2012. 248283

7. Zhao, Q., Sadler, B.M.: A survey of dynamic spectrum access. IEEE Signal Process. Mag. 24(3), 79–89 (2007). https://doi.org/10.1109/MSP.2007.361604

8. Bagheri, H., et al.: 5G NR-V2X: toward connected and cooperative autonomous driving. IEEE Commun. Stan. Mag. 5(1), 48–54 (2021). https://doi.org/10.1109/MCOMSTD.001.2000069

9. Garcia, M.H.C., et al.: A tutorial on 5G NR V2X communications. IEEE Commun. Surv. Tutorials 23, 1972–2026 (2021). https://doi.org/10.1109/COMST.2021.3057017

Exploring the Future of Edge Computing: Advantages, Limitations, and Opportunities

Aneesh Pradeep(✉)

New Uzbekistan University, Tashkent, Uzbekistan
pradeep.aneesh@gmail.com

Abstract. Edge computing is a distributed computing paradigm that enables data processing and analysis to be performed closer to the source of the data rather than in centralized data centers. By bringing computing resources and intelligence closer to the edge of the network, edge computing can provide lower latency, higher bandwidth, and improved privacy and security. Due to the proliferation of Internet of Things (IoT) devices and the demand for real-time analytics and decision-making in several industries, including healthcare, smart cities, and industrial automation, this technology has recently attracted a lot of attention. However, there are also significant obstacles to adopting edge computing, including resource limitations, heterogeneity, scalability, and fault tolerance. As a result, this chapter focuses on resolving these issues and realizing edge computing's full potential.

Keywords: Edge Computing · Edge Computing Architecture · Edge Scalability

1 Introduction

Edge computing has become a promising paradigm in recent years that enables data processing and analysis to be done closer to the data source rather than in centralized data centers. Edge computing has expanded due to the proliferation of Internet of Things (IoT) devices and the demand for real-time analytics and decision-making in various industries, including healthcare, smart cities, and industrial automation. Edge computing is not entirely a new idea; it has existed for a long time in various contexts, including content delivery networks (CDNs), distributed sensor networks, and mobile ad hoc networks (MANETs). However, there has recently been a resurgence in edge computing due to the proliferation of IoT devices and the rising need for real-time analytics and decision-making. As a result, the concept has developed into a more thorough and sophisticated approach designed to address the difficulties associated with data processing at the network's edge. Edge computing has the potential to provide several advantages, including decreased latency, increased efficiency, and improved security and privacy. Edge computing enables faster data processing, better network bandwidth utilization, and lower data transfer and storage costs by moving computing resources closer to the network's edge.

2   Overview of Edge Computing

Due to the rise in Internet of Things (IoT) devices and the demand for real-time analytics and decision-making across various industries, including healthcare, smart cities, and industrial automation, edge computing technology has attracted much attention in recent years. The device, edge, and cloud layers are the three main layers that comprise the edge computing architecture [1]. The sensors, actuators, and other IoT devices that collect and transmit data make up the device layer. While the cloud layer offers extra computing resources and storage for complex tasks that demand more processing power, the edge layer is made up of edge servers and gateways that process and analyze the data close to the source. Edge computing has a number of advantages over standard cloud computing, including lower latency, enhanced safety and confidentiality, and increased efficiency. Edge computing can enable faster response times by analyzing and processing data more closely to its source. [2], lower network bandwidth usage, and lower data transfer and storage costs. However, edge computing poses several challenges, including resource constraints, heterogeneity, scalability, and fault tolerance. These challenges must be addressed for edge computing to achieve its full potential. Researchers are investigating new technologies and standards, such as 5G, edge AI, and fog computing, to address these challenges and improve the performance of edge computing systems.

2.1   Edge Computing vs. Cloud Computing

Edge and cloud computing are distinct computing paradigms that differ in several ways. While cloud computing relies on centralized data centers to perform computation and data storage, edge computing brings computation and data storage closer to the data source at the network's edge. The most significant difference between edge computing and cloud computing is their location. In cloud computing, data is stored and processed in centralized data centers that are typically located far away from the source of data [3]. In contrast, edge computing enables data processing and analysis to be performed closer to the data source, often at the network's edge, such as edge servers, gateways, or IoT devices. This proximity to the source of data results in reduced latency and improved real-time decision-making capabilities. The second difference is the amount of data that needs to be transmitted. In cloud computing, all the data is transmitted to the centralized data center for processing and analysis. This results in high network bandwidth usage and increased latency. On the other hand, edge computing only transmits relevant data to the cloud, reducing the amount of data that needs to be transmitted and processed in the cloud. This reduces network bandwidth usage and improves response times. In cloud computing, data is transmitted and stored in a centralized location, which increases the risk of security breaches and data privacy violations. In edge computing, data is processed and analyzed closer to the source, reducing the risk of security breaches and privacy violations. The scalability of edge computing and cloud computing is different [4]. Cloud computing can scale up or down its resources depending on the computing needs, whereas the size and capacity of the edge devices typically limit edge computing resources [5]. This limitation poses challenges for applications that require significant computing resources.

2.2 Advantages and Challenges

Reduced latency, enhanced security and privacy, reduced network bandwidth usage, and improved efficiency are just a few benefits of edge computing. Resource limitations, heterogeneity, scalability, fault tolerance, data management, and security and privacy are just some of its difficulties. Benefits of edge computing:

- Reduced latency: With edge computing, data processing, and analysis are performed closer to the source of data, resulting in lower latency and faster response times [6]. This is particularly important for applications that require real-time decision-making, such as industrial automation, smart cities, and healthcare.
- Improved security and privacy: Because data is processed and analyzed closer to the source, edge computing can improve security and privacy by lowering the likelihood of data breaches and privacy violations [7].
- Lower network bandwidth usage: By processing data at the edge, edge computing reduces the amount of data that needs to be transmitted to the cloud, resulting in lower network bandwidth usage and reduced costs [8].
- Increased efficiency: Edge computing can increase efficiency by easing the burden on centralized data centers and facilitating more effective use of computing resources
- .

Challenges of edge computing:

- Resource constraints: Edge devices, such as sensors and gateways, often have limited processing power, memory, and storage capacity, posing significant challenges for data processing and analysis [10].
- Heterogeneity: It is challenging to develop a standardized platform for edge computing because edge devices come in various shapes and configurations.
- Scalability: Edge computing resources are constrained by the edge devices' capabilities, making it difficult to scale them up or down to satisfy shifting demands.
- Fault tolerance: The harsh environments that edge devices frequently inhabit, such as industrial sites or remote locations, can cause hardware failures and downtime [11].

- Data management: To ensure that data is accurate and consistent, edge computing requires careful data management, including data transfer, storage, and processing.
- Security and privacy: Edge devices are often connected to the internet, making them vulnerable to security breaches and privacy violations [12].

2.3 Related Work

In recent years, there has been a significant amount of edge computing research and development. Here are some instances of related edge computing research:

- Fog computing: Fog computing is an edge computing that extends cloud computing to the network's edge. It enables data processing and analysis to be performed on devices closer to the data source, such as routers, switches, and gateways.
- Edge analytics: Edge analytics involves performing data analytics and processing at the network's edge, enabling real-time decision-making and reducing the need for data transmission to a centralized cloud. It has been applied in various domains, such as industrial automation, healthcare, and smart cities [13].
- Mobile edge computing: Mobile edge computing is a type of edge computing that focuses on mobile devices, such as smartphones and tablets [14]. It enables data processing and analysis to be performed on the device itself, reducing the need for data transmission to a centralized cloud.
- Edge AI: Edge AI involves deploying artificial intelligence (AI) algorithms and models at the network's edge, enabling real-time decision-making and reducing the need for data transmission to a centralized cloud "Fig. 1". It has been used in a variety of fields, including driverless vehicles, factory automation, and smart buildings.
- Edge security: Edge security focuses on securing edge devices and networks against cyber-attacks and vulnerabilities. It involves deploying security measures at the network's edge, such as encryption, access control, and threat detection.

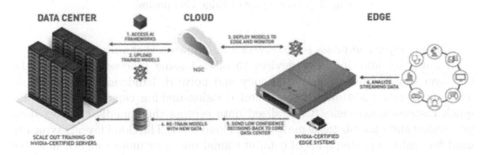

Fig. 1. Lifecycle of an edge AI application

These approaches are addressing various challenges in edge computing, such as reducing latency, improving efficiency, and enhancing security and privacy.

3   Edge Computing Architecture

Edge computing architecture is a distributed computing paradigm that allows data processing and analysis to occur closer to the data source, at the network's edge. It entails deploying computing resources at the network's edge, such as processing power, memory, and memory, commonly on routers, gateways, and edge servers

Edge computing architecture typically consists of three layers: the edge layer, the fog layer, and the cloud layer. The edge layer is the outermost layer, comprising edge devices that collect data from sensors and other sources. The fog layer is an intermediate layer that performs local data processing and analysis on the edge devices, reducing the amount of data that needs to be transmitted to the cloud. The cloud layer is the centralized layer that performs advanced data processing and analysis on the data received from the fog layer. The edge layer is made up of edge gadgets that gather environmental data, like sensors, actuators, and gateways. Completing complex data processing and analysis tasks on edge devices can be difficult because they typically have the limited processing power, memory, and storage. In order to preprocess and filter data before sending it to the fog layer, edge devices are frequently used (Fig. 2).

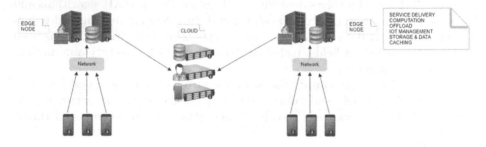

Fig. 2. Three layers of Edge Computing

The fog layer comprises edge servers and gateways that process and analyze local data. By allowing edge devices to offload some processing tasks to the fog layer, fog computing lowers latency and network bandwidth consumption. The fog layer's real-time analytics and decision-making capabilities allow for quick responses to events. Centralized data centers that handle complex data processing and analysis tasks make up the cloud layer. The cloud layer is typically used for tasks requiring a lot of computational power or unique algorithms, like machine learning and artificial intelligence.

3.1   Communication Protocols

To enable communication between edge devices, edge servers, fog nodes, and cloud servers, communication protocols are used in edge computing. These protocols ensure that information can be transferred securely, consistently, and effectively between devices and network nodes. Some of the most popular communication protocols for edge computing are listed below:

- Message Queuing Telemetry Transport (MQTT): MQTT is a lightweight, publish-subscribe protocol designed for use in IoT applications. It enables devices to send messages to each other or to a centralized server, allowing data to be transmitted efficiently and reliably [16].
- Constrained Application Protocol (CoAP): CoAP is another lightweight protocol designed for use in IoT applications [17]. It enables devices to communicate with each other and with the cloud, using a RESTful architecture.
- Advanced Message Queuing Protocol (AMQP): AMQP is a messaging protocol that enables devices and servers to exchange messages in a reliable, secure, and efficient manner [18]. It supports a range of messaging patterns, including publish-subscribe and request-response.
- Hypertext Transfer Protocol (HTTP): HTTP is a widely used protocol for transmitting data over the internet. It is used extensively in cloud computing and is also used in edge computing for communication between edge devices, edge servers, and cloud servers.
- Simple Object Access Protocol (SOAP): SOAP is a messaging protocol that enables devices and servers to exchange XML-based messages [19]. It is used in enterprise applications and is also used in edge computing for communication between devices and servers.

MQTT, CoAP, AMQP, HTTP, and SOAP are some of the most common communication protocols used in edge computing, each with its own advantages and limitations. The choice of protocol depends on the application's specific requirements, such as latency, reliability, security, and efficiency.

3.2   Networking Topologies

Different topologies are used in edge computing, depending on the application's specific requirements. A star topology connects devices to a central hub, such as an edge server or gateway [20]. All communication between devices is routed through the hub, enabling efficient network management and monitoring. This topology is commonly used in edge computing applications where a few devices need to be connected to a central server. Peer-to-peer connections between devices create a self-healing network in a mesh topology. In edge computing applications where numerous devices must be connected but there is no central server, this topology is frequently used. Devices are interconnected in a closed loop when using a ring topology. All devices receive the data because it is sent in a single direction around the loop. This topology is frequently used in edge computing applications when devices need to be connected in a circle. A hybrid topology combines two or more different topologies. For example, a star-mesh hybrid topology might be used in an edge computing application where devices are connected to an edge server in a star configuration while also being connected in a mesh configuration. The choice of networking topology in edge computing depends on various factors, such as the number of devices, the distance between devices, the bandwidth requirements, and the redundancy requirements. Each topology has its own advantages and disadvantages regarding scalability, reliability, and performance. Choosing the suitable topology for the application is crucial to enabling the network to meet the specific requirements of the application.

3.3   Security Considerations

Edge computing involves processing and storing data closer to the source, which brings numerous benefits such as reduced latency and improved scalability. However, this approach also raises several security concerns that must be addressed to ensure the confidentiality, integrity, and availability of data. Here are some of the key security considerations in edge computing:

- Authentication and Authorization: Edge devices and servers should be authenticated and authorized to access the network and data. This involves implementing secure mechanisms for identity and access management, such as multifactor authentication and role-based access control.
- Data Encryption: Data should be encrypted both in transit and at rest to prevent unauthorized access and data breaches. This involves using strong encryption algorithms, such as AES or RSA, to encrypt the data and secure key management systems to ensure the integrity of the encryption keys.
- Network Segmentation: Edge networks should be segmented to limit access to sensitive data and prevent lateral movement in the event of a security breach. This involves implementing network segmentation using firewalls, VLANs, and access control lists.
- Device Management: Edge devices should be managed securely to prevent unauthorized access and data breaches. This involves implementing secure device management protocols, such as Device Management Protocol (DMP) and Lightweight Device Management (LwM2M).
- Threat Detection and Response: Edge networks should be monitored continuously for potential security threats and vulnerabilities. This involves implementing security information and event management (SIEM) systems and security analytics tools to detect and respond to security incidents.
- Physical Security: Edge devices and servers should be physically secured to prevent theft, tampering, or destruction. This involves implementing physical security measures such as access control, surveillance, and intrusion detection systems.

By implementing robust security measures such as authentication and authorization, data encryption, network segmentation, device management, threat detection, and physical security, organizations can mitigate the security risks and achieve the full potential of edge computing.

4   Applications and Use Cases

Edge computing is becoming increasingly popular in a variety of industries due to its ability to process data in real-time and reduce latency. This technology is being used in many different applications, from manufacturing and transportation to healthcare and smart cities. Here are some examples of the applications and use cases of edge computing:

- Industrial Internet of Things (IIoT): Edge computing is used extensively in IIoT applications to process sensor data and enable real-time decision-making. For example, edge computing is used in manufacturing to monitor and analyze production lines, detect anomalies, and optimize machine performance. In the oil and gas industry, edge computing monitors remote drilling sites and performs predictive maintenance on equipment.
- Autonomous Vehicles: For autonomous vehicles to operate safely and effectively, edge computing is necessary. Edge computing lowers the risk of accidents by processing data from sensors and cameras in real time and identifying potential road hazards.
- Healthcare: Edge computing is used in healthcare to improve patient care and lower costs. For instance, wearable technology and sensors can gather data on vital signs and transmit it to edge devices for processing and analysis, allowing for in-depth real-time patient monitoring. Additionally, edge computing can enable remote patient diagnosis and care, lowering the need for hospital visits and enhancing access to care in rural areas.
- Smart Cities: By facilitating in-the-moment data analysis and decision-making, edge computing is used to increase cities' effectiveness and sustainability. For instance, edge computing can process data from cameras and sensors in traffic management to improve traffic flow and ease congestion. By examining data from smart meters and sensors, edge computing in energy management can optimize energy use and lower waste.
- Retail: Edge computing is being used to enhance the customer experience in retail by enabling real-time data analysis and personalized recommendations. For example, edge computing can analyze customer behavior and preferences in a store to offer personalized promotions and product recommendations. In supply chain management, edge computing can track inventory in real time and optimize logistics operations.
- Gaming: Cloud gaming is made possible by edge computing, where games are streamed to edge devices for processing and display. As the processing is done on the edge devices, gamers can play high-quality games without the need for expensive gaming hardware [21].
- Telecommunications: Edge computing can be used in the telecommunications sector to enhance the performance and dependability of various services, including voice over IP, the internet of things (IoT), video streaming, and other applications. Edge computing reduces latency, boosts network efficiency, and improves security by locating computing resources closer to the end users. Edge computing, for instance, can be utilized to cache well-liked

content closer to end users, reducing the need to fetch it from a distant data center and enhancing user experience. Additionally, edge computing can make real-time analytics and automation possible in the network, enabling telecom operators to deliver services better by quickly identifying and addressing network problems.

5   Challenges and Issues

Although edge computing offers numerous benefits, such as reduced latency and improved efficiency, it also presents several challenges and issues that must be addressed. These include the need for robust security measures to protect edge devices and data, the complexity of managing and deploying edge infrastructure, and the potential for data fragmentation and inconsistency.

5.1   Resource Constraints

When deploying and managing edge infrastructure, edge devices are typically small and have constrained memory, processing power, and battery life. Data fragmentation and inconsistency may result from resource limitations on the amount of data that can be processed and stored on edge devices. Furthermore, due to limited resources, it may be challenging to implement adequate security measures to safeguard edge devices and data. These measures often call for a lot of processing power and memory. Furthermore, resource limitations may make adding new devices to a network challenging without overtaxing existing ones, which may restrict the scalability of edge computing systems. This can be particularly difficult when edge devices are placed in harsh or remote locations with insufficient power and connectivity. Researchers and business experts are investigating novel approaches to edge computing that can optimize resource usage and enhance scalability to address these challenges. For instance, resource-intensive tasks like machine learning and data analytics can be offloaded to edge devices by utilizing cloud resources. New edge architectures can also enable distributed data processing and lessen the load on individual edge devices. Examples include edge cloud computing and federated learning.

5.2   Heterogeneity

Different edge devices and platforms may have different architectures, protocols, and capabilities, creating significant interoperability and compatibility issues. For example, edge devices may have different processing capabilities, memory, and storage capacities, making it difficult to implement consistent and scalable data processing and storage strategies. Similarly, different edge platforms may have different communication protocols and security measures, making integrating and managing diverse edge networks challenging. Moreover, the heterogeneity of edge devices and platforms can pose challenges to application development and deployment. The complexity and time required for developing and deploying applications that can operate seamlessly across various edge devices and platforms can restrict the scalability and flexibility of edge computing systems. In order to overcome these challenges, researchers and industry professionals are investigating novel approaches to edge computing that can promote compatibility and interoperability across various edge devices and platforms. Some of these tactics include the use of open-source platforms, modular architectures that can accommodate the integration of a range of edge platforms and devices, and standardization of communication protocols.

5.3   Scalability

Since quickly scaling up or down the infrastructure is necessary to meet the demands of real-time applications, scalability is a crucial issue in edge computing. However, scaling up can be extremely difficult due to the distributed nature of edge computing and the numerous devices involved. It becomes more challenging to control and orchestrate the data flow between devices as a network's edge devices multiply. The flexibility and scalability of edge computing systems may be constrained by the complexity and time required to integrate new edge devices into an already-established network. Demand for real-time data processing and analysis continues to grow; edge computing systems must scale up or down quickly and efficiently to meet changing demands. This requires the ability to allocate resources dynamically across different edge devices and platforms, which can be challenging in a distributed and heterogeneous environment.

5.4   Fault Tolerance

Fault tolerance is a crucial issue in edge computing, as the distributed nature of the infrastructure and the large number of devices involved can make it vulnerable to various types of failures, such as network outages, device malfunctions, and cyber attacks. These failures can lead to significant disruptions in data processing and analysis, as well as data loss and security breaches [22]. Implementing efficient fault tolerance mechanisms can be difficult due to the dynamic and heterogeneous nature of edge computing. For instance, more than traditional fault tolerance techniques like redundancy and backup may be required in a distributed and heterogeneous environment because they may demand a lot of overhead and resources. The application of advanced data replication and synchronization techniques can guarantee data consistency and availability, as well as the use of adaptive and dynamic fault tolerance mechanisms that can detect and mitigate failures in real-time.

6   Future Directions and Opportunities

As edge computing continues to evolve and expand, there are many development and research opportunities that can further enhance the capabilities and applications of this technology. From improving resource management and security to enabling new types of applications and services, there are many areas where researchers and industry professionals can explore and innovate.

6.1   Emerging Technologies and Standards

As edge computing continues to evolve and mature, there are many emerging technologies and standards that are shaping the future of this technology. These technologies and standards are enabling new capabilities and applications, as well as enhancing the scalability, security, and reliability of edge systems. One emerging technology in edge computing is the use of artificial intelligence and machine learning to enable advanced data processing and analysis at the edge. This can enable real-time decision-making and insights, as well as reduce the need for sending data to centralized cloud servers for analysis. Blockchain can provide secure and decentralized data storage and processing capabilities for edge devices. This can enhance the security and privacy of edge systems, as well as enable new types of applications and services. Development of 5G networks is also enabling new opportunities for edge computing [23], by providing high-speed and low-latency connectivity for edge devices. This can enable new types of applications, such as virtual and augmented reality, as well as enhance the performance and scalability of edge systems. There are several initiatives and organizations working to develop standards for edge computing, such as the Edge Computing Consortium, the Industrial Internet Consortium, and the OpenFog Consortium. These standards can help to ensure interoperability, security, and scalability of edge systems, as well as enable new levels of collaboration and innovation in the field of edge computing.

6.2   Integration with Cloud Computing

Integration of edge computing with cloud computing is a growing trend in distributed computing, as it enables organizations to leverage the benefits of both edge and cloud technologies. In the future, we can expect to see several trends in integrating edge computing with cloud computing. A hybrid cloud-edge computing model will emerge, where data processing and storage will be performed at the edge and the cloud, depending on the specific needs of the application [24]. This will enable organizations to achieve the benefits of both edge and cloud technologies while optimizing performance, security, and cost. With the growth of IoT devices and edge computing, we can expect to see an increase in the movement of data from edge devices to the cloud for further processing and analysis. This will require new techniques for data movement and management, as well as optimized network infrastructure and protocols. We can expect to see the emergence of edge computing as a service (ECaaS), where cloud providers will offer edge computing services to their customers. This will enable organizations to easily deploy and manage edge devices and applications while leveraging the scalability and reliability of cloud infrastructure. Cloud services will increasingly incorporate edge computing capabilities to enhance their performance, reliability, and security. For example, cloud providers can use edge devices to perform real-time data analysis and processing, reducing cloud services' latency and bandwidth requirements.

6.3   Edge Computing and Artificial Intelligence

Combining edge computing with artificial intelligence (AI) is a rapidly growing area of research and development, as it enables organizations to leverage the benefits of both technologies. In the future, we can expect several trends in the combination of edge computing and AI, including:

– Edge AI Chips: We expect to see the emergence of specialized edge AI chips that can perform advanced processing and analysis at the edge. These chips will be designed to be energy-efficient and optimized for specific AI applications, such as computer vision and natural language processing.
– Edge-to-Cloud AI Models: With the growth of edge computing and IoT devices, we can expect to see the development of AI models that can run both at the edge and in the cloud. This will enable organizations to leverage the benefits of both edge and cloud computing while optimizing performance, security, and cost.
– Edge AI-as-a-Service: We can expect to see the emergence of edge AI-as-a-service (EAaaS), where cloud providers will offer edge AI services to their customers [25]. This will enable organizations to quickly deploy and manage edge AI applications while leveraging the scalability and reliability of cloud infrastructure.
– Edge AI for Real-Time Decision Making: Edge AI can enable real-time decision-making capabilities in autonomous vehicles, smart cities, and industrial automation applications. In the future, we can expect to see the development of new edge AI applications that can enable faster and more accurate decision-making in real-time scenarios (Fig. 3).

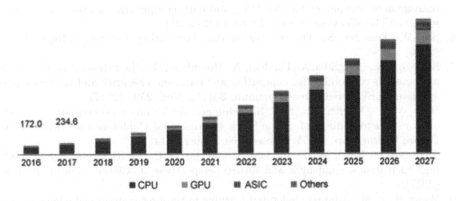

172.0   234.6

2016 2017 2018 2019 2020 2021 2022 2023 2024 2025 2026 2027

■ CPU   ■ GPU   ■ ASIC   ■ Others

Fig. 3. Asia Pacific Edge AI chips market size 2016 -2027(USD Million)

7   Conclusion

Edge computing is expanding quickly and revolutionizing how we process and analyze data. The chapter discussed the architecture and networking topologies, emphasized the benefits and challenges, and provided examples of use cases and emerging technologies. The chapter also provided an overview of the vision and challenges of edge computing. Additional study is required in a number of areas related to edge computing, such as security and privacy, network optimization, and real-time decision-making abilities. Additionally, there is a need for more research into how edge computing can be combined with other technologies like AI, cloud computing, and IoT. As new technologies and standards emerge, it will be important to continue to evaluate and adapt the architecture and networking topologies to ensure that they are optimized for edge computing. While there are challenges and limitations, ongoing research and development are helping to address these issues and pave the way for a more efficient and intelligent future.

References

1. Xiong, Y., Sun, Y., Xing, L., Huang, Y.: Extend cloud to edge with kubeedge. In: 2018 IEEE/ACM Symposium on Edge Computing (SEC), pp. 373–377. IEEE (October 2018)
2. Garg, S., Singh, A., Batra, S., Kumar, N., Yang, L.T.: UAV-empowered edge computing environment for cyber-threat detection in smart vehicles. IEEE Netw. **32**(3), 42–51 (2018)
3. Zhou, Y., Zhang, D., Xiong, N.: Post-cloud computing paradigms: a survey and comparison. Tsinghua Sci. Technol. **22**(6), 714–732 (2017)
4. Liu, J., Wan, J., Zeng, B., Wang, Q., Song, H., Qiu, M.: A scalable and quick-response software defined vehicular network assisted by mobile edge computing. IEEE Commun. Mag. **55**(7), 94–100 (2017)
5. Mijuskovic, A., Chiumento, A., Bemthuis, R., Aldea, A., Havinga, P.: Resource management techniques for cloud/fog and edge computing: an evaluation framework and classification. Sensors **21**(5), 1832 (2021)
6. Shi, W., Dustdar, S.: The promise of edge computing. Computer **49**(5), 78–81 (2016)
7. Shirazi, S.N., Gouglidis, A., Farshad, A., Hutchison, D.: The extended cloud: review and analysis of mobile edge computing and fog from a security and resilience perspective. IEEE J. Sel. Areas Commun. **35**(11), 2586–2595 (2017)
8. Beck, M. T., Werner, M., Feld, S., Schimper, S.: Mobile edge computing: a taxonomy. In Proceedings of of the Sixth International Conference on Advances in Future Internet, pp. 48–55. Citeseer (November 2014)
9. Shahzadi, S., Iqbal, M., Dagiuklas, T., Qayyum, Z.U.: Multi-access edge computing: open issues, challenges and future perspectives. J. Cloud Comput. **6**, 1–13 (2017)
10. Wang, S., et al.: Adaptive federated learning in resource constrained edge computing systems. IEEE J. Sel. Areas Commun. **37**(6), 1205–1221 (2019)
11. Wang, C., Gill, C., Lu, C.: Frame: fault tolerant and real-time messaging for edge computing. In: 2019 IEEE 39th International Conference on Distributed Computing Systems (ICDCS). IEEE (2019)
12. Yi, S., Qin, Z., Li, Q.: Security and privacy issues of fog computing: a survey. In: Xu, K., Zhu, H. (eds.) WASA 2015. LNCS, vol. 9204, pp. 685–695. Springer, Cham (2015). https://doi.org/10.1007/978-3-319-21837-3_67

13. Yi, S., Hao, Z., Zhang, Q., Zhang, Q., Shi, W., Li, Q.: Lavea: latency-aware video analytics on edge computing platform. In Proceedings of the Second ACM/IEEE Symposium on Edge Computing, pp. 1–13 (October 2017)

14. Siriwardhana, Y., Porambage, P., Liyanage, M., Ylianttila, M.: A survey on mobile augmented reality with 5G mobile edge computing: architectures, applications, and technical aspects. IEEE Commun. Surv. Tutorials **23**(2), 1160–1192 (2021)

15. Debauche, O., Mahmoudi, S., Mahmoudi, S.A., Manneback, P., Lebeau, F.: A new edge architecture for ai-iot services deployment. Proc. Comput. Sci. **175**, 10–19 (2020)

16. da Cruz, M.A., Rodrigues, J.J., Paradello, E.S., Lorenz, P., Solic, P., Albuquerque, V.H.C.: A proposal for bridging the message queuing telemetry transport protocol to HTTP on IoT solutions. In: 2018 3rd International Conference on Smart and Sustainable Technologies (SpliTech), pp. 1–5. IEEE (June 2018)

17. Chen, X.: Constrained application protocol for internet of things (2014). www.cse. wustl.edu/jain/cse574-14/ftp/coap

18. Vinoski, S.: Advanced message queuing protocol. IEEE Internet Comput. **10**(6), 87–89 (2006)

19. Box, D., et al.: Simple object access protocol (SOAP) 1.1 (2000)

20. Xiang, B., Elias, J., Martignon, F., Di Nitto, E.: A dataset for mobile edge computing network topologies. Data Brief **39**, 107557 (2021)

21. Zhang, X., et al.: Improving cloud gaming experience through mobile edge computing. IEEE Wireless Commun. **26**(4), 178–183 (2019)

22. Khan, W. Z., Ahmed, E., Hakak, S., Yaqoob, I., Ahmed, A.: Edge computing: a survey, future generation computer systems (2019)

23. Hassan, N., Yau, K.-L.A., Wu, C.: Edge computing in 5G: a review. IEEE Access **7**, 127276–127289 (2019)

24. Qi, Q., Tao, F.: A smart manufacturing service system based on edge computing, fog computing, and cloud computing. IEEE Access **7**, 86769–86777 (2019)

25. Zhang, W., Zeadally, S., Li, W., Zhang, H., Hou, J., Leung, V.C.: Edge AI as a service: configurable model deployment and delay-energy optimization with result quality constraints. IEEE Trans. Cloud Comput. (2022)

Fake Product Review Detection Using Machine Learning

B. V. Santhosh Krishna[1]([✉]), B. Rajalakshmi[1], M. Vijay[2], Donapati Jaswanth Reddy[1],
Bavanasi Abhishek[1], and C. Ashwini Reddy[1]

[1] New Horizon College of Engineering, Bengaluru, India
santhoshkrishna1987@gmail.com
[2] Kalasalingam Academy of Research and Education, Srivilliputhur, Tamil Nadu, India

Abstract. Advancement of technology has surely made our life easier and conve-
nient and E-commerce systems are one of the best gifts of technology. We can now
have anything from any part of the world with just a few taps on our smart devices.
Many E-commerce sites have gained popularity not just in urbanized areas but also
rural areas in many parts of the world. We can have a product or service delivered
in no time without stepping out and at the comfort of our own home. Also, we
have wide range of products and brands which gives us number of options to make
a perfect choice. When it comes to choosing a product, we definitely go through
the reviews given by the customers who have used the products. But how do we
know if they genuine ones? Technology, having it's own advantages, can also be
used for frauds. One such thing is providing fake reviews on products to attract
potential customers and gain popularity amongst them in order to increase sales.
Thus, identifying the fake reviews in an essential thing to do and research should
be effectively done in this particular area. This chapter gives us an approach which
uses machine learning algorithms to tackle this problem. Along with extracting
the characteristics of the reviews it also helps us identify the behavior of the users
who leave a review by using many algorithms like K-Nearest Neighbor, regression and NLP. In addition to these, this chapter is based on data mining to extract
meaningful information. Hence this chapter provides us with a solution on how
we can use machine learning to detect fake reviews while also taking behavioral
patterns of the reviewers into consideration.

Keywords: Fake Reviews · Detection · Supervised Methods · Unsupervised
Methods · Automated · Original · Product reviews

1 Introduction

In this era of arising technology, we are just one tap away to have everything we want.
It is amazing how we can order anything online. Online shopping made it easier to shop
any product from any part of the world, be it a local made one or from a luxury brand.
E-commerce websites [9] are a huge hit and are of a great help when it comes to having
wide variety of styles. In addition, when it comes to decision making in buying a product
or service, people mostly rely on customer reviews. Customer reviews are feedbacks of

© The Author(s), under exclusive license to Springer Nature Switzerland AG 2023
R. N. Shaw et al. (Eds.): ICACIS 2023, CCIS 1921, pp. 210–218, 2023.
https://doi.org/10.1007/978-3-031-45124-9_16

the buyers who have already bought and used a product. People blindly believe the reviews and decide whether to buy a product or not. However, what if the reviews are fake? Yes, it is possible to generate fake reviews on products to attract a customer to buy the product and to gain popularity. Unfortunately, many sellers use third parties, which generate fake reviews so that their products are sold. If we want to have honest and genuine reviews of the customer, it is very important for us to detect the fake ones first [1].

In addition, we can tackle this problem using machine learning. This chapter applies ML classifiers to detect reviews, which are fake. Generally, web-mining techniques are used to find useful information. Content mining, which is also a web-mining task, is also used for extracting relevant content. Machine learning algorithms can use sentiment analysis which helps us determine if they are positive or negative. If huge number of reviews have a similar sentiment then it can be considered fake. Natural language processing (NLP) is used to detect patterns that are most common in reviews using common keywords. Along with this, user behavior is also to be considered to make a decision. For example, if there are more number of reviews posted in a short span then it could be fake. Thus making it possible to eliminate misleading reviews and have only authentic opinions on a product which makes it easier for us with the decision making.

2 Literature Survey

The impact of online reviews as increased with the increase of use of online products and viewing a review and knowing the opinion of previous user to be sure about the product. As this increased, practicing of unethical ways to reach a customer through fake reviews also increased Consumer electronics reviews are analyzed in this article to identify fake reviews. (1) Scraping techniques were used to classify fake reviews in four cities. (2) A feature framework for fake review detection was defined. (3) Develop a fake review classification method based on the proposed framework. (4) A statistical analysis showed that the Ada Boost classifier was the most effective [2]. Online marketplaces have become ubiquitous due to the ease of finding sellers and the trust they facilitate through reputation and feedback systems. Reputation plays an essential role in trust and trade, but it is also susceptible to bias in feedback and reputation systems. It suggests ways to address these problems and suggest directions for future research [3]. Many people around the world use World Wide Web to know information upload and download data. As this data increases, it is becoming difficult to dig patterns and understand patterns. It is very difficult to perform algorithm to extract user queried information is hard. They concluded by telling that using different techniques, tools, approaches, algorithms for discover information from huge bulks of data over the web performed well [4]. With development of web 2.0 Online, reviews have become a valuable resource for decision making, but they also bring with them a curse of deceptive opinion spam. In recent years, fake review detection has attracted significant attention, but most review sites still do not publicly filter fake reviews. Yelp is an exception, and this work attempts to find out what it is doing by analyzing its filtered reviews. They talk about two main approaches to filtering: supervised and unsupervised learning and in terms of features used they talk about linguistic features and behavioral features. They concluded by telling that analysis and experimental results allow us to postulate that Yelp's filtering is reasonable and its filtering algorithm seems to be correlated with abnormal spamming behaviors [5]. It is common for e-commerce sites to allow customers to write reviews of products they have purchased, which provides useful information. However, this can also result in spam as misinformed or malicious reviews are posted since no study has been conducted on review spam and spam detection, the purpose of this chapter is to investigate the issue [6].

3 Methodologies

ML Classifiers

a. **Naïve Bayes**
Naive Bayes algorithm is a probabilistic machine-learning algorithm based on Bayes' theorem. It is com mostly used for classification tasks, such as spam filtering or sentiment analysis.

$$P(A|B) = \frac{P(B|A)P(A)}{P(B)}$$

The algorithm works by calculating the probability of a data point belonging to each class based on the features of the data point. It assumes that the features are conditionally independent of each other, which means that the presence of one feature does not affect the probability of the presence of another feature. This assumption is known as the "naive" assumption, which is where the name "Naive Bayes" comes from. The algorithm is trained using a labeled dataset, which means that each data point is labeled with its corresponding class. During training, the algorithm calculates the prior probability of each class, which is the probability of a data point belonging to that class regardless of its features. It also calculates the conditional probability of each feature given the class, which is the probability of observing that feature given the class. To classify a new data point, the algorithm calculates the posterior probability of each class given the features of the data point, using Bayes' theorem. The class with the highest posterior probability is then assigned as the predicted class for the data point. Naive Bayes algorithm is simple and efficient, and it can be trained quickly even with large datasets. However, the naive assumption of feature independence may not hold true in all cases, and this can lead to suboptimal performance. Nonetheless, it is a popular algorithm due to its simplicity and efficiency.

b. **KNN**
The KNN (k-nearest neighbors) algorithm is a type of supervised machine learning algorithm used for classification and regression tasks. It is a non-parametric algorithm, meaning that it does not make any assumptions about the underlying distribution of the data In the KNN algorithm, given a new data point, the algorithm searches through the training data to find the k-nearest neighbors to the new point, where k is a user-defined parameter. The "nearest" neighbors are defined by a distance metric, such as

Euclidean distance, and can be found using a variety of search algorithms, such as brute force or KD-trees. For classification tasks, the KNN algorithm assigns the class of the new point based on the majority class of its k-nearest neighbors. For regression tasks, the KNN algorithm assigns the output value of the new point as the mean or median value of its k-nearest neighbors. The KNN algorithm is relatively simple and easy to implement, but it can be computationally expensive for large datasets, especially in high-dimensional spaces. Additionally, the algorithm can be sensitive to the choice of the distance metric and the value of k.

c. **Logistic Regression**

Logistic regression is a statistical method used to analyze and model the relationship between a binary dependent variable (a variable with only two possible outcomes) and one or more independent variables (also known as explanatory or predictor variables). The dependent variable is typically coded as 0 or 1, representing the two possible outcomes, and the independent variables can be continuous or categorical. The logistic regression model uses a logistic function, also known as the sigmoid function, to estimate the probability of the dependent variable taking on the value of 1, given the values of the independent variables. The logistic function maps any real-valued input to a value between 0 and 1, which can be interpreted as the probability of the positive class. The parameters of the model are estimated using maximum likelihood estimation, and the quality of the fit is measured using goodness-of-fit tests such as the likelihood ratio test or the Hosmer-Lemeshow test [7]. Logistic regression is commonly used in various fields, including healthcare, social sciences, marketing, and finance, to model and predict binary outcomes, such as the presence or absence of a disease, the success or failure of a marketing campaign, or the likelihood of default on a loan. It is also often used as a baseline algorithm for more complex models, such as neural networks or decision trees.

d. **Data Preprocessing/Data Cleaning**

Data Preprocessing or Data Cleaning is the process of preparing raw data for analysis by cleaning and transforming it into a structured and manageable format. This involves identifying and handling missing or inconsistent data, dealing with duplicate or irrelevant data, and transforming data to a standardized format. The goal of data preprocessing is to ensure that the data is accurate, consistent, and complete before it is analyzed. This can involve a range of tasks, such as removing outliers, resolving missing or incorrect data, and transforming data to a common scale or format. Data preprocessing is a crucial step in the data analysis process because it ensures that the data is of high quality and can be used effectively to answer research questions or make business decisions. It can also help to reduce the risk of errors or bias in the analysis, and improve the overall accuracy and reliability of the results.

Some common techniques used in data preprocessing include:

- Data cleaning: This involves identifying and correcting errors or inconsistencies in the data, such as missing values, outliers, and incorrect data types.
- Data transformation: This involves transforming the data into a more suitable format for analysis, such as normalizing or scaling the data, converting categorical data into numerical data, and reducing the dimensionality of the data.

Data integration: This involves combining data from multiple sources, such as merging data from different databases or data sets.

Data reduction: This involves reducing the size of the data set by removing redundant or irrelevant data (Fig. 1).

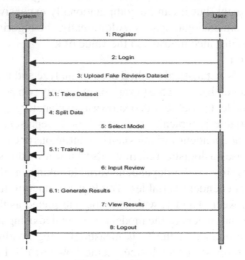

Fig. 1. Architecture

Feature Extraction

Feature extraction is a technique used in machine learning to identify and extra 5 ct relevant information from raw data and transform it into a set of features that can be used as input for machine learning algorithms. The main aim of feature extraction is to reduce the complexity of the raw data and to represent it in a more structured and meaningful way. In many cases, raw data is too complex or too large to be used directly as input for machine learning algorithms. For example, in image recognition tasks, raw image data may be too large and complex to be used directly. Feature extraction can help to identify relevant information in the image, such as edges, corners, and textures, and to represent this information in a set of features that can be used as input for machine learning algorithms.

Feature extraction can be performed using a variety of techniques, such as:

Statistical methods: These involve identifying statistical properties of the raw data, such as the mean, standard deviation, and correlation coefficients.

Dimensionality reduction: These techniques involve reducing the number of dimensions of the data, such as Principal Component Analysis (PCA) or t-distributed stochastic neighbor embedding (t-SNE).

Convolutional neural networks: These are deep learning models that can automatically learn features from raw data, such as images, by using convolutional layers.

Natural language processing techniques: These involve extracting features from text data, such as word frequency or word embedding.

Feature extraction is an important step in the machine-learning pipeline, as it can significantly impact the performance of machine learning algorithms. By identifying and extracting relevant information from raw data, feature extraction can help to improve the accuracy and efficiency of machine learning models.

Python Modules Used

NumPy is a library designed to be efficient and fast, especially when working with large datasets, and it provides many built-in functions for mathematical operations such as linear algebra, Fourier transform, and random number generation. It also has a powerful indexing system for accessing and manipulating elements within arrays, and it provides tools for integrating with other scientific computing libraries, such as SciPy, pandas, and Matplotlib.

Pandas is a library for data manipulation and analysis in Python. It provides a high-level interface for working with structured data, such as CSV files or SQL databases. Pandas includes functions for data cleaning, data filtering, data aggregation, and data visualization. It is widely used in data analysis and data science.

Scikit-learn is a library for machine learning in Python. It provides a range of supervised and unsupervised machine learning algorithms, including classification, regression, clustering, and dimensionality reduction. Scikit-learn also includes tools for data preprocessing, model selection, and evaluation. It is widely used in machine learning and data science.

Python modules are used to organize code into logical and reusable units. They allow you to break down a large program into smaller, more manageable pieces, making it easier to develop, maintain, and debug your code.

The above python modules can contain functions, classes, and variables that can be used by other programs or modules, which can be used by importing them.

4 Functional Diagram

Fake review dataset consists of 2 main interfaces system and user. Under system, first registration details are stored for future. Next, Access login and access to load data, which is used to retrieve data. Based on the data Selected and user preference model is chosen user can logout after the prediction is done Under user registration comes first where every new user need to register themselves in the system with a unique name and email. After registering, a user can login in to the system. After logging in successfully, the user can upload and view their uploaded dataset. The user next has to choose the model to view the result from the dataset. Next, the user can predict outcomes from the system (Fig. 2).

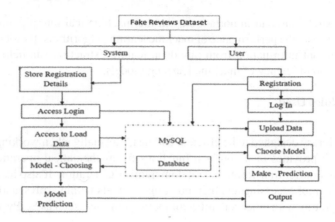

Fig. 2. Functional Block diagram

5   Results

Online reviews have a great impact on decision making of the customer while purchasing a product from an e-commerce site. Hence fake review detection is developed. The output is delivered on time for making better decisions. This system is less complex and does not require any prerequisite skills. The systems goal to develop fast and reliable method which detects and estimates anemia accurately was satisfied. To Design this system powerful algorithm in python based environment with Django framework was used (Figs. 3, 4, and 5).

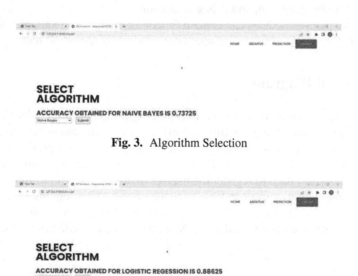

Fig. 3. Algorithm Selection

Fig. 4. Accuracy measure by Logistic Regression

Fig. 5. KNN Accuracy Measure

With the above implementation, we are able to obtain 73% of accuracy when Naive Bayes is used and 88% with Logistic regression and 60% of accuracy when KNN is used. This accuracy we obtained is able to help us to find the fake reviews more efficiently and to remove them to provide original reviews to maintain transparency of the online market. After the working is completed a user can logout of the system. Now the limitations are discussed below, first is technical aspect in text generation and classification of the reviews, which can be improved by future experiments. Now coming to general limitations of fake review detection algorithms, they have no or less awareness, motives or clarity. The text generators understand the language by taking examples of millions of people on how they communicate online, which is then generalized which is then used in reviews online. Sometimes the appearance of the reviews are like they are expressing thoughts which are original, but this is the side effects of imitation or copying but not actual thoughts. The general problem faced by ML models is data specificity. So the human generated reviews are evolving over time. So by frequently updating the classifiers we can maintain high performance. Therefore future experiments need to work on creation of trust worthy baseline datasets to eliminate human generated fake reviews. To validate the performance of the fake review detection researchers use various data sets. Data sets are to be used for the training of the algorithms to identify and find the fake.

6 Conclusion

With the development of web 2.0, online reviews are taken into consideration for making decisions to whether purchase a product, go for a particular movie or booking resorts in an unknown place. Fake reviews detection system takes data from the user and predicts if the review is fake. The system is made user friendly and uses python and Django framework. System is build in such a way where input procedure is easy and output is delivered on time for better decision making. With procedures such as registration and login security is made strong with no pre required skills.

References

1. Meenakshi Sundaram, B., Rajalakshmi, B., Aman Singh, B., Kumar, R.S., Arsha, R.: Disaster relief compensation computational framework. In: Second International Conference on Artificial Intelligence and Smart Energy (ICAIS) (2022). https://doi.org/10.1109/ICAIS53314. 2022.9742829

2. Barbado, R., Araque, O., Iglesias, C.A.: A framework for fake review detection in online consumer electronics retailers. Inf. Process. Manage. **56**(4), 1234–1244 (2019)
3. Tadelis, S.: The economics of reputation and feedback systems in e-commerce marketplaces. IEEE Internet Comput. **20**(1), 12–19 (2016)
4. Santhosh Krishna, B.V., Sharma, S., Devika, K., Sahana, Y., Sharanya, K.N., Indraja, C.: Review of fake product review detection techniques. In: Second International Conference on Artificial Intelligence and Smart Energy (ICAIS), pp. 771–776 (2022). https://doi.org/10.1109/ICAIS53314.2022.9742735
5. Luca, M., Zervas, G.: Fake it till you make it: reputation, competition, and Yelp review fraud. Manag. Sci. **62**(12), 3412–3427 (2015)
6. Jindal, N., Liu, B.: Review spam detection. In: Proceedings of the 16th International Conference on World Wide Web Series (WWW 2007) (2007)
7. Uma, N., Prashanth, C.S.R.: A detailed analysis of the various frequent item set mining algorithms. J. Adv. Res. Dynam. Control Syst. **12**(**2** Special Issue), 448–454 (2020)
8. Jindal, N., Liu, B.: Review spam detection. In: Proceedings of the 16th International Conference on the World Wide Web, pp. 1189–1190 (2017)
9. Hammad, A., Ahmad, S.J.: An approach for detecting spam in Arabic opinion reviews. Doctoral Dissertation. Islamic University of Gaza, Gaza, Palestine. Ahmed, H., Traore, I., Saad, S. Detecting opinion spams and fake news using text classification. e9 Security and Privacy **1**, 1 (2018)
10. Gautam, J., Atrey, M., Malsa, N., Balyan, A., Shaw, R.N., Ghosh, A.: Twitter data sentiment analysis using naive Bayes classifier and generation of heat map for analyzing intensity geographically. In: Bansal, J.C., Fung, L.C.C., Simic, M., Ghosh, A. (eds.) Advances in Applications of Data-Driven Computing. AISC, vol. 1319, pp. 129–139. Springer, Singapore (2021). https://doi.org/10.1007/978-981-33-6919-1_10
11. Rajawat, A.S., Barhanpurkar, K., Goyal, S.B., Bedi, P., Shaw, R.N., Ghosh, A.: Efficient deep learning for reforming authentic content searching on big data. In: Bianchini, M., Piuri, V., Das, S., Shaw, R.N. (eds.) Advanced Computing and Intelligent Technologies. LNNS, vol. 218, pp. 319–327. Springer, Singapore (2022). https://doi.org/10.1007/978-981-16-2164-2_26

A Survey on Designing Efficient WSN Using Duty Cycle Optimization

Sudip Kumar De[1] , Avishek Banerjee[2] , Koushik Majumder[3](✉) ,
Anurag Dasgupta[4], Rabindra Nath Shaw[5], and Ankush Ghosh[5]

[1] Department of Information Technology, Asansol Engineering College, Asansol, WB, India
[2] Department of CSBS, Asansol Engineering College, Asansol, WB, India
[3] Department of Computer Science and Engineering, MAKAUT, Kolkata, WB, India
koushikzone@yahoo.com
[4] Valdosta State University, Valdosta, GA 31698, USA
[5] University Center for Research and Development, Chandigarh University, Mohali, Punjab, India

Abstract. A Wireless Sensor Network (WSN) is a group of wirelessly linked, geographically dispersed sensor nodes. A wireless sensor node is a tiny device that can sense a variety of physical measures from its surroundings and, after translating them into electrical signals, may send and receive a finite amount of data to other nodes or a sink node in the network. Battery-centric wireless sensor nodes typically cannot operate as long as energy-harvesting sensor nodes. A WSN may quickly dry up if the usage of energy is not prioritized for the supplementing of energy to various components of WSN nodes like CPU, radio transceiver, sensors, etc. One of the prime challenges in the WSN network is the minimization of energy consumption of the network. Secondary challenges can be minimization of delays, improving throughput, preserving the quality of service, etc. The duty cycle management can address the primary as well as the secondary challenges of the WSN. This research addresses the impact of the duty cycle in WSN through a survey of several duty cycle designs.

Keywords: Wireless Sensor Network (WSN) · Impact of Duty Cycle · Energy minimization · delay minimization · Throughput maximization · Routing

1 Introduction

A Wireless Sensor Network (WSN) is a distributed collection of wirelessly linked sensor nodes having constrained computing and energy capabilities. WSN networks are gaining popularity because they can be built in regions where normal wireless communications networks are difficult or impossible to deploy. The WSN has been employed for a variety of purposes [1, 2] including environmental monitoring, medical surveillance, military surveillance, engineering surveillance, home automation, agriculture observation, smart city observation [3], etc. Each WSN node generally includes a CPU, a transceiver, a limited amount of memory, a battery, and application-specific sensors [4]. After processing the sensed data in the CPU with the help of the memory unit, it is transmitted to the transceiver unit to initiate communication between surrounding nodes. The battery unit of WSN is responsible for providing power to the entire node. The communication in WSN can be implemented through the use of many layers. The Medium Access Control (MAC) layer is one of them. This MAC layer is controlled by the MAC protocol. The MAC protocol guarantees that transmitting nodes do not interfere with one another and deal with the problem if they do. It is the MAC protocol that is wholly accountable for packet initialization, transmission, and reception in the wireless medium by commanding the radio transition between transmitting and receiving modes. At the time of conventional MAC protocol design, the prime focus is to maximize throughput and reduce delay. On the other side, wireless sensor network protocols are made with an emphasis on reducing energy usage. The main energy source of any sensor node is the battery attached to the node. The source of the required consumed energy for various activities of the nodes (energy needed for data communication, sensing the external environment, etc.) is the limited Li-based battery [5–9]. Besides this limited battery energy, there are also some major obstacles to establishing WSN networks and those are limited processing power, effective deployment strategies, efficient duty cycle optimization, and maintaining service quality.

In a wireless sensor node, the component that consumes the most energy is often the radio or transceiver. If the radio is always put on the high-power active state, then energy will dry out very soon. In practice, radio is not always engaged in communication. Instead, the radio listens idle much of the time to assess the channel. Duty cycling is a process in which a node's radio is routinely put into a high-power active and low-power sleep state. The duty cycle mechanism has long been used in engineering industries to increase the lifespan of equipment like AC, motors, etc. [10]. In wireless sensor networks also, the duty cycle is utilized to minimize the wasting of energy during activities like idle listening (actively monitoring packet arriving), packet overhearing (receiving unintended packets), packet collision (packets are lost due to overlapped transmission), and, as a result, extend the total network durability. Among the high and low-duty cycle approaches a significant amount of research supports the idea of Low-duty cycle operations i.e., keeping sensor node radios mostly in the low-power sleep state. The low-duty cycle approach helps to minimize the energy. However, low-duty cycle operations increase network delay. Selection of the best duty cycle is never easy, especially for applications where latency and energy consumption are key considerations. The authors, [11] investigate the trade-off between network latency and energy efficiency in existing conventional duty cycle MAC protocols and it is observed that for low data rate applications their proposed L-MAC protocol performs better in terms of energy efficiency, and delivery latency. Their research also assists in identifying the lowest duty cycle for L-MAC to meet a certain Quality of Service (QoS) requirement.

Motivation: The factors for energy running out too soon are idle listening, overhearing, and retransmission of collided data. Duty cycle optimization can handle the issue of idle listening, overhearing, and retransmission of colliding data in addition to saving energy by algorithmically shutting off its radio on wsn node. This study has explored several duty-cycle optimization techniques in WSNs, which will be beneficial for researchers.

For the descriptive study of energy management techniques, the authors took into account 48 research publications published between 2002 and 2022, as shown in Fig. 1.

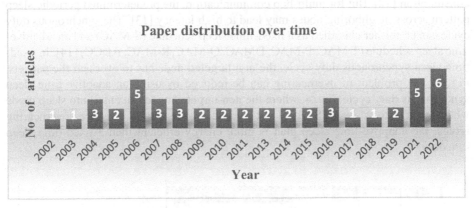

Fig. 1. The distribution of papers from 2002 to 2022

2 Existing Duty Cycle Management Strategies in Designing Efficient WSN

Limitations on battery power, computing power, deployment strategy, duty cycle optimization, and preserving service quality are the primary barriers to the development of WSN networks. These challenges are interconnected, for example, effective duty cycle optimization can reduce network energy consumption and improve throughput and service quality. The types of duty cycle management strategies in the design of Wireless Sensor Networks can be classified as (Fig. 2):

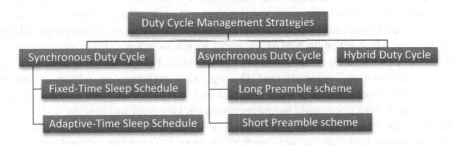

Fig. 2. Types of duty cycle management strategies in designing of WSN

A. Synchronous Duty Cycle Management Strategies

The synchronous duty cycle maintains a predetermined periodic sleep pattern across neighboring nodes such that sensors can sleep on a regular schedule to save power consumption [12]. But for multi-hop communication, the predetermined periodic sleep pattern across neighboring nodes may lead to high latency [13]. The synchronous duty cycle can be further classified as a fixed-time sleep schedule (S-MAC) and an adaptive-time sleep schedule (T-MAC, P-MAC, DMAC, Q-MAC, R-MAC, ADCC) [14]. In fixed-time sleep synchronous duty cycle, the non-targeted node has to overhear the packets, Fig. 3. The problem of overhearing can be reduced by using an adaptive time sleep synchronous duty cycle, Fig. 4, where the non-targeted node can enter into sleep mode whenever it detects the RTS signal not intended for itself. As it reduces overhearing issues, the adaptive-time sleep plan is more energy efficient than a fixed-time sleep schedule.

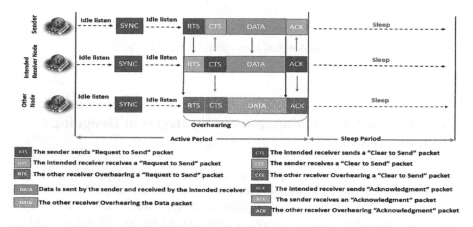

Fig. 3. Synchronous duty cycle with a fixed sleep schedule

The S-MAC or Sensor-MAC was introduced by Wei Ye et al. [15] in 2002. It is a contention-based synchronous fixed-time sleep schedule protocol. Nodes in S-MAC regularly sleep to minimize idle listening time. In 2004, Wei Ye et al. [16] proposed the adaptive-time sleep schedule S-MAC protocol which switches radio to sleep mode to minimize the overhearing events by the untargeted nodes. Because the sleep and listening intervals are fixed and predetermined, the algorithm performs less effectively under varying traffic loads [13]. In S-MAC due to a lack of synchronization between nodes, the node enters into sleep mode before receiving packets from surrounding nodes. This is known as an early sleeping problem. The S-MAC protocol is suitable for situations in which the sensor node can tolerate longer idle periods [17] and low or fixed traffic load [46].

T. van Dam et al. [18] introduced the Timeout MAC (T-MAC) protocol in 2003 to improve the performance of the S-MAC protocol under fluctuating traffic loads. The core concept of T-MAC is to minimize the active duration based on traffic circumstances. When no activation incident is detected for a specified time (TA), the idle listen period

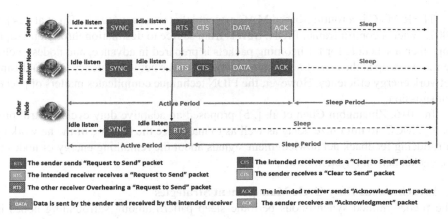

Fig. 4. Synchronous duty cycle with an adaptive sleep schedule

terminates. The least amount of idle listening is determined by TA. Unlike the S-MAC protocol, the early sleeping problem is also tackled in T-MAC, [14]. The T-MAC has low throughput, increased delay, complexity, and scaling issues [19].

In 2005 Zheng et al. [20] proposed an adaptive protocol called Pattern-MAC (P-MAC) protocol. The P-MAC optimizes the wake-sleep time based on the traffic of the node and its neighbors, and the nodes that are genuinely active in the communication wake up often. This method assists in the conservation of energy in non-communicating nodes. But if neighboring nodes could not exchange schedule patterns with each other then nodes will not be able to communicate. In that case, idle listening can be observed [21]. P-MAC protocol delivers higher throughput in high traffic and saves more energy in low traffic than the S-MAC protocol [20].

In 2007 DMAC [22] was introduced to improve the delay issue of S-MAC and T-MAC. Nodes that lose contention do not have to wait for the next upward flow but can attempt again in an overflow slot schedule. The overflow slots boost capacity on demand, enabling DMAC to adjust to traffic load automatically. However the DMAC, like S-MAC and T-MAC, must awaken all wsn nodes during every duty cycle. This is not an energy-efficient approach as lightly-loaded nodes(far away from the sink node) may remain idle during most duty cycles [21].

N. A. Vasanthi et al. introduced the Query-based MAC protocol, Q-MAC [23], in 2006. Two types of duty cycles have been used: static & adaptive. The radios of the nodes use a static schedule and sleep more when there is no query request. The sleep cycle is dynamically altered to adaptive mode whenever a query request is launched. It has been observed that the Q-MAC protocol achieves the minimum latency through adaptive scheduling and energy-efficient data transfer by activating only the nearby nodes during packet transmission. According to simulation data, Q-MAC outperforms S-MAC. In 2009, Chao et al. [21] proposed another QMAC protocol that adjusts node sleep periods based on traffic loads and allows sensor nodes to sleep longer in low traffic to conserve energy. The simulation results show that the suggested QMAC saves more energy than P-MAC, and D-MAC while maintaining a low transmission delay.

The R-MAC is a routing-based MAC protocol that was proposed by Du et al. [24] in 2007. When a control frame, PION, travels from source to destination through multiple hops then a schedule for forthcoming packets is prepared in advance, and nodes intelligently wake up at the predefined planned time to reduce network latency without losing network energy efficiency. However, the PION technique complicates matters of packet transmission.

In 2016, Zhuangbin Chen et al. [25] proposed an adaptive duty cycle control protocol, ADCC, to minimize delay as well as to maximize the lifetime of the network by introducing feedback acknowledgment signals about the remaining energy of nodes in the packet delivery system flow.

B. Asynchronous Duty Cycle Management Strategies

The predetermined synchronous periodic sleep pattern among surrounding nodes in multi-hop communication is not only difficult to implement, but it may also result in significant delay, [13, 26]. Nodes in an asynchronous duty cycle are not needed to agree on a predetermined time frame [27]. As a result, the nodes don't have to memorize their neighbors' schedules, which significantly lowers the storage and energy costs associated with schedule sharing between the nodes [28]. The recipient in the asynchronous duty cycle knows its wakeup period but not its wakeup time. It is also stated that the asynchronous duty cycle protocols are more scalable than synchronous duty cycle protocols [28].

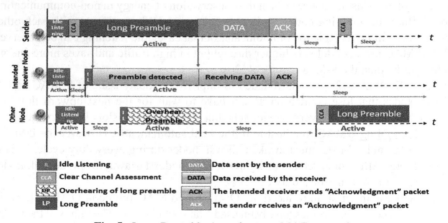

Fig. 5. Long Preamble Asynchronous MAC protocol.

Low power listening (LPL), also known as preamble sampling, is where nodes periodically wake up to detect the potential of transmissions in the network by performing periodic channel sampling. To send data to the intended destination node, the transmitter delivers a preamble packet on the network. Depending on the approaches, the preamble packets can be either a long preamble or a short preamble. The recipient waits for the data to be sent after receiving the preamble packet. To ensure that the receiver will sample the channel during the preamble, the sender uses the long preamble strategy, which is at least as long as the receiver's wakeup period. The sender and recipient exchange data packets following the preamble [29]. However, the large preamble packet size increases the network's listening and receiving overhead and causes a considerable delay [21], Fig. 5. On average, all overhearing nodes must be awake for half of the preamble transmission duration before discovering that the preamble packet is not intended for them [30], as a result, it increases energy requirements.

In 2004, Polastre et al. [31] proposed a sender-initiated asynchronous LPL-based protocol called Berkeley MAC (B-MAC). The B-MAC utilizes a long preamble to make sure the recipient is awake when the data packets arrive. When the channel is idle, this long preamble-sending technique delivers extremely little power usage. Larger delays and overhearing are this protocol's main drawbacks.

To address the drawbacks of B-MAC, the wise-MAC was introduced by El-Hoiydi et al. [32] in 2004. In wise-MAC, instead of fixed length preamble, it uses dynamic preamble length to reduce idle listening and as well as to reduce power consumption. The main drawback of this protocol is low scalability in changing traffic conditions.

In 2006, the X–MAC protocol was introduced by Buettner et al. [33] to address the long waiting time and overhearing problems. Instead of sending a single long preamble, the sender node in X-MAC sends out a time-gapped series of short preambles that include the address of the intended recipient. The time gap between two short preambles enables the intended receiver to send an early acknowledgment (ACK) to the sender so that sender can send the data packet as early as possible. It reduces latency in the network. On the other hand, on receiving the short preamble the non-targeted recipient nodes sleep immediately (Fig. 6) as a solution to overhearing and to minimize energy consumption. Short preamble packet sending technique minimizes network latency and energy waste when compared to B-MAC, but since more preamble packets are delivered, they may still use more energy than synchronous protocols [21].

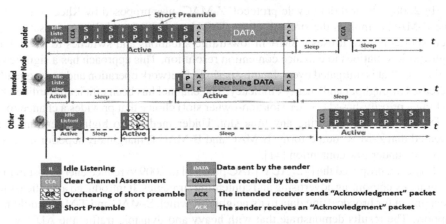

Fig. 6. Short Preamble Asynchronous MAC protocol

Sender-initiated protocols like B-MAC, X-MAC, and C-MAC [34] use a common shared wireless channel, which prevents other sensor nodes from communicating while one sender node searches for a recipient and so consumes additional time and energy. To reduce the burden on the sender nodes the receiver-initiated MAC (RI-MAC) protocol was proposed by Sun et al. [35] in 2008. When a sender node in the receiver-initiated MAC protocol has to transfer data, it first listens to the channel until the recipient sends a preamble, at which point the sender node starts delivering the data. When there is a high volume of traffic, RI-MAC shows a noticeable improvement over X-MAC [35]. The RI-MAC suffers from idle listening by the senders and has a significant end-to-end latency. To overcome the problem of idle listening of senders another receiver-initiated protocol, L-MAC, was proposed by Dinh et al. [11] in 2016. The L-MAC improves end-to-end delivery in low-traffic situations while consuming the least amount of energy possible [36]. In terms of energy balance between transmitter and receiver, it has been found that L-MAC performs better than RI-MAC [11].

In 2011, a receiver-initiated asynchronous protocol called, Predictive-Wakeup MAC (PW-MAC), was proposed by Tang et al. [37] that predicts the receiver's wake-up time to minimize the energy consumption of the sensor node. In the experiment, it was discovered that PW-MAC performed better in terms of energy efficiency than X-MAC, wiseMAC, and RI-MAC in scenarios involving multi-hop traffic, hidden terminals, and wake-up schedule conflicts.

In 2014, [38] another asynchronous protocol, sleep window MAC (SW-MAC), was proposed that predicts the packet arrival time or interval and adjusts the sleep-wake-up schedule. Simulation reveals that in dynamic traffic, with low latency requirements the SW-MAC protocol is particularly suited and exhibits great energy efficiency.

C. Hybrid Duty Cycle Management Strategies

The hybrid duty cycle protocols focus on a composite protocol using multiple channel access techniques (CSMA/CDMA/TDMA) to handle dynamic traffic load in the channel, reduce latency and collision, and achieve energy efficiency. The key strength of the hybrid design is the flexibility of the contention intensities [39].

In 2008, a hybrid duty cycle protocol, Z-MAC, was proposed by Rhee et al. [40]. The Z-MAC combines the strength of the TDMA and CSMA while compensating for their shortcomings. It uses CSMA in low-traffic situations and switches to TDMA in high-traffic situations to enhance contention resolution. This approach has a significant initial cost that is mitigated over a lengthy period of network operation and consequently increases throughput and energy efficiency. The channel has been efficiently utilized by making a priority-based (owner-slot/non-owner slot) choice that provides a chance for a node to communicate during any time slot. Under medium to high contention, it is revealed that Z-MAC outperforms B-MAC and B-MAC is marginally superior in terms of energy under low contention [41].

Ray et al. proposed the [42] ADV-MAC protocol in 2009 to reduce energy lost in idle listening by combining advertising and contention strategies. It introduced a multicasting mechanism for broadcasting data to its neighbors, which S-MAC and T-MAC could not support. The results demonstrate that with heavy and dynamic traffic, the ADV-MAC protocol may save energy while maintaining throughput.

In 2010, Sitanayah et al. [43] proposed an emergency responsive MAC protocol, ER-MAC, by hybridizing the CSMA and TDMA mechanisms to provide low latency with high throughput with greater flexibility in dynamic traffic and network topology. Simulation results show that ER-MAC performs better than Z-MAC in terms of latency, energy consumption, and throughput.

In 2014, Shrestha et al. [44] proposed a single-hop hybridized (CSMA/CA-TDMA) protocol using the MDP technique to access both the contention and contention-free period intelligently. Simulation results demonstrate that this approach works better than CSMA/CA technique in terms of minimization of energy.

In 2015, Zhuo et al. [45] proposed a CSMA-TDMA hybridized MAC protocol iQueue-MAC. It intelligently senses the traffic load and depending on the traffic load it switches to either CSMA or TDMA scheme with minimum control overhead and maximum throughput.

In 2015, a CSMA-TDMA hybridized MAC protocol, the P-Queue-MAC [46] protocol was proposed which can manage dynamic traffic with minimum latency and maximum energy efficiency.

TCH-MAC, a [47] CSMA-TDMA hybridized MAC protocol that boosts throughput while using less energy, was presented in 2018. It effectively manages traffic bursting and energy efficiency using TDMA and CSMA, respectively.

3 Conclusions

In this study, the authors have emphasized mainly different duty cycle management strategies like Synchronous, Asynchronous, and Hybrid Duty Cycle management strategies. In the case of Synchronous duty cycle management, two different sleep schedules namely Fixed-time and Adaptive Time schedules have been discussed and in the case of Asynchronous duty cycle management Long Preamble and Short Preamble, schemes have been discussed. The study will help novice researchers as well as learners to cope with the idea of the field of duty cycle optimization. This study has focused on Duty Cycle Optimization in the context of configuring efficient Wireless Sensor Networks but coverage optimization, topology control optimization, and power control optimization are also some major factors in this context. In the future, any researcher can explore the field and get the motivation to extend the work.

References

1. Banerjee, A., et al.: Construction of effective wireless sensor network for smart communication using modified ant colony optimization technique. In: Bianchini, M., Piuri, V., Das, S., Shaw, R.N. (eds.) Advanced Computing and Intelligent Technologies. LNNS, vol. 218, pp. 269–278. Springer, Singapore (2022). https://doi.org/10.1007/978-981-16-2164-2_22
2. Banerjee, A., Mitra, A., Biswas, A.: An integrated application of IoT-based WSN in the field of indian agriculture system using hybrid optimization technique and machine learning. In: Agricultural Informatics: Automation Using the IoT and Machine Learning, pp. 171–187 (2021)
3. Banerjee, A., et al.: Building of efficient communication system in smart city using wireless sensor network through hybrid optimization technique. In: Piuri, V., Shaw, R.N., Ghosh, A., Islam, R. (eds.) AI and IoT for Smart City Applications. SCI, vol. 1002, pp. 15–30. Springer, Singapore (2022). https://doi.org/10.1007/978-981-16-7498-3_2
4. De, S.K., Banerjee, A., Majumder, K., Shaw, R.N., Ghosh, A.: Use of various optimization algorithms in the energy minimization problem domain of WSN: a survey. In: Shaw, R.N., Das, S., Piuri, V., Bianchini, M. (eds.) Advanced Computing and Intelligent Technologies.

LNEE, vol. 914, pp. 477–488. Springer, Singapore (2022). https://doi.org/10.1007/978-981-19-2980-9_39

5. Banerjee, A., De, S.K., Majumder, K., et al.: Construction of energy minimized WSN using GA-SAMP-MWPSO and K-mean clustering algorithm with LDCF deployment strategy. J. Supercomput. **78**, 11015–11050 (2022). https://doi.org/10.1007/s11227-021-04265-7
6. De, S.K., Banerjee, A., Majumder, K., Chattopadhyay, S.: Minimizing the energy consumption of WSN using noble SMOWA-GA algorithm. Int. J. Appl. Metaheuristic Comput. (IJAMC) **13**(1), 1–22 (2022)
7. Banerjee, A., et al.: Design of energy efficient WSN using a noble SMOWA algorithm. CMC-Comput. Mater. Continua **72**(2), 3585–3600 (2022)
8. Banerjee, A., Das, V., Biswas, A., Chattopadhyay, S., Biswas, U.: Development of energy efficient and optimized coverage area network configuration to achieve reliable WSN network using meta-heuristic approaches. Int. J. Appl. Metaheuristic Comput. (IJAMC) **12**(3), 1–27 (2021)
9. Dey, M., Das, A., Banerjee, A., Kamila, U.K., Chattopadhyay, S.: Construction of efficient wireless sensor networks for energy minimization using a modified ACO algorithm. Int. J. Sens. Wireless Commun. Control **11**(9), 928–950 (2021)
10. Thumann, A., Mehta, D.: Handbook of Energy Engineering. Fairmont Press, Lilburn (2008)
11. Dinh, T., Kim, Y., Gu, T., Vasilakos, A.V.: L-MAC: a wake-up time self-learning MAC protocol for wireless sensor networks. Comput. Netw. **105**, 33–46 (2016). https://doi.org/10.1016/j.comnet.2016.05.015
12. Radha Subramanyam, G., Bala, J., Nagabushanam Perattur, E., Kanaga, G.M.: Energy efficient MAC with variable duty cycle for wireless sensor networks. Int. J. Electron. (2021). https://doi.org/10.1080/00207217.2021.1892202
13. Demirkol, I., Ersoy, C., Alagoz, F.: MAC protocols for wireless sensor networks: a survey. IEEE Commun. Mag. **44**(4), 115–121 (2006). https://doi.org/10.1109/MCOM.2006.1632658
14. Maitra, T., Roy, S.: A comparative study on popular MAC protocols for mixed Wireless Sensor Networks: from implementation viewpoint. Comput. Sci. Rev. **22**, 107–134 (2016). https://doi.org/10.1016/j.cosrev.2016.09.004
15. Ye, W., Heidemann, J., Estrin, D.: An energy-efficient MAC protocol for wireless sensor networks. In: Proceedings.Twenty-First Annual Joint Conference of the IEEE Computer and Communications Societies, vol. 3, pp. 1567–1576 (2002). https://doi.org/10.1109/INFCOM.2002.1019408
16. Ye, W., Heidemann, J., Estrin, D.: Medium access control with coordinated adaptive sleeping for wireless sensor networks. IEEE/ACM Trans. Networking **12**(3), 493–506 (2004)
17. Zhang, P., Sadler, C.M., Martonosi, M.: Middleware for long-term deployment of delay-tolerant sensor networks. In: Proceedings of the International Workshop on Middleware for Sensor Networks, MidSens 2006, pp. 13–18. ACM (2006)
18. van Dam, T., Langendoen, K.: An adaptive energy-efficient MAC protocol for wireless sensor networks. In: 1st ACM Conference on Embedded Networked Sensor Systems (SenSys 2003), Los Angeles, CA, pp. 171–180, November 2003
19. Kumar, P., Güneş, M., Mushtaq, Q., Schiller, J.: Optimizing duty-cycle for delay and energy bound WSN applications. In: 2010 IEEE 24th International Conference on Advanced Information Networking and Applications Workshops, pp. 692–697. IEEE, April 2010
20. Zheng, T., Radhakrishnan, S., Sarangan, V.: PMAC: an adaptive energy-efficient MAC protocol for wireless sensor networks. In: 19th IEEE International Parallel and Distributed Processing Symposium, pp. 8-pp. IEEE, April 2005
21. Chao, C.M., Lee, Y.W.: A quorum-based energy-saving MAC protocol design for wireless sensor networks. IEEE Trans. Veh. Technol. **59**(2), 813–822 (2009)

22. Lu, G., Krishnamachari, B., Raghavendra, C.S.: An adaptive energy-efficient and low-latency MAC for tree-based data gathering in sensor networks. Wirel. Commun. Mob. Comput. **7**(7), 863–875 (2007)
23. Vasanthi, N.A., Annadurai, S.: Energy efficient sleep schedule for achieving minimum latency in query based sensor networks. In: IEEE International Conference on Sensor Networks, Ubiquitous, and Trustworthy Computing (SUTC 2006), pp. 214–219 (2006). https://doi.org/10.1109/SUTC.2006.64
24. Du, S., Saha, A.K., Johnson, D.B.: RMAC: a routing-enhanced duty-cycle MAC protocol for wireless sensor networks. In: IEEE INFOCOM 2007-26th IEEE International Conference on Computer Communications, pp. 1478–1486. IEEE, May 2007
25. Chen, Z., Liu, A., Li, Z., Choi, Y.J., Li, J.: Distributed duty cycle control for delay improvement in wireless sensor networks. Peer-to-Peer Networking Appl. **10**(3), 559–578 (2017)
26. Carrano, R.C., Passos, D., Magalhaes, L.C., Albuquerque, C.V.: Survey and taxonomy of duty cycling mechanisms in wireless sensor networks. IEEE Commun. Surv. Tutorials **16**(1), 181–194 (2013)
27. Liu, Y., Liu, A., Zhang, N., Liu, X., Ma, M., Hu, Y.: DDC: dynamic duty cycle for improving delay and energy efficiency in wireless sensor networks. J. Netw. Comput. Appl. **131**, 16–27 (2019)
28. Foerster, A., Foerster, A. (eds.): Emerging Communications for Wireless Sensor Networks. BoD–Books on Demand (2011)
29. Sha, M., Hackmann, G., Lu, C.: Energy-efficient low power listening for wireless sensor networks in noisy environments. In: Proceedings of the 12th International Conference on Information Processing in Sensor Networks, pp. 277–288, April 2013
30. Raghunathan, V., Ganeriwal, S., Srivastava, M.: Emerging techniques for long lived wireless sensor networks. IEEE Commun. Mag. **44**(4), 108–114 (2006)
31. Paul, A., et al.: A neuro-fuzzy based IDS for Internet-Integrated WSN. In: Bansal, J.C., Paprzycki, M., Bianchini, M., Das, S. (eds.) Computationally Intelligent Systems and their Applications. SCI, vol. 950, pp. 71–86. Springer, Singapore (2021). https://doi.org/10.1007/978-981 16 0407-2_6
32. El-Hoiydi, A., Decotignie, J.D., Hernandez, J.: Low power MAC protocols for infrastructure wireless sensor networks. In: Proceedings of the Fifth European Wireless Conference, pp. 563–569, February 2004
33. Buettner, M., Yee, G.V., Anderson, E., Han, R.: X-MAC: a short preamble MAC protocol for duty-cycled wireless sensor networks. In: Proceedings of the 4th International Conference on Embedded Networked Sensor Systems, pp. 307–320, October 2006
34. Cordeiro, C., Challapali, K.: C-MAC: a cognitive MAC protocol for multi-channel wireless networks. In: 2007 2nd IEEE International Symposium on New Frontiers in Dynamic Spectrum Access Networks, pp. 147–157 (2007). https://doi.org/10.1109/DYSPAN.2007.27
35. Sun, Y., Gurewitz, O., Johnson, D.B.: RI-MAC: a receiver-initiated asynchronous duty cycle MAC protocol for dynamic traffic loads in wireless sensor networks. In: Proceedings of the 6th ACM Conference on Embedded Network Sensor Systems, pp. 1–14, November 2008
36. Shahid, M., et al.: Machine learning-based false positive software vulnerability analysis. Global J. Innov. Emerg. Technol. **1**(2), 29–35 (2022). https://doi.org/10.58260/j.iet.2202.0105
37. Tang, L., Sun, Y., Gurewitz, O., Johnson, D.B.: PW-MAC: an energy-efficient predictive-wakeup MAC protocol for wireless sensor networks. In: 2011 Proceedings IEEE INFOCOM, pp. 1305–1313. IEEE, April 2011
38. Liang, L., Liu, X., Wang, Y., Feng, W., Yang, G.: SW-MAC: a low-latency MAC protocol with adaptive sleeping for wireless sensor networks. Wireless Pers. Commun. **77**(2), 1191–1211 (2014)

39. Ajmi, N., Helali, A., Lorenz, P., Mghaieth, R.: SPEECH-MAC: special purpose energy-efficient contention-based hybrid MAC protocol for WSN and Zigbee network. Int. J. Commun. Syst. **34**(1), e4637 (2021)
40. Rhee, I., Warrier, A., Aia, M., Min, J.: Z-MAC: a hybrid MAC for wireless sensor networks. In: Proceedings of the 3rd International Conference on Embedded Networked Sensor Systems, pp. 90–101, November 2005
41. Yick, J., Mukherjee, B., Ghosal, D.: Wireless sensor network survey. Comput. Netw. **52**(12), 2292–2330 (2008)
42. Ray, S.S., Demirkol, I., Heinzelman, W.: ADV-MAC: advertisement-based MAC protocol for wireless sensor networks. In: 2009 Fifth International Conference on Mobile Ad-hoc and Sensor Networks, pp. 265–272. IEEE, December 2009
43. Sitanayah, L., Sreenan, C.J., Brown, K.N.: ER-MAC: a hybrid MAC protocol for emergency response wireless sensor networks. In: 2010 Fourth International Conference on Sensor Technologies and Applications, pp. 244–249. IEEE (2010)
44. Shrestha, B., Hossain, E., Choi, K.W.: Distributed and centralized hybrid CSMA/CA-TDMA schemes for single-hop wireless networks. IEEE Trans. Wireless Commun. **13**(7), 4050–4065 (2014)
45. Zhuo, S., Wang, Z., Song, Y.Q., Wang, Z., Almeida, L.: A traffic adaptive multi-channel MAC protocol with dynamic slot allocation for WSNs. IEEE Trans. Mob. Comput. **15**(7), 1600–1613 (2015)
46. Wu, L., Zhuo, S., Wang, Z., Wang, Z.: PQueue-MAC: an energy efficient hybrid mac protocol for event-driven sensor networks. Int. J. Distrib. Sens. Netw. **11**(2), 160167 (2015)
47. Yang, X., Wang, L., Xie, J., Zhang, Z.: Energy efficiency TDMA/CSMA hybrid protocol with power control for WSN. Wirel. Commun. Mobile Comput. **2018**, 1–7 (2018)

A Novel Framework for Harnessing AI for Evidence-Based Policymaking in E-Governance Using Smart Contracts

Kamal Upreti[1]($\boxtimes$), Ankit Verma[2], Shikha Mittal[3], Prashant Vats[4], Mustafizul Haque[5], and Shakir Ali[6]

[1] Department of Computer Science, CHRIST (Deemed to be University), Delhi NCR, Ghaziabad, India
kamalupreti1989@gmail.com

[2] Dr. Akhilesh Das Gupta Institute of Technology and Management, Delhi, India

[3] Chitkara University Institute of Engineering and Technology, Chitkara University, Rajpura, Punjab, India

[4] SCSE, Manipal University Jaipur, Jaipur, Rajasthan, India

[5] Dr. D.Y. Patil Vidyapeeth's Centre for Online Learning, Dr. D.Y. Patil Vidyapeeth, Pune (Deemed to be University), Pune, India

[6] Faculty of Digital Business, Lithan Academy (eduCLaaS Pte Ltd.), Singapore, Singapore
info@shakirali.in

Abstract. Harnessing AI for evidence-based policymaking in e-governance has the potential to revolutionize the way governments formulate and implement policies. By leveraging AI technologies, governments can analyze vast amounts of data, extract valuable insights, and make informed decisions based on evidence. This chapter explores the various ways in which AI can be employed in e-governance to facilitate evidence-based policymaking. It discusses the use of AI algorithms for data analysis and prediction, enabling governments to identify patterns, trends, and emerging issues from diverse data sources. Moreover, AI-powered tools can enhance citizen engagement and participation, by facilitating data-driven decision-making processes and providing personalized services. Additionally, AI can assist in policy evaluation and impact assessment, by automating the collection and analysis of data, thus enabling governments to measure the effectiveness of their policies in real-time. Furthermore, AI can contribute to enhancing transparency and accountability in e-governance, by automating processes such as fraud detection and risk assessment. Despite the immense potential, the adoption of AI in e-governance must address challenges such as data privacy, algorithmic bias, and ethical considerations. This chapter concludes by emphasizing the importance of building trust, ensuring fairness, and promoting responsible AI practices to maximize the benefits of AI in evidence-based policymaking for e-governance.

Keywords: Artificial Intelligence (AI) · Evidence-based policymaking · E-governance · Data analysis · Prediction · Citizen engagement · Personalized services

R. N. Shaw et al. (Eds.): ICACIS 2023, CCIS 1921, pp. 231–240, 2023.
https://doi.org/10.1007/978-3-031-45124-9_18

1 Introduction

Governments across the world face the challenge of making informed decisions and formulating effective policies in an increasingly complex and data-driven environment. Traditional methods of policymaking often rely on limited data, anecdotal evidence, and expert opinions, which may not fully capture the intricacies and nuances of modern governance issues. However, with the advent of Artificial Intelligence (AI) technologies, there is a tremendous opportunity to harness the power of data and analytics for evidence-based policymaking in e-governance. AI, with its ability to process vast amounts of data and extract meaningful insights, has the potential to revolutionize the policy-making landscape. By leveraging AI algorithms, governments can analyze diverse sources of data, such as citizen feedback, social media, and government records, to identify patterns, trends, and emerging issues. This data analysis can provide policymakers with a comprehensive understanding of the challenges, needs, and preferences of citizens, helping them make informed decisions based on evidence. One of the key advantages of using AI in evidence-based policymaking is the ability to predict future outcomes. By employing predictive analytics, governments can assess the potential impact of different policy options and identify the most effective strategies. This proactive approach enables policymakers to take preventive measures, optimize resource allocation, and mitigate potential risks. Moreover, AI-powered tools can enhance citizen engagement and participation in the policy-making process. Through data-driven decision-making, governments can solicit feedback from citizens, understand their priorities, and involve them in shaping policies that directly impact their lives. Personalized services can be offered based on individual preferences and needs, fostering a sense of inclusivity and responsiveness. Furthermore, AI can play a crucial role in policy evaluation and impact assessment. Traditionally, policy evaluations have been conducted through manual surveys or limited case studies. AI can automate the collection and analysis of data, providing real-time insights into the effectiveness of policies. This iterative feedback loop allows governments to continuously assess, refine, and adapt their policies to achieve better outcomes. Transparency and accountability are essential pillars of effective governance. AI can contribute to enhancing transparency by automating processes such as fraud detection and risk assessment, ensuring that public resources are used efficiently and effectively. Additionally, AI can provide decision-makers with visibility into the rationale and evidence behind policy recommendations, making the decision-making process more transparent and accountable. However, the adoption of AI in e-governance for evidence-based policymaking also brings challenges. Issues such as data privacy, algorithmic bias, and ethical considerations must be carefully addressed to build trust and ensure fairness. It is essential to strike a balance between leveraging AI's capabilities and safeguarding individual rights and societal values. In conclusion, harnessing AI for evidence-based policymaking in e-governance has the potential to transform governance processes, enabling governments to make data-driven decisions and design policies that address the needs and aspirations of citizens. By leveraging AI's analytical power, governments can unlock valuable insights, enhance citizen engagement, evaluate policy impact, and promote transparency and accountability. To maximize the benefits, it is crucial to adopt responsible AI practices, address potential challenges, and build trust in the use of AI for evidence-based policymaking in e-governance.

2 Related Work

Butterworth, M., et al. [1, 11] explores the various applications of AI in government, including evidence-based policymaking. It provides insights into the benefits, challenges, and potential risks associated with the adoption of AI in e-governance.

Casares, A., et al. [2, 12] discusses the role of data analytics and AI in smart governance and highlights their potential in evidence-based policymaking. It explores the challenges and opportunities associated with utilizing AI technologies for effective policy formulation and implementation.

Čerka, P., et al. [3, 13] examines the opportunities and challenges of using AI for evidence-based policymaking in the public sector. It discusses the potential benefits of AI in improving policy analysis, decision-making, and citizen engagement, while addressing ethical and privacy considerations.

Janssen, Marijn, et al. [4] explores the use of AI and data-driven approaches in policy design and implementation. It discusses the potential of AI technologies to analyze complex data sets, extract insights, and support evidence-based policymaking, highlighting case studies and best practices.

Kouziokas, G., et al. [5] provides practical insights into the application of AI in public policymaking. It covers various aspects, including policy analysis, decision support, and ethical considerations, offering recommendations for policymakers and practitioners interested in leveraging AI for evidence-based policymaking.

Ku, Chih-Hao, et al. [6, 14] examines the applications of AI in promoting good governance, with a specific focus on evidence-based policymaking. It discusses the potential benefits of AI in enhancing policy analysis, citizen engagement, and decision-making processes, while addressing challenges such as data quality, bias, and ethical considerations.

Liu, Shuhua Monica, et al. [7, 15] explores the role of AI in data-driven governance and evidence-based policymaking. It discusses the potential of AI technologies, such as machine learning and natural language processing, in analyzing large datasets, extracting insights, and informing policy decisions. It also addresses challenges related to data privacy, algorithmic bias, and accountability.

Matheus, Ricardo, et al. [8] provides an overview of AI-assisted policymaking in various domains, including e-governance. It examines the use of AI technologies, such as data analytics, machine learning, and decision support systems, in generating evidence for policy formulation and evaluation. This chapter also discusses challenges and future research directions in this field.

Ozoegwu, C., et al. [9] explores the implications of AI adoption in public administration, focusing on evidence-based policymaking. It discusses the potential of AI to improve policy analysis, citizen engagement, and decision-making processes. This chapter also addresses the challenges of algorithmic transparency, fairness, and accountability that need to be considered when harnessing AI for e-governance [16].

Singh, Prabhsimran, et al. [10] examines the ethical implications of using AI in evidence-based policymaking. It discusses issues such as fairness, transparency, accountability, and privacy, highlighting the need for ethical frameworks and guidelines to ensure responsible and trustworthy use of AI technologies in e-governance.

These related works provide valuable insights into the application of AI for evidence-based policymaking in e-governance. They explore the potential benefits, challenges, and ethical considerations associated with harnessing AI technologies, offering recommendations and guidelines for policymakers and practitioners to navigate the complexities of integrating AI into policy-making processes.

3 Proposed Methodology

In this section we will define the proposed methodology for Harnessing AI for Evidence-Based Policymaking in E-Governance. The detailed components of the proposed framework are given in Fig. 1.

3.1 Define Policy Objectives

Clearly define the policy objectives and the specific areas of focus where AI can contribute to evidence-based decision-making in e-governance. Identify the policy domains and the specific challenges that AI can address. By identifying the relevant data sources needed to support evidence-based policymaking. This can include government databases, open data sources, citizen feedback platforms, social media, and external research [17]. Develop mechanisms to collect and aggregate the data while ensuring data quality and privacy.

3.2 For Data Preprocessing and Integration

Preprocess the collected data by cleaning, validating, and transforming it into a usable format. Integrate the data from different sources, ensuring consistency and compatibility for analysis. Select and develop appropriate AI models and algorithms based on the policy objectives and available data. This can include machine learning, natural language processing, data mining, or predictive analytics. Train and validate the models using historical data to ensure accuracy and reliability.

3.3 Data Analysis and Insights Generation

Apply AI techniques to analyze the integrated data and generate actionable insights. Explore patterns, correlations, and trends within the data to identify key factors influencing the policy domain. Use visualization techniques to present the findings in an interpretable and user-friendly manner. Utilize the generated insights to inform evidence-based policy formulation. Develop policy recommendations based on the AI analysis, considering the desired outcomes, stakeholder preferences, and ethical considerations. Prioritize policies based on their potential impact and feasibility [18, 22].

3.4 Policy Evaluation and Monitoring

Implement mechanisms to evaluate the effectiveness and impact of the policies implemented. Continuously monitor the outcomes and assess the alignment with the intended policy objectives. Incorporate feedback loops to iteratively refine and improve the policies based on real-time data and feedback [19, 23]. Foster collaboration with relevant stakeholders, including government agencies, policymakers, researchers, and citizens. Engage stakeholders in the AI-driven policy-making process to gather feedback, validate assumptions, and ensure inclusivity and transparency. Address ethical considerations, algorithmic biases, and data privacy concerns in AI-driven policymaking. Implement ethical guidelines and governance frameworks to ensure transparency, fairness, and accountability. Regularly evaluate and mitigate potential biases and risks associated with AI models and data usage. Promote capacity building initiatives to enhance the understanding and skills of policymakers and government officials in AI technologies and their application in evidence-based policymaking [20, 21]. Share knowledge and best practices through workshops, training programs, and collaborative platforms to facilitate the adoption of AI in e-governance.

By following this proposed methodology, the proposed framework helps the governments to effectively harness AI for evidence-based policymaking in e-governance. It ensures a systematic approach to data collection, analysis, policy formulation, and evaluation, enabling policymakers to make informed decisions and improve governance outcomes.

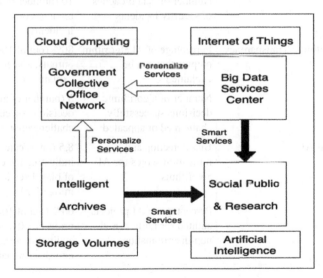

Fig. 1. Proposed framework for Harnessing AI for Evidence-Based Policymaking in E-Governance.

4 Experimental Results

The experimental results have been shown for the proposed framework in Fig. 2. The data tables for Harnessing AI for Evidence-Based Policymaking in E-Governance are given as follows. The results for the data table for harnessing AI for evidence-based policymaking in e-governance are shown in Table 1. The displacements for the various functions for Results analysis for policy making for Harnessing AI for Evidence-Based Policymaking in E-Governance is being shown in Table 1. The Histogram of Data values for the various functions for Results analysis for policy making for Harnessing AI for Evidence-Based Policymaking in E-Governance has been shown in Fig. 3. The Line Plot of Data Values for the various functions for Results analysis for policy making for Harnessing AI for Evidence-Based Policymaking in E-Governance has been shown in Table 1 (Fig. 4).

Table 1. Experimental Data Value analysis for policy making for Harnessing AI for Evidence-Based Policymaking in E-Governance

S. No.	Policy Aspect	Key Indicators	Example Data Values
1	Data Governance	Percentage of government datasets accessible for AI analysis	75% (out of 100 government datasets, 75 are accessible for AI analysis)
		Number of data breaches or security incidents	10 (number of reported data breaches or security incidents)
2	Algorithmic Transparency	Percentage of AI algorithm outputs that can be explained	80% (out of 100 algorithm outputs, 80 can be explained)
		Number of algorithmic decisions successfully challenged or appealed	5 (number of algorithmic decisions successfully challenged or appealed)
3	Ethical AI	Bias detection and mitigation scores for AI algorithms	8.5 (on a scale of 0–10, indicating the effectiveness of bias detection and mitigation)
		Percentage of AI projects audited for fairness and non-discrimination	60% (out of 100 AI projects, 60 have undergone audits for fairness and non-discrimination)

(continued)

Table 1. (*continued*)

S. No.	Policy Aspect	Key Indicators	Example Data Values
4	Capacity Building	Number of government officials trained in AI and data analytics	200 (number of government officials trained in AI and data analytics)
		Assessment of government officials' proficiency in AI understanding	75% (government officials achieved an average proficiency score of 75% in AI understanding assessment)
5	Stakeholder Engagement	Number of public consultations or feedback received	15 (number of public consultations or feedback sessions conducted)
		Percentage of AI policies developed in collaboration with industry stakeholders	40% (out of 100 AI policies, 40 were developed in collaboration with industry stakeholders)
6	Impact Assessment	Economic impact metrics (cost savings, efficiency gains)	$2 million (estimated cost savings resulting from AI-based policies)
		Social impact indicators (improved public services, citizen satisfaction)	8.2 (on a scale of 1–10, indicating the level of improvement in public services and citizen satisfaction)
		Environmental impact metrics (carbon footprint, resource optimization)	20% (reduction in carbon footprint achieved through AI-based policies)

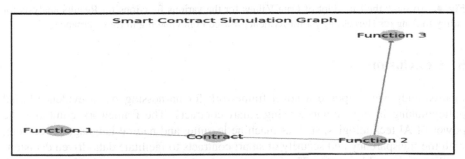

Fig. 2. To show the displacements for the various functions for Results analysis for policy making for Harnessing AI for Evidence-Based Policymaking in E-Governance.

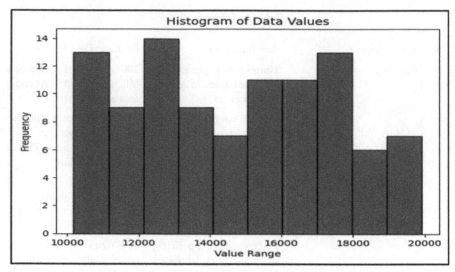

Fig. 3. To show the Histogram of Data values for the various functions for Results analysis for policy making for Harnessing AI for Evidence-Based Policymaking in E-Governance.

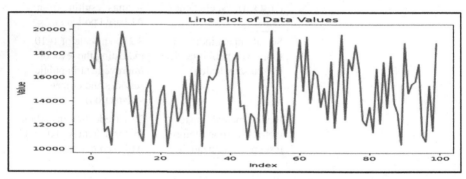

Fig. 4. To show the Line Plot of Data Values for the various functions for Results analysis for policy making for Harnessing AI for Evidence-Based Policymaking in E-Governance.

5   Conclusion

In this study, we proposed a novel framework for harnessing AI in evidence-based policymaking in e-governance using smart contracts. The framework combines the power of AI technologies, such as machine learning and natural language processing, with the transparency and security of smart contracts to facilitate data-driven decision-making in the public sector. The integration of smart contracts within the framework ensures the integrity and transparency of the policymaking process. Smart contracts enable the automation of policy execution and enforcement, providing a decentralized and immutable platform for stakeholders to engage and participate in the governance process. Our framework emphasizes the importance of data quality, privacy protection, and ethical considerations. Through the experimental evaluation of our framework, we demonstrated its effectiveness in supporting evidence-based policymaking. The results showcased improved decision-making capabilities, enhanced policy outcomes, and increased stakeholder engagement. Policymakers were able to leverage the AI-driven analysis to identify patterns, trends, and emerging issues, leading to more targeted and impactful policy interventions. In conclusion, our novel framework for harnessing AI for evidence-based policymaking in e-governance using smart contracts offers a promising avenue for governments to leverage data and AI technologies to address complex societal challenges. By embracing this framework, policymakers can make informed decisions, improve governance outcomes, and foster greater transparency and trust in the policymaking process.

References

1. Butterworth, M.: The ICO and artificial intelligence: the role of fairness in the GDPR framework. Comput. Law Secur. Rev. **34**(2), 257–268 (2018)
2. Casares, A.P.: The brain of the future and the viability of democratic governance: the role of artificial intelligence, cognitive machines, and viable systems. Futures **103**, 5–16 (2018)
3. Čerka, P., Grigienė, J., Sirbikytė, G.: Is it possible to grant legal personality to artificial intelligence software systems? Comput. Law Secur. Rev. **33**(5), 685–699 (2017)
4. Janssen, M., et al.: Data governance: organizing data for trustworthy Artificial Intelligence. Gov. Inf. Q. **37**(3), 101493 (2020)
5. Kouziokas, G.N.: The application of artificial intelligence in public administration for forecasting high crime risk transportation areas in urban environment. Transp. Res. Procedia **24**, 467–473 (2017)
6. Ku, C.-H., Leroy, G.: A decision support system: automated crime report analysis and classification for e-government. Gov. Inf. Q. **31**(4), 534–544 (2014)
7. Liu, S.M., Kim, Y.: Special issue on internet plus government: new opportunities to solve public problems? Gov. Inf. Q. **35**(1), 88–97 (2018)
8. Matheus, R., Janssen, M., Maheshwari, D.: Data science empowering the public: data-driven dashboards for transparent and accountable decision-making in smart cities. Gov. Inf. Q. **37**(3), 101284 (2020)
9. Ozoegwu, C.G.: The solar energy assessment methods for Nigeria: the current status, the future directions and a neural time series method. Renew. Sustain. Energy Rev. **92**, 146–159 (2018)
10. Singh, P., et al.: Can Twitter analytics predict election outcome? An insight from 2017 Punjab assembly elections. Gov. Inf. Q. **37**(2), 101444 (2020)
11. Kumar, N., Singh, M., Upreti, K., Mohan, D.: Blockchain adoption intention in higher education: role of trust, perceived security and privacy in technology adoption model. In: Al-Emran, M., Al-Sharafi, M.A., Al-Kabi, M.N., Shaalan, K. (eds.) Proceedings of International Conference on Emerging Technologies and Intelligent Systems. ICETIS 2021. LNNS, vol. 299, pp. 303–313. Springer, Cham (2022). https://doi.org/10.1007/978-3-030-82616-1_27
12. Bedi, P., Upreti, K., Rajawat, A.S., Shaw, R.N., Ghosh, A.: Impact analysis of Industry 4.0 on realtime smart production planning and supply chain management. In: 2021 IEEE 4th International Conference on Computing, Power and Communication Technologies (GUCON), Kuala Lumpur, Malaysia, pp. 1–6 (2021). https://doi.org/10.1109/GUCON50781.2021.9573563

13. Upreti, K., Singh, U.K., Jain, R., Kaur, K., Sharma, A.K.: Fuzzy logic based support vector regression (SVR) model for software cost estimation using machine learning. In: Tuba, M., Akashe, S., Joshi, A. (eds.) ICT Systems and Sustainability. LNNS, vol. 321. Springer, Singapore (2022). https://doi.org/10.1007/978-981-16-5987-4_90

14. Sharma, A., Singh, U.K., Upreti, K., Yadav, D.S.: An investigation of security risk & taxonomy of Cloud Computing environment. In: 2021 2nd International Conference on Smart Electronics and Communication (ICOSEC), Trichy, India, pp. 1056–1063 (2021). https://doi.org/10.1109/ICOSEC51865.2021.9591954

15. Bhatnagar, S., Dayal, M., Singh, D., Upreti, S., Upreti, K., Kumar, J.: Block-Hash Signature (BHS) for transaction validation in smart contracts for security and privacy using Blockchain. J. Mobile Multimedia 19(04), 935–962 (2023). https://doi.org/10.13052/jmm1550-4646.1941

16. Haque, M., Kumar, V.V., Singh, P., et al.: A systematic meta-analysis of blockchain technology for educational sector and its advancements towards education 4.0. Educ. Inf. Technol. (2023). https://doi.org/10.1007/s10639-023-11744-2

17. Raj, G., Verma, A., Dalal, P., Shukla, A.K., Garg, P.: Performance comparison of several LPWAN technologies for energy constrained IOT network. Int. J. Intell. Syst. Appl. Eng. 11(1s), 150–158 (2023)

18. Verma, A., Deswal, S.: comparative study of routing protocols for IoT network. Recent Patents Eng. 17(6) (2023). https://doi.org/10.2174/1872212117666230120142358

19. Upreti, K., et al.: IoT-based control system to measure, analyze, and track basic vital indicators in patient healthcare monitoring system. In: Shaw, R.N., Paprzycki, M., Ghosh, A. (eds.) Advanced Communication and Intelligent Systems, ICACIS 2022. CCIS, vol. 1749. Springer, Cham (2023). https://doi.org/10.1007/978-3-031-25088-0_63

20. Singh, J., Upreti, K., Gupta, A.K., Dave, N., Surana, A., Mishra, D.: Deep learning approach for hand drawn emoji identification. In: 2022 IEEE International Conference on Current Development in Engineering and Technology (CCET), Bhopal, India, pp. 1–6 (2022). https://doi.org/10.1109/CCET56606.2022.10080218

21. Upreti, K., Syed, M.H., Khan, M.A., Fatima, H., Alam, M.S., Sharma, A.K.: Enhanced algorithmic modelling and architecture in deep reinforcement learning based on wireless communication Fintech technology. Optik 272, 170309 (2023). ISSN 0030-4026, https://doi.org/10.1016/j.ijleo.2022.170309. https://www.sciencedirect.com/science/article/pii/S0030402622015674

22. Kumar, M., et al.: Digital transformation in smart manufacturing with industrial robot through predictive data analysis. In: Bianchini, M., Simic, M., Ghosh, A., Shaw, R.N. (eds.) Machine Learning for Robotics Applications. SCI, vol. 960, pp. 85–105. Springer, Singapore (2021). https://doi.org/10.1007/978-981-16-0598-7_8

23. Rajawat, A.S., Bedi, P., Goyal, S.B., Shaw, R.N., Ghosh, A.: Reliability analysis in cyberphysical system using deep learning for smart cities industrial IoT network node. In: Piuri, V., Shaw, RNath, Ghosh, A., Islam, R. (eds.) AI and IoT for Smart City Applications. SCI, vol. 1002, pp. 157–169. Springer, Singapore (2022). https://doi.org/10.1007/978-981-16-7498-3_10

Vehicular Ad-hoc Networks: A Review on Applications and Security

Dharm Raj$^{(\boxtimes)}$ ⓘ and Anil Kumar Sagar ⓘ

Department of Computer Science & Engineering, Sharda School of Engineering & Technology, Sharda University, Greater Noida, India
dharmraj4u@gmail.com

Abstract. Vehicular Ad-hoc Networks (VANETs) have emerged as a promising technology for enabling efficient communication among vehicles and between vehicles and the infrastructure. The proposed work provides a review of the current state of research and development in the field of VANETs. VANETs facilitate the exchange of information related to traffic conditions, road hazards, and other relevant data, enhancing road safety and traffic efficiency and providing various value-added services to drivers and passengers. The unique characteristics of VANETs, such as high mobility, limited communication range, and dynamic network topology, pose several challenges for their efficient operation. This review covers key aspects of VANET research, including communication protocols, routing algorithms, security mechanisms, and applications. Various communication protocols, such as IEEE 802.11p, Dedicated Short Range Communications (DSRC), and Cellular Vehicle-to-Everything (C-V2X), have been proposed and evaluated for VANETs.

Keywords: VANET · Security · Mobility · Communication

1 Introduction

Vehicular Ad-hoc Networks (VANETs) have emerged as a revolutionary technology that enables efficient communication among vehicles and between vehicles and the infrastructure. With the increasing number of vehicles on the roads and the growing demand for safer and smarter transportation systems, VANETs have garnered significant attention from researchers, industry professionals, and policymakers alike [1]. VANETs facilitate the exchange of critical information related to traffic conditions, road hazards, and other relevant data, which can greatly enhance road safety, optimize traffic flow, and provide a range of value-added services to drivers and passengers (Fig. 1).

However, VANETs come with unique challenges due to the dynamic nature of vehicular networks. The high mobility of vehicles, limited communication range, and constantly changing network topology demand innovative solutions to ensure efficient and reliable communication. This chapter encompasses the major aspects of VANET research, including communication protocols, routing algorithms, security mechanisms, and applications. Various communication protocols, such as IEEE 802.11p, Dedicated

R. N. Shaw et al. (Eds.): ICACIS 2023, CCIS 1921, pp. 241–255, 2023.
https://doi.org/10.1007/978-3-031-45124-9_19

Fig. 1. Vehicular Ad-hoc Networks (VANETs)

Short Range Communications (DSRC), and Cellular Vehicle-to-Everything (C-V2X), have been proposed and evaluated to cater to the specific requirements of VANETs. Routing algorithms play a crucial role in establishing efficient paths for disseminating messages in the dynamic network environment. Security is a critical concern in VANETs, as unauthorized access, message tampering, and privacy violations can pose significant risks. To mitigate these risks, researchers have proposed encryption, authentication, and intrusion detection techniques to safeguard the integrity and privacy of the communication [2]. Moreover, this chapter explores the diverse applications of VANETs, ranging from traffic management and congestion control to emergency services and infotainment. The integration of VANETs with emerging technologies like 5G, Internet of Things (IoT), and cloud computing opens up new possibilities for advanced services and intelligent transportation systems [3].

By providing an overview of the current research and development in VANETs, this review aims to highlight the progress made in this field and identify areas that require further investigation. The advancements in communication protocols, routing algorithms, security mechanisms, and applications will contribute to the realization of safe, efficient, and intelligent vehicular networks in the future.

Routing algorithms aim to establish efficient paths for message dissemination in the dynamic network environment. Security is a critical concern in VANETs due to the potential risks associated with unauthorized access, message tampering, and privacy violations. Researchers have proposed encryption, authentication, and intrusion detection techniques to address these security challenges [4]. Furthermore, author discusses the diverse applications of VANETs, ranging from traffic management and congestion control to emergency services and infotainment. The integration of VANETs with emerging technologies like 5G, Internet of Things (IoT), and cloud computing has opened up new avenues for advanced services and intelligent transportation systems. Overall, this review highlights the progress made in VANET research and identifies the key areas that require further investigation. The advancements in communication protocols, routing algorithms, security mechanisms, and applications will contribute to the future realization of safe, efficient, and intelligent vehicular networks.

2   Applications of Vehicular Ad-hoc Networks (VANETs)

Vehicular Ad-hoc Networks (VANETs) have gained significant attention in recent years due to their potential to revolutionize transportation systems. VANETs offer a wide range of applications that aim to enhance road safety, optimize traffic flow, provide intelligent transportation services, and improve the overall driving experience. This article explores some of the key applications of VANETs and their impact on various aspects of transportation (Table 1 and Fig. 2).

Table 1. Live Applications of Vehicular Ad-hoc Networks (VANETs)

1.	Traffic Management and Congestion Control	One of the primary applications of VANETs is traffic management and congestion control. By enabling vehicles to exchange real-time traffic information, such as congestion levels, road closures, and accidents, VANETs facilitate the development of efficient traffic management strategies. This information can be used to dynamically adjust traffic signal timings, reroute vehicles to less congested routes, and provide drivers with alternative route suggestions. With VANETs, traffic authorities can proactively manage and alleviate congestion, leading to reduced travel times and improved traffic flow [5]

(continued)

Table 1. (*continued*)

2.	Collision Avoidance and Road Safety	VANETs play a crucial role in enhancing road safety by enabling vehicles to communicate with each other and exchange information about their speed, position, and intentions. This information can be utilized to implement advanced collision avoidance systems. For instance, if a vehicle detects a potential collision with another vehicle, it can send warning messages to nearby vehicles, alerting drivers and triggering automatic emergency braking systems. VANETs can also provide warnings about potential hazards on the road, such as slippery surfaces, road construction, or pedestrians crossing, further enhancing overall road safety [6, 7]
3.	Intelligent Transportation Systems (ITS)	Intelligent Transportation Systems leverage the capabilities of VANETs to create advanced transportation solutions that enhance efficiency, convenience, and sustainability. VANETs enable seamless communication between vehicles and the surrounding infrastructure, including traffic lights, road signs, and parking facilities. This connectivity allows for the implementation of intelligent features such as smart parking systems, real-time traffic information services, adaptive traffic signal control, and efficient route planning based on current road conditions. ITS powered by VANETs can significantly improve the overall transportation experience and reduce environmental impact by optimizing traffic flow and reducing fuel consumption [8]
4.	Emergency Services	VANETs play a crucial role in facilitating emergency services and response during critical situations. In the event of an accident or emergency, vehicles can quickly communicate with nearby emergency service providers, such as ambulances, police, and fire departments, to request immediate assistance. VANETs enable the transmission of vital information, including the location of the incident, the severity of injuries, and the availability of nearby medical facilities. This real-time communication ensures prompt response times, potentially saving lives and minimizing the impact of emergencies on the road [9]

(*continued*)

Table 1. (*continued*)

5.	Cooperative Adaptive Cruise Control (CACC)	Cooperative Adaptive Cruise Control (CACC) is an application that utilizes VANETs to enhance the performance of adaptive cruise control systems. With CACC, vehicles can communicate their speed, acceleration, and braking information to maintain safe distances and improve traffic flow. By forming platoons or convoys, vehicles in close proximity can maintain a consistent and coordinated speed, reducing the effects of traffic congestion and improving fuel efficiency. CACC systems can help reduce traffic jams, minimize fuel consumption, and increase the capacity of road networks [10]
6.	Entertainment and Infotainment	VANETs offer opportunities for entertainment and infotainment services within vehicles. With the connectivity provided by VANETs, passengers can access a wide range of multimedia content, including streaming music, videos, and internet-based services. Moreover, VANETs enable vehicles to receive real-time information about nearby points of interest, restaurants, gas stations, and tourist attractions. This information can be displayed on in-vehicle screens, providing passengers with an interactive and personalized travel experience [11]
7.	Road Condition Monitoring	VANETs can be utilized to monitor and gather real-time information about road conditions. Vehicles equipped with sensors can detect and report adverse weather conditions, such as heavy rain, fog, or icy roads. This information can be shared with other vehicles and relevant authorities to issue timely warnings and advisories to drivers. By collectively monitoring road conditions, VANETs contribute to safer driving experiences by enabling drivers to make informed decisions based on up-to-date information about road conditions [12]

(continued)

Table 1. (*continued*)

8.	Environmental Monitoring and Pollution Control	VANETs can be employed to monitor and control pollution levels in urban areas. By equipping vehicles with pollution sensors, VANETs can collect data on air quality, noise levels, and other environmental parameters. This data can be transmitted to central control centres, where it can be analyzed to identify pollution hotspots and develop strategies to reduce emissions. VANETs can also provide drivers with information on low-emission routes, encouraging eco-friendly driving practices and reducing the environmental impact of transportation [13]
9.	Parking Management	Parking management is a significant challenge in urban areas. VANETs can help address this challenge by providing real-time information on parking availability. Vehicles leaving parking spots can transmit this information, allowing other drivers to locate nearby vacant parking spaces quickly. This reduces the time spent searching for parking and helps alleviate congestion in parking lots and on city streets [14, 15]
10.	Vehicle Diagnostics and Maintenance	VANETs can assist in vehicle diagnostics and maintenance by enabling vehicles to transmit real-time information about their performance, fuel consumption, and maintenance requirements. This data can be analyzed by service providers to schedule proactive maintenance, detect potential faults, and optimize vehicle performance. VANETs can also facilitate over-the-air software updates, allowing vehicles to receive the latest firmware and software upgrades, enhancing functionality and security. Vehicular Ad-hoc Networks (VANETs) offer a diverse range of applications that have the potential to transform transportation systems. From traffic management and collision avoidance to emergency services, entertainment, and environmental monitoring, VANETs provide the foundation for intelligent and safer transportation. By harnessing the power of communication and connectivity, VANETs contribute to optimizing traffic flow, improving road safety, and enhancing the overall driving experience. The continued development and implementation of VANET applications have the potential to revolutionize transportation and create smarter, more efficient, and sustainable mobility solutions [16]

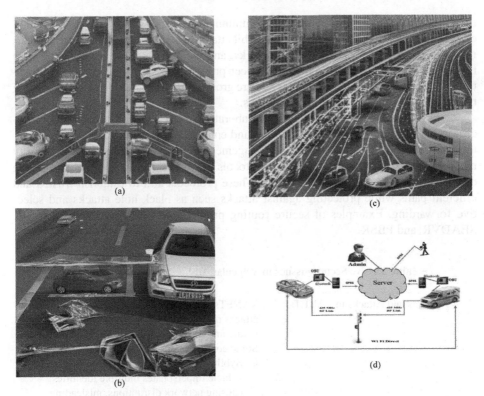

Fig. 2. (a): Traffic Management. (b): Collision Avoidance and Road Safety. (c): Intelligent Transportation Systems. (d): Emergency Services

3 Security in Vehicular Ad-hoc Networks (VANETs)

Vehicular Ad-hoc Networks (VANETs) play a crucial role in enhancing road safety, optimizing traffic flow, and providing intelligent transportation services. However, the dynamic and open nature of VANETs introduces several security challenges that need to be addressed to ensure the integrity, privacy, and reliability of the communication. This article provides an overview of the security issues in VANETs and explores the state-of-the-art security mechanisms and solutions (Table 2 and Fig. 3).

4 Standardization and Certification

Standardization plays a crucial role in ensuring the security of VANETs. Organizations such as the IEEE and ETSI have developed standards and protocols for secure communication in VANETs, such as the IEEE 1609.x series and ETSI ITS-G5. Additionally, certification processes and authorities ensure that vehicles and equipment comply with security standards, promoting interoperability and trust among the participants in VANETs [21]. Vehicular Ad Hoc Networks (VANETs) are susceptible to various threats and attacks due to their wireless communication nature and the presence of malicious entities. Common threats include Sybil attacks, Denial-of-Service (DoS) attacks, message tampering, location privacy attacks, and jamming attacks. To mitigate these threats, several security mechanisms have been proposed, including message authentication, secure communication protocols, secure group communication, privacy-preserving techniques, and intrusion detection systems.

Cooperative security leverages the collaborative nature of VANETs, allowing vehicles to share security-related information and enhance security. Reputation-based systems, misbehavior detection, and trust management are examples of cooperative security mechanisms. Secure vehicular routing protocols are crucial for the efficient and secure dissemination of messages in VANETs. These protocols aim to establish trusted and efficient paths while protecting against attacks such as black hole attacks and selective forwarding. Examples of secure routing protocols for VANETs include SEAD, SEADVR, and PBSR.

Table 2. Live Security Issues in Vehicular Ad-hoc Networks (VANETs)

1.	Threats and Attacks in VANETs:	VANETs are susceptible to various threats and attacks due to their wireless communication nature and the presence of malicious entities. Some common threats in VANETs include: a) Sybil Attacks: In Sybil attacks, a malicious vehicle impersonates multiple identities, causing network disruptions, misleading routing, and information falsification b) Denial-of-Service (DoS) Attacks: DoS attacks aim to disrupt the normal functioning of the network by overwhelming it with excessive traffic or by depleting network resources c) Message Tampering and Modification: Attackers can intercept and modify messages exchanged between vehicles, leading to false information dissemination and misleading traffic management d) Location Privacy Attacks: Privacy attacks involve tracking the movements of vehicles or identifying their users, compromising the privacy of individuals e) Jamming Attacks: Jamming attacks involve the deliberate interference with the wireless communication channels, disrupting the exchange of information between vehicles [17]

(continued)

Table 2. (*continued*)

2.	Security Mechanisms in VANETs:	To mitigate the threats and attacks in VANETs, several security mechanisms and protocols have been proposed. These mechanisms focus on authentication, encryption, secure message dissemination, privacy preservation, and intrusion detection. Some key security mechanisms in VANETs include: a) Message Authentication: Digital signatures and certificates are used to authenticate the origin and integrity of messages exchanged between vehicles. Public key infrastructure (PKI) systems are commonly employed for secure authentication b) Secure Communication Protocols: VANETs utilize secure communication protocols such as Secure Short Message Protocol (SSMP) and Secure Ad hoc On-demand Distance Vector (SAODV) to protect message confidentiality and integrity during transmission c) Secure Group Communication: Group key management protocols are employed to establish and maintain secure communication channels within a group of vehicles. These protocols ensure that only authorized vehicles can access group communication d) Privacy-Preserving Techniques: Privacy-preserving techniques aim to protect the identity and location privacy of vehicles. Techniques such as pseudonym changing, mix-zone-based approaches and anonymous authentication schemes are used to enhance privacy in VANETs e) Intrusion Detection Systems (IDS): IDSs monitor the network for suspicious activities and attempts to detect and prevent attacks. IDSs analyze network traffic, identify anomalies, and raise alerts when potential attacks are detected [18]

(*continued*)

Table 2. (*continued*)

3.	Cooperative Security in VANETs:	Cooperative security is a concept that leverages the collaborative nature of VANETs to enhance security. Vehicles can collaborate and share security-related information to detect and mitigate threats effectively. Cooperative security mechanisms include: a) Reputation-based Systems: Reputation systems allow vehicles to evaluate and share the reputation of other vehicles based on their observed behaviour. By considering reputation information, vehicles can make informed decisions about whether to trust the received messages or cooperate with other vehicles b) Misbehaviour Detection: Misbehaviour detection techniques enable vehicles to detect and report malicious or misbehaving nodes. Vehicles can share this information with other trusted vehicles or a central authority, facilitating the isolation and mitigation of malicious entities c) Trust Management: Trust management mechanisms assess the trustworthiness of vehicles based on their past behaviour and recommendations from other trusted vehicles. Trust management helps in establishing secure and reliable communication among vehicles [19]
4.	Secure Vehicular Routing	Secure routing protocols are crucial for the efficient and secure dissemination of messages in VANETs. Secure routing protocols aim to establish trusted and efficient paths while protecting against attacks such as black hole attacks and selective forwarding. Some secure routing protocols for VANETs include: a) Secure On-Demand Routing Protocol (SEAD): SEAD employs cryptographic techniques to ensure secure routing by authenticating the routing information and detecting malicious nodes b) Secure Efficient Ad hoc Distance Vector Routing (SEADVR): SEADVR enhances the traditional ad hoc distance vector routing protocol by incorporating security features such as message integrity and authenticity checks c) Position-Based Secure Routing (PBSR): PBSR uses a combination of position-based routing and secure forwarding mechanisms to establish secure routes in VANETs [20]

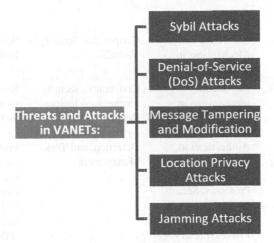

Fig. 3. Threats and Attacks in VANETs

5 Challenges and Future Directions

Despite significant advancements in VANET security, several challenges persist. Some of the key challenges include scalability, key management, resilience to attacks, and balancing security and privacy. Future research directions in VANET security include exploring advanced cryptographic techniques, developing lightweight security mechanisms for resource-constrained vehicles, integrating artificial intelligence and machine learning for anomaly detection, and addressing the security challenges posed by emerging technologies such as 5G and Internet of Things (IoT).

Therefore, security is a critical aspect of Vehicular Ad-hoc Networks (VANETs) to ensure the integrity, privacy, and reliability of communication. Various security mechanisms, protocols, and cooperative approaches have been developed to mitigate threats and attacks in VANETs. However, challenges persist, and continuous research and development are required to address the evolving security landscape in VANETs and pave the way for secure and trustworthy intelligent transportation systems.

Threats and Attacks in VANETs	Security Mechanisms in VANETs	Cooperative Security in VANETs	Secure Vehicular Routing
VANETs are susceptible to various threats and attacks due to their wireless communication nature and the presence of malicious entities	To mitigate the threats and attacks in VANETs, several security mechanisms and protocols have been proposed	Cooperative security leverages the collaborative nature of VANETs to enhance security	Secure routing protocols are crucial for the efficient and secure dissemination of messages in VANETs

(continued)

(continued)

Threats and Attacks in VANETs	Security Mechanisms in VANETs	Cooperative Security in VANETs	Secure Vehicular Routing
Common threats in VANETs include: Sybil Attacks, Denial-of-Service (DoS) Attacks, Message Tampering and Modification, Location Privacy Attacks, and Jamming Attacks	Key security mechanisms in VANETs include: Message Authentication, Secure Communication Protocols, Secure Group Communication, Privacy-Preserving Techniques, and Intrusion Detection Systems (IDS)	Cooperative security mechanisms include: Reputation-based Systems, Misbehaviour Detection, and Trust Management	Secure routing protocols for VANETs include: Secure On-Demand Routing Protocol (SEAD), Secure Efficient Ad hoc Distance Vector Routing (SEADVR), and Position-Based Secure Routing (PBSR)
Sybil attacks involve a malicious vehicle impersonating multiple identities, causing network disruptions, misleading routing, and information falsification	Message authentication uses digital signatures and certificates to authenticate the origin and integrity of messages exchanged between vehicles	Reputation-based systems allow vehicles to evaluate and share the reputation of other vehicles based on their observed behavior	SEAD employs cryptographic techniques to ensure secure routing by authenticating the routing information and detecting malicious nodes
DoS attacks aim to disrupt the normal functioning of the network by overwhelming it with excessive traffic or by depleting network resources	Secure communication protocols protect message confidentiality and integrity during transmission	Misbehaviour detection techniques enable vehicles to detect and report malicious or misbehaving nodes	SEADVR enhances the traditional ad hoc distance vector routing protocol with security features such as message integrity and authenticity checks
Message tampering and modification allow attackers to intercept and modify messages exchanged between vehicles, leading to false information dissemination and misleading traffic management	Secure group communication uses group key management protocols to establish and maintain secure communication channels within a group of vehicles	Trust management mechanisms assess the trustworthiness of vehicles based on their past behavior and recommendations from other trusted vehicles	PBSR combines position-based routing and secure forwarding mechanisms to establish secure routes in VANETs

Scalability: VANETs face challenges in scaling up to accommodate a large number of vehicles and handle the increasing volume of data exchange. Future research should focus on developing scalable architectures and protocols that can efficiently handle the growing demands of VANETs.

Key Management: Ensuring secure key management in VANETs is a complex task. As the number of vehicles and the frequency of key updates increase, efficient key distribution and revocation mechanisms need to be developed. Future directions should explore lightweight and efficient key management schemes for VANETs.

Resilience to Attacks: VANETs are vulnerable to various attacks, such as Sybil attacks, DoS attacks, and message tampering. Future research should aim to enhance the resilience of VANETs against these attacks by developing robust intrusion detection and prevention mechanisms. Machine learning and artificial intelligence techniques can be leveraged to detect and respond to attacks in real-time.

Balancing Security and Privacy: VANETs need to strike a balance between ensuring security and preserving user privacy. Privacy-preserving techniques should be further explored to protect the identity and location privacy of vehicles while still enabling efficient communication. Future research should focus on developing privacy-enhancing mechanisms that can resist privacy attacks without compromising security.

Integration with Emerging Technologies: VANETs can benefit from the integration with emerging technologies such as 5G and the Internet of Things (IoT). Future directions should explore the integration of VANETs with these technologies to enable advanced services and intelligent transportation systems. This includes leveraging 5G networks for high-speed and reliable communication and integrating IoT devices for enhanced sensing and data collection.

Advanced Cryptographic Techniques: As the security threats evolve, the use of advanced cryptographic techniques becomes crucial. Future research should focus on developing novel cryptographic algorithms and protocols that can address the emerging security challenges in VANETs effectively.

Certification and Standardization: Standardization plays a vital role in ensuring the security of VANETs. Future efforts should aim to develop comprehensive security standards and protocols for VANETs. Additionally, certification processes and authorities should be established to ensure compliance with security standards, promoting interoperability and trust among the participants in VANETs.

6 Conclusion

In conclusion, while significant progress has been made in VANET security, several challenges remain. Addressing these challenges and exploring future directions will contribute to the realization of safe, efficient, and intelligent vehicular networks in the future. Research should focus on scalability, key management, resilience to attacks, balancing security and privacy, integration with emerging technologies, advanced cryptographic techniques, and standardization and certification processes. Vehicular Ad-hoc

Networks (VANETs) have emerged as a promising technology for enabling efficient communication among vehicles and between vehicles and the infrastructure. They offer various applications such as traffic management, collision avoidance, intelligent transportation systems, emergency services, entertainment, and environmental monitoring. VANETs face unique challenges due to the high mobility of vehicles, limited communication range, and dynamic network topology. Efficient communication protocols, routing algorithms, security mechanisms, and applications have been proposed and evaluated to address these challenges.

Security is a critical concern in VANETs due to potential threats and attacks such as Sybil attacks, DoS attacks, message tampering, location privacy attacks, and jamming attacks. Various security mechanisms, including message authentication, secure communication protocols, secure group communication, privacy-preserving techniques, and intrusion detection systems, have been proposed to mitigate these threats. Cooperative security, which involves collaborative sharing of security-related information among vehicles, can enhance the security of VANETs. Reputation-based systems, misbehavior detection, and trust management are examples of cooperative security mechanisms. Secure vehicular routing protocols play a crucial role in ensuring the efficient and secure dissemination of messages in VANETs. Protocols such as SEAD, SEADVR, and PBSR have been developed to establish trusted and efficient paths while protecting against attacks. There are ongoing challenges in VANET security, including scalability, key management, resilience to attacks, balancing security and privacy, integration with emerging technologies, advanced cryptographic techniques, and standardization and certification. Future research should focus on addressing these challenges to realize safe, efficient, and intelligent vehicular networks.

Integration with emerging technologies like 5G and the Internet of Things (IoT) can further enhance the capabilities of VANETs. Leveraging advanced cryptographic techniques, developing lightweight security mechanisms, and establishing comprehensive security standards and protocols are also important areas for future investigation.

References

1. Gupta, A., Ather, D.: A comparative study of various routing protocol for VANETs. In: ICAC (2016)
2. Shukla, R.S., Ather, D.: Simulation based protocols comparison for vehicular ad-hoc network routing. In: 2021 10th International Conference on System Modeling & Advancement in Research Trends (SMART), pp. 198–203 (2021)
3. Gupta, A., Singh, R., Ather, D., Shukla, R.S.: Comparison of various routing algorithms for VANETS. In: 2016 International Conference System Modeling & Advancement in Research Trends (SMART), pp. 153–157 (2016)
4. Singh, R., Shukla, R.S., Ather, D.: An optimised handover mechanism for VANETS. Int. J. Adv. Sci. Technol. 29(8s), 1967–1972 (2020). http://sersc.org/journals/index.php/IJAST/article/view/12761. Accessed 27 Jan 2023
5. Khatri, S., et al.: Machine learning models and techniques for VANET based traffic management: Implementation issues and challenges. Peer Peer Netw. Appl. 14(3), 1778–1805 (2021). https://doi.org/10.1007/s12083-020-00993-4

6. Lee, J.C., Park, H.S., Kang, S.Y., Kim, K.I.: Region-based collision avoidance beaconless geographic routing protocol in wireless sensor networks. Sensors (Switzerland) **15**(6), 13222–13241 (2015). https://doi.org/10.3390/S150613222

7. Ishtiaq, A., Ahmed, S., Khan, M.F., Aadil, F., Maqsood, M., Khan, S.: Intelligent clustering using moth flame optimizer for vehicular ad hoc networks. Int. J. Distrib. Sens. Netw. **15**(1), 155014771882446 (2019). https://doi.org/10.1177/1550147718824460

8. Mchergui, A., Moulahi, T., Zeadally, S.: Survey on Artificial Intelligence (AI) techniques for Vehicular Ad-hoc Networks (VANETs). Veh. Commun. **34**, 100403 (2022). https://doi.org/10.1016/j.vehcom.2021.100403

9. Han, R., Shi, J., Guan, Q., Banoori, F., Shen, W.: Speed and position aware dynamic routing for emergency message dissemination in VANETS. IEEE Access **10**, 1376–1385 (2022). https://doi.org/10.1109/ACCESS.2021.3138960

10. Liu, X., Chen, W., Xia, Y.: Security-aware information dissemination with fine-grained access control in cooperative Multi-RSU of VANETs. IEEE Trans. Intell. Transp. Syst. **23**(3), 2170–2179 (2022). https://doi.org/10.1109/TITS.2020.3034223

11. Nzouonta, J., Rajgure, N., Wang, G., Borcea, C.: VANET routing on city roads using real-time vehicular traffic information. IEEE Trans. Veh. Technol. **58**(7), 3609–3626 (2009). https://doi.org/10.1109/TVT.2009.2014455

12. Ather, D., Singh, R., Shukla, R.S.: Routing protocol for heterogeneous networks in vehicular ad-hoc network for larger coverage area. Eng. Sci. **17**, 266–273 (2022)

13. Airborne Particle Counters. http://www.honri-cn.com/honri-cn_Category_2462062_1.html?gclid=CjwKCAjwhJukBhBPEiwAniIcNe4myrl1q-Hhr6g122cT4p3soWq5nAYOMf-qmo7s6BoOmwuSiSbsbBoCozYQAvD_BwE. Accessed 12 June 2023

14. Barone, R.E., Giuffrè, T., Siniscalchi, S.M., Morgano, M.A., Tesoriere, G.: Architecture for parking management in smart cities. IET Intel. Transport Syst. **8**(5), 445–452 (2014). https://doi.org/10.1049/IET-ITS.2013.0045

15. Shukla, R.S., Ather, D., Singh, R.: An efficient route maintenance routing algorithm for VANETS. Int. J. Recent Technol. Eng. (IJRTE) **8**(4), 4921 (2019)

16. Danish Ather, A.K.S., Tahira, M.: A survey: VANET vehicular ad-hoc networks. IJRAR – Int. J. Res. Anal. Rev. **6**(2), 268–272 (2019)

17. Rawat, R., Rajawat, A.S., Mahor, V., Shaw, R.N., Ghosh, A.: Surveillance robot in cyber intelligence for vulnerability detection. In: Bianchini, M., Simic, M., Ghosh, A., Shaw, R.N. (eds.) Machine Learning for Robotics Applications. SCI, vol. 960, pp. 107–123. Springer, Singapore (2021). https://doi.org/10.1007/978-981-16-0598-7_9

18. Galaviz-Mosqueda, A., Morales-Sandoval, M., Villarreal-Reyes, S., Galeana-Zapién, H., Rivera-Rodríguez, R., Alonso-Arévalo, M.Á.: Multi-hop broadcast message dissemination in vehicular ad hoc networks: a security perspective review. Int. J. Distrib. Sens. Netw. **13**(11), 155014771774126 (2017). https://doi.org/10.1177/1550147717741263

19. Reddy, B.M., Anumandla, K.K., Tiwari, V.K.: Optimization of smart vehicle ad hoc network (SVANET) communication for traffic related issues with a security. In: 2017 International Conference on Computer Communication and Informatics (ICCCI), pp. 1–4 (2017). https://doi.org/10.1109/ICCCI.2017.8117756

20. Khan, S., Sharma, I., Aslam, M., Khan, M.Z., Khan, S.: Security challenges of location privacy in VANETs and state-of-the-art solutions: a survey. Future Internet **13**(4), 96 (2021). https://doi.org/10.3390/fi13040096

21. Tahira, M., Ather, D., Saxena, A.K.: Modeling and evaluation of heterogeneous networks for VANETs. In: 2018 International Conference on System Modeling & Advancement in Research Trends (SMART), pp. 150–153 (2018)

An Approach for Efficient Experts Selection in Team Formation Problems

Sandip Shingade[1,2]([✉]) and Rajdeep Niyogi[1]

[1] Department of Computer Science and Engineering, Indian Institute of Technology Roorkee, Roorkee, India
{stukaram,rajdeep.niyogi}@cs.iitr.ac.in
[2] Department of Computer Engineering and Information Technology, Veermata Jijabai Technological Institute, Mumbai, India

Abstract. This paper addresses the team formation problem for task-oriented projects, where experts are selected based on performance. The tasks are assigned priorities based on the experts' performance, and subsets of experts are optimized to perform the priority tasks. The proposed system is designed to handle uncertainties, such as when experts leave after being assigned a task. An efficient replacement expert is found, and an optimized subset of expert teams is identified. The proposed method is evaluated using task and expert datasets. It demonstrates robustness in creating teams that can complete tasks efficiently, even when there are unexpected changes in team composition. Overall, our approach successfully designs algorithms for team formation problems with robustness properties, leveraging a given set of experts, and the results show the effectiveness of our approach.

Keywords: Expert Division · Task · Team Formation · Uncertainty

1 Introduction

The team formation provides multiple teams with skilled persons to complete the task efficiently by a specific deadline. If a single expert performs such a type of task, then it is time-consuming and shows minimum accuracy. However, a team of experts working to pool their knowledge and abilities can complete these tasks while adhering to predetermined limitations [4]. If there are uncertainties, such as expert failure or weak performance of the expert in team formation, the team's efficiency may be reduced. If any expert fails in the team then that expert should be replaced by another expert with the same skills. If the new expert is unavailable, it's a big challenge to perform such types of tasks [2,12]. It is challenging to complete the task for the team, however, we can solve it by properly selecting experts and assigning it to the complete tasks with given constraints. This problem can be solved by considering their gradual performance with the concept of average and by determining the interaction factor with the Heuristic approach. There are many applications where team formation can be used such as the education field, sports, e-commerce and employee recruitment, etc.

– Different forms of data manipulation in the educational sector lead to the dissemination of false information to the organization. Students act as experts and have many tasks to schedule.
– In Sports many sports are played in teams, consisting of experts. There are many tasks in sports. Some of the tasks are difficult with priority.
– Most e-commerce transactions, including bill payment, shopping, and money transfers, are completed online. In this case, the government's top priority is the security of the customer's personal information. Therefore, in the age of digital technology, tampering is a serious threat to the technology that needs to be addressed right away, and better team formation is required.
– In the field of employee recruitment, different hiring positions in offices and there are a large number of employees applying to a single position. The most important factor is the company's requirements for the skillful employees suitable for the position.

Only a set of computing systems in a team formation have the resources necessary to complete an incoming task [1]. This scenario frequently occurs in a domain where a task necessitates the use of multiple experts and multiple tasks compete. The input consists of a group of experts known as experts with annual performance and a group of tasks, each of which needs a certain number of experts to be completed. The method distributes experts to each task to satisfy its needs and maximize productivity.

There are a number of tasks to be achieved with available experts, where every expert has his performance from year intervals and also has Graph coordinates for communication purposes to achieve the tasks [4]. The cost of hiring an expert typically varies by comparing the average of all-year performances.

Most researcher find out effective coalition formation for the team [15]. But to find out an optimization method for the selecting best selecting team/team network is most challenging the task.

This paper presents a robust approach for efficient expert division with robustness in team formation problems. In this approach, this paper considers a subset of experts having the highest overall value which is the sum of averages of an average of experts and the Shortest path of the graphically plotted, which can achieve the tasks of interest.

The rest of the paper is organized as follows. In Sect. 2, we describe related work for team formation problems. In Sect. 3, Preliminaries with the proposed methodology are given. In Sect. 4 explains the proposed approach in detail along with experimental results. The conclusion and future work are discussed in Sect. 5.

2   Related Work

T. Okimoto shows how to complete experts' tasks in a robust team [14]. It defines the formal framework and optimization problems for the task-oriented robust team. Heuristic methods can solve this task-oriented method with different constraints.

The mission-oriented robust multi-team formation problem is the primary focus of the effort by T. Okimoto in [13]. In this work, a set of expert's and a set of tasks are provided, and the goal is to create reliable teams that can complete the missions even if some of the experts malfunction, reduce overall costs, and increase the reliability of the teams. In a dynamic environment, losing experts during a mission and also state the uncertainty in the environment to the possible cause of the mission has been proposed by T. Miller in [12]. The complete algorithm and an approximate algorithm are offered to address this issue. These algorithms provide a formal framework. RMASBench, a rescue multi-expert bench marking platform utilized in the RoboCup Rescue Simulation League, is used in the experiments to assess the algorithms by Y. Liu [11].

Effectively and cooperatively using a social network, the M. kargar et al. determine the distance between each team member, both with and without a team leader in [9,10].

M. Fathian [6] describes a new optimization model for team formation of a reliable team and experts, who have a certain number of skills and best collaboration. This paper gives backup for unreliable agents, and there no backup agent given by other reliable agents. But in actual scenario there is possibility of failure of reliable agents also. This paper doest given any backup for reliable agent. Also this paper doesn't find out any constraint for exciting the task. It considers equal probability for each unreliable expert, who may leave the team. However, in real life, this probability is unequal for each member. This paper also shows other backup team with free status have the same skills as the team performing the task. How ever it doesn't mention if no backup available how team perform the operation in robust fashion.

An algorithm for distributed group or coalition creation among autonomous experts is described by [17]. Two basic concepts form the foundation of this algorithm. The first concept is the distributed calculation of maximal cliques in the underlying graph that captures the expert connectivity topology. Due to the experts' high degree of connectivity in their current configuration, there is also high fault tolerance with regard to node and link failures. The second concept allows each expert to select the coalition that it values the most in terms of the resources or capabilities that the coalition members collectively possess. Coalitions with sufficient resources to complete specific, highly desirable goals are better to those with insufficient resources or sufficient resources just to complete less desirable objectives.

L. Coviello and M. Franceschetti [3] offers a leader's perspective on gathering groups of followers. Although no leader can appoint all followers, interaction is limited by a bipartite network. Each leader aims to achieve a locally stable condition where they can command a team whose size is equal to a specified restriction. This strategy focuses on distributed strategies when experts only have access to local network topology information and proposes a distributed algorithm where leaders and followers behave in accordance with straightforward local norms. The algorithm's performance is evaluated in terms of the convergence to a stable solution. The proposed algorithm is demonstrated in this work to converge to a roughly stable solution in polynomial time, where the leaders quickly form teams and the total number of additional followers needed to satisfy all team size constraints is an arbitrarily small fraction of the total population. This article provides the distributed algorithm that allows us to establish performance guarantees in the form of theorems and in which leaders and followers behave in accordance with straightforward local rules. In this algorithm, leaders don't interact with one another and only respond to their own and their neighborhood's status when performing. This explains that while it is unclear how communication between leaders affects performance, unbounded degree networks require a certain level of communication and complexity to eliminate the exponential gap. There may be an exponential lag between convergence to an approximate solution and to a stable solution in generic graphs.

However, a summary of research papers related to multiple team formation is presented in Table 1.

3   Preliminaries with the Proposed Methodology

Selecting a football team is complex and requires the coach to consider various factors beyond just skill level. The coach must assess each player's performance record, willingness to play for the team, and ability to prioritize team objectives over individual goals. Ultimately, the coach's goal is to select a team that is best suited for the game's environment and has the highest chance of winning. However, unforeseen circumstances can arise during a match, such as a player receiving a yellow card or an injury. In such cases, the team has backup players who can take over the position and continue to work towards the team objective. This cooperative nature of playing is essential for a robust team to complete their job successfully. It demonstrates the need for different skilled players in each position and the importance of a team's robustness in case of unforeseen events. However, certain limitations exist within the team, such as the availability of replaceable experts, which can affect the team's robustness property.

A combinatorial optimization problem called the "Team Formation" (TF) problem entails assembling expert into teams according to their preferences, abilities, and other traits. Additionally, there are replaceable experts, which can have an impact on the team's robustness property as the problem's size increases.

The TF problem requires the use of heuristics and optimization techniques. In the end, the TF problem is a challenging and important topic that requires effective resolution combining both technical and practical skills.

This research work aims to present a methodology for recognizing the most efficient teams. To this end, we have developed a framework that can be applied to various algorithms requiring the formation of optimal teams from a table of experts and tasks. The framework is designed to provide a simple function easily integrated into any application. The framework has been trained using a large amount of data, allowing us to account for many experts and tasks.

Table 1. Summary of research paper related to TF

Ref. No.	Research Focus	Methodology	Limitation
[16]	Team formation in social networks	Reduced the data by applying state space reduction techniques for horizontal and vertical reduction	Multi objective optimization meta heuristic algorithm required
[5]	Team formation with mata-heuristic approach	Finding optimized team using different mata-heuristic approach to using minimum communication time between different expert	Only consider minimum communication time for team formation
[6]	New optimization model for team formation of a reliable team and experts	Gives backup for unreliable agents, and there no backup agent given by other reliable ageny	In actual scenario there is possibility of failure of reliable agents also
[1,8]	To solve Task Oriented Robust Team Formation (TORTF) problem	ART (Algorithm for Robust Team) and AORT (Algorithm for Optimal Robust Team)	The computational complexity of TORTF is identified
[3]	Distributed team formation in multi-expert systems to reach a state of local stability Focus on distributed strategies and propose a distributed algorithm	A distributed algorithm for team formation Time is divided into rounds, each composed of two stages	How communication between leaders affects performance is an open question Determining what amounts of communication and complexity is necessary to remove the exponential gap in the case of unbounded degree networks
[14]	Organization-Based Cooperative Coalition Formation To solve coalition formation problem	a sample hierarchical organization	The optimal algorithm will need exponential time in the worst case
[7]	The Multiple Team Formation Problem using Social networks Two new dimensions of the TFP are added and to produce An optimization model	Three algorithms: Constraint programming, Local search, Variable neighborhood Search	Different Skills are required If the skill is not match then the task will be incomplete. Also, not significant performance issue as the problem grows in size

Furthermore, the framework is highly scalable and can operate on any operating system without limitations. The system can produce accurate results with a large dataset stored in a CSV file.

3.1 Average[A]

Figure 1 shows how to calculate the averages of all experts in the dataset by using the following formulas.

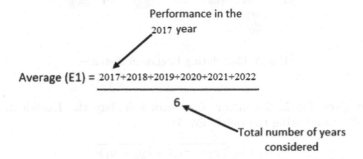

Fig. 1. Calculate the averages of experts.

We are putting the data frame in the average column's descending order. so that we may first concentrate on the performance's foundation. Our system defined experts' performance considering the average yearly performance of corresponding experts. If we arrange in descending order, we can schedule maximum performance experts for the task.

3.2 Highest Required Expert to Perform Task[EN]

To optimize for efficiency while minimizing complexity, we need to identify the highest required expert to perform a task, denoted as EN. This value represents the maximum number of experts needed to complete the task, and can be determined by examining the "Number of experts" column in the dataset. In this example, EN is equal to 9 as shown in Fig. 2. Our goal is to select a small yet robust set of experts that can maximize performance while minimizing complexity. We can achieve this objective by choosing the maximum required expert for each task from all entries in the expert dataset.

3.3 Confusion Matrix for Euclidean Distance

After determining the highest average number of experts, our next step is to calculate the Euclidean distance between each expert to measure their level of coordination. This distance metric provides valuable insights into how well the experts work together as a team.

Tasks	Remaining experts	
T1	9	
T2	4	
T3	5	(Max : EN=9)
T4	6	
T5	1	

Fig. 2. Select the Highest required expert to perform task(EN).

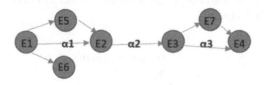

Fig. 3. Calculating Euclidean distance.

In the given Fig 3, for instance, we can calculate the Euclidean distance between e1 and e2 using the below Eq. 1:

$$\alpha_1 = \sqrt{(x_2 - x_1)^2 + (y_2 - y_1)^2} \tag{1}$$

3.4 Problem Statement

Let a set of n experts denoted by $E = \{e_1, e_2, \ldots, e_n\}$, and their yearly performance is recorded in set $P = \{p_1, p_2, \ldots, p_m\}$. $T = \{t_1, t_2, \ldots, t_k\}$ is a set of tasks. Set of subsets those perform the team task after calculating $S = \{s_1, s_2, \ldots, s_m\}$. If a task required $T_1 \, to \, T_n = \{e_1, e_2, \ldots, e_k\}$. set of experts completed by a group of experts teams.

In a team formation problem, different tasks require different sets of experts with specific skills to be completed. We propose a model to assign experts to tasks, such that the subset of experts with the highest overall value, which is calculated as the sum of the average expertise level of the experts [A], and the negative of the shortest path in the graph connecting the experts [–B], can accomplish the required tasks. Additionally, we aim to find suitable replacement experts in case any of the selected experts quit the task.

In a real-world scenario, it's important to prioritize completing tasks in order of their importance. To achieve this, we assign the maximum value to the set of teams for the highest priority task, and subsequently assign the next maximum value to the set of experts for the next priority task, ensuring that the probability of task completion for each expert is maximized. The team formation problem, where the number of teams is denoted by $Teams = \{e_1, e_2, \ldots, e_k\}$, results in 2^n possible teams, making it an NP-hard problem. To efficiently identify the subset of teams with the highest overall average, we propose an algorithm for scheduling experts to tasks.

Problem Steps to Evaluaiton. Let $T = \{t_1, t_2, ..., t_k\}$ be set of Tasks, $E = \{e_1, e_2, ..., e_n\}$ be set of Expert/experts, $S_n = \{e_1, e_2, ..., e_m\}$ subset of set with expert. $S = \{s_1, s_2, ..., s_m\}$ be a set of subsets after calculating, **EN:** Number that represents highest required expert to perform the task **EP:** no of expert needed for the selected task The proposed System consists of three main parts:

1. Calculating value **A**: Calculate the average of each Expert represented in each subset as shown in Fig. 4. Suppose the Subset $S_1 = \{e_1, e_2, ..., e_5\}$ Average $(e_1) = 20$ Average $(e_2) = 25$ Average $(e_3) = 20$ Average $(e_4) = 10$ Average $(e_5) = 25$. We find out that the Average A is **20**.
2. Calculating value **B** By using the Heuristic method for consideration of interaction factor, the graph with x and y co-ordinate as follows; we need to find the value B by Euclidean distance. Consider subset $S_1 = \{e_1, e_2, ..., e_5\}$ with 5 experts.

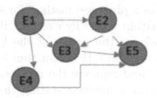

Fig. 4. Subset of 5 experts

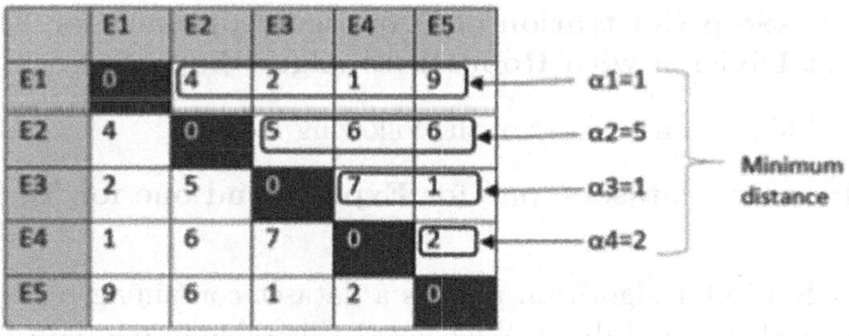

	E1	E2	E3	E4	E5	
E1	0	4	2	1	9	⬅ α1=1
E2	4	0	5	6	6	⬅ α2=5
E3	2	5	0	7	1	⬅ α3=1 Minimum distance
E4	1	6	7	0	2	⬅ α4=2
E5	9	6	1	2	0	

Fig. 5. Confusion matrix for Euclidean distance

Confusion matrix of Euclidean distance of expert e_1, e_2, e_3, e_4, e_5 is illustrated as shown in Fig. 5. Let $\alpha_1, \alpha_2, \alpha_3, \alpha_4, \alpha_5$ be the minimum Euclidean distance of expert e_1, e_2, e_3, e_4, e_5. The Euclidean distance is determined by equation (1).
B $= \alpha_1 + \alpha_2 + \alpha_3 + \alpha_4 + \alpha_5$ is **9**

3. Calculating value **C** Overall value = **A** + (−**B**) Our overall value of **C** is **11**. i.e. we find out the Subset S_1 value is **11** In the best case, we noted that Value B is small if the interaction is high. In the worst case: Value B is large if the interaction weakens. So, Value B is inversely proportional to the performance, and value B becomes negative

4   Proposed Approach for Efficient Expert Division with Robustness Algorithm

Figure 6 shows the flow of the proposed method for selecting the expert set. It starts by reading the task dataset and then proceeding to read the expert dataset. The average performance of each expert on the given task is calculated, and the highest average experts are selected for each task, with the selected experts being removed from the expert dataset. The expert is then selected as "EN," and the highest average experts for the given task are chosen. The confusion matrix for Euclidean distance is then calculated, and the user is prompted for the task, followed by getting the expert's performance (EP). The subset is a set of A and B calculated, followed by the overall score. The team with the highest overall score is finalized, and the completed task and selected experts are removed. The algorithm then prompts to proceed to the next task or end the algorithm if all tasks are completed.

Figure 7 shows the flow of a proposed method for selecting the Set of experts with Robustness. The algorithm starts by checking if there is a leaving expert, and if so, it proceeds to ask for the names of the leaving experts and checks their validity. If the names are valid, the algorithm finds a replacement expert, updates the expert dataset, and removes the replaced expert. If the names are invalid, the algorithm displays a message stating that the expert is not valid. Once the update is complete, the algorithm proceeds to the next task. Finally, the algorithm ends.

4.1   Step-by-Step Illustration of Proposed Approach for Efficient Expert Division with Robustness Algorithm

The proposed algorithm consists of the following steps:

1. **Introduce two datasets, one for Experts and one for Tasks.**

Task Data Set. Our algorithm utilizes a dataset containing tasks numbered from 1 to n as shown in Table 2. We convert this table into a data frame using the pandas' library, enabling us to perform operations on all columns. The task table is structured as follows: Column A represents the tasks, while Column B indicates the number of experts required to perform each specific task.

Expert Data Set. Our analysis involves the use of an expert table containing experts numbered from 1 to n as shown in Table 3. This table is stored in a CSV file and is structured as follows. We choose to evaluate expert performance every year due to the patterns of gradual increase or decrease or sometimes consistent performance annually. This information helps us to make informed decisions when selecting a team. Additionally, personal accidents or health issues may result in a temporary decrease in expert performance, but this does not necessarily indicate that the expert will not perform at their best in the future.

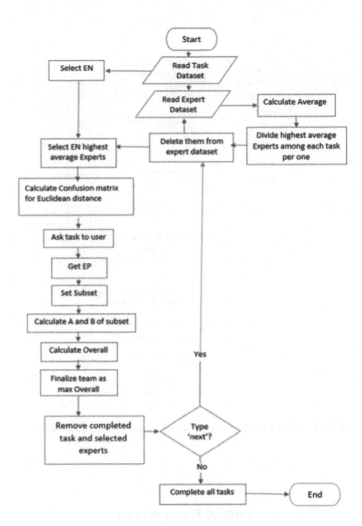

Fig. 6. Flow for Selection of Efficient Experts.

Table 2. Task data set

SN	Task	No expert to perform the respective Task
1	T1	10
2	T2	5
3	T3	6
4	T4	7
5	T5	2

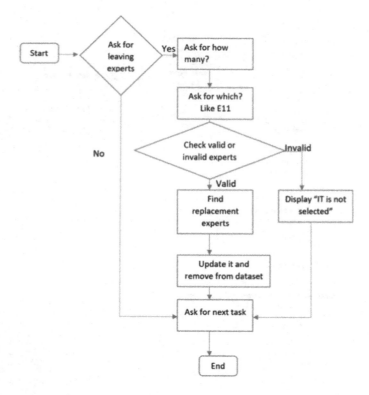

Fig. 7. Flow of Selection of Set of experts with Robustness

Table 3. Expert data set

SN	Expert	Expert year of Performance (varies from 0–100)						Graph coordinate	
		2017	2018	2019	2020	2021	2022	x	y
0	E1	20	30	70	50	80	90	0	0
1	E2	30	20	50	80	90	50	1	5
2	E3	40	70	80	90	50	80	15	10
3	E4	10	50	90	50	70	52	12	12
4	E5	50	80	52	80	20	93	13	14
-	-	-	-	-	-	-	-	-	-
999	E1000	89	56	89	89	78	86	15	18

2. **Set the initial values for Average, the first expert of each task, and EN.**
3. **Sort the expert dataset based on their average and create a confusion matrix. Select the task to be performed by the user as shown in Table 4, Table 5 and Table 6.**

Table 4. Expert data set with average

SN	Expert	Expert year of Performance (varies from 0–100)						Graph coordinate		Yearly Average
		2017	2018	2019	2020	2021	2022	x	y	
0	E44	74	78	51	81	39	99	21	34	71.0000
1	E43	74	75	52	93	93	33	27	30	70.0000
2	E13	15	58	91	96	62	95	27	30	69.5000
3	E18	35	91	84	61	58	96	38	40	69.1666
4	E15	34	82	86	81	75	52	32	34	68.3333
–	–	–	–	–	–	–	–	–	–	
999	E37	54	63	67	11	27	55	36	50	61.6666

Table 5. Expert with Euclidean distance

	e1	e2	e3		e8	e9	e10
e1	0.000000	7.211103	7.211103	...	10.000000	22.472205	10.770330
e2	7.211103	0.000000	0.000000	...	2.828427	19.209373	6.324555
e3	7.211103	0.000000	0.000000	...	2.828427	19.209373	6.324555
e4	18.027756	14.866069	14.866069	...	15.000000	4.472136	20.615528
e5	11.000000	6.403124	6.403124	...	6.708204	12.806248	12.206556
e6	24.738634	23.323808	23.323808	...	22.803509	41.868843	17.204651
e7	15.000000	21.931712	21.931712	...	24.758837	30.265492	25.553865
e8	10.000000	2.828427	2.828427	...	0.000000	19.104973	5.656854
e9	22.472205	19.209373	19.209373	...	19.104973	0.000000	24.758837
e10	10.770330	6.324555	6.324555	...	5.656854	24.758837	0.000000

4. **Set EP (expert Pool) and a subset of experts.** if task $t1$ selected maximum value overall for task $t1 = -2.4221450672778104$ so now set no S_5 having the following expert assigned to task $t1$ ['E11', 'E44', 'E43', 'E13', 'E18', 'E15', 'E10', 'E47', 'E12', 'E19'], $t2$ ['E50'], $t3$ ['E22'], $t4$ ['E34'], $t5$ ['E8']
5. **Calculate the values of A, B, and the overall value for each expert in the subset group for the selected task as shown in Table 7.**
6. **Remove the corresponding task and experts from the datasets and repeat steps 2–6 for the remaining tasks.** Any expert to want leave the assigned task $E11$ so $E11$ is replaced by $E3$ as shown in Table 8 and Table 9.

Table 6. Highest required expert to perform task

	Total expert	remaining Expert	—	x of first	y of first
task	...				
t1	10	9	...	28	26
t2	5	4	...	15	18
t3	6	5	...	33	48
t4	7	6	...	45	41
t5	2	1	...	19	20

Table 7. Subset of sets

sr. no	Subset	EX1	EX2	EX3	EX4		EX8	EX9	A	B	Over-all
0	S1	e1	e2	e3	e4	...	e8	e9	68.833333	96.095427	−27.262093
1	S2	e1	e2	e3	e4	...	e8	e10	68.796296	99.196333	−30.400036
2	S3	e1	e2	e3	e4	...	e10	e9	68.777778	105.089906	−36.312129
3	S4	e1	e2	e3	e4	...	e8	e9	68.740741	82.729200	−13.988459
4	S5	e1	e2	e3	e4	...	e8	e9	68.703704	71.125849	−2.422145
5	S6	e1	e2	e3	e4	...	e8	e9	68.703704	100.181282	−31.477579
6	S7	e1	e2	e3	e10	...	e8	e9	68.611111	107.099464	−38.488353
7	S8	e1	e2	e10	e4	...	e8	e9	68.574074	107.250633	−38.676558
8	S9	e1	e10	e3	e4	...	e8	e9	68.518519	107.250633	−38.732114
9	S10	e10	e2	e3	e4	...	e8	e9	68.407407	94.236099	−25.828691

7. **Find replacement expert for any experts who leave the task.** We need to assign replacement for expert $E11$ already present in $t1$
$t1$ ['E44', 'E43', 'E13', 'E18', 'E15', 'E10', 'E47', 'E12', 'E19', 'E3'] $t2$ ['E50'], $t3$ ['E22'], $t4$ ['E34'], $t5$ ['E8'] when LEAVING EXPERTS ['E11']
The maximum value of overall for task $t2 = 46.61671408036955$ So, now set of No. $S4$ having following expert assigned to task $t2$. $t1$ ['E44', 'E43', 'E13', 'E18', 'E15', 'E10', 'E47', 'E12', 'E19', 'E3'] $t2$ ['E50', 'E40', 'E7', 'E5', 'E6'] $t3$ ['E22'] $t4$ ['E34'] $t5$ ['E8']. Note that the algorithm aims to efficiently schedule experts to tasks based on their average performance and coordination with other experts, while also considering the priority of tasks and the possibility of expert replacements.

4.2   Limitation

The efficiency of our project is affected if the data of an expert is not found or is null or incomplete in the required format. Therefore, detailed data must be provided in the required format for the proper functioning of our algorithm.

Table 8. Select replacement expert

	EX	2017	2018	2019	2020	2021	2022	x	y	avg
0	E40	36	96	59	54	82	62	28	18	64.833333
1	E7	44	64	93	86	15	87	17	18	64.833333
2	E5	50	80	52	80	20	93	13	14	62.500000
3	E48	71	12	49	83	85	74	13	49	62.333333
4	E29	99	99	73	22	15	64	48	26	62.000000
–	–	–	–	–	–	–	–	–	–	–
34	E37	54	63	67	11	27	55	36	50	46.166667

Table 9. Select replacement expert

	Subset	EX1	EX2	EX3	EX4	A	B	Over-all
0	S1	e1	e2	e3	e4	63.625000	51.656854	11.968146
1	S2	e1	e2	e3	e5	63.541667	53.656854	9.884812
2	S3	e1	e2	e3	e6	63.458333	51.642566	11.815768
3	S4	e1	e2	e3	e7	63.458333	16.841619	46.616714
4	S5	e1	e2	e3	e8	63.416667	37.751877	25.664789
–	–	–	–	–	–	–	–	–
24	S25	e10	e2	e3	e4	62.500000	56.181029	6.318971

5   Conclusion and Future of Work

In summary, we successfully developed an optimized algorithm for team formation that involved the efficient division of subsets of experts to perform priority tasks. Additionally, we created an innovative approach that allowed for the replacement of left-out experts and the formation of an optimized team schedule. Our integrated approach proved highly effective in forming teams from a given set of experts and allocating tasks to them with maximum efficiency. This methodology showcases promising potential for addressing challenges in team formation and lays the groundwork for future research in meta-heuristic and parallel computing approaches.

References

1. Abdallah, S., Lesser, V.: Organization-based cooperative coalition formation. In: Proceedings of IEEE/WIC/ACM International Conference on Intelligent Agent Technology (IAT 2004), pp. 162–168. IEEE (2004)
2. Ben-Tal, A., Nemirovski, A.: Robust convex optimization. Math. Oper. Res. **23**(4), 769–805 (1998)
3. Coviello, L., Franceschetti, M.: Distributed team formation in multi-agent systems: stability and approximation. In: 2012 IEEE 51st Annual Conference on Decision and Control (CDC), pp. 2755–2760. IEEE (2012)

4. Dos Santos, F., Bazzan, A.L.C.: Towards efficient multiagent task allocation in the robocup rescue: a biologically-inspired approach. Auton. Agent. Multi-Agent Syst. **22**, 465–486 (2011)

5. El-Ashmawi, W.H., Ali, A.F., Slowik, A.: An improved jaya algorithm with a modified swap operator for solving team formation problem. Soft. Comput. **24**(21), 16627–16641 (2020)

6. Fathian, M., Saei-Shahi, M., Makui, A.: A new optimization model for reliable team formation problem considering experts' collaboration network. IEEE Trans. Eng. Manage. **64**(4), 586–593 (2017)

7. Gutiérrez, J.H., Astudillo, C.A., Ballesteros-Pérez, P., Mora-Melià, D., Candia-Véjar, A.: The multiple team formation problem using sociometry. Comput. Oper. Res. **75**, 150–162 (2016)

8. Juárez, J., Santos, C., Brizuela., C.A.: A comprehensive review and a taxonomy proposal of team formation problems. ACM Comput. Surv. (CSUR) **54**(7), 1–33 (2021)

9. Kargar, M., An, A.: Discovering top-k teams of experts with/without a leader in social networks. In: Proceedings of the 20th ACM International Conference on Information and Knowledge Management, pp. 985–994 (2011)

10. Kargar, M., Zihayat, M., An, A.: Finding affordable and collaborative teams from a network of experts. In: Proceedings of the 2013 SIAM International Conference on Data Mining, pp. 587–595. SIAM (2013)

11. Liu, Y., Wang, L., Huang, H., Liu, M., Xu, C.-z.: A novel swarm robot simulation platform for warehousing logistics. In: 2017 IEEE International Conference on Robotics and Biomimetics (ROBIO), pp. 2669–2674. IEEE (2017)

12. Miller, T., Oren, N., Sakurai, Y., Noda, I., Savarimuthu, B.T.R., Cao Son, T. (eds.): PRIMA 2018. LNCS (LNAI), vol. 11224. Springer, Cham (2018). https://doi.org/10.1007/978-3-030-03098-8

13. Okimoto, T., Ribeiro, T., Bouchabou, D., Inoue, K.: Mission oriented robust multi-team formation and its application to robot rescue simulation. In: IJCAI, pp. 454–460 (2016)

14. Okimoto, T., Schwind, N., Clement, M., Ribeiro, T., Inoue, K., Marquis, P.: How to form a task-oriented robust team. In: Proceedings of the 2015 International Conference on Autonomous Agents and Multiagent Systems, pp. 395–403. International Foundation for Autonomous Agents and Multiagent Systems (2015)

15. Rahwan, T., Michalak, T.P., Wooldridge, M., Jennings, N.R.: Coalition structure generation: a survey. Artifi. Intell. **229**, 139–174 (2015)

16. Rehman, M.Z., et al.: A novel state space reduction algorithm for team formation in social networks. Plos one **16**(12), e0259786 (2021)

17. Tošić, P.T., Agha, G.A.: Maximal clique based distributed coalition formation for task allocation in large-scale multi-agent systems. In: Ishida, T., Gasser, L., Nakashima, H. (eds.) MMAS 2004. LNCS (LNAI), vol. 3446, pp. 104–120. Springer, Heidelberg (2005). https://doi.org/10.1007/11512073_8

Cybersecurity Model for Mobile and Web Application Banking Sectors

Pavithran Velirsamy[1]([⊠]), Syed Hamid Hussain Madni[1], Muhammad Faheem[2],
and Siti Hajar binti Othman[1]

[1] Faculty of Computing, Universiti Teknologi Malaysia, Skudai, Malaysia
pavithransamy97@gmail.com, {hamidhussainsyed,hajar}@utm.my
[2] School of Technology and Innovations, University of Vaasa, Vaasa, Finland
muhammad.faheem@uwasa.fi

Abstract. Cybersecurity risk has an impact on a company's bottom line, just like financial and reputational threats do. Banking cybersecurity is becoming a key concern as the world transitions to a digital economy. Using data-protection methods and processes is important for a successful digital revolution. The Cybersecurity model is essential for banking industries. The findings of the research result in a higher level of cybersecurity model being implemented in banking sectors. Thus, banks will have an easier workload ensuring that they adhere to the required procedures in order to forestall the occurrence of cybercrime within their own institutions.

Keywords: Cybersecurity · Banks · Banking Sectors · Model · Application

1 Introduction

Banking cybersecurity is becoming a key concern as the world transitions to a digital economy. Using data-protection methods and processes is important for a successful digital revolution. Whether it is an unintentional breach or a well-planned attack, the effectiveness of bank cybersecurity affects the protection of our Personally Identifiable Information (PII). Banking and finance have high stakes since massive sums of money are at stake, as well as the prospect of significant economic upheaval if banks and other financial systems are hacked [1].

2 Definition of Terms

- Cybersecurity Readiness: Cybersecurity readiness is being prepared to minimize and manage risk [2].
- Cybersecurity Threats: A negative activity that is designed to damage, steal from, or otherwise interfere with digital life in general [3].
- Cybersecurity Practices: Protecting networks, computers, mobile devices, and servers, as well as data, from hostile assaults, is the goal of the cybersecurity measures that have been implemented [4].

R. N. Shaw et al. (Eds.): ICACIS 2023, CCIS 1921, pp. 271–279, 2023.
https://doi.org/10.1007/978-3-031-45124-9_21

- Cyber Crime: The term "Cyber Crime" refers to any illicit activity that takes place using a computer or any other device that is networked [5].
- Cybersecurity Framework: It is a collection of information that covers the standards, the best practices, as well as the fundamentals of controlling the risks that are associated with cybersecurity [6].

3 Cybersecurity

Cybersecurity is the process of protecting sensitive data and important computer systems from harmful online actors. Information technology (IT) security, usually referred to as cybersecurity measures, is used to thwart assaults on networked systems and applications. These precautions are made to be successful whether threats are internal or external to an organization [7]. There are two branches of cybersecurity as described in detailed below:

3.1 Cybersecurity Capability

The main goal is to allow all the organization and companies all over the globe to assess national cybersecurity capabilities in a comprehensive way in order to identify investment and capacity-building priorities. All this is based on CMM which is known as Cybersecurity Capacity Maturity Model for nations [4].

The CMM reviews a countrys cybersecurity capacity in terms of five dimensions. The first dimension is cybersecurity policy and strategy. Where it is creating a cybersecurity plan and ensuring that it is resilient. The second department is cybersecurity education, training, and skills. This is where your cybersecurity knowledge will grow. The third dimension is cyberculture and society. This is the process of instilling a responsible cybersecurity culture in a company. The fourth dimension is the legal and regulatory framework. The final dimension in this dimension is standards, organization, and technologies, as well as effective legal and regulatory structures. Controls, standards, and technology are used to manage hazards [4].

3.2 Cybersecurity Breaches

Security breaches are any incidents that allow unauthorized access to computer data, applications, networks, or devices. Information is therefore accessed without authorization. Typically, it occurs when a hacker bypasses security precautions. From a technological perspective, a security breach and a data breach are different. When a cybercriminal steals sensitive data, the incident is referred to as a data breach as opposed to a security breach, which is only an intrusion [8].

It should not be surprising that security lapses be quite expensive for enterprises. There are just a handful of different kinds of security lapses. Weak passwords are the most popular. Simple coding or cracking techniques make it simple to break weak passwords. A malware assault is the second. For instance, phishing emails might be used to get access. It just takes one person opening a link in a phishing email for dangerous malware to spread across the network. Additionally, an exploit focuses on a system fault, such as an obsolete system. Devices with outdated operating systems that have not been upgraded, such as those in businesses using unsupported and out-of-date versions of Windows, are particularly susceptible to assaults [8].

4 Security in Banks

Customers' worries about the security of their financial and personal information that can be available online are understandable. The community of online financial institutions recognized the need for security precautions. A variety of important factors, security being one of the most crucial of them, have an impact on customers' intents to use internet banking. The discussion about online banking is mostly driven by worries about the dependability of internet banking services and insufficient data protection [9].

The potential security risks associated with using online banking but also the numerous ways in which individuals might be affected by these risks, making this topic a fascinating one. This is since such content illustrates to readers the numerous vulnerabilities that are present in digital platforms as well as how to take advantage of them. This sheds light on a facet of cybersecurity and online banking that the vast majority of customers are often oblivious to. This problem is extremely important since it relates to the financial security of average people, the money that banks have worked so hard to obtain and which they are obligated to protect at all costs. If they are aware of the numerous ways in which cybercriminals frequently exploit these platforms, the majority of those involved with digital banking platforms can try to assist these programs in modernizing themselves and getting rid of their flaws in order to prevent criminals from using them unlawfully. This would prevent criminals from utilizing these platforms in an unlawful manner. The relevance of the topic can be seen from the fact that financial institutions stand to benefit from having access to such information.

4.1 Unencrypted Data

One of the main issues for the majority of users of internet banking services is the fact that their data is not secure on such platforms. This issue arises because the vast majority of people lack the knowledge necessary to properly encrypt their data, which ultimately results in the data being exposed. As a result, hackers can more easily steal people's data and even use it to withdraw money straight from their bank accounts [10].

4.2 Malware

The vast majority of malicious actors on the internet trying to break into users' accounts by putting malicious software onto the users' computers or mobile devices and then accessing the accounts. Mobile devices and laptops that are already infected with malware pose a significant risk to the cybersecurity systems utilized by financial institutions. As a consequence of the availability of such systems in the hands of customers or even in the custody of a bank, there have been several instances in which computer systems belonging to banks have been hacked. These incidents occurred for the following reasons: When such software is utilized, hackers are provided with the opportunity to steal massive quantities of money from bank accounts without fear of being discovered [10].

4.3 Spoofing

Hackers are increasingly resorting to new techniques, such as posing as account owners in order to steal money from accounts on websites. In most cases, hackers will carry out this activity after gaining the login credentials of a victim for a digital financial network. It is possible that the operations of a bank cannot be negatively impacted by this assault but a person can suffer considerable financial losses as a result of these attacks [10].

4.4 Manipulated Data

In order to steal money from other people's accounts, hackers can alter certain information connected to digital platforms or cybersecurity systems. This makes it simpler for them to trick others into giving them money. This will ultimately cause banks to suffer significant financial losses, and claims [11].

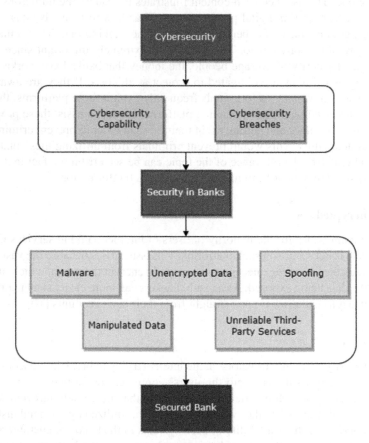

Fig. 1. Block Diagram of Cybersecurity for Banking Sectors.

4.5   Unreliable Third-Party Services

Many banks and other types of financial institutions are able to provide their customers with superior online services thanks to the utilization of third-party suppliers. However, if the people being hacked do not have solid cybersecurity processes in place, it can be simple for hackers to steal money from other individuals by leveraging the systems of third parties. According to Antoine Bouveret, the most significant effect of this is the irreparable damage done to the reputation of the banks [11].

4.6   Findings

A significant number of conclusions emerged from the review of the relevant literature. The progression of all of the discoveries made while conducting this survey is depicted in Fig. 1.

5   Conceptional Cybersecurity Model for Banking Sectors

The cybersecurity model for banking sectors stands for the highest level of abstraction that is possible. There are five different functions, two platforms, six organization or individuals and 3 types of banks as stated in Fig. 2.

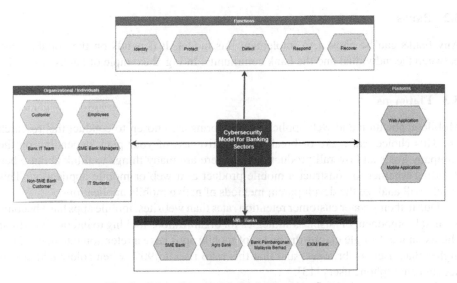

Fig. 2. Cyber Security Model for Banking Sectors.

5.1   Functions

First and foremost, the Identify Function aids a company in developing an understanding of how to manage cybersecurity risk to its assets, people, systems, data, and capabilities.

An organization can focus and priorities its efforts in a way that is consistent with its risk management strategy and the needs of the business when it has a complete awareness of the business environment, the resources that support important functions, and the associated cybersecurity threats [12].

Second, the Protect Function outlines the appropriate safety measures to take to ensure the provision of crucial infrastructure services. By supporting this feature, the Protect Function enables users to limit or control the consequences of a potential cybersecurity event [12].

Thirdly, the actions that need to be taken in order to recognize the emergence of a cybersecurity incident are defined by the Detect Function. It is possible to quickly find cybersecurity incidents thanks to the Detect Function [12].

The Respond Function, which comes after that, entails actions that are intended to be taken in response to a detected cybersecurity event. The Respond Function aids in ensuring that a company is able to contain the harm brought on by a potential cybersecurity incident [12].

The final stage, the Recover Function, is in charge of deciding whether any actions are required to keep up resilience plans and to restart any capabilities or services that are interrupted as a result of a cybersecurity incident. The Recover Function makes it easier to quickly resume regular business operations in order to lessen the negative effects of a cybersecurity incident [12].

5.2 Banks

Any banks can be chosen to implement this model. It depends on the collaboration between the individual and the bank community. In Fig. 2 example of banks is stated.

5.3 Platforms

Mobile application and web application platforms are chosen to conduct this research on. This choice can make or break the effectiveness of your plan, depending on the company goals and overall product goals. There are many things to think about when deciding whether to construct a mobile product as a web or mobile application. This article will analyze the development methods of native mobile applications.

Due to their greater customer retention rates than websites, mobile apps have become a crucial component of business strategies for organizations looking to interact with their clients online. Google claims that users of mobile apps have a retention rate that is 50% higher than users of browsers and that this ratio rises to 90% when solely taking into account smartphone users [13].

Compared to websites that users must access using a mobile Web browser, mobile applications provide a more participatory experience. This enables businesses to provide material that is not already accessible on their website. Additionally, they could have competitions or games where users can win rewards.

Furthermore, websites need an Internet connection to function, however, mobile applications can operate offline and be utilized on many mobile devices. Because of this, apps are far more adaptable than websites, enabling them to reach more people and perhaps boost revenue. When a user's Internet connection malfunctions while they are on a website, the website does not work correctly. Since most mobile applications can function without a network connection, they often have an edge in terms of dependability.

Moreover, push notifications are a feature that users can configure in their mobile applications to personalize them and enable companies to notify customers of any modifications to their products or services. Brands don't have to worry about sending out an email or text messages to efficiently and rapidly distribute fresh information because such alerts show up on the user's device as soon as the device gets them.

Users of mobile applications can frequently move across a whole app in a way that seems natural to them. The team can create a mobile app that will display optimally on consumers' mobile devices by being designed to fit precisely on a small screen.

The main advantage of having a website rather than a mobile app is that everyone can view a website, regardless of whether they have access to mobile technology. Web pages are also accessible even when a user's cellular service is down and don't require users to download an app in order to utilize them.

Making websites suit the branding is simple. You won't need to employ a developer every time you want to make changes, which can be expensive, because websites are also simpler to update. In comparison to an app that people might not get around to installing, the business will have more possibilities of turning visitors into customers when it is accessible online. An app is less likely to be downloaded unless a user deliberately seeks it out, therefore users are more likely to click links on a website than in an app.

Other than that, users should not be concerned about compatibility difficulties because they can visit websites on all platforms and in all browsers. In order to establish the resolution of the device being used and modify the delivery and presentation of the website content appropriately, responsive web design is the idea of utilizing media queries and CSS, a style sheet language for specifying the appearance of web pages [14]. Each time a device receives an update to its operating system or web browser, users must also update their apps on the device. Costly and time-consuming work can be involved in this.

SEO is essential to the success of the website because it increases traffic and helps you become more visible. Compared to a mobile app, the website can be optimized for search engines considerably more rapidly and easily. Because monitoring and upgrading the content on a website is absolutely free, SEO services and tools are not required. However, you can get this done for you by using subscription-based services. A mobile app must be submitted to many app marketplaces.

5.4 Organizational/Individual

A well-rounded picture of the present level of cybersecurity model in banking sectors can be obtained by conducting a survey with a diverse range of individuals such as customers, employees, IT professionals, managers, and students.

It is possible to gain valuable insight into the perceived level of security of online banking services and the level of confidence customers have in the bank's ability to protect their personal and financial information by soliciting feedback from customers of cooperating banks.

The responses of staff members, especially those working in information technology (IT) and managers, can provide valuable information regarding the internal policies and procedures of the bank for addressing cybersecurity issues, as well as the level of training and awareness among staff members.

Input from students majoring in information technology can provide a perspective on current best practices in the business as well as new trends in the field of cybersecurity. This can be helpful in identifying areas in which the bank may need to enhance its preparation.

Surveying customers of banks can give a benchmark for comparing the level of cybersecurity preparedness of banks to that of other banks.

This enables to gain a comprehensive understanding of the various aspects of cybersecurity model within the banking sector and identify areas where improvements can be made if you conduct a survey with a diverse group of individuals. This will allow to achieve the aforementioned goal.

6 Discussion

The research is to provide a well-designed cybersecurity model for banks. The research will involve conducting a survey of customers, employees, IT staff, managers, IT students, and bank customers to assess the current level of cybersecurity model within the banking sector. The survey results will be used to identify the model level of different types of banks. This will enable a comparison of the cybersecurity level of different banks, providing insights into the strengths and weaknesses of the different types of banks in terms of cybersecurity. Based on the survey results, recommendations can be provided to improve the cybersecurity of banks.

7 Conclusion

Overall, this research aims to contribute to the body of knowledge on cybersecurity model in the banking sector and to provide practical guidance for banks to improve their cybersecurity posture. This research be conducted based on existing papers, articles and journals.

Acknowledgement. The authors are thankful to Universiti Teknologi Malaysia (UTM) for supporting this research through RUG grant No. IFRS 7873.

References

1. Naz, Z.: Cybersecurity in Banking: Importance, Threats, Challenges. India, Knowledgehut (2022)
2. Eilts, D.: An empirical assessment of cybersecurity readiness and resilience in small businesses (2020)
3. Tunggal, A.T.: What is a Cyber Threat? UpGuard (2022)
4. Bartsch, M.: Cybersecurity Best Practices. Springer, Germany (2018)

5. Zhang, Y.X.: A survey of cybercrimes. Secur. Commun. Netw., 422–437 (2012)
6. Shen, L.: The NIST cybersecurity framework: overview and potential impacts. Scitech Lawyer **16** (2014)
7. IBM: What is cybersecurity? Retrieved from IBM, 20 December 2022. https://www.ibm.com/my-en/topics/cybersecurity
8. Johns, E.: Cyber Security Breaches Survey 2020. Department for Digital, Culture, Media & Sport, London (2020)
9. Ramayah, T.: Investigating the Impact of Security Factors In. KIIE, Malaysia (2019)
10. Rawat, R., Rajawat, A.S., Mahor, V., Shaw, R.N., Ghosh, A.: Surveillance robot in cyber intelligence for vulnerability detection. In: Bianchini, M., Simic, M., Ghosh, A., Shaw, R.N. (eds.) Machine Learning for Robotics Applications. SCI, vol. 960, pp. 107–123. Springer, Singapore (2021). https://doi.org/10.1007/978-981-16-0598-7_9
11. Bouveret, A.: Cyber Risk for the Financial Sector: A Framework for Quantitative Assessment. International Monetary Fund., pp. 1–29 (2018)
12. NIST: Framework for improving critical infrastructure cybersecurity. The National Security Archive (2014)
13. Mukherjee, M.: Mobile app versus web site: which is better for your business? UXmatters **1** (2022)
14. Jobe, W.: Native apps vs. mobile web apps. Int. J. Interact. Mob. Technol. (iJIM), 1–7 (2013)

Author Index

R. N. Shaw et al. (Eds.): ICACIS 2023, CCIS 1921, pp. 281–283, 2023.
https://doi.org/10.1007/978-3-031-45124-9

Printed in the United States
by Baker & Taylor Publisher Services